LANGUAGE IDEOLOGIES AND THE VERNACULAR IN COLONIAL AND POSTCOLONIAL SOUTH ASIA

This volume critically engages with recent formulations and debates regarding the status of the regional languages of the Indian subcontinent vis-à-vis English. It explores how language ideologies of the "vernacular" are positioned in relation to the language ideologies of English in South Asia.

The book probes into how we might move beyond the English-vernacular binary in India, explores what happened to "bhasha literatures" during the colonial and post-colonial periods and how to position those literatures by the side of Indian English and international literature. It looks into the ways vernacular community and political rhetoric are intertwined with Anglophone (national or global) positionalities and their roles in political processes.

This book will be of interest to researchers, students and scholars of literary and cultural studies, Indian Writing in English, Indian literatures, South Asian languages and popular culture. It will also be extremely valuable for language scholars, sociolinguists, social historians, scholars of cultural studies and those who understand the theoretical issues that concern the notion of "vernacularity".

Nishat Zaidi is a professor and former head of the Department of English, Jamia Millia Islamia, New Delhi. She has authored/translated/edited 16 books. Some of her recent publications include *Karbala: A Historical Play* (translation of Premchand's play *Karbala* with a critical introduction and notes) (2022), *Ocean as Method: Thinking with the Maritime* (with Dilip Menon et al. 2022), *Literary Cultures and Digital Humanities in India* (with A. Sean Pue 2022), *Makers of Indian Literature: Agha Shahid Ali* (2016), *Day and Dastan* (with Alok Bhalla, 2018) and *Between Worlds: The Travels of Yusuf Khan Kambalposh* (with Mushirul Hasan, 2014).

Hans Harder is a professor of Modern South Asian Languages and Literatures at the South Asia Institute, Heidelberg University, Germany. His research interests include modern literatures in South Asia, particularly Bengali, religious movements, and colonial and post-colonial intellectual history. He has written and/or edited *Bankimchandra Chattopadhyay's Śrīmadbhagabadgītā: Translation and Analysis* (2001); *Literature and Nationalist Ideology: Writing Histories of Modern Indian Languages* (2010); *Sufism and Saint Veneration in Contemporary Bangladesh* (Routledge 2011); *Asian Punches: A Transcultural Affair* (with Barbara Mittler, 2013) and *Literary Sentiments in the Vernacular* (with Charu Gupta, Laura Brueck and Shobna Nijhawan, Routledge 2021).

LANGUAGE IDEOLOGIES AND THE VERNACULAR IN COLONIAL AND POSTCOLONIAL SOUTH ASIA

Edited by Nishat Zaidi and Hans Harder

Routledge
Taylor & Francis Group
LONDON AND NEW YORK

Designed cover image: Hans Harder

First published 2024
by Routledge
4 Park Square, Milton Park, Abingdon, Oxon OX14 4RN

and by Routledge
605 Third Avenue, New York, NY 10158

Routledge is an imprint of the Taylor & Francis Group, an informa business

British Library Cataloguing-in-Publication Data
A catalogue record for this book is available from the British Library

ISBN: 978-1-032-24724-3 (hbk)
ISBN: 978-1-032-24734-2 (pbk)
ISBN: 978-1-003-27992-1 (ebk)

DOI: 10.4324/9781003279921

Typeset in Times New Roman
by SPi Technologies India Pvt Ltd (Straive)

CONTENTS

List of Figures *viii*
List of Contributors *ix*
Acknowledgements *xiii*
Note on Transliteration *xiv*

Introduction: Language Ideologies and the 'Vernacular': A Critical Perspective 1
Nishat Zaidi and Hans Harder

PART I
Ideologies of Vernaculars and English **15**

1 Beyond Hegemonic Binaries: English and the 'Vernaculars' in Post-liberalization India 17
Javed Majeed

2 Urdu Language Ideologies and Pakistani Identity 34
Arian Hopf

3 "Mother English": Savitribai Phule on Caste Patriarchy and the Ideology of the English Vernacular 57
Christian Lee Novetzke

4 The Location of Theory: *Bhāṣa* Literatures in Indian and North American Postcolonialism 75
Suddhaseel Sen

5 A Vernacular Archive of Sex and Sexuality: Personal Annotations 90
Charu Gupta

6 Political Reform, Territorialising Language: Re-casting Difference, Constitutional Categories and Developmental Goals, 1905–1950s 115
Veena Naregal

PART II
Lost/Found in Translation between Vernaculars and English **139**

7 Linguistic Estrangement: When Is a Language My Own? 141
Sudipta Kaviraj

8 British Translators, Bhagat Singh, and 'Atheism': How 'Reverse Translation' Alters the Meaning of Philosophical Concepts 165
Ruth Vanita

9 Telling Lives in Forked Tongues: Reading Shanta Gokhale's and Nabaneeta Dev Sen's Autobiographical Writings 180
Dhrupadi Chattopadhyay

10 Vernacularizing Science in Colonial Bengal: A Translational Site of 'Other' Archives 198
Indrani Das Gupta

11 Multilingual Locals in Transnational Geographies: *Vaijñānik Upanyās* and the Cosmopolitanisation of Hindi in Late Colonial North India 217
Ishita Singh

PART III
Language Ideology, Literature and the Vernacular Public Spheres **235**

12 Vernacularizing Emotions: Mohammed Ali's *Comrade* and *Hamdard* 237
Margrit Pernau

13 In Defence of the *Prem'sāgar*: Re-evaluating the Narrative of the Hindi–Urdu Split 255
Gautam Liu

14 Vernaculars across Texts: Modern Islam and Modern Literature in Bengal 273
Neilesh Bose

15 Reading Caste in Vernacular Journals 295
Meenakshi Yadav

16 A South Asian Vernacular Public Overseas: Tamil in the Straits Settlements, c. 1870–1942 311
Torsten Tschacher

Index *330*

FIGURES

5.1 'Our Midwives' 96
5.2 Benefits All Around for the Muslim Bangle Seller 97
5.3 'Tending the Feet' 98
5.4 Christian-Hindu Untouchable Woman 100
5.5 Madam Lady and Fish Seller 101
5.6 (a and b): Women Buying Medicines from Devi and Women Sharing Medical Knowledge 108
16.1 Number of Tamil publications in the Straits Settlements per five-year period, 1887–1942 315

CONTRIBUTORS

Neilesh Bose is an associate professor of History and Canada Research Chair of Global and Comparative History at the University of Victoria. With interests in modern South Asia, cultural history and the history of religion, his recent publications include the edited volumes *India after World History: Literature, Comparison, and Approaches to Globalization* (Leiden, 2022) and *South Asian Migrations in Global History: Labor, Law, and Wayward Lives* (London, 2020). He has written on various aspects of vernacular religion, nationalisms and decolonisation in his monograph *Recasting the Region: Language, Culture, and Islam in Colonial Bengal* (Delhi, 2014) and numerous articles and book chapters.

Dhrupadi Chattopadhyay is an assistant professor at the Department of English, SNDT Women's University, Mumbai. She has been trained in literary studies at Lady Shri Ram College, New Delhi, Jawaharlal Nehru University, New Delhi and Ruprecht Karls Universitat, Heidelberg. Post-colonial studies, culture studies, digital humanities and emerging literatures are her areas of interest.

Charu Gupta is a professor in the Department of History, University of Delhi. The focus of her work is gender, sexuality, masculinity, caste, religious identities and vernacular literatures in early twentieth-century north India. Her publications include *Sexuality, Obscenity, Community: Women, Muslims and the Hindu Public in Colonial India* (Permanent Black, 2001 & Palgrave, 2002) and *The Gender of Caste: Representing Dalits in Print* (Permanent Black & University of Washington Press, 2016; paperback 2017). She is presently working on the social histories of particular genres and subjects through life narratives in Hindi in early twentieth-century north India.

Indrani Das Gupta is an assistant professor in the Department of English, Maharaja Agrasen College, University of Delhi. She is currently pursuing her doctoral research in the field of Indian science fiction from Department of English, Jamia Millia Islamia, New Delhi. Her articles have been published in Routledge, Bloomsbury and Macmillan. Her recent publications include a co-edited book on Gandhi and chapters on Bollywood dance, Rudyard Kipling and science fiction. She was also the Fiction editor of *Mithila Review: An International Journal of Science Fiction and Fantasy*.

Arian Hopf is a Lecturer in Urdu at the South Asia Institute, Heidelberg. He holds a PhD on the concept of religion in colonial South Asia with focus on the Aligarh Movement. His PhD has been published as *Translating Islam, Translating Religion*.

Sudipta Kaviraj is a specialist in intellectual history and Indian politics. He works on two fields of intellectual history: Indian social and political thoughts in the nineteenth and twentieth centuries and modern Indian literature and cultural production. His other fields of interest and research include the historical sociology of the Indian state and some aspects of Western social theory. He holds a PhD from Jawaharlal Nehru University, New Delhi. Prior to joining Columbia University, he taught at the Department of Political Studies at the School of Oriental and African Studies, University of London. He has also taught Political Science at JNU and was an Agatha Harrison Fellow at St. Antony's College, Oxford. He is a member of the Subaltern Studies Collective.

Gautam Liu, Mag.phil., studied Indology at the University of Vienna, where he taught Hindi from 2000 till 2007. In 2007, he was appointed as a full-time lecturer in Hindi at the South Asia Institute of Heidelberg University, where he teaches Hindi language and literature till date.

He co-authored the two-volume textbook *Hindi bolo – Hindi für Deutschsprachige* and translated Uday Prakash's novel *Mohandas* into German.

Javed Majeed is a professor of English and Comparative Literature at King's College London. His books include *Ungoverned Imaginings: James Mill's the History of British India and Orientalism* (1992); *Autobiography, Travel and Postnational Identity: Gandhi, Nehru and Iqbal* (2007) and *Muhammad Iqbal: Islam, Aesthetics and Postcolonialism* (2009). His two-volume study of G. A. Grierson's *Linguistic Survey of India* was published as *Nation and Region in Grierson's Linguistic Survey of India* and *Colonialism and Knowledge in*

Grierson's Linguistic Survey of India (2019). He is the author of 31 peer-reviewed articles and essays on South Asian literature, politics and intellectual history. He was elected as a fellow of the British Academy in 2021.

Veena Naregal is a professor in the Institute of Economic Growth, University of Delhi. Her research interests include language and Indian democracy, disciplinary/institutional histories and regional theatre histories.

Christian Lee Novetzke is a professor of South Asia Studies, Religious Studies, Global Studies and the Comparative History of Ideas at the University of Washington, Seattle, USA.

Margrit Pernau is a senior researcher at the Center for the History of Emotions at the *Max Planck Institute for Human Development* in Berlin. She has published a number of edited volumes, among which are the following: *The Delhi College: Traditional Elites, the Colonial State and Education before 1857* (Delhi, OUP 2006), *Civilizing Emotions: Concepts in Nineteenth Century Asia and Europe* (Oxford, OUP) in 2015, with Helge Jordheim et al., and *Monsoon feelings: A history of emotions in the rain* with Imke Rajamani and Katherine Schofield (Delhi, Niyogi Books 2018). She has brought out several special issues, among them *Feeling Communities* (IESHR, 2017) and *Emotions in South Asia* (SAHC, 2021). Her most recent monographs are *Emotions and Modernity: From Balance to Fervor* (Delhi, OUP 2019) and *Emotions and Temporality* (Cambridge, Cambridge UP 2021). Besides, she has written numerous articles on the history of emotions, historical semantics, comparative studies and translation studies.

Suddhaseel Sen is an assistant professor of English in the Department of Humanities and Social Sciences at IIT Bombay. He holds a PhD in English (Collaborative Programme in South Asian Studies) from the University of Toronto and a second PhD, in Musicology, from Stanford University. Sen has been a Research Fellow for the Balzan Research Project, Towards a Global History of Music. His publications include the monograph *Shakespeare in the World: Cross- Cultural Adaptation in Europe and Colonial India, 1850–1900* (Routledge, 2020) and essays on cross-cultural exchanges between Indian and British musicians; Richard Wagner and Germa Orientalism; nineteenth-century Bengali literature and culture; and films by Satyajit Ray and Vishal Bhardwaj, among others.

Ishita Singh is an assistant professor in the Department of English at Jesus and Mary College. She is currently a PhD candidate in the Department of History at the University of Delhi. She has presented her research at various international conferences and has published with peer-reviewed journals. Her research interests include anti-caste politics, Ambedkarite and women's writing, speculative fiction, science fiction, fantasy, utopia and dystopia, and Hindi Literature. She has formerly been the managing editor at *Mithila Review, The Journal of International Science Fiction and Fantasy*.

Torsten Tschacher is currently a Heisenberg Fellow of the German Research Foundation (DFG) at the Department of Modern South Asian Languages and Literatures of the University of Heidelberg. His research focuses on the history, society and discursive traditions of Tamil-speaking Muslims around the Bay of Bengal. He has published widely on questions of identity and community formation in Tamil Muslim societies as well as Muslim literature in Tamil. A research monograph entitled *Race, Religion, and the 'Indian Muslim' Predicament in Singapore* was published in 2018 with Routledge. Currently, he is preparing a book-length study of Islamic textual cultures in the Tamil-speaking world between 1572 and 1842, and has recently edited (with Pushkar Sohoni) a volume on non-sectarian traditions of celebrating Muharram with Routledge (2022) entitled *Non-Shia Practices of Muḥarram in South Asia and the Diaspora: Beyond Mourning*.

Ruth Vanita has taught at Delhi University and the University of Montana. She is the author of many books, including *Love's Rite: Same-Sex Marriage in Modern India*; the novel *Memory of Light* (2020), *The Dharma of Justice: Debates on Gender, Varna and Species in the Hindu Epics* (2022) and *The Broken Rainbow: Poems and Translations* (2022), and over 70 scholarly articles on British and Indian literatures. She has translated many works from Hindi and Urdu to English, most recently Mahadevi Varma's *My Family*. Her next novel, *A Slight Angle*, will appear in 2023, and thereafter a book on Shakespeare.

Meenakshi Yadav is an assistant professor in the Department of English at Shivaji College, University of Delhi. She holds an MPhil from the Department of English, University of Delhi. She is pursuing PhD from the Department of English, Jamia Millia Islamia. She is currently working on Hindi Print Media in the late nineteenth to twentieth century.

ACKNOWLEDGEMENTS

The editors would like to acknowledge the funding received from the Ministry of Education, Government of India, through its Scheme for the Promotion of Academic and Research Collaboration (SPARC), which allowed us to conduct the collaborative project on "Debating and Calibrating the Vernacular in Colonial and Postcolonial South Asian Literature and Culture" with Hans Harder (Heidelberg University, Germany) as the foreign PI and Nishat Zaidi (JMI, INDIA) as the Indian PI. This edited volume owes its existence to the project and the two-day international conference organised under the aegis of the project from 15 to 17 March 2021.

We would also like to express our gratitude to the administration of Jamia Millia Islamia, especially the vice chancellor and conference patron Professor Najma Akhtar, who always supported the project. We are grateful to the research scholars of the Department of English, JMI, in particular Kashish Dua and Meenakshi Yadav, for their unstinting support and hard work in organising the conference. Kashish Dua also deserves a special mention for handling all email communications and her help in organising the volume material.

NOTE ON TRANSLITERATION

Diacritical marks are sometimes perceived as disruptive and as the antithesis of smooth reading; but when it comes to accurately rendering words and passages from their original languages into Latin script, they are indispensable. In this book, we have used diacritics economically in the main body of the texts, restricting them to titles of works, periodicals and certain non-English terms. Names of authors, associations, place names etc. are given in the common, non-diacritical English transliteration. In the bibliographies attached to the individual chapters, however, bibliographical details for works in South Asian languages are given in standard academic transliteration. The common systems of transliteration are used for languages using Indic (Hindi, Bengali, Marathi, Tamil etc.)[1] and Arabic scripts (Urdu).

Note

1 This includes the additional convention, in most cases, of marking unpronounced, inherent -a- inside Hindi and Bengali words by the omission sign ˡ introduced by Rahul Peter Das (cf. *Indo-Iranian Journal* 27.1984, p. 66, n. 2). We use, e.g., *Svargˡpurī* rather than *Svargapurī*, in a Hindi context, and *Premˡsāgar* rather than *Premasāgar* or *Premsāgar*: transliterating प्रेमसागर as *Premasāgar* could suggest that the -a- is pronounced, and *Premsāgar* that -m- and -s- form a conjunct (प्रेम्सागर). While *Premˡsāgar* is highly unlikely to be misread, there are cases where this difference matters. To prevent such misunderstandings and warrant an exact transliteration that allows us to reconstruct the original form of the word or phrase while not deviating from the word's pronunciation, marking these omissions is necessary. However, cases are few; and where authors have objected to this convention, we have not insisted.

INTRODUCTION

Language Ideologies and the 'Vernacular': A Critical Perspective

Nishat Zaidi and Hans Harder

Languages rarely exist in an unmarked state of just being there. Communication about communication is probably as old as communication itself; likewise, reflection on language is not a new thing, especially if it comes to languages in the plural. Various perceptions, narratives and stereotypes add up to a thick conundrum of attributes that get attached to a language and its community of speakers, and languages come to stand for their communities and symbolize them (Rahman 2008: 44). This may not be so tangible in situations where there is a high degree of monolingualism and an uncontested dominance of a national language, as was the common case in parts of Europe until recently (Blommaert & Verschueren 1998: 117–47). It is more acutely apparent in situations in which languages exist in close proximity and overlap in terms of geography and communicative domains. The South Asian situation is such.

South Asian Languages and English

Multiple overlaps are hard to pin down on a two-dimensional map. It is common knowledge now that the linguistic maps of South Asia as found in school books and shown in introductory literature to the subcontinent, presenting neatly divided linguistic areas, are, on closer investigation, often inadequate in rendering the data of actual language use. This is obviously so for urban agglomerations, but also for other areas such as rural Punjab, the Kathmandu valley, parts of Bengal, Jharkhand, Karnataka/Kerala and so on – not to speak of Assam or Kashmir. Language use differs a lot along the lines of community, religion and caste. It involves interstices as well as divisions in both a horizontal and a vertical sense, in a spatial metaphorical sense, and in the latter there exist plenty of hierarchies. In certain cases, this close coexistence of many

DOI: 10.4324/9781003279921-1

languages side by side, or on top of each other, may appear as a direct product of modernity with its features of labour migration and increased interregional connectivity. But, as such, it is hardly a new phenomenon.

So what is new in the language situation of colonial and post-colonial South Asia? Obviously the introduction of a new superposed linguistic variety with its very specific, thus far unmatched presence. No doubt the pre-colonial situation was also characterized by much multiplicity and overlap, but this new presence took the complexity of the linguistic landscape to yet another level. This new superposed variety is, of course, English – the language which, unlike other colonial languages such as French and Portuguese, was there to stay, proliferated, and is still proliferating. South Asian regional languages in colonial and post-colonial times have come to coexist in a close neighbourhood with English. In the colonial age of the nineteenth and twentieth centuries, contact with English and the culture and literature connected with it stimulated many features of their standardization, reform and modernization. Simultaneously, anti-colonialism triggered in some cases a polemical response against the English language, asserting the regional languages as the true and authentic spheres of South Asian cultures. Nonetheless, even staunch anti-English language nationalists in those days would have admitted that the give and take – and probably more the take than the give – these languages had with English in so many fields has been very considerable.

Post-Independence developments have significantly altered this setup. While a certain nationalist consensus regarding the authenticity of regional languages and the relative foreignness of English seems to have held the scene well until the end of the twentieth century, post-liberalization India for sure, and arguably also other South Asian countries, has come to accept English in many realms of life. An indicator of this trend in the realm of literature can be found in the changed and more appreciative way English literature from the subcontinent is dealt with in literary histories (Harder 2017: 323–352). The signs are all set in the direction of what has been called a vernacularization of English.

Language Ideologies

The contributions to this book do not focus on the quantitative data of language use, but on the perceptual, identitarian and political dimensions that accompany and drive linguistic dynamics. These could be summarized as the ideological aspects of language situations. 'Ideology', of course, is a loaded term that has undergone much theorization and debate ever since Karl Marx. 'A set of interrelated ideas' is perhaps the most basic definition, a set that is meant to represent something and simultaneously to appeal for something – the risk being that ideology may reduce complexity to such an extent that it either fails to represent or, depending on one's take, contrives to represent tendentiously. Marx and Engels (1970: 47) famously characterize ideology as false consciousness and speak of "phantoms formed in the human brain". Althusser (2014: 38, 45) follows suit in stating that, "[i]deology is a 'representation' of the imaginary relation of individuals with their real life conditions", but adds that ideology is inescapably built into the human nature, humans being "ideological animals". Mannheim (2013: 183) sees the difference between ideology and utopia largely as sets of ideas about how things are and how they should be, admitting that these often permeate each other and can be hard to separate. Eagleton defends the concept as well as the critique of ideology against post-structural thinkers, or "Derrida's children", claiming that it provides an important firewall against an unleashed arbitrariness of representations and against non-committal political stances (Eagleton 1991: 198). Ideology, it seems, is situated between complete reduction and full representation (to the extent that any one of these are feasible), and between description and norm, or referential vs emotive and conative statements (I. A. Richards, acc. to Eagleton) or again constative vs performative ones in J. L. Austin's terminology (ibid.: 19). As a common denominator, it emerges that ideology means the interplay of connected notions and assumptions about society in a systemized way – notions and assumptions that are usually shared among groups or whole societies and relate to the political and social spheres of life.

Accordingly, among sociolinguists, language ideologies are understood as sets of assertions and beliefs about a language in a given milieu or society. Kathryn Woolard (1998: 3) furnishes a basic definition: "Representations, whether explicit or implicit, that construe the intersection of language and human beings in a social world are what we mean by 'language ideology'". Summarizing different standpoints, she goes on to differentiate between language ideologies that focus on linguistic structure, on contact and conflict, or on sets of ideas developed by professional linguists (ibid.: 3–4). Of these, it is clearly the second category that is at the centre of the present book. As Woolard shows, ideologies of language contact and conflict involve common sociolinguistic topics such as "language maintenance and shift, contact-induced linguistic change, the linkage of language to ethnicity and nationalism, language attitudes, and language planning and development" (ibid.: 16).

Language ideologies in this sense refer to the sets of ideas linguistic communities form about their own and other languages, and put into practice in various ways: right from scripturalization, formalization through grammars and adoption of new genres and media, to agitations and movements for official language recognition. Writing a language into its scriptural existence, forcing it to progress and gearing it towards excellence is a very common set of actions that characterize the careers of scripted languages by definition. This process of intentional solidification and enrichment is what sociolinguists have labelled by the very technical term of 'corpus planning'. In a comparative study of such corpus planning measures, Joshua Fishman describes these as rather universal features across many communities, quoting ample examples of how negative attributes regarding one's own language are downplayed, how its aesthetic value is celebrated and how language planning will lead it to perfection (Fishman 1996: 3–16). The mechanisms at work and the parallelity of both the processes and the terms in which they are perceived are striking indeed.

But beyond such decontextualized shared structures of linguistic self-assertion, any investigation of particular language ideologies of course has to dig deeper and thoroughly contextualize the linguistic data socially and historically. As would have become apparent from the preceding paragraph already, South Asia has plenty of languages on the move. While the colonial age saw the dynamic processes of standardization and modernization of many of the major languages on the subcontinent, at present it is the self-assertion of smaller languages, some deemed as dialects, that seems the most virulent. But this does not mean that the larger regional languages, whose relation to English is the prime focus of this volume, have remained immobile once their middling status was achieved. The forms of language ideologies vary greatly, and our volume aims to capture some of this diversity, no matter whether the ideologies in question are fluid and agitational or whether they have been sedimented and become doctrinal. Do the South Asian 'vernaculars' still aspire to the full-fledged autonomous status twentieth-century nationalist movements had claimed for them, or do they dive off into parochial bubbles? How are language ideologies of the 'vernaculars' positioned vis-à-vis language ideologies of English in South Asia?

The focus on language *ideologies* provides a good entry point for investigating the trajectories of languages on the subcontinent in the colonial and postcolonial periods. It allows us to look at languages as consciously modelled, positioned, set against others and invested with attributes, and implies a direct link to agents, or ideologues, behind such processes. If language as such is always a shared intermediate space and intersubjective by definition, it may lend itself well to structural analysis and depersonalized systemic observation. This is the level of grammar and linguistics. Ideologies on Woolard's second level, however, in stressing the metalinguistic level and focusing on the way we think about languages and use them for certain goals, reach out into the fields of sociolinguistics, history, literature and social sciences. In other words, the basic sense of ideology as a set of ideas to describe a situation and to call for action is suited well to describe our concerns. Tracing the ideologies and their carriers, investigating their validity, questioning basic assumptions regarding linguistic belonging and observing these ideologies at work in colonial and postcolonial South Asia is what brings our concerns together.

The 'Vernacular'

Why not leave it at multilingualism? Why have 'vernacular' in the title? Multilingualism of course also covers up a host of hierarchical relationships, contact scenarios and historical and ongoing entanglements. But the 'vernacular' as it is commonly used today has the sharpest edge to it, provoking us to vector hierarchy into our considerations right from the start. The shortest way to evoke the relation between South Asian languages and English is to resort to this ambivalent, or some would say contentious category straight away. The 'vernacular' as a category commands a whole range of ambivalent meanings and has been a contested term ever since the colonial age. It is overshadowed by its etymology and colonial history and causes unease, prompting many authors to add disclaimers and apologies when using it, or using inverted commas – a practice we also heed in this introduction. But while implying a hierarchical setup and the subjugation of 'lower' languages under the 'high variety' of English with its cosmopolitan positioning, the 'vernacular' has also received empowering impulses and has been invested with qualities like groundedness and expressive strength. Thus, in the thoroughly multilingual literary and public spheres of South Asia, and in the context of the ongoing rise of literary Anglophonia in South Asia and particularly in post-liberalization India, a re-examination of the notion of 'vernacularity' in terms of competing language ideologies seems relevant.

Today the term 'vernacular', hosted by the English language, is the only one that has the potential, at least in some of its uses, to divide up the complex linguistic landscape of South Asia into an English realm on the one hand and a large plurality of languages of the subcontinent on the other – unlike 'South Asian languages', which would immediately provoke questions about whether English shouldn't be included, unless, as in our first sub-heading, both figure in an additive construction; also unlike *bhāṣā*s, which would preferably be used for non-Sanskrit literary languages; and even unlike 'regional languages', which would again convey the larger languages with some official status.

The term 'vernacular' has quite a complex history. Derived from Latin *verna*, domestic slave, it came to be employed to Latin itself as the language of the house as opposed to superposed Greek in Ancient Rome already, shedding its connotations with slavery to a large extent (Pollock 2006: 22). In the Renaissance, it was the adjective *vernaculum* in its language-related sense, not the noun *verna*, that was borrowed by various emerging European languages. Its meaning shifted and now encompassed the regional, or non-classical languages of Europe in contrast to Latin (and Greek and Hebrew). This was how it was mainly (and infrequently) used in English until, in colonial South Asia, it underwent another shift in administrative use, now denoting the native South Asian languages in contradistinction to English itself.[1]

If this reflects common usage in South Asia until date, it does not mean that the 'vernacular' is limited to such denotations, neither in the past nor at present. By the side of such ways of functioning as an umbrella category for a variety of languages – the 'vernaculars' – there has also been a trend to restrict its linguistic uses to spoken and not-yet formalized language, and to set it against refined, literarized language. Traces of such usage are there in Orientalist work on South Asian languages, from end eighteenth to the twentieth centuries, by authors like Halhed and Colebrooke, and up to Grierson (Harder, Zaidi & Tschacher 2022: 7–9). Such usage relates to states of languages rather than to languages as discrete units, meaning that a language can be vernacular in certain situations and formal in others.

Apart from these language-related uses, the 'vernacular' has also been deployed increasingly in recent years in the fields of architecture, culture and arts, by the side or as a replacement of terms like 'native', 'folk', 'indigenous' etc., and as the opposite of 'polite architecture', 'high tradition', 'cosmopolitan practice' and so on. As such, the 'vernacular' has come to operate in oppositions between global and local, and undergone a positive re-evaluation within models of glocalization. It has been connected with groundedness and assimilative and still resilient local practice, thus circumventing the purist claims of authenticity (Brosius & Michaels 2020).

Untying the 'vernacular' from the fixed set of languages it has come to stand for in South Asia is also partly facilitated by such changed uses and positive re-evaluations. It has led to moves of opening the doors for considering certain ways of using English as the 'vernacularization of English' (Kothari 2011) and to consider literature such as R. K. Narayan's as 'vernacular' even though it is written in English (Shankar 2012: 36–49).

Vernacularization

Highly influential, and in some part responsible for the general trend of engaging again with the 'vernacular', is Sheldon Pollock's model of vernacularization. The idea is that around the end of the first millennium AD, regional languages started moving into many domains of use, particularly literary ones, in which formerly Sanskrit had been dominant. It is certainly not the language of 'cosmopolitan' Sanskrit which is vernacularized, but the respective domains of communication, culture and art – meaning that Pollock's vernacularization is very differently conceived from the 'vernacularization of English' mentioned above. In fact, according to Pollock's model, the point is that when the regional languages push into these new realms, they do not do so just as they are but *become* in that process the literary 'vernaculars' that are the agents of this process. They do so not by liquidating the cultural and aesthetical norms connected with Sanskrit, but by gradually appropriating them and adapting many of Sanskrit's (or Persian or Arabic) formal and generic features. Thus, it is not the extinction of Sanskrit but the creative tension between it and the regional languages that brings forth Pollock's literary 'vernaculars'. Unlike other literary historians, Pollock foregrounds courtly poetry and etiquette, not bhakti poetry with its more (but never entirely) iconoclastic tendencies.[2]

The languages comprised by Pollock's notion of 'vernaculars' (Kannada, Bengali, Oriya, Avadhi etc.) largely overlap with the 'vernacular' languages the

Vernacular Press Act refers to. But this resemblance is deceptive since what is at stake in Pollock's notion is the creative tension between cosmopolitan Sanskrit and regional 'vernaculars', whereas in British administrative parlance at least since Macaulay – and in sync with the shift of meaning outlined above – it is the juxtaposition of those languages to English which is intended.

As Pollock diagnoses, the 'vernacular millenium' in South Asia and elsewhere comes to an end with the advent of capitalist globalization, 'a form of transregional cultural change far more powerful and coercive than what marked the age of empires and civilizations' (Pollock 1998: 69). If we zoom into his macro-historical panorama to the colonial and postcolonial scenery a little bit, however, an uneven picture emerges. In a first wave, exposure to English goes along with language reforms and much 'corpus planning' in the regional languages, often fueled by nationalist sentiment. In a second wave long after colonialism has ended, English solidifies its presence no longer as any sort of colonial master's tongue, but as a link language of the educated and, in Pollock's terms, the lingua franca of international capitalism. While English has in various ways assumed the role Sanskrit, Persian and Arabic had held for centuries in supplying models of aesthetical production and public as well as private language use, it has simultaneously penetrated the system to a greater extent than arguably any of those ever did – up to the point that it has indeed also established itself as a 'vernacular' for so many practical purposes especially in India. It is this scenario and its different phases that the contributions in our volume address.

Ideologies of Vernaculars and English

As Raymond William observed, "a definition of language is always, implicitly or explicitly, a definition of human beings in the world" (Williams 1977: 21). Not only linguistic forms but also social institutions such as the nation-state, education, juridico-legal structures and religious institutions hinge on the ideologization of language use. The chapters in this volume explore diverse ways in which ideology impinges on language use and is in turn shaped by language forms in South Asia. The authors in Section I of the volume, 'Ideologies of Vernaculars and English', broadly focus on language politics and the function of language ideology in colonial India.

The first chapter, 'Beyond Hegemonic Binaries: English and the "Vernaculars" in Post-Liberalization India', by Javed Majeed probes the English-'vernacular' binary and explores possibilities of what he calls emancipatory multilingualism as opposed to hierarchical multilingualism. Majeed teases out the possibility of de-hegemonizing English as well as those Indian languages that are privileged in hierarchical multilingualism, by moving away from the monolingual paradigms rooted in the notion of the 'native speaker'. In doing so, Majeed's chapter tests the limits of postcolonial paradigms by drawing attention to how the knowledge economy and the global spread of neoliberal free-market doctrines have naturalized the use of English as the language of global competitiveness in post-liberalization India and in the global South. In the process Majeed also prompts us to re-think the term 'India' in wider, more imaginative ways which are not coterminous with the bounded territorialities of the political map of the subcontinent.

If India's multilingualism is widely acknowledged, the formation of the Islamic State of Pakistan showed the tendency to obliterate its multilingualism under the perceived Islamization of Urdu. In his chapter 'Urdu Language Ideologies and Pakistani Identity', Arian Hopf examines the politics of identity formation in Pakistan and its visceral connection with Urdu language ideologies. Considering the tensions inherent in the idea of Pakistan, envisioned as a country for the Muslims of undivided India comprising the territories encompassing the Muslim-majority provinces in the North-East and North-West, Hopf highlights the resultant fissures and ruptures. He does so by juxtaposing the counter-narratives which were significant and simultaneously present in the early years of Pakistan's independence, to the meta-narrative of an Islamic identity. In this regard, Urdu was deemed as symbol or essence of an Indo-Muslim culture. Yet, this blurred the strongly needed demarcation to India, Urdu historically being based in what is present India.

Christian Lee Novetzke takes the argument about the 'spectre of English' to the discourses about Dalit identity initiated by Savitribai and Jotirao Phule. His chapter, '"Mother English": Savitribai Phule on Caste Patriarchy and the Ideology of the English Vernacular', examines the role of English in the making of the social thought of these significant figures in India's intellectual, social and political history, and key voices in India's genealogy of political liberalism that attended to the conditions of subaltern communities. Drawing our attention to how Savitribai Phule referred to English as "mother's milk", and how Jotirao Phule sometimes wrote in English and also gave his major Marathi manifestos English titles, Novetzke argues that English was more than a language of opportunity for them. In conflict with dual structures of power, colonial domination and the Brahmanical hegemony, they viewed English as a discursive realm wherein through Western liberal idioms, the illiberal fields of the Marathi public hegemonized by Brahmanical, Sanskrit-based discourses could be challenged.

Suddhasil Sen approaches the aspect of paradigm shift in philosophical and theoretical concepts as viewed from the location of language in his chapter 'The Location of Theory: *Bhāṣa* Literatures in Indian and North American Postcolonialism'. Acknowledging that the literary developments in modern Indian languages are inextricably tied to the cultural encounter with European literature from the colonial period onwards, Sen argues that what usually gets ignored in scholarly investigations of such encounters is their reading in terms of the canonical postcolonial concepts of cultural hegemony and colonial mimicry. Sen's chapter charts the reception history of postcolonial theory in India and examines the implications of its hegemony on current Indian scholarship.

Charu Gupta takes more than 30 years of her research on disparate subjects forward, to reflect on how and why the vernacular has been her constitutive archive to study sex and sexuality in colonial India. Questioning the authority and authenticity of the official archive, and inspired in part by the intellectual provocations of Dalit and feminist studies, she argues that it is crucial to recognize the vernacular as a malleable concept, whose meanings are contingent on its contexts. Gupta states that a vernacular signifying practice has critical problems as it can offer disquieting elements that uphold dominant and normative values. At other moments, however, it can be liberatory and act as a vehicle of dissent.

Veena Naregal's chapter draws attention to the indexing of linguistic differences as a territorial category in a polity marked by as much of linguistic diversity as South Asia. Naregal examines the constitutional debates, higher educational policy and regional discourse in Marathi between 1920s and 1950s, to understand official and elite efforts to establish political coherence and exercise control via a modicum of connect with popular will. Furthermore, the chapter also dwells upon the drawn-out temporal intersections between the logic of linguistic territorialization and simultaneous leveraging of development agendas in the decades between 1920s and 1950s.

Lost/Found in Translation between Vernaculars and English

The term 'ideology' underlines the partiality, contestability and the contested nature of our cultural conceptions. It reminds us that what is often paraded as universal or natural is "interest-laden" and has roots in historical context (Woolard and Schieffelin 1994: 58). In the next section of the book, 'Translation Issues Between Vernacular and English', we move on to investigate the multiple manifestations of ideology operating though translations from English into the vernacular and vice versa. The section is overall oriented towards tracing historical roots of what is often seen as natural and universal.

Languages we speak embody the life-worlds we inhabit. However, in historical conditions like colonization, where a rupture occurs between the spoken language and the language of education, the result can be what Ngugi Wa Thiong'O terms as "colonial alienation" (Thiong'O 1992: 17). In the first chapter of this section, 'Lingual estrangement: When Is a Language My own?', Sudipta Kaviraj examines the phenomenon of lingual alienation. Reflecting on the subject though his own experience as a social scientist, where his Bengali identity collaborates with his work of doing social science in English, Kaviraj dwells on what he calls a 'translational' situation, and discusses its advantages and disadvantages.

Ruth Vanita's chapter, 'British Translators, Bhagat Singh, and 'Atheism': How Reverse Translation Alters the Meaning of Philosophical Concepts', investigates another angle of this problematic, a phenomenon she terms 'reverse translation'. This occurs when a philosophical concept, such as *dharma*, is repeatedly translated into English, using terms from a Judeo-Christian lexicon, such as 'religion', and then the English word is translated, or the concept it encapsulates is projected, back into South Asian languages including Sanskrit. In this process, which is largely "unwitting and unmarked," Vanita argues that the Indian-language word and concept shift their connotations both for English and for non-English speakers, often resulting in altered philosophical frameworks.

Dhrupadi Chattopadhyay in her chapter focuses on the autobiographical writings of Shanta Gokhale and Nabaneeta Dev Sen to highlight the gendered aspect of language ideology. As both these writers chose to inscribe their lives in 'vernaculars' as well as English, Chattopadhyay argues that their attempt to produce 'new' subjectivities in their writings was a reflection of their desire to accommodate novel frameworks of experience in colonial and postcolonial times. The chapter further argues that the writers cautiously choose the in-between (translational) spaces of the vernacular and English as their preferred site of identity production.

The next two chapters of the section probe the question of language ideology from the perspective of the manner in which science, the bedrock of colonial modernity, was translated and amalgamated into the vernacular life-worlds in colonial India. Indrani Das Gupta, in her chapter 'Vernacularizing Science in Colonial Bengal: A Translational Site of "Other" Archives', analyses Sukumar Ray's text, *Heśorām Hūśiyārer ḍāiri* (1922), first published in the Bengali Children's magazine, *Sandeś*, to understand how Bengali science fiction actively engaged in production and reception acts accommodating, assimilating, critiquing, or resisting Western science's authority and legality.

Ishita Singh's chapter, 'Multilingual Locals in Transnational Geographies: *Vaijñānik Upanyās* and the Cosmopolitanisation of Hindi in Late Colonial North India', focuses on terms for Science Fiction (SF) in Hindi such as *vijñān-kathā* or *vijñān-galp*. Singh traces the genealogy of Hindi science fiction through the nineteenth century, when in colonial North India, Allahabad and Benaras became the intellectual centres of this new knowledge, and Hindi journals like *Sarasvatī* published by the Arya Samaj and the *Nāgarī pracārinī patrikā* published by the Nagari Pracharani Sabha played significant roles in the proliferation of scientific education along with the promotion of Hindi in colonial North India. She enquires into the articulation and reinvention of wonder in colonial Hindi SF texts and links them to double estrangement due to both the SF sublime and the colonial encounter with the new strange and alien.

Language Ideology, Literature and the Vernacular Public Sphere

Literary texts do not exist in a historical vacuum. They are contingent upon the historical, sociopolitical and cultural conditions in which they materialize.

Literary language is produced within a network of value categories. A "particular generic constellations of field, tenor, and mode" is operative in the production of linguistic nodes, and the lexical 'core' of a word is no more than an "aggregate or average produced by the interlocking and overlapping of genres of discourse at any point of time" (Frow 1986: 72). The next section of the book, 'Language Ideology, Literature and the Vernacular Public Spheres', examines these interlocking patterns by which several genres of discourse act upon linguistic codes used in literary texts and result in formation of public spheres.

Ideology can often be grasped in literary language use, choice of linguistic 'raw materials' and so on, producing what Raymond Williams termed as "structures of feeling".[3] Implying an interactive relationship between individuals and society in both historical and material perspectives, "structures of feelings" refer to the lived experience and sentiments of social consciousness in a certain historical period. Williams believes that a "structure of feeling" is "often indeed not yet recognized as social but taken to be private, idiosyncratic, and even isolating, but which in analysis has its emergent, connecting, and dominant characteristics, indeed its specific hierarchies" (Williams 1977: 132). Thus, ideology in literature often operates through an affective landscape, as feeling is the best mode of coming to terms with the intricacy among the residual, dominant and emergent ideologies.

In the first chapter of this section titled, 'Vernacularizing Emotions: Mohammed Ali's *Comrade* and *Hamdard*', Margrit Pernau focuses on Urdu newspapers in the twentieth century such as Abul Kalam Azad's *Al-Hilāl*, Zafar Ali Khan's *Zamīndār*, Mehdi Hasan's *Madina* and Muhammad Ali's twin publications, the English *Comrade* and the Urdu *Hamdard*. Tracing their genealogy from the nineteenth century, *Delhi Urdu Akhbār* and the reformist journals like *Tahzīb al-Akhlāq, Awadh Akhbār* and the *Paisā Akhbār*, Pernau investigates not only the impact of vernacularization on the linguistic but also the emotional and political style of newspapers.

The following chapter, 'In Defense of the *Prem'sāgar*. Re-evaluating the Narrative of the Hindi-Urdu Split' by Gautam Liu questions the common narrative of the divide of a common Hindi-Urdu prose at the beginning of the nineteenth century. Through his close examination of the work of Fort William's Bhākhā Munshi Lallu Lal, *Prem'sāgar*, Liu questions the existence of common Hindi-Urdu prose and suggests that the language of *Prem'sāgar* is a rather organic development of a vibrant prose tradition in the Hindi heartland.

The next chapter of the book by Neilesh Bose titled 'Vernaculars across Texts: Modern Islam and Modern Literature in Bengal' dwells on the ways in which language ideology impinges on understanding of religion. The chapter highlights the role of the vernacular condition or vernacularization as a model for understanding religion, which, he argues, has yet to appear in tandem with studies of literary history. His chapter is oriented towards tying together the field of religious history and literary history through a look at Islam in Bengal from the first Koran in Bengali of Girish Chandra Sen in the 1880s to the poetry of Nazrul Islam, especially his poems in the 1920s, fusing imagery from Islam into a larger framework. Bose argues that both developments – the vernacularization of Islam and the Islamicization of Bengali poetry – belong in the same framework of a condition in which religion and literature must be seen as indispensable to one another.

Meenakshi Yadav's chapter, 'Reading Caste in Vernacular Journals', surveys the Hindi print sphere to analyze how caste ideologies exerted themselves on the operation of linguistic codes in these journals. The support for Sanskritized Hindi in late nineteenth century as the pure language (owing to its traditional association with Hinduism) and *mātṛbhāṣā* (mother tongue) did not necessarily result in its uncritical acceptance by all sections. Yadav demonstrates how the relative appropriation of Sanskritized Hindi by the periodicals was in tandem with the *varṇa* status of their editors and authors.

Finally, Torsten Tschacher's chapter, 'A South Asian Vernacular Public Overseas: Tamil in the Straits Settlements, c. 1870–1942', shifts the focus of discussion to overseas settlements. Pushing the idea of a 'South Asian vernacular' beyond its popularly assumed hierarchical relationship with English as the dominant idiom of colonial power, Tschacher examines it from the perspective of South Asians settled overseas as traders or labourers in another colony. By undertaking a close analysis of Tamil print and publishing in the Straits Settlements (Singapore, Penang and Melaka) between the late nineteenth century and the Japanese occupation in 1942, Tschacher suggests that the diasporic location of these writings added yet another layer to the English vernacular binary where 'vernacular' status became aspirational, and the local Tamil public sphere became more dependent on discourses produced in India.

Contested Terrains of Consciousness

Language ideologies in South Asia, in short, have played a pivotal role in the dynamics of power politics. Ever since the colonial 'welfare'-driven administrative intervention made languages instruments of arbitrary distribution of favours and neglect through administrative, education and pedagogical policies, linguistic groups have competed with each other to earn maximum recognition of the state. The accompanying technologies of print capitalism and the hegemonic position of English vis-à-vis the vernaculars ordered the rechanneling of creative energies in vernacular languages and invigorated new modes of aesthetic perception often engendering condescension for indigenous aesthetic principles in favour of 'modern' rational, secular aesthetics. No matter whether we think of the Partition of India, the birth of the sovereign nations in the subcontinent, state formation processes in independent India, language scenarios in post-Partition Pakistan with Urdu as the national language, or the *Bhāṣā Āndolan* in Bangladesh, language ideologies have continued to play a key role in shaping the history of South Asia which has ever since revolved around extra-linguistic resonances attached to languages and the concomitant identity politics. The chapters in this volume have attempted to expose the multilayered and deeply entangled existence of language ideologies in South Asian history and culture. Though drawn from different realms of language experiences, they converge on one point which is their assertion of what Terry Eagleton viewed as 'performative' aspect of ideology whereby "ideology creates and acts in a social world while it masquerades as a description of that world" (Eagleton 1991: 19). Duly cognizant of the fact that the South Asian language situation with its cultural plurality, linguistic heterogeneity and complex history and geography defies simple local vs global dialectics that often dominate our perception of vernaculars vs English, the contributions in this volume complicate such binaries. They probe the intersectionality of languages with human beings and their worlds and attempt to comprehend the ways in which individuals, institutions and the interrelationship they share is often an outcome of language ideologies. The very making of the category of the vernacular is immersed in ideology, so much so that one may even claim that language ideology is not significantly distinct from operations of ideology in other domains of human activity. In the process they unravel terrains of consciousness that are sites of continued contestations, claims and counterclaims and defy any easy logic of pure language or putative categorization.

Notes

1 For a detailed account, see Harder, Zaidi and Tschacher (2022).
2 This has met with some resistance; cf., for instance, Williams, Malhotra and Hawley (2018: Introduction).
3 The phrase 'structures of feeling' was first used by Williams in 1954 in his book (with the documentary filmmaker Michael Orrom) *Preface to Film*.

Bibliography

Althusser, Louis. 2014. *On the Reproduction of Capitalism: Ideology and Ideological State Apparatuses*. London: Verso.

Blommaert, Jan, and Jef Verschueren. 1998. *Debating Diversity: Analysing the Discourse of Tolerance*. London and New York: Routledge.

Brosius, Christiane and Axel Michaels. 2020. 'Vernacular Heritage as Urban Place-Making. Activities and Positions in the Reconstruction of Monuments after the Gorkha Earthquake in Nepal, 2015–2020: The Case of Patan.' *Sustainability*, 12(20), 8720; https://doi.org/10.3390/su12208720. Accessed 1 May 2023.

Eagleton, Terry. 1991. *Ideology: An Introduction*. United Kingdom: Verso.

Frow, J. 1986. *Marxism and Literary History*. Oxford: Basil Blackwell Ltd.
Harder, Hans (ed.). 2017. *Literature and Nationalist Ideology: Writing Histories of Modern Indian Languages*. London: Routledge.
Harder, Hans, Nishat Zaidi and Torsten Tschacher. 2022. *The Vernacular; Three Essays on an Ambivalent Concept and its Uses in South Asia*. Working Papers in Modern South Asian Languages and Literature 5, 2022. Heidelberg: Department of Modern South Asian Languages and Literatures.
Fishman, Joshua A. 1996. "Perfecting the Perfect: Improving the Beloved Language", in: Laura García Moreno and Peter C. Pfeiffer (eds): *Text and Nation: Cross-Disciplinary Essays on Cultural and National Identity*. Columbia: Camden House.
Kothari, Rita. 2011. *Chutnefying English: The Phenomenon of Hinglish*. India: Penguin Books Limited.
Mannheim, Karl. 2013. *Ideology and Utopia*. United Kingdom: Taylor & Francis.
Marx, Karl and Friedrich Engels. 1970. *The German Ideology. Part 1*. Ed. J. C. Arthur. New York: International Publishers.
Pollock, Sheldon. 1998. "India in the Vernacular Millennium: Literary Culture and Polity, 1000–1500." *Daedalus* 127, no. 3: 41–74. http://www.jstor.org/stable/20027507.
———. 2006. *Language of the Gods in the World of Men: Sanskrit, Culture, and Power in Premodern India*. Berkeley: University of California Press.
Rahman, Tariq. 2008. *Language, Ideology and Power: Language Learning Among the Muslims of Pakistan and North India*. Karachi: Oxford University Press Karachi.
Shankar, S. 2012. *Flesh and Fish Blood. Postcolonialism, Translation and the Vernacular*. Berkeley: University of California Press.
Thiong'O, Ngugi wa. 1992. *Decolonising the mind the politics of language in African literature*. London: Currey.
Williams, R. 1977. *Marxism and Literature*. Oxford: Oxford University Press.
Williams, Tyler, Anshu Malhotra and John Stratton Hawley (eds). 2018. *Text and Tradition in Early Modern North India*. New Delhi: Oxford University Press.
Woolard, Kathryn A. 1998. "Introduction: Language Ideology as a Field of Inquiry", in: Schieffelin, Bambi B. et al. (eds): *Language Ideologies: Practice and Theory*. NewYork/Oxford: Oxford University Press.
Woolard, Kathryn A. and Baby B. Schieffelin. 1994. "Language Ideology'. *Annual Review of Anthropology* 23: 55–82.

PART I

Ideologies of Vernaculars and English

1

BEYOND HEGEMONIC BINARIES

English and the 'Vernaculars' in Post-liberalization India

Javed Majeed

This chapter questions the validity and usefulness of the English-vernacular binary in India. It begins by addressing the global context of the changing relations between English and Indian languages in the subcontinent. I argue that we need to distinguish the colonial legacy of English in contemporary India from the way in which the spread of neoliberal doctrines in the 1980s and the liberalization of the Indian economy have contributed to its dominance. Without fully displacing the earlier colonial/post-colonial dynamic, the conditions of late capitalism after the end of the Cold War and the liberalization of the Indian economy have created another dimension to the relations between English and Indian languages. The spread of neoliberal ideas has naturalized English as the language of global competitiveness in India, and this has had an impact on its language economies.

As an index of globalism, English is often seen as 'neutral'. This is reflected in the use of Business English Lingua Franca (BELF) as a shared communication code within the global business community and in the continuing use of English as a medium of instruction in Institutes of Management in India and elsewhere. This 'neutrality' is reinforced by political perceptions of English as ethnically, culturally, and religiously 'neutral' in key domains. In India, such political perceptions extend to how some regional language elites oppose what they see as 'Hindi imperialism' by supporting English. This support of English in opposition to Hindi does not fit with the English-vernacular binary.

The English-vernacular binary tends to invest the latter with a grounded 'native' authenticity in opposition to English as a permanently 'colonial' and non-native language. This ignores how English has acquired functional nativeness in India. It also impedes the decolonization of English, because it reinforces channels of authentication and authority with reference to the native

DOI: 10.4324/9781003279921-3

speaker. In fact, the way the two terms in the binary operate indicates that they share an ideology of nativism, and in both the cases of English and the vernaculars, the figure of the 'native speaker' is instrumental in defining the boundaries of authentic belonging. The binary also mystifies the ways in which languages as indices of ancestral group identities are entangled with economic discourses of profit. Moreover, the binary disguises how English and some Indian languages have both been hegemonized in a hierarchical form of multilingualism in India. It also distorts another dimension in the construction of the term 'vernaculars', namely how the term 'vernacular' is juxtaposed with and posited in relation to 'classical' languages. In this regard, English is a vernacular too.

My chapter concludes by considering ways in which we might move beyond the English-vernacular binary in India, at least conceptually. In doing so, it ends on a utopian note, by considering what the term 'India' might mean. It also asks if English could have progressive potential as a global language. While the spread of English as a global language can be correlated with globalization as an economic process and the inequalities it has created, English is not in and of itself an actual cause of these inequalities. Positing English as a cause of these inequalities runs the risk of occluding the material structures of domination and pre-empting critiques of economic systems.

Economic Liberalization and English as an Index of Global Competitiveness

It is not possible to take a nation-centric or region-centric approach when considering the status of regional languages vis-à-vis English in India because the position of English as a global lingua franca has had an impact on the relationship between the 'vernaculars' and English. While the so-called regional languages in the subcontinent are themselves transnational languages due to their presence in the South Asian diasporas across the world, here I will focus on English as a global language. This is because its spread across the globe is a world historical phenomenon which has affected many other languages and their relationships to it as well. Moreover, the function of English has changed primarily from communication between non-native and native English speakers to communication between non-native speakers (Graddol 2006; see also Seidlhofer & Jenkins 2003), and so the relationship between 'regional' languages and English in India also has to take into account the changing function of English as a medium of exchange between non-native speakers of English.

In considering the global context, we should distinguish the colonial legacy of English in India from other factors contributing to its current dominance. Phillipson (1992) and de Swaan (2002) have argued that it was only after 1945 that English became globally dominant. The key factor here was the decisive rise of the US as the major global power of the advanced capitalist economies. This was reflected in the way American foundations and institutions laid the groundwork for MBA programmes and management studies in India in the 1950s and 1960s, as a result of which English became the language of instruction in Indian Institutes of Management (Jammulamadaka 2019). This collaboration in management studies led to the transfer of management knowledge and pedagogy from the US to India, and it included the transfer of curriculum, teaching methods, hiring policies, and the tenurial system (Kothiyal, Bell & Clarke 2018). It is also likely that the Cold War played a role in the sponsoring of management studies as part of a diplomatic and cultural policy of expanding US influence and the ideology of capitalism against the Soviet bloc, especially given India's non-aligned foreign policy and its relations with the USSR during that period.

The dominance of English in management studies has been further reinforced by the spread of neoliberal free market doctrines from the 1980s onwards, which has naturalized the use of English as the language of global competitiveness around the world. For example, after the 1997–98 Asian financial crisis and the IMF-led economic restructuring in South Korea, English was promoted as the medium of instruction in higher education because it was seen as an index of competitiveness and as the inevitable side effect of globalization (Piller and Cho 2015). In Singapore, the decision to make English the official language was also motivated by its perception as a mark of global competitiveness and by Singapore's aim to position itself as a global city (Wee 2012). Similarly, the switch from French to English as a medium of instruction in Rwanda in 2008 was partly justified with reference to English as the language of globalization and the need to attract FDI in the service sector (Spowage 2018). The naturalization of English as the language of global competitiveness is evident in India, where the US patronage of management studies in English has been reinforced by the spread of neoliberal free-market doctrines, particularly after the liberalization of the Indian economy, which accelerated after the economic crisis during the Congress government of 1991–1996 (Frankel 2005). The preference for English as a global lingua franca has also been conditioned by and correlates with the expansion of the digitalized knowledge economy (Ricento 2015b). Hence, leading entrepreneurs in the Indian IT industry view English as an index of globalization, and they see its dominance in Indian business and management as the Indian economy coming of age (Sonntag 2015).

This has clearly had an effect on the relations between English and regional languages in India. Frankel (2005: xiii) describes India as 'an enclave economy with islands of excellence distributed between regions, states, and urban and rural areas'. These enclaves are the knowledge-based sector, involving some 15% of the population who are also India's privileged consumer classes, which absorbs well-trained industrialists, managers, laboratory scientists, and software engineers and competes in the global market. This sector has a high international profile and is concentrated in major cities in a few states, one of which is Bangalore in Karnataka, well known as a centre of India's IT and business processing outsourcing industries. As a result, there are competing linguistic hegemonies in Bangalore, between the local Kannadiga identity of 'Bangaluru' as a regional city and the cosmopolitan identity of 'Bangalore' as an English-speaking international metropolis celebrated by the city's bourgeoisie and English press (Nair 2009, Sonntag 2015). Bangalore is thus indicative of how the predominance of English as a global language (EGL) within a global labour market co-exists with the existence of regional and state labour markets, with the upper lucrative levels of this labour market focusing on the knowledge economy and demanding a knowledge of EGL and the lower levels of the agricultural and the industrial economy operating in state and regional languages (Williams 2015, Romaine 2015).

We see the particularities of English as an index of globalism at work in call centres in India. In many ways, 'language workers' in call centre workers are emblematic figures of late capitalism (Boutet 2012). The key features of English language work in call centres have been well-studied; these include accent reduction, location masking, scripting, and voice standardization (Boutet 2012, Mirchandani 2004). This language work involves what Boutet has called 'the extreme merchandising' of speech in English (209). Call centre operatives are in effect English language workers, who through accent reduction and the neutralization (in multiple senses) of Indian English are converted into 'a resource that can face the customer in any part of the world' (Mirchandani 2004: 360). We might think of call centres as nodes of 'language trafficking', which reproduce the spread of a particular type of global English throughout the world (359).

Thus, in recalibrating the notion of vernacularity in relation to English in post-liberalization India, the colonial legacy of English needs to be distinguished from the key factors which have contributed to the dominance of English in India since 1945. Without fully displacing the earlier colonial/post-colonial dynamic between Indian languages and English, the conditions of late capitalism after the end of the Cold War and the liberalization of the Indian economy have created another dimension to this dynamic, which has to be taken into account.

The 'Neutrality' of English and the English-Vernacular Binary

Given the global context in which English has operated since the end of the Cold War and with the spread of neoliberalism, our understanding of its dominance of English and how it is reproduced can be enhanced by de Swaan's (2002) world-systems approach to language. De Swaan argued that the world language system, held together by English as the 'hypercentral language', has oligopolistic features. These include privileged markets, communication savings effects, and language learning saving effects. He also compared language loyalty to brand loyalty: in some ways, the dominant languages of the world-system operate like prestigious brands. The reconceptualization of language as branded goods is evident in how the post-war global expansion of English is described in reports by the British Council as an 'asset' comparable to North Sea Oil, a 'world commodity', and a 'brand [...] highly sought after' (Phillipson 1992). De Swaan further argues that users of dominant languages benefit from legitimization effects (134–135), that is, from the automatic advantages enjoyed by the mother tongue speakers of dominant languages in situations involving negotiation, competition, and conflict. In such situations, using the dominant language is intrinsically legitimizing, while the use of other languages requires explanation (see also Bourdieu 1977 on linguistic production in the language market and the role of 'symbolic capital' in authorizing dominant languages). The legitimizing effects accruing to English extend to its being posited as 'neutral' in terms of conducting business in a language which transcends ethnic and cultural diversity (Wright 2015). In management studies, this has been reinforced by BELF as a shared communication code within the global business community, which is not tied to a cultural identity rooted in a narrowly defined ethnos (Tietze 2008).

Political imperatives to use English as ethnically and culturally 'neutral' dovetail with the dominance of English as a lingua franca (ELF) in the global economy. Thus, the perception of English as a pragmatic, inter-ethnic, and neutral lingua franca also underlay its choice as the official language of Singapore (Wee 2012), while the switch from French to English in Rwanda was partly motivated by perceptions of French as tainted by its association with the Hutus and the genocidal Francophone government (Romaine 2015). As is well known, the Constituent Assembly framed and adopted the Indian Constitution in English, and there is no version in an Indian language which has legal standing. Part of the reason for this was the perception that English was not tied to a particular region, unlike Hindi, which faces the challenge of being a regional language that simultaneously aspires to be a 'national' language (Gupta 1970, Kudaisya 2006, Austin 2009). In addition, Hindi, like Urdu, has been communalized along religious lines from the late nineteenth century onwards (King 1994, Dalmia 1997, Orsini 2002; for the parallel communalization of Urdu, see Rahman 2011), and this has limited its ability to function as a point of identification for different communities (Sarangi 2009). In arguing that English should be viewed as the Latin of the twenty-first century, Waquet (2001) has pointed out that unlike Latin which was closely associated with the Catholic Church as a liturgical language until the Vatican II Council of 1962 to 1965, English does not have specific sacerdotal associations. As such, in South Asia as a whole, English is more readily seen as 'secular' than its rivals Hindi and Urdu.

Moreover, the Official Language (Amendment) Act of 1967, which legalized assurances on the continuation of English in addition to Hindi for all official purposes of the Union and for the transaction of business in Parliament, was partly designed to placate those who were resistant to what they saw as the imposition of Hindi, especially in South India, where some activists saw and continue to see efforts to expand Hindi's influence as language 'imperialism'. These tensions were evident in the Constituent Assembly debates about Hindi as an official language (Dasgupta 2013, Austin 2009). This opposition to Hindi was not confined to speakers of South Indian languages alone. Bengali intellectuals and politicians also shared these views (for an interesting account particularly of S. K. Chatterji's views, see Husain 2017). The opposition extends to non-Hindi-speaking states supporting English in advanced education in order to equalize the opportunities of their regional elites in relation to elites from Hindi-speaking regions (Brass 2009). Tamil Nadu has gone the furthest in eschewing Hindi, and it has one of the highest levels of bi- and tri-lingualism in English in the country (ibid.). So, while English is a key issue in the competition between established elites and proto-elites, it is also a key factor in the competition between the Hindi-speaking elite and regional language elites, some of whom actively support English in order to limit the power and influence of Hindi at a national level. This active support of English on the part of some regional language elites, as well as the competition between other regional languages and Hindi, is clearly at odds with the English-vernacular binary.

Vernacular 'Authenticity' and 'Inauthentic' Globality

The English-vernacular binary also evokes a contrast between the rooted authenticity of the latter, distant from the workings of the political economy, and the rootless inauthenticity of the former, entangled with oppressively global economic processes. As the original Concept Note for the Conference put it, the 'vernaculars' are 'invested with qualities like grounded-ness and expressive strength'. We can add that they evoke a specific 'structure of feeling', to use Raymond Williams' term. However, language economists have argued that languages have become a factor in the production process and language learning has been reconceptualized as an economic decision in the 'cognitive capitalism' of the knowledge economy (Duchêne & Heller 2012, Ricento 2015a, Spowage 2018). With tertiarization and the emergence of the knowledge economy, communication is central to the market's functioning, and the role of language, culture, and identity in the creation of added value has increased (Bale 2015). At the same time, while it is clear that the new centrality of linguistic form and practice in economic production has affected our ideas of language, and language and culture are increasingly treated in economic terms (Holborow 2015), this has not replaced older discourses which treat language as indexing cultural identity, allegiance, and peoplehood

(Duchêne & Heller 2012). In fact, as the latter convincingly argues, the discourses of pride in which language is framed as a cultural heritage, and of profit, in which language is a means to material gain, are co-constituted tropes (Duchêne & Heller 2012, 16; see also Susan Gal 2012, Percio & Duchêne 2012). As a source of symbolic added value in the globalized economy, language is tied to the commodification of national identities and the marketing of authenticity. These identities are mobilized in the construction of niche markets, and language is corralled into branding, through the use of characteristic scripts, the iconic naming of places, people, and objects, and in the language of service in which speaking in a particular accent is crucial to selling certain goods (Duchêne & Heller 2012, 10–14). The association of pride with rootedness and authenticity can be and is commercialized and consumed (Percio & Duchêne 2012).

In South Asia, the dialectical interaction between discourses of profit and ancestral pride has another dimension. Given the multilingual nature of the subcontinent, in the political competition between established and emerging elites language issues attain a high degree of saliency (Sonntag 2009, Sheth 2009, Rahman 1996). In this intra-elite competition, language is both an economic asset and a communal symbol in the pursuit of economic advancement, social status, and political power. The political competition over official language status in India is in part economic competition over public sector employment. This fuels political mobilization on the basis of language, particularly as the state sector in South Asia accounts for a larger share of GDP than in economically advanced democracies. The economic value of public sector employment for aspiring white-collar workers means linguistic federalism is key in attempting to equalize opportunities for different language groups in that sector (Choudhry 2009). Thus, the investing of 'vernaculars' with qualities like authentic groundedness and expressive strength in opposition to English's inauthentic globality obscures how the former is simultaneously constituted in terms of ancestral pride, community identity, and economic advancement and profit.

It is also worth noting at this point Peter Ives' discussions (2006, 2010) of how Gramsci did not valorize what he called the 'spontaneous' grammar of vernacular languages as authentic or natural, or even inherently more in tune with a particular group of people. For Gramsci, the vernacular is not necessarily free from unequal power relations, nor is it necessarily a natural expression of one's being in opposition to the artificial imposition of a normative grammar which originates from the ruling class. In fact, the apparent spontaneity of the vernacular may not be the result of free choice at all but could be indicative of the subjugated nature of subaltern conditions and the fragmentary and episodic character of the history of subaltern groups instead. Indeed, it could also be argued that the positing of 'vernaculars' as grounded and authentic forms of belonging, and hence in opposition to a free-floating global English, in fact reinforces a politics of identity which polices forms of belonging deemed appropriate for subaltern groups. As Hany Babu (2017) has insightfully pointed out, Article 351 in the Indian Constitution is committed to developing Hindi as one of the official languages of the Union but not English. This could be interpreted as perpetuating unequal access to English, and therefore as reinforcing English-speaking elite closure in India, while simultaneously intensifying the investment of structures of feeling in the vernaculars as 'authentically' Indian. From one perspective at least, the latter could be seen as a way of keeping subalterns in their (authentic) place as part of the processes of English-speaking elite closure.

English as Permanently Colonial and the Ideology of Nativism

The English-vernacular binary also mystifies the ways in which, as Kachru (2005: 115) puts it, 'on the one hand, we have nativized English discourse, and on the other hand we have Englishized discourse in South Asian languages'. By perpetuating the notion of English as always foreign in India, and as a permanent colonial legacy, the binary impedes the decolonization of English and reifies it as non-Indian. It obscures how English has acquired functional nativeness in India, and how it has developed its own sub-varieties and regional variations (ibid.), indicating widespread penetration across various social, functional, and educational levels in the subcontinent. It fixes language as a static phenomenon, whereas the functional nativeness of India's English is a sociolinguistic phenomenon which has emerged in a dynamic interactional context of language contact between English and Indian languages (ibid.).

In doing so, the English-vernacular binary also reinforces channels of authentication and authority with reference to the native speaker of English and thereby perpetuates subordination to the 'ELT mythology, imposed by the ELT Empire' (ibid.: 19). However, although the vernaculars in India index an autochthonous legitimacy, the way the two terms in the English and vernacular binary operate indicates that they both share an ideology of nativism. Despite widespread bilingualism in India, language movements and the very notion of the linguistic states in India are implicitly premised on the category of the monolingual native speaker. Similarly, even though world Englishes are pluricentric, monolingual paradigms continue to cast a long shadow over the representation and teaching of English. As Seidlhofer and Jenkins (2003) have stressed, until recently the default descriptive reality when approaching English as a world language was that English is a native language. It was only with VOICE, the Vienna-Oxford International Corpus of English, that we had the first corpus capturing ELF spoken interactions between L2 speakers, which enabled us to conceptualize ELF as a language use in its own right. In the case of both English and the vernaculars, the figure of the 'native speaker' is instrumental in defining the apparently common-sense linguistic boundaries of authentic belonging, in relation to which the 'non-native speaker' is positioned (to paraphrase Martin Gill (2021: 273), discussing English and immigration in Britain).

The Joint Hegemonization of English and the Vernaculars

In addition, the English-vernacular binary ignores the hegemonization of Indian languages in the Eighth Schedule, which institutionalizes a particular kind of hierarchical multilingualism in India (for this hierarchy, see Agnihotri 2015, Hany Babu 2017). As the latter argues, the constitutional scheme and official language policy of the Indian state, rather than envisaging a complementary relationship between languages, envisages a hierarchical system of languages. The Indian Constitution has created a four-tier order of languages, with Sanskrit, Hindi, scheduled, and non-scheduled languages occupying different rungs of the ladder. The Eighth Schedule has accorded differential status to Indian languages, which is reflected in differential institutional and societal support for and attitudes towards these languages (Hany Babu 2017). It has also been argued that the multilingual ethos that is constitutive of Indian society was largely ignored in the Constituent Assembly debates, when decisions about language were incorporated into the Constitution. Moreover, the Directive Principles of State Policy contain no specific directions concerning minority languages (Agnihotri 2015). Thus, the listing of languages in the Eighth Schedule has opened up a competitive inter-lingual dynamic between the 'vernaculars', which again does not fit the English-vernacular binary model. This oppositional binary also obscures the hierarchical and hegemonic form of multilingualism defined by the state in India, in which both English and the Eighth Schedule languages, with Hindi at its apex, have joint, if fluctuating and variable, forms of hegemony.

The Ideology of Classicism

The English-vernacular binary ignores another dimension in the construction of the term 'vernaculars', namely how the term 'vernacular' is juxtaposed with and posited in relation to 'classical' languages. In the case of the Indo-Aryan family of languages, the latter refers to Sanskrit, Greek, and Latin. In this context, English is a vernacular too. The English-vernacular binary therefore obscures the placing of vernaculars, including English, in an evaluative hierarchy in relation to these classical languages. The anxiety of this placing with regard to English is evident in the tensions around the term 'English' in Macaulay's 1835 Minute on Education. On the one hand, this Minute argues that English is the language of progress and science, in short of techno-modernity. On the other hand, and in tension with this, English is compared to Greek and Latin: 'What the Greek and Latin were to the contemporaries of

More and Ascham, our tongue is to the people of India' (Macaulay 1835: 167). Moreover, for Macaulay one of the 'memorable instances' in history of a 'great impulse given to the mind of a whole society, of prejudices overthrown, [...] of arts and sciences planted in countries which had recently been ignorant and barbarous', is the Renaissance or the 'great revival of letters among the Western nations [...]. At that time almost everything that was worth reading was contained in the writings of the ancient Greeks and Romans'. He adds that in this period had only Anglo-Saxon chronicles and romances in Norman French been printed in England, then 'would England ever have been what she is now?' (Macaulay 1835: 166–67). English will create a 'Renaissance' in India, like Greek and Latin did in the 'revival of letters' in Europe. In Macaulay's Minute, then, English is the language of modernity and progress, and yet it also has to borrow some of its prestige from the aura of Greek and Latin to which it is compared. These contradictions are intensified by Macaulay's tendency to put English into competition with Greek and Latin. For example, he asserts that 'The literature of England is now more valuable than that of classical antiquity' (167), and more hesitantly, that it 'abounds with works of imagination *not inferior* to the noblest which Greece has bequeathed to us' (166, emphasis mine), the hesitancy here signalling some degree of uncertainty as to the valuation of English in relation to classical languages.

More might be said about the contradictions in Macaulay's ideology of language, particularly with regard to his references to Sanskrit, which complicates the category of classical antiquity in the Minute by instituting a competitive relationship between Greek and Latin on the one hand and Sanskrit on the other. Here we can note the tensions in Macaulay's Minute stemming from positing English as a living language indexing science and progress, which at the same time has to borrow some of its prestige from the 'dead' languages of Greek and Latin to which it is compared. English is pre-eminently modern and yet has to have the aura of classical antiquity. What we see in Macaulay's Minute is therefore the contradictory marking of the value of English as a vernacular. This contradictory placing is also evident in the case of Hindi. On the one hand, Hindi is pre-eminently modern; on the other hand, it has to be purified by Sanskritizing it. It operates simultaneously as an index of India's coming to age in the epoch of modernity, and yet it must continually showcase and extend its links to Sanskrit as the pre-eminent language of antiquity. This has led to what Agnihotri (2015: 53) has called the 'puritanical fanaticism involved in Sanskritising Hindi'. It has also created a wide gap between the Hindi used in schools and that in homes, making it difficult for the language to serve as a vehicle for mass literacy (Sheth 2009). Snell (2011) has argued that the over-formal register of Hindi promoted in official circles has even encouraged the importation of English words into the language. Moreover, the main impetus behind this official Hindi is to shape it as a symbol of a particular version of Indian nationhood, rather than to extend its communicative competence

(Gupta 1970), and as such, this further narrows the possibilities of identifying with it as a would-be 'national' as opposed to an official language. The point here, though, is that treating English as not vernacular obscures how the ideology of classicism has operated in relation to both English and some Indian languages, both of which are 'vernaculars' in this context.

Moving beyond the English-Vernacular Binary

Is it possible to move beyond the English-vernacular binary, at least conceptually? Annie Montaut (2006) points out that what causes a language to be separatist is not language diversity per se but the notion of language as a monolithic entity, territorially bounded, and as an index of cultural identity, allegiance and peoplehood (for languages as indices of group identities, see Schieffelin, Woolard & Kroskrity 1998). This concept of language is partly tied to the figure of the native speaker with exclusive rights to the language in question. Hence, dismantling the category of the native speaker will help us to move beyond the English-vernacular binary. One way to do this, as Ayesha Kidwai (2008: 5) has argued, is to capitalize on the persistent and pervasive bi- and multilingualism in India. In fact, all the states in the Indian Union are plurilingual units. Pervasive multilingualism engenders a positive attitude towards using and learning new languages, without prejudice to whether they are 'native' to the community a speaker belongs to – as multilingual speakers know, they do not have to use all their languages in identical domains for identical purposes. This reduces language conflict, because functionally specialized multilingualism allows new languages to be added on for specialized domains.

Undoing the distinction between native and non-native speakers will also have an effect on how we think about English as an entity in India. As Gill (2021: 279) has pointed out, the construct of the 'native' speaker forms 'part of the hidden ideological apparatus by which the English language has secured its frontiers and identities against incursion by non-native others'. The binary of the native and non-native speaker of English ignores how English has been indigenized in countries like India, which has institutionalized varieties with a history of acculturation and a range of functions in local education, administration, and legal systems (Kachru 1986, Phillipson 1992). Undoing the distinction between native and non-native speakers would counter the normative and ideological narratives of authenticity grounding the notion of languages (Brutt-Griffler & Samimyi 2001, Myhill 2003), both English and the Indian vernaculars, as bounded unitary entities and their speakers as a well-defined, homogenous, and monolingual community, in contrast to the 'inauthenticity of the bilingual, the hybrid, the non-standard and the non-native' (Gill 2021: 272).

Similarly, Montaut (2006) makes a powerful argument for the recovery of grassroots multilingualism in India, by drawing on the insights and methodologies of Creole linguistics, which counters the reification of languages as objects tied to native speakers. She cites de Selva and Sugathpala (1975) to the effect that the Prakrits could be seen in terms of the creolization of Sanskrit. She also argues for the importance of areal (horizontal) contact in India blurring the boundaries between genetic grouping of languages. It is this which led Dil (1980) to posit an Indian linguistic area in which all four original families of languages (Indo-Aryan, Dravidian, Austric, Tibeto-Burman) in contact on the subcontinent today share more specific features among themselves than any single one of them does with an external member of the family (Montaut 2006; Dil 1980).

Thus, creole linguistics as opposed to cladistics might help us to move beyond the reification of languages as objects tied to native speakers in India. The recovery of grassroots multilingualism as opposed to institutionalized hierarchical multilingualism inevitably leads us to consider how we can reactivate the fluid continuum of languages and dialects in South Asia. Masica (1993) has stressed that the entire Indo-Aryan realm except Sinhalese is one dialectal continuum, where continued contact inhibits crystallization, and differentiated dialects continue to influence one another. The speech of each village differs slightly from the next without loss of mutual intelligibility all the way from Assam to Afghanistan. Although of course cumulatively the differences are great, this does mean that it is difficult to draw clear boundaries between dialects, not to mention languages (Masica 1993: 23–25). This continuum is implicitly rejected by identity claims tied to territorially bounded languages, and also by the struggle between languages for recognition in the Eighth Schedule, in which languages are construed as rigid entities, in conflict and competition with each other. Montaut (2006) suggests one way to activate this continuum and therefore a grassroots multilingual ethos with its functional heterogeneity is to build on the linguistic experience of diversity and hybridity, in order to cultivate a specific cognitive and cultural mode of relationships from the viewpoint and stance of the historical legacies of creolized cultures in India itself (Montaut 2006: 101–2). The interaction between languages as flexible and adjustable systems, and a stress on their hybrid features and functional heterogeneity, fits a narrative of plural identities and belongings, and is at odds with the notion of a single unitary identity and a single mode of belonging (ibid.). In such a scenario, speakers will not be defined as one-language users but shifting users of shifting multilayered repertoires, with flexible and constant adjustments between speaker and addressee taking place, aiming more at communicational performance than correctness (ibid.: 95). In this scenario, therefore, languages would be approached as products of dynamic interaction and not as static phenomena.

As Bagchi (2012: 6) notes, utopian thinking tends to think beyond national boundaries. We can work with this in two ways. First, as a linguistic region 'India' is at odds with the post-Partition political map of the subcontinent (Majeed 2015). The Indian languages of the Indo-European family of languages are an obvious example of a group of languages that do not fit the political boundaries of the subcontinent, while languages such as Punjabi and Bengali, which are geographically contiguous with each other, span across the political borders of the subcontinent. Other languages that are not geographically contiguous are related in families that span political boundaries. Brahui, spoken in the highlands of Baluchistan and contiguous parts of Sind in present-day Pakistan, with speakers in contiguous parts of Iran and Afghanistan, is related to the Dravidian language family of South India. This language, described as 'the most-interest exciting of the languages of the Dravidian family' (Dil 1980: 315), is a good example of how India as a linguistic region does not fit with India and Pakistan as political entities created out of competing nationalisms. That is, already built into the idea of 'India' as a linguistic region is a transnationalism that is at odds with the 'national' in the subcontinent.

The second way to work with this is to consider, as Peter Ives (2006, 2010) has done, whether the global spread of English might have progressive potential as a global language. While English is a crucial element of an international business class structure, it is not necessarily the case that global English will always be connected to the apparatus of global capitalism. For example, Michael Toolan (2003) points out that while globalization has anti-democratic effects, it has also resulted in the spread of a worldwide rights-oriented culture – English could be the vehicle for this culture's articulation and maintenance. That is, English can just as easily be an instrument in the democratization of global governance as it is an instrument in anti-democratization that characterizes much current globalization. As Richard Alexander (2003) also points out, the formulation of alternatives to globalization can and, perhaps in view of the increasing internationalization of the opposition to global institutions, must proceed in part through English – this is a dialectical aspect of the global reach English has achieved. The progressive potential of English is also evident in India. Oppressed groups like Dalits view English as an instrument of socio-economic mobility, and as a form of resistance to dominant regional languages and their Sanskritization (Sarangi 2009, Sonntag 2015). The 'castelessness' of English promises agency, articulation, recognition, and justice to Dalit writers, and its potential to translate 'the Dalit life from fatalism to an identity of rights outweighs considerations of its distance from Indian reality' (Kothari 2013: 67). Similarly, Hany Babu argues that because English is outside the four-tier order of languages defined by the Constitution, it has emancipatory potential, and hence 'to attain a casteless society, it is essential that we enable the citizens to wield a language that has no memory of caste' (Hany Babu 2017: 118). Thus, just as the vernaculars in India are not intrinsically connected to freedom, so English is not intrinsically connected to oppression. We should not slide into the mistake of assuming that Englishization is a cause of global inequalities. Replacing English with another language will not in and of itself change material structures of domination. While the spread of

English as a global language can be correlated with globalization as an economic process and the inequalities it has created, it is important to resist the temptation to posit English as an actual cause of those inequalities, otherwise we run the risk of both occluding and pre-empting critiques of material structures of domination.

References

Agnihotri, R.K. 2015. "Constituent Assembly Debates on Language". *Economic & Political Weekly*, 50(8), 47–56.

Alexander, R. 2003. "Global Languages Oppress But Are Liberating, Too: The Dialectics of English". In: Mair, C. (ed.) *The Politics of English as a World Language*. Amsterdam & New York: Editions Rodopoi B.V., pp. 87–95.

Austin, G. 2009. "Language and the Constitution: The Half-hearted Compromise". In: Sarangi, A. (ed.) *Language and Politics in India*. New Delhi: Oxford University Press, pp. 41–92.

Bagchi, B. 2012. "Introduction". In: Bagchi, B. (ed.) *The Politics of the (im)Possible: Utopia and Dystopia*. Los Angeles: Sage, pp. 1–19.

Bale, J. 2015. "Language Policy and Global Political Economy". In: Ricento, T. (ed.) *Language Policy and Political Economy: English in a Global Context*. Oxford: Oxford University Press, pp. 72–96.

Bourdieu, P. 1977. "The Economics of Linguistic Exchanges". *Social Science Information*, 16(6), 645–668.

Boutet, J. 2012. 'Language Workers. Emblematic Figures of Late Capitalism'. In: Duchêne, A. & Heller, M. (eds.) *Language in Late Capitalism: Pride and Profit*. New York and London: Routledge, pp. 207–229.

Brass, P.R. 2009. 'Elite Interests, Popular Passions, and Social Power in the Language Politics of India.' In: *Language and Politics in India*, Ed. Asha Sarangi, New Delhi: OUP, 183–217.

Brutt-Griffler, J. & Samimyi, K.K. 2001. "Transcending the Nativeness Paradigm". *World Englishes*, 20(1), 99–106.

Choudhry, S. 2009. Managing Linguistic Nationalism through Constitutional Design: Lessons from South Asia". *International Journal of Constitutional Law*, 7(4), 577–618.

Dalmia, V. 1997. *The Nationalization of Hindu Traditions: Bhāratendu Hariśchandra and Nineteenth-Century Benares*. New Delhi: Oxford University Press.

Dasgupta, J. 2013. "Language Policy and National Development in India". In: Brown, M.E. & Ganguly, S. (eds.) *Fighting Words: Language Policy and Ethnic Relations in Asia*. Cambridge, MA: MIT Press, pp. 21–50.

de Selva, A.M. & Sugathpala, W.M. 1975. *Linguistic Diversity*. Annamalainagar: Annamalai University.

de Swaan, A. 2002. *Words of the World: The Global Language System*. Cambridge: Polity Press.

Dil, A.S. (ed.) 1980. *Language and Linguistic Area: Chapters by Emeneau B. Murray*. Stanford: Stanford University Press.

Duchêne, A. & Heller, M. 2012. "Pride and Profit: Changing Discourses of Language, Capital and Nation-State". In: Duchêne, A. & Heller, M. (eds.) *Language in Late Capitalism: Pride and Profit*. New York and London: Routledge, pp. 1–21.

Frankel, F. 2005. *India's Political Economy 1947–2000: The Gradual Revolution.* New Delhi: Oxford University Press.

Gal, S. 2012. "Sociolinguistic Regimes and the Management of Diversity". In: Duchêne, A. & Heller, M. (eds.) *Language in Late Capitalism: Pride and Profit.* New York and London: Routledge, pp. 22–42.

Gill, M. 2021. "Nativeness, Authority, Authenticity: The Construction of Belonging and Exclusion Debates about English Language Proficiency and Immigration in Britain". In: Percy, C. & Davidson, M.C. (eds.) *The Languages of Nation: Attitudes and Norms.* Bristol: Multilingual Matters, pp. 271–291.

Graddol, D. 2006. *English Next: Why Global English May Mean the End of 'English as a Foreign Language'.* British Council.

Gupta, J.D. 1970. *Language Conflict and National Development: Group Politics and National Language Policy in India.* Berkeley: University of California Press.

Hany Babu, M.T. 2017. "Breaking the Chaturvana System of Languages: The Need to Overhaul the Language Policy". *Economic & Political Weekly*, 52(23), 112–119.

Holborow, M. 2015. *Language and Neoliberalism.* New York: Routledge.

Husain, I. 2017. "Countering Hindi Nationalism: Reflections on Political and Intellectual Response of Bengal to Hindi after Independence". *Proceedings of the Indian History Congress*, 78, 1137–1146.

Ives, P. 2006. "'Global English': Linguistic Imperialism or Practical Lingua Franca?" *Studies in Language and Capitalism*, 1, 121–141.

Ives, P. 2010. "Cosmopolitanism and Global English: Language Politics in Globalisation Debates". *Political Studies*, 58, 516–535.

Jammulamadaka, N. 2019. "Indian Management. A Modernization Experiment". In: Bowden, B. & Murray, A. (eds.) *The Palgrave Handbook of Management History.* Cham: Palgrave Macmillan, pp. 1–20.

Kachru, B.B. 1986. "The Power and Politics of English". *World Englishes*, 5(2/3), 121–140.

Kachru, B.B. 2005. *Asian Englishes: Beyond the Canon.* Hong Kong: Hong Kong University Press.

Kidwai, A. 2008. "Managing Multilingual India". *The Marxist*, 24(2), 1–7.

King, C.R. 1994. *One Language, Two Scripts: The Hindi Movement in Nineteenth Century North India.* Bombay: Oxford University Press.

Kothari, R. 2013. "Caste in a Casteless Language? English as a Language of 'Dalit' Expression". *Economic & Political Weekly*, 48(39), 60–68.

Kothiyal, N., Bell, E., & Clarke, C. 2018. "Moving Beyond Mimicry: Developing Hybrid Spaces in Indian Business Schools". *Academy of Management Learning & Education*, 17(2), 137–154.

Kudaisya, G. 2006. *Region, Nation, 'Heartland': Uttar Pradesh in India's Body Politic.* New Delhi: Sage.

Macaulay, T.B. 1835. "Minute Recorded in the General Department by Thomas Babington Macaulay, Law Member of the Governor-General's Council, dated 2 February 1835". In: Zastoupil, L. & Moir, M. (eds.) *The Great Indian Education debate: Documents Relating to the Orientalist-Anglicist Controversy, 1781–1843.* Richmond: Curzon, pp. 161–173.

Majeed, J. 2015. "'A State of Affairs which is Essentially Indefinite': The Linguistic Survey of India (1894–1927)". *African Studies*, 74(2), 221–234.

Masica, C.P. 1993. *The Indo-Aryan Languages.* Cambridge: Cambridge University Press.

Mirchandani, K. 2004. "Practices of Global Capital: Gaps, Cracks and Ironies in Transnational Call centres in India". *Global Networks*, 4(4), 355–373.
Montaut, A. 2006. "Colonial Language Classification, Post-colonial Language Movements, and the Grassroots Multilingualism Ethos in India". In: Hasan, M. & Roy, A. (eds.) *Living Together Separately: Cultural India in History and Politics*. New Delhi: Oxford University Press, pp. 75–116.
Myhill, J. 2003. "The Native Speaker, Identity, and the Authenticity Hierarchy". *Language Sciences*, 25, 77–97.
Nair, J. 2009. "Language and the Right to the City". In: Sarangi, A. (ed.) *Language and Politics in India*. New Delhi: Oxford University Press, pp. 368–415.
Orsini, F. 2002. *The Hindi Public Sphere 1920–1940: Language and Literature in the Age of Nationalism*. Delhi: Oxford University Press.
Percio, A.D. & Duchêne, A. 2012. "Commodification of Pride and Resistance to Profit: Language Practices as Terrain of Struggle in a Swiss Football Stadium". In: Duchene, A. & Heller, M. (eds.) *Language in Late Capitalism: Pride and Profit*. New York and London: Routledge, pp. 43–72.
Phillipson, R. 1992. *Linguistic Imperialism*. Oxford: Oxford University Press.
Piller, I. & Cho, J. 2015. "Neoliberalism as Language Policy". In: Ricento, T. (ed.) *Language Policy and Political Economy: English in a Global Context*. Oxford: Oxford University Press, pp. 162–186.
Rahman, T. 1996. *Language and Politics in Pakistan*. Karachi: Oxford University Press.
Rahman, T. 2011. *From Hindi to Urdu: A Social and Political History*. Karachi: Oxford University Press.
Ricento, T. (ed.) 2015a. *Language Policy and Political Economy: English in a Global Context*. Oxford: Oxford University Press.
Ricento, T. 2015b. "English: The Global Lingua Franca". In: Ricento, T. (ed.) *Language Policy and Political Economy: English in a Global Context*. Oxford: Oxford University Press, pp. 276–304.
Romaine, S. 2015. "Linguistic Diversity and Global English: The Pushmi-Pullyu of Language Policy and Political Economy". In: Ricento, T. (ed.) *Language Policy and Political Economy: English in a Global Context*. Oxford: Oxford University Press, pp. 252–275.
Sarangi, A. (ed.) 2009. *Language and Politics in India*. New Delhi: Oxford University Press.
Schieffelin, B.B., Woolard, K.A., & Kroskrity, P.V. (eds.) 1998. *Language Ideologies: Practice and Theory*. New York: Oxford University Press.
Seidlhofer, B. & Jenkins, J. 2003. "English as a Lingua Franca and the Politics of Property". In: Mair, C. (ed.) *The Politics of English as a World Language*. Amsterdam & New York: Editions Rodopoi B.V., pp. 139–165.
Sheth, D.L. 2009. "The Great Language Debate: Politics of Metropolitan Versus Vernacular India". In: Sarangi, A. (ed.), *Language and Politics in India*. New Delhi: Oxford University Press, pp. 267–295.
Snell, R. 2011. "Hindi: Its Threatened Ecology and Natural Genius". In: Kothari, R. & Snell, R. (eds.) *Chutnefying English: The phenomenon of Hinglish*. New Delhi: Penguin, pp. 22–36.
Sonntag, S.K. 2009. "The Political Saliency of Language in Bihar and Uttar Pradesh". In: Sarangi, A. (ed.) *Language and Politics in India*. New Delhi: Oxford University Press, pp. 221–242.

Sonntag, S.K. 2015. "Narratives of Globalization in Language Politics in India". In: Ricento, T. (ed.) *Language Policy and Political Economy: English in a Global Context.* Oxford: Oxford University Press, pp. 209–227.

Spowage, K. 2018. "English and Marx's 'General Intellect': The Construction of an English-Speaking Élite in Rwanda". *Language Sciences*, 70, 167–178.

Tietze, S. 2008. "The Work of Management Academics: An English Language Perspective". *English for Specific Purposes*, 27, 371–386.

Toolan, M. 2003. "English as the Supranational Language of Human Rights?" In: Mair, C. (ed.) *The Politics of English as a World Language*. Amsterdam & New York: Editions Rodopoi B.V., pp. 53–65.

Waquet, F. 2001. *Latin or the Empire of a Sign from the Sixteenth to the Twentieth Centuries*. London & New York: Verso.

Wee, L. 2012. "Prescribing Pastoral and Pragmatic Orientations: Challenges for Language Policy". In: Percy, C. & Davidson, M.C. (eds.) *The Languages of Nation: Attitudes and Norms*. Bristol: Multilingual Matters, pp. 63–80.

Williams, G. 2015. "Language, Hegemony, and Economy". In: Ricento, T. (ed.) *Language Policy and Political Economy: English in a Global Context*. Oxford: Oxford University Press, pp. 97–115.

Wright, L. 2015. "Why English Dominates the Central Economy: An Economic Perspective on 'Elite Closure' and South African Language Policy". In: Ricento, T. (ed.) *Language Policy and Political Economy: English in a Global Context*. Oxford: Oxford University Press, pp. 187–208.

2

URDU LANGUAGE IDEOLOGIES AND PAKISTANI IDENTITY

Arian Hopf

Pakistan was founded in 1947 as a separate country from India and struggled for an autonomous identity right from its beginning. It was founded as a country for the Muslims of undivided India and comprised the Muslim-majority provinces in the North-East and the North-West. Yet, most supporters of the Pakistan movement came from outside the eventual territory – at least with regard to West Pakistan –that internal differences came to the surface soon after independence. Thus, the question of what unites this country was posed right after 1947 and seems to remain unanswered till date. Without doubt, Islam served as a central aspect for defining Pakistani identity. However, the political category of *Muslim* was still new, and soon after partition from 'Hindu'-India, it lost its appeal, while ethnic or linguistic bonds were increasingly emphasised. Another essential part of the identity of Pakistan hinges on its distinction from India – a country which now inherited most of the geographical places connected to Muslim history in the subcontinent. Urdu was declared Pakistan's national language – a language that had no dissemination as the first language in the territory of Pakistan but was spread in the area of Delhi and Uttar Pradesh, now part of the Indian territory. Despite the essentiality of distinguishing its identity from India, Pakistan also could not eliminate its historical and linguistic link to India – a dilemma that shall be analysed in this chapter.

The central aim of the following reflections is to widen the perception of the debate about Pakistani identity in the academic literature, which seems to be restricted to a narrow perspective of Pakistan as an Islamic country. Even though the significance of this aspect cannot be denied, still this chapter aims at exposing the counter-narratives to the meta-narrative of an Islamic identity, which were significant and simultaneously present in the early years of

DOI: 10.4324/9781003279921-4

Pakistan's independence. This first of all requires a more differentiated perspective on Islam as not being confined to a mere religion, in the sense of a metaphysical philosophy. For one significant counter-tendency of the identity of Pakistan was the emphasis of an Indo-Muslim culture that had to be protected through the foundation of Pakistan. In this regard, Urdu was deemed as symbol or essence of this culture. Yet, this blurs the strongly needed demarcation to India with Urdu being based in present-day India. In this chapter, I will discuss different narratives to tackle this dilemma. Another strand of narratives focuses on Pakistan's present geographical location and tries to define it within these borders. This approach requires us to also consider historical landmarks of the pre-Islamic period, which pose another dilemma of blurring the Islamic identity of Pakistan.

The following sections will discuss these three strands of narratives with reference to prominent examples of how to solve the implied dilemmas of blurring either the demarcation to the Other of Pakistani identity, i.e., India, or its Islamic identity. To begin with, I will concisely review a few titles of the vast academic literature on Pakistan with regard to the overemphasis of Islam as a single identity marker.

Islam

In order to reconstruct the pre-history of the Pakistan movement, one has to look at the Hindi–Urdu controversy which emerged in the late 1860s in Northern India over the official language of government offices and the lower courts. The immediate reason is argued to be found in the government's contradictory language policy and its implications for job opportunities. The government encouraged Hindi in the Devanagari script as well as Urdu in the Nastaliq script as media of school education. Yet, only Urdu in the Nastaliq script was used for government jobs, which had adverse implications on the job market for those educated in Hindi. This contradiction and conflict was first expressed in a memorandum in 1868 highlighting the antiquity of Hindi and its link to India in contrast to Urdu and its connection not only to foreign languages but also to Islam. Thus, the application of Urdu for government use would impose a Muslim impact and "destroy our Hindu nationality" (King 1992: 124), as Babu Shiva Prasad wrote in 1868.

The Hindi–Urdu controversy has already been discussed extensively and thus shall not be elaborated here in all its intricacies. However, what concerns our present topic and what can already be discerned from this concise reference is the linking of religion with language – a process that was subsequently extended also to the nation during the following decades. Urdu was increasingly perceived to be in need of protection, which first resulted in the formation of the Anjuman-i Taraqqī-i Urdū in defence of its official status, while the two-nation theory of Hindus and Muslims being distinct nations gained in importance. While hitherto Muslims had not conceived of themselves as a separate nation, the idea of religion being a defining criterion of nationality was increasingly propagated. Muslims were presented as distinct from Hindus in every regard, from having their own customs and traditions up to their distinct language: Urdu. Hindi was consequently not only linked with India (Hindustan) but also with Hinduism, while Urdu came to represent Islam as well as Pakistan. Hence, Urdu received the status of a symbol for a separate nation (Pakistan) as well as Islam (Ayres 2009: 18).

Even though Urdu could not lay any claim on being a sacred language like Arabic, the dichotomic chain of associations with Hindi and Urdu opposing two religions and nations allowed for its high symbolic status as representative of Islam in South Asia. Since the demand for Pakistan was perceived as an outcome of this linguistic controversy and most supporters of this demand were to be found in this very area of its dissemination, it was to be deemed natural that Urdu would become Pakistan's national language, while Islam was perceived as the basis of Pakistan's identity (Ayres 2009: 28; Ali 2009: 19).

In his *Muslim Zion*, Faisal Devji describes an anti-historical stance of Muhammad Ali Jinnah, leader of the Muslim League, neglecting any reference to a glorious Muslim past or to an Indo-Muslim history. Instead, he promoted a uniform notion of Islam and Muslim, thus aiming for unravelling internal differences among the Muslims of South Asia. He propagated a united category of Muslim that would bring together "the merchants of Gujarat and Bombay [...] with gentry, aristocrats and professional men from other regions" (Devji 2013: 146). Jinnah wanted to overcome the varying regional and class-specific notions for the benefit of a single category of Muslims – "identity in purely juridical terms" (Devji 2013: 100). Hence, Jinnah, Ameer Ali and others whom Devji does not mention,[1] describe a concept of Islam that aims at overcoming also the internal sectarian differences for the benefit of a united Islam. On this basis, Jinnah could argue for the majority-position of Muslims at least in a number of provinces, which weakened the position of the all-over Hindu majority and justified the demand for a separate country for Muslims (Devji 2013: 87).

Yet, this anti-historical notion of identity, based as it was on a unified Islam reduced to its social function as identity category, could provide only "an abstract idea of belonging together" (Devji 2013: 123). This abstract notion apparently dissolved with independence; the dichotomy to the Hindu-Other faded into the background and left behind a fragmented society (Devji 2013: 154, 239).

Devji's critique of the Islamic narrative as insufficient to form a Pakistani identity, adequate as this critique may be, accepts as its premise that this Islamic narrative was the only one available. Devji does not look into any other national narratives, but focusses his study on the most prominent and powerful one. He neglects, or rather overlooks, alternative national narratives that focus on history, culture and language. This lacuna, notable in Devji's analysis as well as with many other authors on the topic, is the entry point for the present chapter. I will point out a number of counter-narratives that exist by the side of the most prominent Islamic narrative, and are usually elided in studies on Pakistan.

Yet, before passing to counter-narratives to this meta-narrative of Islam, as paradigmatically foregrounded in Devji's account, we will concisely discuss a few examples of this Islamic narrative as propaganda in literature (Hamzić 2016: 289).

Taḥrīk-i adab-i islāmī

Soon after the formation of Pakistan, the Taḥrīk-i adab-i islāmī emerged as a literary movement for the promotion of an Islamic literature. Many of its writers were sympathisers or members of the Jamaat-i Islami (Jamāʿat-i islāmī), whose aim was the establishment of an Islamic state in Pakistan. The formation of this literary movement has to be read within the literary context of the 1940s. The Progressive Writer's Movement, initially devoted to social criticism but gradually adopting a socialist outlook, was the most influential literary movement in 1930s and 1940s India and fought for the country's independence. Social ills like poverty or iniquity were admonished, and also religion and its customs and traditions were frequently criticised. However, soon after independence, the movement lost momentum with its main aim having been obtained.

Many of its writers had opposed the creation of Pakistan and depicted the cruelty of Partition in their writings.

> This naturally enraged those who saw the dawn of independence as a dream come true. The Marxists were committed to other ideologies and had their own philosophy of loyalty. Against this backdrop, some writers began criticising the progressive movement and their literature, especially their disregard for morals, religion and traditions. Though some protesting voices against the progressive literature had always been there, the new critics based their criticism on moral and Islamic values and raised the question of patriotism, too. It soon gathered the momentum of a movement and was called 'Islami adab ki tehrik'.
>
> *(Parekh 2010)*

The crucial motive of this latter movement was their opposition to the influence of the Progressives. Hence, it also lost momentum with the steady decline of the Progressives in the years after Independence. The main focus was to produce a literature that propagated Islamic values. Even though its writers did not aim to pen sermons, but evoke a change in people's mind, their literature was not so much a realistic depiction of the society but rather a portrayal of how society should be (Sadīd 1985: 603).

Although this quest for an Islamic literature has to be read in the backdrop of the search for a Pakistani identity, some pioneers can also be sighted in the pre-Independence period. Mahir-ul-Qadri, a poet, critic and author of short stories, novels and other genres, made his first step towards a career in the world of letters in various newspapers and magazines and also spent some time in Bombay and made a name for himself as writer of stories and lyrics for a few movies. However, in retrospect he regretted the time spent in the film industry, and in 1946 he decided to launch a literary magazine in Delhi. Due to the events of Partition, the launch had to be postponed until 1949 in Karachi. Here he resumed his plan and started the magazine *Fārān* and established "Halqa-i-adab-i-Islami", or Islamic literary circle. "'Faaraan' remained a regular publication till his death, in 1978, fighting for the cause Mahir had envisioned" (Parekh 2010).

Yet, *Faran* was not just a literary magazine, but carried a clear intention of disseminating Islamic values – a policy that was conspicuously reflected not only in the selection of the contributions to be printed with regard to their content as well as their language but also in the choice of ads: "Every literary piece received for publication, for instance, whether prose or verse, had to conform to a certain standard of morality. No ads were accepted for publication from banks and no ads carrying any pictures were published" (Parekh 2010).

Another renowned representative of this movement is Nasim Hijazi. Born in 1914, he was a prolific writer who had published several historical novels and short stories and preceded Mahir-ul-Qadri by one decade. His first short story was published in 1936 and his first novel was finished in 1938. All plots of his works are located in a historical setting and revolve around "brave, courageous and righteous heroes who either are Muslims right from the start or embrace Islam in the course of the action. Most villains are non-Muslims [...]" (Oesterheld 2009: 104). With his reference to the glorious past of Islam, Hijazi was not a pioneer, but could draw on a literary tradition that evoked a Golden Age of Islam. In the backdrop of nineteenth-century reform movements, this topic had frequently been drawn upon ever since Altaf Husain Hali's famous *Musaddas* on the Ebb and Flow of Islam. In this long poem, the author depicts a Golden Age of Islam which is to be found first and foremost in the days of the Prophet Muhammad. Islam and its achievements are juxtaposed to pre-Islamic Arabia, thus evoking the "progressive" nature of Islam. This is compared in the second part with Islam's present situation as contrasted to Europe. Muslims had sacrificed the "progressive" nature for stagnancy in ossifying Islam (Hopf 2017: 117–121). Subsequently, this topos came to be a favourite "to mobilize and consolidate the Muslim community. Starting with the novels of Abdul Halim Sharar (1860–1926) [...] and continued by Muhammad Iqbal (1877–1938), the glorious past was used as counter-image to the desolate present" (Oesterheld 2009: 97).

Hijazi has to be seen in this context. He also aimed at propagating a message through his historical novels. Hence, all his stories have a reference and message for the present. He pursued two motives – "to gain Pakistan and, after 1947, to work for the stability of Pakistan and the introduction of an Islamic order in the country" (Oesterheld 2009: 99). Yet, Hijazi knew that he had to grip and enthral the reader in order to convey his message. Thus, he utilised the genre of the historical novel wherein he did not depict violence in battles in too much detail and constructed a plot with twists and turns as well as some romantic interludes in order to capture and keep the reader's attention. The message is conveyed mainly through the speeches and dialogues of the protagonists (Oesterheld 2009: 97–8, 100, 103–5).

Although Hijazi's novels are very popular till date and have run through several editions, his name is not included in the literary canon of Urdu – a fate also suffered by Mahir-ul-Qadri and the Taḥrīk-i adab-i islāmī in general. Both authors draft a society based on Islamic values. Pakistan is imagined as a country where an Islamic way of living has materialised. Hence, Islam is their answer to the quest for a Pakistani identity. Although we find here a narrative that confines the idea of Pakistan to Islam, as also described by Devji, Hijazi's historical novels and the entire tradition behind him call Devji's narrowing into question even within the Islamic narrative. For, Hijazi's idea of Pakistan is crucially based on evoking a Golden Age and a glorious past of Islam – an aspect entirely ignored in Devji's narrow representation. The latter emphasises the anti-historic stance whereupon Pakistan is based:

> But Pakistan did so with the claim of having made a radical and unprecedented beginning, of having inherited nothing from the past, not even from the past of Islam by which it justified its existence.
>
> *(Devji 2013: 89)*

This statement appears to be highly questionable after the preceding analysis and shows the necessity to present counter-narratives to the unchallenged meta-narrative of Pakistan's Islamic identity.[2]

Geography

While we have seen in the previous section a centralist approach to define Pakistan's identity, we will now discuss a narrative of Pakistan on the basis of its existing, geographical realities. For, the Islamic narrative was facing two crucial challenges. On the one hand, Pakistan's particularity in relation to other Muslim countries was always at stake. If Islam was the crucial marker of identity, in how far was Pakistan then distinct from other Muslim countries? On the other hand, this centralist approach also entirely ignored the regionally distinctive cultures of the Sindhis, Balochis, Pashtuns, Punjabis, Siraikis etc.

In her *Speaking like a State*, Alyss Ayres describes the official elaboration of the history of the pre-Independence movement for Pakistan as a process entirely neglecting the territorial realities of the current country. The official historiography presented Pakistan's roots being located outside the present territory, while the regions within its territory are paid only little attention to. Instead, Pakistan's history is traced back to the Hindi–Urdu controversy which took place in a region now being comprised in the Indian territory. The reasons for this development are twofold. First, most support for Pakistan came from exactly those regions where the Hindi–Urdu controversy had taken place, while most regions of (West-)Pakistan's current territory only lately supported the foundation of this new country. Second, as a result of the Hindi–Urdu controversy, Urdu came to be inextricably associated with Islam. It acquired the status of the language of Islam in South Asia and had to be protected through the creation of a new country (Ayres 2009: 121–3).

While it is frequently argued that only under the regime of Zia-ul-Haq such a centralised stance to Pakistan's history had been propagated, Ayres argues that Zia was quite consistent with most of his predecessors: "The proceedings of the first Pakistan Educational Conference, held in December 1947, show that the new state's education planners felt it urgent to forge a truly *national* culture, something they clearly felt could not exist within the terms of regional ethnicities" (Ayres 2009: 129).

Thus, right from the beginning, Pakistan saw a centralist model that was interrupted only in the period of Zulfiqar Ali Bhutto in the early to mid-1970s. During this period, regional identities came to be viewed as a legitimate contribution in the search of a redefined national identity after the independence of former East-Pakistan as Bangladesh. The freedom struggle in East-Pakistan was crucially initiated by the insistence on Urdu as Pakistan's national language while denying Bengali an equal status despite being the most widely spoken language of Pakistan. In this backdrop, a redefinition of a national identity with concessions to regional cultures and languages was perhaps deemed as legitimate and necessary. Bhutto advocated the recognition of Sindhi culture, while other regions were allowed equal rights to promote their language and culture (Ayres 2009: 76).

Yet, this was only a short intermezzo incisively suspended with Zia's assumption of power. Zia aimed at enforcing an Islamic state wherein regional identities had no place. Instead, Islam was proclaimed the centre of Pakistan's identity, while Urdu – in contrast to any regional language – was pushed as a symbol of Muslim identity. Only after Zia's death in a plane crash in 1988 did the emphasis on regional identities re-emerge, and since the 1990s several historical studies of regional aspects in Pakistan's history have come forth. The crucial point about those studies is their revisionist character with regard to previous state-instantiated histories, as they deliberately do not aim at excluding or understating non-Muslim aspects of history or downplaying the significance of the current territories in the struggle for Pakistan. In general, these histories argue for a more composite character of Pakistan's society and its identity (Ayres 2009: 132–3, 138–40).

One narrative within this context is the inclusion of the pre-Islamic history of the current territory of Pakistan. Most histories hitherto either saw the beginning of Pakistan's history in its independence in 1947 or in the prelude of the Hindi–Urdu controversy, or otherwise in the first Muslim invaders in South Asia in the eighth century, while others even began Pakistan's history with the Prophet Muhammad. By contrast, these new tendencies aimed at including not only regional histories such as the history of Sindh or Punjab etc., but went even further back in time and began Pakistan's history with the Indus Valley Civilisation. One such example can be found in Fahmida Riaz's *Pakistan: Literature and Society* (1986), a rather late publication in this strand. Riaz tries to deconstruct a centralist or singular narrative of Pakistani culture and aims instead at "giving voice to the often marginalized regional literary traditions" (Yaqin 2009: 129). In her book, she tries to view Pakistani culture from the perspective of the regional literatures and thus tries to present a counter-narrative to the centralist narrative emphasising the role of Urdu as lingua franca and epitome of the Indo-Muslim culture. Instead, she paints a multifaceted and pluralistic picture of Pakistan (Yaqin 2009: 132–3).

Yet, as will become clear from the following analysis, the geographical perspective was neither entirely new nor exclusively monopolised by rather liberal-minded thinkers, but was equally instrumentalised in conservative circles (Ali 2009: 35).

Urdu in the Indus Valley Civilisation

In his contribution "Urdū kā tahẕībī pas-manẓar" (The Cultural Background of Urdu) to the volume *Pākistānī Adab*, published in 1981, the well-known literary critic and poet Wazir Agha (1922–2010) presents an innovative perspective on the history of Urdu. He commences his article with a rather traditional introduction of the history of Urdu as a pidgin that evolved in the context of the Muslim invasion in the military camps of the Mughals as a lingua franca between the natives and the soldiers consisting of speakers of Arabic, Persian and Turkish. I will not debate all the linguistic intricacies of this assertion, as much has been written on this topic already, and rather focus on the associations tied with Urdu. Agha proceeds by describing the naming history of Urdu and emphasises the denomination of *reẖta*,[3] which literally describes a hybridity of the language or blend (*āmezish* and *āvezish*). Here Agha deviates from the traditional view:

> The assertion […] that the [history] of *reẖta* begins with the arrival of the Muslims on the Indian Subcontinent [*barr-i ṣaġīr-i hind-o-pāk*] is incorrect

> [...]. In fact, the [history] of *reẖta* begins thousands of years ago when different ethnicities mixed up here.
>
> *(Āġā 1981: 236)*

As we learn from the following lines, "here" refers to the Indus Valley Civilisation in Mohenjo Daro and Harappa:

> The human skeletons that were found in the excavation places of Mohenjo Daro and Harappa are related to the Proto-Australoid [...], Mediterranean and Armenoid ethnicities wherefrom this conclusion can be drawn that a mingling of these various ethnicities had taken place at some time [even] before the Indus Valley Civilisation.
>
> *(Āġā 1981: 236)*

Subsequently, the first stage of a linguistic blending process took place. This language was developed and refined to such a state that its speakers designed a script for it. Agha then describes another linguistic blend in the course of the immigration of the Aryans in 1500 BC. Although he admits that the aforementioned script has not been deciphered hitherto, still he assumes the continued existence of this language, blended with the Vedic language of the Aryans:

> Their [i.e. the Aryans'] language was the Vedic language [...]. They were successful in influencing the indigenous [*desī*] language in many ways, even though the ancient linguistic structure [*qadīm lisānī ḍhānca*] remained unaltered. Yet, due to the arrival of these tribes a tremendous blending took place in the Indus Valley Civilisation, which resulted in another occurrence of "*reẖta*" between the Vedic and the indigenous languages.
>
> *(Āġā 1981: 237)*

Apparently, Agha implies an equation of this ancient *reẖta* and Urdu:

> This was the second, important stage of the gradual development of *reẖta* (Urdu). The third important stage occurred when the Muslims arrived on the Subcontinent.
>
> *(Āġā 1981: 237)*

By mingling the particular term of Urdu with *reẖta* in its more literal sense, Agha aims subsequently at construing a basis for a common Pakistani culture independent of regional aspirations:

> West-Pakistan is with regard to traditions and customs [*kalcar yā s̱aqāfat*] split into various small regions. [...] But with regard to the national culture

> [*qaumī aur tahzībī iʿtibār se*] one can observe a magnificent unity in the entire West-Pakistan.
>
> (*Āġā 1981: 239*)

Despite all its local and regional differences not only in culture and customs but also in the languages of Pakistan, Agha argues for a unity which is based on the unifying character of Urdu – a language which is, according to Agha, not spoken in any particular region, apart from a few cities, and which is the lingua franca of communication between the different ethnicities of Pakistan. But not only are the people of Pakistan compelled to use this language as a medium of communication between different language communities, but all people of Pakistan feel a strong connection to this language and its literature. For, "anyone feels a strong relation to the cultural character [*mizāj*] of Urdu [...]". "Urdu is the flag-bearer of our country's shared culture heritage" (Āġā 1981: 239–40).

This example showcases an instrumentalisation of Urdu for a shared Pakistani culture and identity surpassing the regional languages and cultures. This is argued in a twofold manner. First, Urdu is presented as an ancient language which reaches back to the Indus Valley Civilisation – a highly questionable claim based on a language whose written remains could not be deciphered to this day. Still, Agha argues that this very language of the Indus Valley Civilisation has passed through three major stations of mingling with various cultures and languages: first, in the Indus Valley Civilisation itself or even before; second, during the invasion of the Aryans in South Asia; and lastly, with the arrival of the Muslims in the eighth century. In referring to one of Urdu's historical names, *rehta*, and drawing on this term's literal meaning of mixing, mingling etc., Agha does not leave it at tracing back the origin of Urdu to the Muslim invasions in South Asia, but creates a continuous lineage of such mingling back to the Indus Valley Civilisation. This allows him, on the one hand, to claim great antiquity for Urdu and provides him, on the other, a link to the current territory of Pakistan as well. Due to Agha's refutation of the assertion that Urdu is based in Indian territory and thus foreign to Pakistan, Urdu is now on the same footing as the regional languages; and surpasses them by being the unifying factor between the various regional languages – not just as a necessity of communication, but rather as a cultural link between the regions. Although not explicitly stated, Agha seems to argue for a superiority through historic precedence, as Urdu predates the other languages with its lineage to the ancient culture of the Indus Valley Civilisation. In constructing an antiquity of Urdu as well as its provenience from the territory of present Pakistan, Agha supercedes the territorial narrative with its emphasis of the regional histories as well as the ancient (pre-Islamic) history of Pakistan's territory, its critique of the state-instantiated history, and its focus on the Islamic character of Pakistan.[4]

Indo-Muslim Culture and Urdu

Agha's presentation of Urdu as an antique language is indeed conservative with respect to its implications for regional definitions of Pakistan's identity. Yet, Agha takes an unconventional stance with regard to the characterisation of Urdu and its conservative interpretation as an Islamic language. As we have seen, on the backdrop of the Hindi–Urdu controversy, Urdu came to be increasingly perceived as a symbol of Muslim identity and Islam in South Asia. This assertion is reflected in many historiographies and eventually ossified in "Pakistan studies" as a compulsory subject at the Secondary School and Higher Secondary school levels of education:

> This new subject thus built on a set of ideas already contained in earlier policy plans, ideas about the necessity for this new nation to know particular representation of its history (that which had let to its creation) and therefore appreciate the struggles that had led to its independence.
>
> *(Ayres 2009: 133; cf. i.a. Fatehpuri 1981)*

In his article, "The Language of Love: A Study of the Amorous and Erotic Associations of Urdu", Tariq Rahman discusses the associations of decadency and love Urdu came to be negatively connoted with in the context of religious reform movements in the nineteenth century. What is more, Rahman proceeds by describing this as a process of pushing "Urdu towards an Islamic orientation" (Rahman 2009: 60) – an assertion that shall be concisely discussed here, as it concerns our discussion of a narrowing of the identity of Pakistan. While we have seen a narrowing to Islam in the example of Devji, we here observe the other side of the coin with Urdu being narrowed down to a merely Islamic language. Rahman argues that

> the erotic associations of Urdu are suppressed by the Urdu-using community in both Pakistan and India in order to protect itself against charges of obscenity, decadence and backwardness. The construction of the modern, sanitized Urdu (Muslim) community needs re-examination and the restitution and acceptance of the erotic, rather than its suppression.
>
> *(Rahman 2009: 30)*

> The reformers of Muslims society [...] tried to break it [i.e. the association of Urdu with decadence and the eroticism] and, instead, strengthened the association with Islam [...]. Thus, in order to regenerate a powerful Muslim 'nation' (*qaum*) a new literature, chaste and moral, had to be created.
>
> *(Rahman 2009: 32)*

But even though those reformers held a prominent position at the time concerned, neither did they represent the whole Urdu literary scene nor did they entirely succeed in their efforts. Rahman's statements refer to their intentions of narrowing Urdu down to Islamic topics and of its de-eroticisation.

Rahman's assertions regarding what the reformers' intentions were, however, have to be further qualified in two regards. First of all, one has to ask how far the reformers' only aim was to get rid of the tag of eroticism. In fact, the main aim of the Aligarh Movement around Sir Sayyid Ahmad Khan (1817–1898) was first and foremost to create a link with European modernity, symbolised primarily through science. Thus, their aim was in the first instance to catch this train without abolishing Islam. This, however, required translations of scientific texts into Urdu. Hence, the mentioned sanitisation of Urdu was first and foremost related to enable Urdu to become part of this new discourse in creating an appropriate vocabulary.

Subsequently, a "natural" (*necarī*) literature was also propagated, i.e., a literature released of the tradition of the classical poetry which revolved around highly conventionalised themes, sometimes losing touch with reality. The most important advocate of this new literary style was Altaf Husain Hali (1837–1914). While this style perhaps comes close to what Rahman describes, yet one has to ask how successful this endeavour to establish a new literary style eventually was. For in fact, the *dāstān*, a genre with magical and romantic elements, was at its peak of popularity at the same period. Also the future impact of Hali's literary-reformist ideas on Urdu literature remained rather limited: even graduates of the Muhammadan Anglo-Oriental College, later Aligarh Muslim University, the flagship of the Aligarh Movement, and supporters or admirers of the Aligarh Movement perceived this newly propagated literature as dry and preferred to turn to Romanticism, a literary trend much in vogue in the beginning of the twentieth century in Urdu. Although this trend cannot be described as erotic or obscene, still the woman as the object of romantic love was the main topos it revolved around (Parekh 2019).

Altogether, Rahman's assertion of an Islamisation of Urdu in course of nineteenth-century reformist movements remains highly questionable and covers only a very narrow part of the literary history of Urdu, while ignoring other more popular trends in Urdu literature at the same time. This underscores the necessity to broaden the associations linked with Urdu and re-evaluate the meta-narrative of a solely Islamic identity of Pakistan with Urdu being nothing else than a symbol of Islam, hence, an Islamic language, as Rahman argues. In the following paragraphs, I will discuss another counter-narrative of the idea of Pakistan ascribing to Urdu entirely different associations.

Muhammad Hasan Askari and Urdu as Symbol for Indo-Muslim Culture

Scenarios, as we find in the retrospective assessments of Devji, Rahman and others, were not as simplistic as they present them. Shortly before and after the creation of Pakistan, the Islamic narrative was by no means the only or even most prevalent idea of how Pakistan would be. In fact, liberal and secular forces were in the leading position, as epitomised in Muhammad Ali Jinnah's speech delivered on 11th of August:

> You are free; you are free to go to your temples, you are free to go to your mosques or to any other place of worship in this state of Pakistan. You may belong to any religion or caste or creed – this has nothing to do with the business of the state [...]. In the course of time, Hindus would cease to be Hindus and Muslims would cease to be Muslims not in the religious sense, because that is the personal faith of each individual, but in the political sense as citizens of the state.
>
> *(Ali 2009: 19–20)*

This very speech by none other than the founder of Pakistan refuted right from the beginning any religious ambitions of creating Pakistan as an Islamic state, but underlined its secular character. Yet, it also cannot be denied that the subsequent governments more and more played the card of Islam as a firm identity marker. A first climax was reached in the period of Bhutto, only surpassed by Zia.

Yet, in the first years of the creation of Pakistan we find several expressions of apprehensions regarding an Islamisation of the country with the power in the hands of the Maulvis. A very early example of such worries can be identified in Saadat Hasan Manto's short story or rather satirical essay *Allāh kā baṛā faẕl hai* (It is a great grace of Allah), published in 1949. Manto (1912–1955), perhaps the most famous short story writer of Urdu literature, herein lets the protagonist proudly describe that any kind of art has been abolished in his country:

> God is great. The era of ignorance has been brought to a close. There used to be dance halls, cinemas, art galleries in every nook and corner. Now by the grace of Allah you can't come across any poet or musician. All sorts of curses including music exist no more. You will not find any barber shop using razors anymore. However, halwa, the religious food of our religious leaders is available everywhere in abundance.
>
> *(Nayyar 2018)*

In a long story, Dhanak (Rainbow), by the famous writer Ghulam Abbas (1909–1982), similar worries are expressed. In this story, written in the late 1960s, the author describes a revolution of the Maulvis. Yet, as soon as they come to power, the sectarian differences come to light, eventually leading to the devastation of the entire country.[5]

As these examples show, by the time of the creation of Pakistan, the Islamic narrative as the only idea of Pakistan was by no means an established fact, as Devji or Rahman want to make us believe. Citing the example of Muhammad

Hasan Askari, I will provide another counter-narrative of Pakistan as a heaven for Urdu literature.

Muhammad Hasan Askari (1919–1978) was a writer of short stories and perhaps the most eminent literary critic of Urdu in the twentieth century. Askari was by no means a staunch supporter of the creation of Pakistan right from the outset, but since 1946 he began to discuss this topic discerningly and to some degree positively in his monthly column 'Jhalkiyā̱n' in the literary journal *Sāqī* (Farooqi 2012: 116). In his 1946 column titled *Pākistān*, Askari discusses his support for the case of the Muslim League, yet also expresses his restrictions and conditions. For, he perceived Pakistan as a dream where

> he would find an ideal Islamic democracy where intellectuals would lead the way, where Urdu would find a homeland, and where the state would be liberal toward intellectual and artistic dissent. He dreamed that the Urdu language and its writers would define Pakistani culture and that Urdu writers there need not be defensive about any minority status as they would in fact be leaders of the pack, not underdogs.
>
> *(Farooqi 2012: 6)*

In the same breath, he also made clear the restrictions for his support. For, he would not tolerate any strictures or limitations on literature and artistic freedom in Pakistan – fears we have seen above in many other artists as well and not without any reason. Under these circumstances, Pakistan would prove to be a blessing for literati. For, Muslims would no more be compelled to play the role of a minority as in undivided India. This would breathe new life into Urdu literature, as its writers would gain a (political) significance so far unknown to them. Critique of the government would have an impact, as it could no more be played down as the voice of a minority ('Askarī 2015: 1041–43).[6]

Askari bases his idea of Pakistan on the idea of Indo-Muslim culture, thus arguing that "Pakistan is basically old" ('Askarī 2015: 1119) and not a country only recently founded. Thus, he intervenes in a debate about whether the Muslim reformer Ameer Ali can be described as Pakistani. Since Ali had passed away already in 1928, the debate may at first sight appear to be obscure. But it also reflects a prevalent idea of Pakistan, not as a geographically defined country, but rather culturally or by religion. The former definition seems to be what Askari has in mind when he ironically but also anxiously asks whether then the two eminent poets of Urdu literature, Mir and Ghalib, also have to be excluded from the Pakistani heritage. According to Askari, Pakistan was not only claimed for the Muslims of its present territory but for all Muslims of the Indian subcontinent. In the same context, he also expresses his anxiety about an Islamisation of Pakistan and about the exclusion of Urdu from the realm of Pakistani heritage by labelling it a foreign language originally not spread in present-day Pakistani territory ('Askarī 2015: 1123, 1141).

Instead of an idea of Pakistan based either on religion or on geographical restrictions, Askari advocated a different conception of Pakistan based on the Indo-Muslim culture with Urdu as its identity marker. He makes clear that one must not confuse this as a simplistic equation with Islam, as he also underscores the contribution of non-Muslims to this culture and language (ʿAskarī 2015: 1135). If Askari does not inextricably link Indo-Muslim culture with Islam, so how does he define it? Askari makes clear that one has to distinguish between Islam and Muslims. Islam must not be restricted to its notion of a metaphysical philosophy, but has to be seen as a cultural force (*tahẕībī quvvat*). Although this culture was represented first and foremost by Muslims, it was not confined to them and many non-Muslims made crucial contributions to it (ʿAskarī 1998: 308).

Herewith Askari presents a narrative for Pakistan which is based on a non-territorial identity. Askari tries to consolidate this identity of Pakistan by endorsing the claim for the creation of a separate country, while at the same time the Muslim culture of the subcontinent is, according to Askari, epitomised in Urdu.

Askari also propagated the idea of a *Pākistānī adab*, a Pakistani literature – a unique literature or literary style of the Muslims of South Asia. He believed this distinct cultural identity to be based on the fundaments of Islam. After 1949, the term *Islāmī adab* also appears in his writings. Both seem to be used synonymously, which again underscores his understanding of Islam not merely as a religion and metaphysical thought, but as a cultural force. He also makes clear that this literature must not be confused with a literature preaching any ideology, as we have seen in the preceding paragraphs, but would rather be based on a distinct Muslim identity. Hence, Askari too took a strong stand against the Progressives, who were still very influential shortly after Partition, and refused their literary style as purpose driven and propagating a particular ideology. Askari did not so much refuse their particular ideology of socialism than a literature with a didactic purpose. Instead, he realised that Urdu literature had to change urgently. But Askari never made clear what this Pakistani/Islamic literature should look like. Although he saw in Rumi, Hafiz, Iqbal, Hali and Sayyid Ahmad Khan examples for this literature, still he never gave an unequivocal definition of this proposed literary style (Manẓar 2008: 269–75).

Askari equally draws on the ideologically created link between Urdu and Islam, even though he does not approve to the notion of Islam as presented by the Islamic narrative. He rather proposes a cultural notion of Islam. This involves some difficulties in the context of Pakistan Askari does not seem to have considered:

> Askari and some of his colleagues appear to have not appreciated, far less addressed or questioned, the obvious challenges lurking in the new state's

> future, represented by the profound ethnic differences and divisions out of which Pakistan was formed. His conception of Urdu as the ideal language for this culture did not take into account the inherent resistance among ethnic groups whose primary language was not Urdu. All of this suggests that he had not conceived of separatism on cultural and linguistic lines; in other words, he was unable – or unwilling – to foresee the possibility of a Pakistan fractured by internal tension.
>
> *(Farooqi 2012: 35–6)*

Askari was unable to see the upcoming conflict between the Muhajirs, the Muslims immigrants from present India, and the "locals" of Pakistan. He tried to foster Pakistan with a narrative of the superiority of the former. For him, the essence of Muslim culture was reflected in the Muhajir's language. This tallies with that group's self-perception, since the Muhajirs as early and emphatic supporters of the demand for Pakistan perceived themselves as "the 'real' creators of Pakistan" (Farooqi 2012: 173–4).

In Askari, we see another important and influential narrative of Pakistan which explicitly was not based on Islam as a religion, but on a distinct culture of South Asian Muslims. Yet, Askari's linking of this culture only with Urdu gave birth to critique by proponents of the regional languages. While Askari does not further elucidate or substantiate this assertion of Urdu being an epitome of this Indo-Muslim culture, I will now discuss a linguistic approach which aims at substantiating this claim.

Jamil Jalibi

In the preceding section, we have seen that Askari's linking of Islam with Urdu evoked resistance on the part of the regional languages of Pakistan. Askari did not further justify this assertion, as the Hindi–Urdu controversy and the linking of the religious associations to the respective language had by his time already sedimented as general knowledge, requiring no further reasoning. Some years later, when Jameel Jalibi (1929–2019), a prominent linguist and scholar of Urdu literary history, engaged in the still pending quest for a national identity/culture and wrote his *Pākistānī kalcar* (*Pakistani culture*) in 1964, he had already realised some of these shortcomings in Askari's claim.

Jalibi recognises inner conflicts in Pakistan after its foundation, based on the fact that "[f]rom the cultural point of view Pakistan came into being in a vacuum" (Jalibi 1984: 2). Instead of referring to an own cultural stock, Jalibi perceives a search for cultural identity in the "West" – a process he strongly condemns. In a similar vein as Askari, Jalibi too refers to the Indo-Muslim culture without which Pakistan would be meaningless. For, "without a past no people can become a nation and no land a country" (Jalibi 1984: 10). Again, Jalibi too recognises Urdu as epitome or product of this culture:

> It is Indo-Muslim culture which is the source of our solidarity, our spiritual unity and our conception of ourselves as a nation. Of it has been born the Urdu language and our music, our building, our architecture, painting and calligraphy are expressions of its spirit.
>
> *(Jalibi 1984: 57)*

Yet, he also recognises geographical limitations implied by the Partition with crucial historical places now being located in India. But as part of Indo-Muslim culture, Jalibi does not exclude these places for merely geographical reasons. Apart from this geographical separation, he also acknowledges the regional cultures and languages of the Pakistani territory, but questions their ability to form a national identity. In fact, he sees the unity of Pakistan endangered by overemphasising regional nationalisms (Yaqin 2009: 123). Only Urdu can bridge Pakistan's inner contradictions as a lingua franca known by all. Still, he suggests the introduction of a two-language formula in the school curriculum, which would give recognition to one regional language and a national language. Thus, the learning of two languages as a compulsory means would, in his estimation, bring both East and West Pakistan away from a disruptive model of nationalism. For him, English as state language is the crux of the problem because it symbolises a colonisation of the mind (Yaqin 2009: 125).

Hence, Jalibi recognises three crucial difficulties in the search for a Pakistani culture: first, the regional aspirations, which, in his opinion, cannot serve as a national identity, while, secondly, the reference to the Indo-Muslim culture, perceived to be common to all South Asian Muslims, is to a large extent separated from the current territory of Pakistan and located in India. Lastly, English and the search for cultural identity in the "West" are seen as pernicious to the national project.

In his *Pākistānī kalcar*, Jalibi does not further substantiate his preference of Urdu over the regional languages and cultures, aside from its character as a lingua franca. He does not elaborate either how to bridge the geographical detachment of Indo-Muslim history as well as its language, Urdu, being located in Northern India. Yet, a reading of his voluminous history of the Urdu literature, *Tārīḵẖ-i adab-i Urdū* (1977), reveals some intriguing insights into his understanding of Urdu, its relation to the other languages of Pakistan as well its origin (Jalibi 1984: 1–10, 46, 57, 172).

In his history of the Urdu literature, Jalibi in the first instance seems to argue that Urdu has originated from Punjabi. Referring to older proponents of this claim like, e.g., Hafiz Mahmood Khan Shirani's *Panjāb meṉ Urdū*, Jalibi bases this assertion on old texts of the Dakhani tradition of Urdu – a variety of Urdu that came to be used for literary writings in the Deccan region since the fifteenth century, long before Urdu came in vogue in Northern India as a literary language since the eighteenth century. Apart from lexical peculiarities as a comparatively less-advanced Persianisation and influences from southern languages like Marathi and Telugu, this variety is also characterised by some grammatical features which Jalibi ascribes to Punjabi (Jālibī 1977: 664). With reference to Multan as the first capital of a Muslim reign in South Asia, Jalibi sees Punjab as the place of origin of Urdu:

> The basic accent [*lahja*] of Urdu was in its period of origin strongly influenced by the Punjabi accent.
>
> In the period of the origin of Urdu, the people of Punjab and Multan had a great influence on the politics and society of the Subcontinent. Therefore, the accent [*lahja*], melody [*āhang*] and tone [*lai*] of Punjabi was contained in the blood of this language [i.e. Urdu] right from the beginning.
>
> *(Jālibī 1977: 153)*

Without discussing the linguistic intricacies of this claim, one can see here Jalibi's attempt to geographically relocate Urdu in the current territory of Pakistan. In this vein, Urdu can fulfil its role as epitome of the Indo-Muslim culture without its geographical location being confined to current Indian territory. In fact, Urdu is rather presented as something inherently Pakistani, as this is its actual origin:

> [N]ow after 1200 years, it [i.e. Urdu] has returned to its land of origin, thus closing the circle that was started right after Muhammad bin Qasim's conquest of Sindh in 712.
>
> *(Jālibī 1977: 680)*

And Jalibi does not end with this claim. As we have seen in earlier paragraphs, according to him Punjab was always perceived as the best-developed and most-powerful province of Pakistan. Perhaps this is the reason why Jalibi does not want to link Urdu only to Punjab, but emphasises the encompassing claim for the origin of Urdu in all languages of Pakistan:

> One of its forms [*hayūlā*] emerged in Sindh and Multan. Afterwards, this linguistic process happened in Punjab and the border region [to Afghanistan, i.e. probably the then North Western Frontier Province] from where it arrived ca. two centuries later in Delhi. Here it mingled and was mingled with the present languages and spread over the entire Subcontinent. [...] This relation with various languages as well as the claim of various regions on [the origin of] this language proves that it [i.e. Urdu] has profited from all

> these [languages] and created its own unique character. Therefore, this language is the language of all subcontinental languages and is now as then the *lingua franca* of the entire subcontinent.
>
> (*Jālibī 1977: 3–4*)

Jalibi relates the four main regional languages of Pakistan, Pashto, Balochi, Sindhi and Punjabi, with Urdu. While he can do this more or less convincingly for Sindhi and Punjabi, he faces some difficulties with Pashto and Balochi being related to another linguistic family. In the case of Pashto, Jalibi relates Hindko, a close relative of Punjabi, with this process, while he does not present any detailed discussion on behalf of Balochi. While Sindhi, Punjabi and Hindko could be related linguistically, he characterises Pashto first and foremost as a contact language increasing the lexicon of Urdu.

In the same vein, Jalibi seems to argue for a shared Indo-Muslim lexicon which is to quite some extent common to all these four languages – a fact which he bases on a shared vocabulary to express the basic tenets of Islam (Jālibī 1977: 710). Furthermore, all these languages and their shared lexicon are an expression of the Islamic spirit:

> What is common to all languages of West Pakistan is Urdu and its lexicon wherein the Islamic spirit has been implanted of this sort that Islam and Urdu have become each other's representative and symbol.
>
> (*Jālibī 1977: 669*)

Jalibi does not only relocate Urdu to the territory of Islam, but furthermore describes it as a representative and symbol of Islam as well as a conglomerate of all languages of Pakistan. Urdu comes to be the glue between the different languages as it is a product of blending. Hence, Jalibi deliberately does not conclusively decide between the different claims on Urdu, but rather lets them coexist as an expression of the shared participation in its genesis and development. This way, Urdu is not only a Pakistani language, but *the* Pakistani language which has profited from all other regional languages. Though Urdu is not described as superior to the other languages, it still receives a prominent position among equals. Jalibi seems to broaden the notion of lingua franca being not only a language known to all as a medium of communication but also the outcome of a collective development. This relocates Urdu not only geographically but also linguistically in the territory of Pakistan. On this basis, Jalibi can bypass the location of Urdu as a foreign language to Pakistan, on the one hand, and aspirations of regional languages, on the other. In his line of argument, Urdu is the only language that can claim to be a Pakistani language common to all citizens on the national level.

Conclusion

Is Islam the only identity category that unites Pakistan? In the beginning of this chapter, I have discussed Devji's *Muslim Zion* critically with regard to this assertion. Even though the significance of Islam as crucial aspect of Pakistani identity cannot be denied, this chapter aimed, first, to broaden the notion of Islam as it was perceived in the imagination of Pakistan, and, second, to point out also such narratives which do not or only secondarily refer to Islam. While we have seen that Islam was also propagated in a literary movement as the crucial identity category, there are at least two other strands defining Pakistan differently.

Within the geographical narrative, we could observe two different strands. The first aims at also including pre-Islamic history on the present territory of Pakistan, while the second focuses on the various regional cultures, thus criticising a centralist narrative that focuses on the Hindi–Urdu controversy. While the centralist narrative is characterised by the necessity of the protection of Urdu as an epitome of Islam in South Asia, the regional tendencies aim at imagining Pakistan as a composite society. However, in the example of Wazir Agha, we have seen how these two strands of the geographical narrative have been undermined for the benefit of the narrative of Urdu. Agha claimed an antiquity of Urdu that can be traced back to the Indus Valley Civilisation, thus undercutting the revisionist implications of this tendency.

In the strand focusing on Indo-Muslim culture as identity of Pakistan, we again find a centralist narrative strongly favouring Urdu, however with different arguments. In Muhammad Hasan Askari, we saw a strong proponent of Urdu as epitome of this culture. Hence, he imagined Pakistan as heaven for Urdu literature, neglecting or rather overlooking regional languages of Pakistan with equal ambitions. Askari also strongly advocates the Islamic identity of Pakistan, but in an entirely different way than Devji, for whom Islam is merely a social category of solidarity. Neither does Askari conceive of Islam as religion or metaphysical philosophy, as he terms it, but rather as a culture being based on the fundamental tenets of Islam.

While his narrative entirely overlooked the regional languages and cultures, Jamil Jalibi included all the various opposing strands and aimed to present an all-encompassing narrative bringing together these opposing forces. He again discusses the origin of Urdu and aims at geographically relocating it in the territory of Pakistan, thus refuting descriptions of Urdu as a foreign language. Not only that in his narrative Urdu returns in Pakistan to its land of origin, Jalibi is also cautious enough to allow all regional languages of Pakistan a share in its development. Thus, Urdu cannot be claimed by a single region. What is more, Urdu seems to be construed as a shared language between all these languages, not only due to their acquaintance with it but also with regard to its origin. Urdu does not merely remain a symbol of Indo-Muslim culture, but is rather a product of the same.

As could be observed in the preceding discussion, a confinement of Pakistani identity solely to Islam is not warranted. Even though Islam is undeniably a crucial category, one at least has to broaden it conceptually, since limiting it to a merely social category is not justifiable for the various narratives of Pakistan. The equation of Urdu and Islam in the aftermath of the Hindi–Urdu controversy has created other narratives which still refer to Islam but only through the linguistic and/or cultural backdoor of Urdu and Indo-Muslim culture.

Notes

1 Two other prominent and much earlier proponents in this regard are Sir Sayyid Ahmad Khan (1817–98), founder of the Aligarh Movement that aimed for a reform of Islam in accordance to scientific findings, and Nazir Ahmad (1830–1912), who is famed for having penned Urdu's first novel but also many religious tracts. None of them is mentioned by Devji, although both of them were important proponents of the process of homogenising Islam and overcoming sectarian boundaries.

2 In Ameer Ali, we find another exponent who is quoted by Devji to substantiate a process of uniformisation of Islam. This can indubitably be found in Ameer Ali. Yet, another fact Devji does not mention is that Ali presented his notion of Islam in the form of a history of Islam. Herein, Ali aims at silencing particular strands of Islam in order to highlight a rational essence of Islam. He also seeks to substantiate his notion of Islam through history (Hopf 2017).

3 "Poured out; scattered; mixed; — […] 'The mixed dialect,' the Hindūstānī or Urdū language" (Platts 2006: 611).

4 Since this text mentions West-Pakistan, one can assume that it was originally written before 1971.Thus, it apparently precedes the tendency when upholding territorial narratives had become prominent in the mid-1970s during Zulfiqar Ali Bhutto's term of office. Yet, it cannot be finally clarified whether those tendencies were perhaps already present before that time and Agha is in fact referring to them.

5 Another story, *Ānandī*, by the same author shall also be shortly mentioned in this context, although it was written quite some time before the creation of Pakistan – sources vary from 1933 to 1940. The story revolves around the exclusion of the red-light quarter of a pulsating city, as this quarter is positioned in the centre of the city. In a municipality session it is argued that this disturbs the inhabitants' morality. Subsequently, the residents of this quarter are forced to leave the city and are offered a plot outside the city in return. When the author describes the development of a new, flourishing city around this new-established red-light quarter, one is reminded of an allegory for Partition. Yet, in the end of the story, its circularity turns out, as the municipality of this new city gather to discuss the immoral character of this quarter being located just in the centre of the city. By this time, the founding role of these ladies seems to be entirely forgotten. Having the association to Partition in mind, one could read this story as an exclusion of the cultural elite out of the newly established country of Pakistan, ignoring the crucial role of the cultural elite for the latter's creation. For, one has to keep in mind that by the 1930s and 1940s, the *ṭavāʾif* was not just a prostitute, but oftentimes a highly educated woman with many artistic skills, while prostitution was, if at all, only a minor part of this profession. Yet, this interpretation has to be put in brackets, as the association with Partition cannot be anticipated by the author at the time he had penned the story. Still, a reader of the 1948 publication could have read it in this perspective.

6 It is, however, another topic that Askari only shortly after the creation of Pakistan bemoans the incompatibility of Urdu literati to adapt to these new requirements, leading him even to announce the death of Urdu literature (ʿAskarī 2015: 1112–13, 1115; ʿAskarī 1998: 497–8).

Bibliography

ʿAbbās, Ġulām. 2018. *Ġulām ʿAbbās ke be-miṡāl afsāne*. Lāhaur: al-Ḥamd.

Āġā, Vazīr. 1981. "Ūrdū kā tahẕībī pas-manẓar." In *Pākistānī adab*, vol. 1, edited by Rašīd Amjad, Fārūq ʿAlī, 235–240. Rāvalpinḍī: Feḍaral Gavarnminṭ Sir Sayyid Kālij.

Ali, Choudhary Rahmat. 1946. *Pakistan. The Fatherland of the Pak Nation*. Lahore: Book Traders.

Ali, Mubarak. 2009. *Pakistan. In Search of Identity*. Karachi: Pakistan Study Centre.

ʿAskarī, Muḥammad Ḥasan. 2015. *Majmūʿa*. Lāhaur: Sang-i Mīl.

———. 1998. *ʿAskarī-nāma. Lāhaur: Sang-i Mīl.*

Ayres, Alyssa. 2009. *Speaking Like a State. Language and Nationalism in Pakistan*. Cambridge: Cambridge University Press.

Devji, Faisal. 2013. *Muslim Zion. Pakistan as a Political Idea*. Cambridge: Harvard University Press.

Faiz Aḥmad Faiẓ. 1981. "Pākistānī tahẕīb ke ajzāʾ-i tarkībī." In *Pākistānī adab*, vol. 1, edited by Rašīd Amjad, Fārūq ʿAlī, 107–121. Rāvalpinḍī: Feḍaral Gavarnminṭ Sir Sayyid Kālij.

Farooqi, Mehr Afshan. 2012. New York: Palgrave Macmillan.

Fatiḥpūrī, Farmān.1981a. "Urdū aur Pākistānī zabāneṉ." In *Pākistānī adab*, vol. 1, edited by Rašīd Amjad, Fārūq ʿAlī, 254–260. Rāvalpinḍī: Feḍaral Gavarnminṭ Sir Sayyid Kālij.

———. 1981b. *Pakistan Movement and Hindi-Urdu Conflict*. Lahore: Sang-e-Meel.

Hamzić, Vanja. 2016. "Faisal Devji, Muslim Zion. Pakistan as a Political Idea." *South Asia Research* 36(2): 288–290.

Hopf, Arian. 2017. "(Re)constructing the Origin. Countering European Critique with Historiography in Hali's Musaddas and Ameer Ali's The Spirit of Islam." *Zeitschrift für Indologie und Südasienstudien* 34: 145–184.

Jaffrelot, Christophe. 2002, "Introduction. Nationalism without a Nation. Pakistan Searching for its Identity." In *Pakistan: Nationalism without a Nation*, edited by Christophe Jaffrelot, 7–48. New Delhi: Manohar.

Jālibī, Jāmil. 1977. *Tārīḫ-i adab-i Urdū*. Dihlī: Ejukešanal Pablišing Hāʾus.

Jalibi, Jamil. 1984. *Pakistan. The Identity of Culture*. Karachi: Royal Book Company.

King, Christopher R. 1992. "Images of Virtue and Vice. The Hindi-Urdu Controversy in Two Nineteenth-century Hindi Plays." In *Religious Controversy in British India: Dialogues in South Asian Languages*, edited by Kenneth W. Jones, 123–150. Albany: State University of New York Press.

Manẓar, Šahzād. 2008. "Muḥammad Ḥasan ʿAskarī. Pākistānī adab, Islāmī adab." In *Muḥammad Ḥasan ʿAskarī aur muʿāṣir tanqīd*, edited by Ištiyāq Aḥmad, 269–277. Lāhaur: Bait al-Ḥikmat.

Nayyar, Nasir Abbas. 2018. "Fiction as Alternate History." *The News on Sunday*, March 11, 2018. https://www.thenews.com.pk/tns/detail/565090-fiction-alternate-history

Oesterheld, Christina. 2016. "Mullā Vajhī's Sab Ras." In *Islam, Sufism and Everyday Politics of Belonging in South Asia*, edited by Deepra Dandekar and Torsten Tschacher, 279–293. London and New York: Routledge.
———. 2009. "Jihādī Literature? Some Novels of Nasim Hijazi." In *Cracow Indological Studies*, vol. XI, edited by Agnieszka Kuczkiewicz-Fraś, 97–122. Kraków: Ksiegarnia Akademicka.
Platts, John T. 2006. *A Dictionary of Urdū, Classical Hindī and English*. New Delhi: Manohar.
Pande, Aparna. 2018. "Escaping India. Pakistan's Search for Identity." In *Routledge Handbook of Contemporary Pakistan*, edited by Aparna Pande, 15–40. London and New York: Routledge.
Parekh, Rauf. 2010. "Mahir-ul-Qadri. A Movement unto Himself." *Dawn*, May 10, 2010. https://www.dawn.com/news/972513/mahir-ul-qadri-a-movement-unto-himself
———. 2019. "Literary Notes. Romanticism in Urdu literature and Mehdi Ifadi." *Dawn*, November 26, 2019. https://www.dawn.com/news/1518797
Pemberton, Kelly and Michael Nijhawan (eds.). n.d. *Articulation of Identities in South Asia*, 115–139. New York, London: Routledge.
Rahman, Tariq. 2006. "Urdu as an Islamic Language." *The Annual of Urdu Studies* 21: 101–119.
———. 2009. "The Language of Love. A Study of the Amorous and Erotic Associations of Urdu." In *Cracow Indological Studies*, vol. XI, edited by Agnieszka Kuczkiewicz-Fraś, 29–66. Kraków: Ksiegarnia Akademicka.
Rai, Alok. 2001. *Hindi Nationalism*. London, Hyderabad: Sangam Books.
Rais, Rasul Bakhsh. 2017. *Imagining Pakistan. Modernism, State, and the Politics of Islamic Revival*. Lanham, Boulder, New York, London: Lexington Books.
Riaz, Fahmida. 1986. *Pakistan. Literature and Society*. New Delhi: Patriot Publishers.
Sadīd, Anvar. 1985. *Urdū adab kī taḥrīkeṉ. Ibtidā'-i Urdū se 1975 tak*. Karācī: Anjuman-i Taraqqī-i Urdū Pākistān.
Šerānī, Ḥāfiẓ Maḥmūd. 1998. *Panjāb meṉ Urdū*. Islāmābād: Muqtadara qaumī zabān.
Šīrīṉ, Mumtāz. 1963. *Mi'yār. Tanqīd*. Lāhaur: Nayā Idāra.
Vajhī. 1964. *Sab ras*. Lāhaur: Lāhaur Akeḍimī.
Yaqin, Amina. 2009. "Variants of Cultural Nationalism in Pakistan. A Reading of Faiz Ahmad Faiz, Jamil Jalibi, and Fahmida Riaz." In *Shared Idioms, Sacred Symbols, and the Sacred Symbols, and the Articulation of Identities in South Asia*, edited by Kelly Pemberton, Michael Nijhawan, 115–139. New York, London: Routledge.

3

"MOTHER ENGLISH"

Savitribai Phule on Caste Patriarchy and the Ideology of the English Vernacular

Christian Lee Novetzke

In 1854, Savitribai Phule (1831–1897) published a book of poems in Marathi that included two poems dedicated to the culture and language of English. She personified her subject through the address, "Mother English." This is poem number 28 in a collection of 42 poems titled *Kāvyaphule* or "Flowers of Poetry":

Mother English (*Iṅgrajī Māulī*)
(*abhaṅg*)

Mother English and the English language
Resolve to uplift Shudras;
Mother English, not the Mughals,
Not the Peshwai, that foolhardy reign.
Mother English grants real knowledge
And with care offers Shudras a life.
Mother English feeds mother's milk (*pānhā*) to Shudras
And nurtures Shudras like a Grandmother (*ājī*).
Mother English breaks brutality (*paśutva*)
And offers humanity (*manuṣyatva*) to the Shudra people.[1]

With this publication, Savitribai Phule became one of the first women to enter the modern public sphere as a published author, and perhaps the very first non-Brahman woman to do so. Born into the Mali *jāti*, she identified as a Shudra, a caste identity she shared with her husband, Jotirao Phule (1827–1890), one of the most important leaders and thinkers of non-Brahman politics in the modern period. Though Savitribai Phule often has been relegated to the shadow of her more famous husband, with this publication in 1854, Savitribai

DOI: 10.4324/9781003279921-5

Phule likely preceded her husband into the public sphere by some 15 years—Jotirao Phule would not publish his first major work until 1869.[2] Her collection exemplifies her complex approach to her key subjects, which include, most prominently, the effects of caste patriarchy on women, Shudras, and Dalits; the title plays with her husband's last name demonstrating how she both inhabits caste patriarchy and critiques it from within.[3] Indeed, Jotirao Phule is a key subject of both this book of poetry and the final one she would write a year after his death in 1891 entitled *Bāvannakaśī Subodh Ratnākar*, or "A Refined Collection of Wisdom." Though Phule only ever published these two books of poetry—one 15 years before her husband fully entered the public sphere as an author and the last a year after his death—they together constitute a key intellectual, political, and theoretical perspective within modern Indian thought that opposed caste patriarchy. However, very few scholars writing in English have engaged with the extraordinary work of Savitribai Phule.[4]

What struck me the first time I read this poem is the skill Phule displays in unraveling a set of complicated positions about the ideology of language and culture. The poem is composed in a simple, straightforward way, and in the *abhaṅg* meter, known throughout Maharashtra as a medium for non-elite devotional or *bhakti* sentiments. Phule's choice to use this meter, one of the oldest and most common meters of poetry in Marathi, signals her interest in tapping into a quotidian Marathi public. Given that Phule's entire repertoire of poetry attacked caste patriarchy (not just Brahmanical patriarchy), I was also interested to see the construction of a kind of anti-caste matriarchy—a poem using the metaphors of mothers and grandmothers. Phule took this approach even while she positioned herself as Jotirao Phule's wife—she signed her work "Savitri Jotiba," for example. Phule demonstrated an ability to inhabit but also critique patriarchy, which she did here through matriarchal metaphors. Perhaps she drew her inspiration from women in Indian history and mythography about whom she wrote, such as Vindhyavati, a mythic figure who ruled with her King Bali, and Tarabai Bhosale, the wife of Rajaram Bhosale and a Maratha warrior queen who commanded Maratha forces in the early eighteenth century.

Through gendering her engagement with English as a language and a culture of place, Phule embraced a tradition in Maharashtra around vernacularization. As I have argued in recent work, the history of vernacularization in Marathi involved an immanent critique of caste and gender inequality.[5] I posit that this is the case because vernacularization involves a deepening of engagement with everyday life and non-elite worlds. The long history of cultural critique in Marathi began with the earliest iterations of vernacular literature in the thirteenth century in texts that presented sophisticated conceptualizations of gender, power, language, and culture.[6] Marathi itself—as with many of India's vernacular languages—is often ascribed a feminine gender, especially when juxtaposed to Sanskrit, a "masculine" language "in the world of men."[7]

As I argue in my work, the process of vernacularization in Marathi in the thirteenth century grew in part from critiques of gender inequality; gender/power dynamics are, therefore, essential to the process of vernacularization, a process ongoing into the present.[8] This does not mean that all Marathi vernacular iterations engage these subjects or agree on their value, but a critique of social inequality, nonetheless, was a point of origin for Marathi vernacularization and remains one of its strongest subjects. I position Savitribai Phule's poetry within the context of this long genealogy of vernacularization in Marathi that takes account of caste and gender inequality as a fundamental subject of critique in everyday life, what I call the quotidian revolution. Savitribai Phule's poetry sustains this tradition and deepens the vernacularization of Marathi in the modern period, but it also draws English into this process.

If caste and gender are essential aspects of the ideology of vernacularization in Maharashtra, then the coming of English as a language and culture of place—a vernacular—would be positioned within this analytical matrix and judged within this stream of critical thought. Phule reflects deeply on this new vernacular on the subcontinent, which she sees not in line with the cosmopolitan masculinist, casteist elitism of Sanskrit, but rather allied with a gendered criticism of inequality that favored the vast majority of people who make up the world of everyday life, a group Phule refers to as "women, Shudras, and Dalits" (*strī-śūdra-atiśūdra*). Certainly, the reality of the effects of English on Indian society are vast and conflicting; my aim here is only to show how this one person, Savitribai Phule, understood those effects in her poetry.

Savitribai Phule's personification of English as a mother not only provided a matriarchal counterpoint to caste patriarchy, but it also elided the distinction between English as a language of place and English as a culture, especially a ruling, dominant, and colonial culture. This elision is essential to vernacularization, and one can see this with "Marathi," a word that names both a language of place and of culture as well. This is a fact well known to anyone who has studied the ongoing history of vernacularization in Maharashtra from thirteenth-century works like the *Jñāneśvarī* and the *Līḷācaritra* to contemporary political projects within the "vernacularization of democracy," such as the Shiv Sena. What links together these very distinct conceptual worlds is an emphasis on the experiences of everyday life and the non-elites who populate this world. In a similar way, Phule sees English as a language and a culture of place proposing a distinct ideology. What does this ideology of English as a vernacular look like in Savitribai Phule's thought and poetry?

The Mother English of Phule's imagination is intent on the "upliftment" (*uddhārī*) of women, Shudras, and Dalits and granting them the opportunity for just and equal treatment and a good life. Her poem stages an aspiration and articulates a hope for the present and future. It espouses that English as a cultural form stands in opposition to caste inequality and injustice. Mother English is also compared with the cultural-political formations of the past—the Mughals and the Brahmanical Peshwa period of the Maratha Empire—implying that "Mother English" is a political formation like these others of the region's past. The last lines juxtapose how Phule sees women, Shudras, and Dalits subjected to brutality or "animality" (*paśutva*) under previous political formations on the subcontinent with the humanity (*manuṣyatva*) or even "humanism" that Phule associates with English as a language and culture of place. For Savitribai Phule, the vernacular Mother English bears an ideology of humanistic ethics, equal rights, and social justice that emerges from its particular history and location and is actualized in relation to the inhumanity, inequality, and injustice that Phule describes in her work as endemic within orthodox Hindu Indian society.

In order to understand how Savitribai Phule conceives of the English, a colonial, dominating force, as also a harbinger of social justice and equality, we have to understand her theorization of colonialism, which is also taken up by Jotirao Phule in his writings as well. I argue that the Phules theorize colonialism through the prism of a *colonial palimpsest*, the overlaying of several simultaneous forms of colonialism, each interacting and affecting the other, creating multiple subjectivities for any one individual, community, or collective. This concept is essential to how Savitribai Phule understands "history" (*itihās*); in many ways, the entire aim of Phule's work is encapsulated in her own words, to produce "a noble history (*itihās nāmī*) of an enslaved people (*gulāmī jan*)."[9] In other words, she is a thinker of comparative colonialisms rather than a thinker who sees colonialism as an essentialized dialectic between two parties, Indians and colonizers.

The first form of colonialism that Savitribai Phule identifies is that of the "Aryan" invader to the subcontinent.[10] Here is a pithy summary from an *abhaṅg* included in her second and last book of poems published in 1891:

Thoughtfully examine the history (*itihās*) of India:
The conquering Aryans of the hinterlands were immoral (*adharmī*).
These Tartar (*tārtarī*)[11] people were uncivilized (*rānaṭī*).
They invaded and remained (*ghusunī rahāte*) among the righteous (*sadharmī*) people they defeated. || 5 ||

Because of their victory, the Aryas apply marks (*ṭiḷā*) of distinction,
Saying, "We are superior to Shudras, who are born from inferior wombs (*kaḍū yonī*)."[12]
They imposed on us the custom of slavery and called it *dharma*.
Shudras and women endured living like animals. || 6 ||

Savitribai Phule, like Jotirao Phule, presented the origin of caste patriarchy as a result of the hoary invasion and subsequent cultural hegemony they identify with the Aryans and the theory of their invasion of the subcontinent. Some

Orientalists, in particular some German Indologists of the nineteenth–mid-twentieth centuries,[13] and some Brahman intellectuals, such as B. G. Tilak, would read through the Aryan Invasion theory a history of their own cultural superiority as direct descendants of the Aryans. The Phules took this same historical theory of the invasion and domination of the subcontinent by Aryans, but turned it upside down to argue for a kind of perduring settler colonialism of India's indigenous population by a ruthless invading polity. The entry of various European companies and states and ultimate domination of the subcontinent by the British East India Company and later the British Crown are layers of colonialism that rest upon the much longer, deeper, and more hegemonic colonialism of the "Aryan invasion," which the Phules (and others) see as the origin point for caste patriarchy. Their use of the Aryan invasion theory does not rest on whether it is true, but rather on the currency of the idea among Brahman and Orientalist thinkers. The Phules used the Aryan invasion theory to present caste patriarchy as something like a mode of settler colonialism already in place for millennia before the British arrived.

One key way that Savitribai Phule engages a critique of caste patriarchy predicated on this originary invasion theory is through the word *dharma*. Phule draws this word from the depths of Indian cultural forms—such as Hinduism, Buddhism, Jainism, and the Sanskrit sphere—but also situates it in the fields of governance, politics, and ethics. Phule uses this word in multiple, dialectical, ways, which we can see in the brief passage above. She refers to the invading Aryans as *adharmī*, as the opposite of *dharma*, which I have rendered as immoral. Phule uses *sadharmī*, or "possessing *dharma*," to describe the "righteous" indigenous people whom the immoral Aryans colonized. Elsewhere she uses *svadharma* to describe sacred obligations incumbent on individuals that are "the gateway to slavery."[14] Phule uses *dharma* in two ways: firstly, as a relative and aberrant morality bent to serve a system of domination through moralizing caste patriarchy as religious obligation; and secondly, as a kind of absolute morality, in the mode of a kind of Kantian universal law, a concept of equality and justice that has been overwritten by other forms of *dharma*. In the second verse, Phule uses *dharma* in this first way, as a relative concept that names a set of beliefs and practices—religion, ritual, custom, practice—which all buttress the "slavery" or *gulāmī* of caste patriarchy instituted by the Aryans. In other words, for Phule, *dharma* is both the objective truth of what is right and the subjective socio-religious constructions of an oppressive social order that "enslaves" women and Shudras to endure "living like animals."

When the Phules trace this history of caste patriarchy, they see it exemplified in the Brahmanical Peshwa period of the Maratha Confederacy when the Maratha polity with its capital in Pune was ruled by a dynasty of Chitpavan Brahmans. The Peshwa period, particularly in its later years, is regularly configured by Brahman and non-Brahman scholars and writers as a time of heightened oppression of Shudras, Dalits, and women, as well as a period marked by the failure of the Peshwas to resist encroaching British rule and retain a unified Confederacy.[15] The latter Peshwa, in other words, comes to typify the worst aspects of Brahmanical caste patriarchy in Maharashtrian socio-political history as it intersects with governance, rule of property, religion, and social order in general.

A key feature of this long genealogy of Brahmanical caste patriarchy, supported by the subjective relativist structures of *dharma* from Savitribai Phule's point of view, is the denial of education to women, Shudras, and Dalits. Though she has a capacious understanding of the functioning of the caste–gender nexus, what is highlighted in her engagement with English is how caste and gender oppression function as a system of selective knowledge access, as a social hierarchy of knowledge. Phule understands caste–gender hegemony as a knowledge regime that denies education to women, Shudras, and Dalits. The "higher" that one is placed on the hierarchy of the caste–gender nexus, the more one has access to knowledge; conversely, a lower placement is marked by the denial of access to knowledge of all kinds. This lack of knowledge is then used to justify enslavement and servitude on a balance of relative "merit" for different kinds of labor. The often-cited injunction in the *Laws of Manu* to Shudras and women hearing the Vedas (and suffering violent consequences in the breach of the injunction) exemplifies the function of caste as a system of knowledge hegemony. The arrival of British power—metonymically represented by English as a language and culture of place—is laid over this caste and gender system.

It is in this context that we can read the second of Savitribai Phule's two poems about "Mother English" in *Kāvyaphule*:

Mother English
(*padya*)

Peshwa rule is gone. ||
Mother English has arrived. ||

A dense darkness of despair,
The excessive fear of heaven and hell,
The mind plagued with thoughts of inferiority,
Thus is the age into which Mother English has arrived. ||

Throw custom far away,
Break down the doors of tradition.
Take education in writing and reading.
Good times have come, Mother English has arrived. ||

Because of ignorance the Shudra people are susceptible to
The many contrivances of the Brahman *dharma* (*bhaṭadharma*).

The Shudras were twisted and tormented.
Peshwa rule is dead, Mother English has arrived. ||

The regime of Brahman rule (*bhaṭaśāhī*) has been burned down
And the intelligent English have prevailed.
This has benefitted the Shudra people.
The *Manusmṛti* is dead, Mother English has arrived. ||

[The English gave] knowledge to the Shudra people like a protective shade.
They are advocates for the Untouchables (*atiśūdra*),
English rule has become a boon.
The state of terror (*bhayānakatā*) is over, Mother English has arrived.

The land of India belongs to no one,
Not Iranis, Brahman, foreigners (*yavan*), or Huns.
This is the truth of the blood of India (*iṇḍi raktācā*).
Loudly proclaim that Mother English has arrived. ||[16]

This second poem about Mother English fully expresses the vernacular politics that Savitribai Phule associates with English as a language and culture of place.[17] The arrival of the English unseats "Brahman rule" and "Brahman *dharma*" associated with not only the recent Peshwa reign but also the kinds of ritual, textual, religious, and social ideas associated with the *Laws of Manu*. English rule is the antidote to a pre-existing form of dominance, a "state of terror" that is also psychological and that produces a "mind plagued with thoughts of inferiority." Phule's concept of the psychological damage wrought by the colonialism of caste patriarchy presages arguments later made by scholars such as Ashis Nandy about the psychological effects of British colonial domination.[18] Phule's concept of comparative colonialisms, forming what I have called a palimpsest in any given moment, helps us understand her dialectical technique in this poem, portraying a protagonist, a gendered English rule, set against a rule of the Peshwa, the Brahman, and its attendant patriarchy. The final lines of this poem reflect her position that Shudras and Dalits (*atiśūdra*) were the first peoples of India and this is the "truth of the blood of India." As she says in another poem in this collection:

The word Shudra means a *native*
Because the powerful applied the term Shudra to those they defeated.[19]

Phule uses the English word "native" in this poem, phonetically spelled in Marathi (*neṭivh*). One of the reasons she uses this English word in her Marathi poem is to reference British (and broadly European) philological history around the theory of the Aryan migration/invasion thesis, which posits a native or indigenous population against a migratory or invading one. Her politics regarding the British rests on this assumption of indigeneity and the subsequent conquest and subjugation of an indigenous population through her version of settler colonialism. Mother English *is* an instrument of colonialism, of course, and Phule clearly sees the British colonizing and usurping the power of the Mughals and the Peshwas. But she does not see the English in opposition to a homogenous "Indian" people nor does she appear to identify with the elites whose power has been usurped, such as the Peshwas. Instead, she sees in place an already-bifurcated world that British colonialism enters, a world that distinguishes women, Shudras, and Dalits from a "high caste" male patriarchy. Her view of colonialism is prismatic; she views the English through a wider glass, encountering a society already bent and dispersed by the Aryan conquest that produced caste patriarchy. Through the palimpsest of colonialism, Phule sees a past of freedom that can be revived in the present. Her hope that Mother English will nurture women, Shudras, and Dalits is also a hope to return to a time before all colonialism on the subcontinent.[20] However, it is also the case that Phule does not appear to recognize in her writing the violence, despotism, indentured servitude, racism, white supremacy, and cruelty of British colonialism either. Whatever her position in terms of Indian nationalist thought, it should be clear that her perspective on "the nation" in a nationalist frame is primarily informed by her view of colonialism as a layered formation on the subcontinent, what I refer to as palimpsestic.

As a vernacular of culture and language emerging from a place and time, Phule believes that Mother English provides the chance for new freedoms she identifies have been impossible since the advent of the Aryan presence on the subcontinent. One key aspect of this new set of possible freedoms is access to knowledge and education, a theme throughout Savitribai Phule's poems. Phule uses "Mother English" to mean not only a language that is a medium for knowledge and power but also a culture that she understands to promote the education of women, Shudras, and Dalits, which she sets against a cultural discourse—"Brahman *dharma*"—that prohibits education and knowledge for these communities. One reason for this juxtaposition of colonial powers is to show that the rule of Mother English does not require the subservience of women, Shudras, and Dalits, which "Brahman rule" is predicated upon, enacted through the forced ignorance of subjugated communities. If Phule did understand caste patriarchy as a system of knowledge access, then opening access to knowledge for those denied learning is a key weapon against caste patriarchy. For her, English as a culture and a language represents a different system of knowledge access. Though one may feel she romanticizes her subject—she is a poet after all—this is the gist of her theory of language, power, and freedom.

Learning English was central to Phule's prescription for setting the power of one colonial force (the British) against another (caste patriarchy). The most direct call for Shudras and Dalits to learn English comes from a brief *abhaṇg* in her collection:

Study English
(*abhaṅga*)

In life self-reliance takes diligent work.
Make an effort to acquire knowledge and prosperity.

Without education life is wasted, like an animal's life.
Don't sit idle; get an education.

Shudras and Untouchables (*atiśūdra*) can relieve their suffering (*duḥkha*).
The opportunity has arrived to learn English.

Learn English and break caste hierarchy (*jātibheda*).
Throw away the tiresome stories (*bhārūḍā*) of the Bhataji [Brahman].

As Shailaja Paik has shown in her work, the political effort toward emancipation from caste patriarchy in modern India required a movement through education, and the suffering caused by caste patriarchy for non-Brahmans and women is directly related to the denial of education to these communities.[21] These are strategies of a knowledge system designed to create inequalities. Phule's poem returns to the theme of her first Mother English *abhaṅg* as she argues that women, Shudras, and Dalits are rendered "animal-like" without education and so fit for inhumane subjugation at the hands of others. The idea that Shudras and Dalits are rendered "subhuman" or "without humanity" is a point Shailaja Paik makes in relationship to Dr. B. R. Ambedkar's question for *māṇusakī*, what she glosses as "being regarded as human in society."[22] Savitribai Phule's emphasis on how caste patriarchy reduces some people—Dalits and Shudras in particular—to a social ontology of animality follows a similar vein. Phule directly argues here that learning English will break "caste hierarchy" (*jātibhed*) because it will assert a discursive power that can contradict another discursive power, that of "tiresome stories of the Bhataji," Phule's metonym for Brahmanical texts, histories, myths, and rituals.

In her second and last book of poetry, Savitribai Phule returned to these many critiques and diagnoses of power in a poetic form that served as an elegy for her husband who had died a year before the book's publication. In this work, a single extended poem that narrates the history of sequential oppression faced by women, Shudras, and Dalits, Savitribai Phule devotes 11 quatrains to the subject of "The English" or *āṅglāī*. She positions this section after engaging other epochs in Indian history—from the Aryan invasion to the Brahmanical suppression of Buddhism to the Peshwa period. Following her treatment of the time of the English, she concludes with the era of "Jotiba" that she argues is made possible by the advent of British rule. Here is her subsection of verses on the "English":

The English

Even though non-Shudras were employed for English work
Shudras and women were not treated like Shudras.
English rule arose in this land of India
To improve things for the people in the region of Maharashtra. || 23 ||

They wrote history shaped by the truth (*satye*).
And that's how we understand Jotiba's historical work.
Just as surpassing English is pleasing and honest,
In this way Jotiba's story energizes us. || 24 ||

As humans are beings eligible for education:
The English declare such noble sentiments.
Therefore, we must study [to open our] eyes.
Let women, Shudras, and everyone else learn to read. || 25 ||

Observe the thunderous drumming of the English language!
Thus, we feel awestruck by their rule.
They give opportunities to the uneducated to learn.
Thievery, murder, robbery, and crime is prohibited. || 26 ||

The priests (*bhaṭa*) of the schools of the Lord Jesus Christ
Appeal to the Shudra children with education.
Some say, "Oh how the Christians lead them like sheep!"
This disparagement is vacuous; such talk is empty. || 27 ||

Thus, Shudras have been deprived "age after age."[23]
Without an iota of happiness, always enduring misery,
They are made voiceless just like an animal.
This is their condition and no one feels ashamed. || 28 ||

Such people learn nothing about birth and death.
Therefore, they don't [even know] that their suffering is like that of an animal.
They have no awareness, and they have no knowledge.
Humans in this condition can never be happy. || 29 ||

One says, "See the extent of my farm and my well.
See my crop and how nice my sorghum is!

I have a fair and lovely wife and a sweet daughter."
Such an egotistical man is not a worthy person. || 30 ||

One who acts in such sub-human (*pāśavī*) and very vile ways
Is always jealous of the happiness of other people.
He is fixated by greed for wealth and the wives of others.
The truth is that he is not civilized but instead he is like a beast. || 31 ||

Such a person has no ethics (*dharma*) or morality (*nītī*)
He has a mean demeanor like a brute.
His life goes to waste.
This is how the Shudra becomes a zero-man (*śūnya māṇūs*). || 32 ||

See here: it was the English year twenty-seven.
Twenty-seven: a year that people speak of with fondness,
An era of progress (*sudhāraṇ*), one of good fortune:
In Pune Jotiba was born in his own home (*svagṛhī*). || 33 ||[24]

This final paean to English as a language and culture of place rehearses many themes we have already seen and presents the English as a vernacular culture of liberality and the English language as a medium for liberal ideas. The poem sequence begins with a rejection of the association of labor and caste—the idea that one's hereditary occupation and ascribed gender position a person in a naturalized hierarchy of labor. Phule notes that even though the British employed non-Shudras—Brahmans and other "high caste" men—this did not also mean that Shudras and women were treated as inferior beings. In today's parlance, we might see this as Savitribai Phule's critique of the association of "merit" and caste.[25]

The second poem targets another key issue Phule weaves throughout her work: a history of caste patriarchy composed to underwrite Aryan conquest and normalize caste patriarchy. As noted above, the Phules adopt this concept from European Orientalist scholarship, though Savitribai Phule here cites English historiography in particular. Her perspective is that history in India before the arrival of the English (and of English language) was a prejudicial construction that served caste patriarchy, not "truth," or history based on facts.

The next two poems together elaborate Savitribai Phule's understanding that the liberalist concepts of equality, justice, and human rights she associates with English as a culture and political power are exemplified in its language. Hence, learning English is a way to access these potential avenues of social justice and good governance. The right to education in particular is essential here, and Phule dwells on the criticism that English education is nothing more than Christian indoctrination. Phule's position on English as a liberatory vernacular should be seen in the light of the English Education Act of 1835. Scholars, influenced by Michel Foucault's engagement with education and social order,[26] have rightly pointed to the instrumentality of English education to produce, as Thomas Macaulay (in)famously argued, "a class of persons Indian in blood and colour, but English in tastes, in opinions, in morals and in intellect."[27]

In addition, Phule does not decry the rejection of Indian literatures that Macaulay places in the shadow of "a single shelf of a good European library" because, as a Shudra woman, she does not appear to take either ownership or pride in an elite caste male-dominated Marathi literary history or that of any other Indian language, including Sanskrit (which there is reason to believe she knew as well).[28] The palimpsest of colonialism allows Phule to see in the kinds of sentiments expressed in the English Education Act and in Macaulay's speech a rejection of the discursive edifice of her own oppression. There may yet be the oppression of British colonialism and English cultural arrogance—or even Christian proselytization—but from her point of view it would appear that the English presence in India is the lesser of evils. Phule seems to propose that the subjugation of Indian languages by English literature is the corollary to the subjugation of caste patriarchy and its ideology to the more egalitarian language and ideology of English culture and rule.

At the core of Phule's endorsement of the English as purveyors of a liberalist position and policy on universal education is, I have argued, her idea that caste operates as a system of knowledge hierarchy. As she clearly argues here and elsewhere in her work, when one is generationally deprived of knowledge and education, that deficit reduces a person to the status and intellect that is animal-like (*pāśavī*), subhuman on a scale of humanity, rendering a person without happiness, a person suffering and voiceless. Phule is making a civilizational critique of caste patriarchy and its strategies of oppression through hierarchies of knowledge. Phule argues that English breaks this chain of oppression because it introduces a language and culture that is distinct from "India" constructed in Brahmanical terms, that is, as an elite and elitist *vernacular*. Therefore, English can be used as a weapon against the discursive forms of oppression existing in India that Phule articulates. This is why she calls not just for education, but for education *in English*, in a vernacular she argues is imbued already with liberalist concepts that challenge the hegemony of an unjust social order articulated with the frames of Brahmanical caste patriarchy. This is a position at odds with the idea of English as a cosmopolitan language of domination.

The four quatrains that then follow lay out Phule's argument about the highly evocative "zero-man" (*śūnya māṇūs*), which is her criticism of her fellow (male) Shudras who choose to remain within the thrall of caste patriarchy, who do not develop caste consciousness. She identifies a false consciousness engendered by ignorance, a lack of self and social awareness that keeps Shudras suffering in a subhuman condition. Phule again genders her subject here, a caricature of a Shudra male antagonist obsessed with materiality and possession, a man who boasts of possessing a "fair and lovely wife and a sweet daughter" who nonetheless seeks "the wives of others." While she has, up to this point, established her understanding of the historical and social conditions that enforce caste patriarchy, here she turns her critique to those Shudras who continue to allow their lives to be ruled by caste patriarchal norms, especially in relationship to gender inequality, and do not strive for an education and the development of caste consciousness. In this critique, Phule recovers the use of *dharma* to name an objective moral and ethical position, the rejection of which renders a person animal-like (*paśūsārakhī*), a "brute." In other words, knowing and living by this absolute *dharma* that demands equality and justice is what makes a person "human" (*manuṣye*). Anyone who does not possess consciousness of caste patriarchy and does not work to eradicate caste–gender injustice is termed by Phule a "zero-man," a person without humanity, a life gone to "waste." The "zero-man" is a product, too, of caste patriarchy, and Phule argues that the palimpsest of colonialism allows the zero-man to be revealed because English as a language and culture of place produces one possibility for caste–gender consciousness. Savitribai Phule instrumentalizes English power to critique the older and more enduring "colonialism" of caste patriarchy embodied not only in the "high caste" male figure but in the Shudra "zero-man" as well.

Conclusion

Toward the end of the *Bāvannakaśī Subodh Ratnākar* of 1891, Phule returns to a theme we saw in the first "Mother English" poem cited above from *Kāvyaphule* in 1854:

Jotiba says that English is mother's milk (*māy pānhā*).
Drink, dear child, and grow strong like a high-born person (*abhijāt*).
Take great effort with your academic lessons
Seize peace and satisfaction in this worldly life (*saṁsār*).[29]

This reference to Jotirao Phule may be drawn from one of his own poems, an *abhaṅg* that appears with two others as a coda to his most famous work, *Gulāmagirī* (1873). Here is the relevant portion:

With similar minds and bodies,
Why has [only] the Brahmin
received comfort? || 13 ||
Intoxicated by power,
they denied education to Shudras
Who have obeyed through the ages. || 14 ||
[Now] Manu[30] has been thrown into the fire and
English has become our Mother of Knowledge (*jñānācī māūlī*)
Who nourishes us with her milk (*pānhā pājī*). || 15 ||

Now then, do not back down.
Vociferously reject
The Manu mindset (*manūmatāṃ*). || 16 ||
You will find happiness once you're educated.
Accept my writing,
Joti says. || 17 ||

The Phules hoped that English—as a language and a culture—could undo the restrictions of birth, equalize the playing field for those not "high born," and create new opportunities for women, Dalits, and Shudras in the spinning wheel of life (*saṁsāra*). Jotirao Phule provocatively names the mental anguish he hopes English education will eradicate as the "Manu mindset," a rephrasing of the "mind plagued with inferiority" that Savitribai Phule captured in her second Mother English poem. The language here of mother's milk, birth, and the turning of life draws us back to Savitribai Phule's gendered imagination of English as a mother, protector, educator, and source of new life, a theme Jotirao Phule adopts as well. Known throughout her own life as a motherly figure who fought for educational opportunities for all Indians, the call to learn, and especially to learn English, education advocacy remains a hallmark of Savitribai Phule's public memory.[31]

Savitribai Phule theorized caste patriarchy as the power to construct a language of inferiority and a cultural of inequality that enforced a knowledge hierarchy and disenfranchised women, Shudras, and Dalits. She understood "the English" to be a linguistic and cultural sphere that espoused a liberality toward women, Shudras, and Dalits, and produced historiography that revealed the operations of caste patriarchy. English power for Phule was not only the political power of British colonialism but also the cultural power of a new linguistic sphere, a vernacular, that accessed new ideas around human rights and provided a language to both express those ideas and actualize them. Yet, her understanding of this new linguistic and political sphere was not taken in isolation but layered over what she understood to be the pre-existing colonialism of caste patriarchy with its origins in the Aryan conquest of the subcontinent. She articulates this understanding of colonialism as layered, what I refer to as a palimpsestic, as someone who is already subsumed under several strata of domination. For this reason, she genders English power as "Mother English" and juxtaposes this gendered force against a masculinist Brahmanical caste patriarchy. In her work, "Mother English" is a *caste and gender* critique of language and knowledge. At the same time, she offers an internal critique of Shudra culture, holding up her caricature of the unreconstructed male Shudra, the "zero-man," who refuses education and insists on understanding women as property. Phule's analysis in this way is fundamentally intersectional—all caste violence is predicated on a pre-existing gender violence even when it occurs within and among people of the same caste community.

My aim in this chapter has not been to excuse British colonialism or judge the positive or negative effects of European colonial power in India. It would not be my place to do so anyway. While I think of myself as a scholar informed by postcolonial critique, I am not seeking here to enter into debates about the nature or function of British colonialism. The fact of colonialism's extractive brutality or its relationship to white supremacy and patriarchy I would never dispute. Instead, I have attempted to show how one of the most important thinkers of modern India viewed the English language and its culture as a colonial power that colonized a pre-existing and more insidious colonial power, from her point of view. Shailaja Paik has pointed out that Dalit political positions in Maharashtra, especially in relationship to Dr. B. R. Ambedkar's thought, understood the dichotomy between British colonialism and Indian nationalism to be a false dichotomy because it ignored the "internal" colonialism of caste patriarchy.[32] This is a fundamental principle of analysis for Savitribai Phule, whose published work preceded Ambedkar's by nearly a half-century.

In that same vein, I do not query here the historical validity of the Aryan Invasion theory. And in any case, Phule's use of this idea is to turn a rationalization of Aryan superiority against its progenitors, which means the critique functions both in registers of myth as in history. Rather, I aim to show how Savitribai Phule used this concept strategically. Phule was not alone in making this argument, while at the same time there were important non-Brahman critics of this "native" interpretation of the Aryan Invasion position, most famously Dr. B. R. Ambedkar, who rejected this aspect of the thought espoused by Savitribai and Jotirao Phule and others.[33]

Rather than engage with the validity of these ideas, I have taken Savitribai Phule's work itself as eminently worthy of inclusion in the consideration scholars make of how some Indians experienced and understood the English presence in the time of European colonialism and the function and power of the English language. I do not argue that Savitribai Phule speaks for all non-Brahmans or *bahujan*s or for all women or others subjected to caste patriarchy. Savitribai Phule's is but one voice among so many. Yet her voice is powerful, prescient, and original; her ideas seeded in much of the political thought that followed her, and her legacy apparent in India today. This chapter is one attempt to draw the extraordinary thought of Savitribai Phule more fully into our scholarly present and help find its place within the "Mother English" that held so much of her hope.

Acknowledgements

I am thankful to Nishat Zaidi for the kind invitation to join this volume, and for Hans Harder's editorial suggestions. I am grateful to several people who commented on the arguments of this chapter and on the Marathi translations, especially Shobha Kale, Sunila S. Kale, Anup Hiwrale, Shailaja Paik, Rohini

Mokashi-Punekar, and Rohini Shukla. I bear all responsibility for the content of this essay and translations, including all errors and omissions.

Notes

1 All translations are mine and are based on the Marathi original poems in Mali, M. ed. 1988.
2 This claim is based on the publication record contained in the Government of Maharashtra's edition of Jotirao Phule's work edited by Phadke, Keer, and Malshe. See Phadke, et al., 2006. I am aware of other claims of publications attributed to Jotirao Phule that are of an earlier date. For example, see S. Gundekar 2002 and 2010. My thanks to Surajkumar Thube for these references. I am also aware of the claim that the work attributed to Savitribai Phule is not attributable to her, though I find this claim's evidence to be spurious. For more on this claim, see for example S. G. Malshe 1987:47-62
3 Phule also followed the practice of taking her husband's first name as her second name, which she used as her authorial signature, as in "Savitri Jotiba."
4 Two volumes in English engage with Savitribai Phule: Mani, B. and P. Sardar, eds. 2008. *A Forgotten Liberator*, and Sudhakar, G. 2018. *Savitribai Phule: Pioneer of Women Empowerment*. There is one translation of Phule's *Kāvyaphule* in English (Mhatre, U., trans. and L. Dhara, ed. 2012: *Kavyaphule: Poetic Blossoms)*. There is no English translation of the *Bāvannakaśī Subodh Ratnākar*, but I am preparing one for publication.
5 Novetzke 2016.
6 My reference here is to the two earliest texts of Marathi, the *Līḷācaritra* and the *Jñāneśvarī*.
7 See Pollock, Sheldon I. 2006.
8 Novetzke, Christian Lee. 2016.
9 See poem 4 of the *Bāvannakaśī Subodh Ratnākar* in Mali, M. ed. 1988.
10 In this chapter, I do not adjudicate the authenticity of the claims of the Aryan Invasion theory. For more on this, see Bryant, Edwin. 2003.
11 The term "Tartar" or "Tatar" refers to many communities, but in general this refers to people with an historical origin in northern or central Asia, roughly corresponding to Turkey. I believe her reference is to the fact that the term "Tartar" would often be used as a designation of the region of the Caucasus, the origin of the term "Caucasian," and so associated with the migration of the Aryans, even though many of the languages of the region, like Turkish, are not Indo-European languages. She is also referencing the idea common in the nineteenth century that Tartar people were "barbarians" and uncivilized.
12 Cf. the *Bhagavad Gītā* 9.32 and references to the lowly born from *pāpayoni*, "wombs of sin."
13 Pollock, Sheldon. 1993.
14 See poem 12 of the *Bāvannakaśī Subodh Ratnākar* in Mali, M. ed. 1988.
15 Vijay Tendulkar's play *Gashiram Kotwal* (1972) is a paradigmatic example of this critique.
16 See poem 38 in *Kāvyaphule* in Mali, M. ed. 1988.
17 Another poem in this collection reflects many of these same ideas: Poem 34 in *Kāvyaphule*, Śikaṇesāṭhī Jāge Vhā or "Wake Up to the Need for Education."
18 Nandy, Ashis. 1983.
19 See poem (*abhaṅg*) 30 in *Kāvyaphule*. I supplied the lines "to those they defeated" to clarify the meaning of this verse extracted from the one that follows in Phule's original text, which indicates this meaning.
20 See Omvedt, Gail. 2008.

21 Paik, Shailaja. 2014: 119 ff., and 241 ff.
22 Paik, 2021: 129.
23 Quotation marks in the original as "yugānuyuge," likely a reference to the famous phrase in the *Bhagavad Gītā*, Chapter 4, verse 8: "I come into being from age to age with the purpose of fixing *dharma*—as a refuge for those who do good and as a doom for those who do evil." (Translation by Laurie Patton 2008). Phule here is perhaps critiquing the *Gītā*'s message.
24 *Bāvannakaśī Subodh Ratnākar* in Mali, M. ed. 1988.
25 See Subramanian, Ajantha. 2019.
26 For example, see Viswanathan, Gauri. 1989.
27 T. B. Macaulay, February 2, 1835, online here: http://www.columbia.edu/itc/mealac/pritchett/00generallinks/macaulay/txt_minute_education_1835.html.
28 I have not read a statement by Phule or her biographers that she knew Sanskrit, but Marathi collection of her work reproduces Sanskrit text she read and transcribed into the Marathi script *moḍī*.
29 See Poem 46 of *Bāvannakaśī Subodh Ratnākar* in Mali, M. ed. 1988.
30 This is a reference to the purported author of the *Manusmṛti*.
31 Pune University was renamed Savitribai Phule Pune University in 2014 in honor of Phule and in recognition of her role in the promotion of education.
32 Paik, S. 2021: 131.
33 See "Who were the Shudras?" by Dr. B. R. Ambedkar (1946).

Bibliography

Bryant, Edwin. 2003. *The Quest for the Origins of Vedic Culture: The Indo-Aryan Migration Debate*. New York: Oxford University Press.

Gundekar, Shriram. 2002. *Mahātma Jotibā Phule: Sāhitya āṇi Sāhityamūlye*. Puṇe: Pratimā Prakāśan.

———. 2010. *Satyaśodhakī Sāhityācā Itihās*. Vol. I. Lātūr: Satyaśodhak Sāhitya Prakāśan.

Mali, M. ed. 1988. *Sāvitrībāī Phule Samagra Vāṅmay* [Savitribai Phule Collected Works]. Mumbaī: Mahārāṣṭra Rājya Sāhitya āṇi Saṃskṛti Maṇḍal.

Malshe, S. 1987. *Tāratamya*. Mumbaī: Prakāśan Mandir.

Mani, B. and P. Sardar, eds. 2008. *A Forgotten Liberator*. New Delhi: Mountain Peak.

Mhatre, U., trans. and L. Dhara, ed. 2012. *Kavyaphule: Poetic Blossoms*. Mumbai: Dr. Ambedkar College of Commerce and Economics.

Nandy, Ashis. 1983. *The Intimate Enemy: Loss and Recovery of Self under Colonialism*. Delhi: Oxford University Press.

Novetzke, Christian Lee. 2016. *The Quotidian Revolution*. New York: Columbia University Press.

Omvedt, Gail. 2008. *Seeking Begumpura: The Social Vision of Anticaste Intellectuals*. New Delhi: Navayana Publishers.

Paik, Shailaja. 2021. "Dalit Feminist Thought." *Economic and Political Weekly* LVI(25): 127–136.

———. 2014. *Dalit Women's Education in Modern India: Double Discrimination*. New York: Routledge, and in particular 119ff, and 241ff.

Patton, Laurie L. 2008. *The Bhagavad Gita*. London; New York: Penguin.

Phadke, Y., D. Keer, and S. Malshe, eds. 2006. *Mahātmā Phule Samagra Vāṅmaya* [Mahatma Phule Collected Works]. Mumbaī: Mahārāṣṭra Rājya Sāhitya āṇi Saṃskṛti Maṇḍal.

Pollock, Sheldon. 1993. "Deep Orientalism? Notes on Sanskrit and Power beyond the Raj." In Breckenridge, Carol Appadurai (ed.) *Orientalism and the Postcolonial Predicament: Perspectives on South Asia*, 76. University of Pennsylvania Press.

———. 2006. *The Language of the Gods in the World of Men: Sanskrit, Culture, and Power in Premodern India*. 1st ed. Berkeley: University of California Press.

Subramanian, Ajantha. 2019. *The Caste of Merit Engineering Education in India*. Cambridge, MA: Harvard University Press.

Sudhakar, G. 2018. *Savitribai Phule: Pioneer of Women Empowerment*. New Delhi: Avni Publications.

Viswanathan, Gauri. 1989. *Masks of Conquest: Literary Study and British Rule in India*. New York: Columbia University Press.

"Who were the Shudras?" by Dr. B. R. Ambedkar (Ambedkar, Bhimrao Ramji. 1946. Who Were the Shudras? Vol. item 07744. Bombay: Thacker & Co.). n.d.

4

THE LOCATION OF THEORY

Bhāṣa Literatures in Indian and North American Postcolonialism

Suddhaseel Sen

> The value of the postcolonial idea as a discursive concept is appealing to me because it allows me to see common ground between writings from different cultures and histories. It is a much more demanding methodology than it might seem if practised without an adequate interest in context.
>
> (Abdulrazak Gurnah, quoted in Mohan and Datta [2019: 6])

There are some fundamental methodological asymmetries between the scholarship on literature and other art forms from North America and Europe, on the one hand, and India, on the other. Western scholarship on the former is characterised by a far greater and rigorous attention to historical, social, and formal contexts and requires scholars to be able to cite primary and secondary texts in the relevant European languages. In contrast, an increasing number of contemporary Indian postcolonial literary scholars draw primarily upon top-down theoretical approaches, focusing less on historical details or the empirical record provided by modern Indian-language responses. As we shall see, the latter approach was by no means dominant in India in the late 1980s and early 1990s, when several scholars from the subcontinent took exception to some of the methodological moves adopted by postcolonial theorists such as Homi Bhabha and Gauri Viswanathan, who were (and remain) located in North America, and in whose work the neglect of writings in modern Indian languages is particularly noticeable. Yet, these early Indian responses, which brought much-needed internal diversity to postcolonial theory, gradually made way for the hegemony of what could be called the North American model of postcolonial studies in Indian academia.

Neil Lazarus has argued that postcolonial theorists, focused as they are on the unifying theme of colonial victimhood, tend to ignore the linguistic,

DOI: 10.4324/9781003279921-6

literary, and historical specificities of various literatures from colonised or ex-colonised communities (Lazarus 2011: 73–74). This kind of mainstream postcolonial theorising, which drew upon poststructuralist methodological assumptions, became *dominant* first in North American academia in the 1980s and 1990s, and eventually spread elsewhere. It is characterised by its overwhelming focus on the coloniser vis-à-vis the colonised divide; its emphasis on discursive formations, often seen in isolation from the specific historical contexts from which they emerge; and its overdependence on English-language writings even where anticolonial movements are concerned, which leads to the virtual erasure of histories of anticolonial resistance in modern Indian languages (or the languages of other colonised communities, for that matter).

It would be incorrect to imply that early postcolonial scholarship in the UK or elsewhere shared none of these features: after all, the essays that constitute Bhabha's *The Location of Culture*, a book that exemplifies all of these tendencies, were written when Bhabha was teaching in the UK. Nevertheless, such ahistoricist approaches were also strongly contested from the beginning in the UK by several scholars, as did their Indian counterparts. Nor will it be accurate to argue that the work of North American postcolonialists working on various aspects of India show, without exception, the traits I have outlined. But, as Timothy Brennan has recently pointed out, "deconstruction was less a French invasion (as the media would have you believe) than an American invention, beginning with the recruitment of Derrida, lured to the United States only after his influence was 'beginning to wane' in Europe."[1] It is in this sense that the characteristic features of what I have called mainstream postcolonial theory, based on the poststructuralist/deconstructionist turn, found acceptance much more readily in North American literature departments than elsewhere in the first two decades of its global spread.

This historical background provides one of the most important clues behind our understanding of why the body of literature and criticism in modern Indian languages—variously termed *bhāṣa* or vernacular literatures[2]—became increasingly marginalised by postcolonial theorising in the metropolitan centres of power and cultural capital—and eventually by Indian postcolonial theorising as well. This chapter is, at one level, an attempt to examine the reasons why a substantial number of Indian academics fell in line with the methodologies of North American postcolonialism, whether willingly or otherwise, despite the insightful caveats offered in the early 1990s. It also analyses the implications of this marginalisation of *bhāṣa* literatures in theorising cross-cultural exchanges by postcolonial theorists from India and what steps need to be taken to redress what seems to me to be a serious matter for concern.

Postcolonialism: North American Theorising, Indian Responses

One of the most important contributions of what is arguably the foundational text for postcolonial studies, Edward Said's book *Orientalism* (first published

1978), was to demonstrate that "deep-seated biases about non-Western cultures permeate Western works of art, scholarship, and political policies about non-Western cultures and societies," thereby reminding us "about the need for examining a range of disciplines in the humanities with a new degree of self-reflexivity that was hitherto missing" (Sen 2018: 276). Nevertheless, *Orientalism* also poses methodological problems, of which one that is particularly relevant in this context is that it presents a historically uninflected and one-sided view of the aims and methods of establishing a hierarchy of power by the coloniser, making only the discourse of the colonialist relevant for analysis.[3] As Aijaz Ahmad rightly observed:

> A notable feature of *Orientalism* is that it examines the history of Western textualities about the non-west quite in isolation from how these textualities might have been received, accepted, modified, challenged, overthrown or reproduced by the intelligentsias of the colonized countries: not as an undifferentiated mass but as situated social agents impelled by our own conflicts, contradictions, distinct social and political locations, of class, gender, religious affiliation, and so on.
>
> *(1993: 172)*

This is partly because *Orientalism* is methodologically indebted to the work of Michel Foucault, who tended to focus more on the workings of power than on resistances to it. Said recognised this one-sidedness and later distanced himself from Foucault once *Orientalism* had started to make its transformative impact upon academia.[4]

This one-sided focus on domination vis-à-vis resistance, one that takes modern Indian-language responses outside of the purview of postcolonial theorising, can be seen in Gauri Viswanathan's *Masks of Conquest* (1989, rpt. 2014), which sought to examine the impact of British colonial education on Indians without taking into account how Indians "actually received, reacted to, imbibed, manipulated, reinterpreted, or resisted the ideological content of British literary education" (1989:11). Viswanathan acknowledged this to be an important omission when she stated "how the native *actually* responds [...] can, and perhaps must, be told separately for its immensely rich and complex quality to be fully revealed" (1989: 12; emphasis in the original). The omissions of Viswanathan and Said are startling, and their troubling implications were pointed out early on not only by Ahmad but also by other theoretically sophisticated scholars from India. Consider, for instance, Jasodhara Bagchi's response from 1991, *before* Ahmad's book was first published:

> It will be far from adequate to think that English literary studies were a colonizer's plant on the Indian consciousness to gag it into the torpor of slavery. What Macaulay proposed was only a formal recognition by the state apparatus of a cultural input that was already entrenched in Bengal. Even

> recent critiques of the institution of English literary studies in colonial India have been deficient because of the exclusive attention being given to the explicit design of the colonial masters.[5] Without giving recognition to the initiative of the Bengali elite in the introduction of English studies in Bengal it will not be possible to understand the deep ambivalence in our approach to English studies.
>
> *(Bagchi 1991: 146–7)*

Bagchi by no means whitewashed the Bengali elite's interest in English studies in her essay. Instead, she situated the growth of English studies in a period when the Bengali elite began "to question colonial domination" and started "working out the parameters of its own hegemonic possibilities" (Bagchi 1991: 146).

Bagchi's reading was spot-on for at least three reasons. Firstly, her analysis went on to provide reasons as to why British education did not result in cultural crawling on the part of the Bengali elite *as a whole*, and why it gave birth to a nationalist freedom struggle, even though its ideological underpinnings were far from perfect. Secondly, Bagchi presciently drew attention to the inadequacy of the concept of colonial hegemony, and instead brought back to the term "hegemony" a firmly Marxist, class-based orientation. Doing so brought her work into consonance with that of Svati Joshi, who connected the establishment of English studies with the rise of the Indian urban middle class and *its* attempts to form an ideological hegemony, one in which *anti*colonial sentiments played an important role (1991: 5–6). In turn, drawing attention to the consistently high levels of illiteracy in the Indian subcontinent both in the nineteenth and twentieth centuries, Modhumita Roy questioned the role played by English education, especially of the *literary* kind, regarding the degree to which Indians were "disciplined" in colonial India through English education (Roy 1994: 85), while Joshi interrogated the extent to which the "homogenization of cultural processes" occurred (Joshi 1991: 5). These counterviews to Said's and Viswanathan's positions are important points to note, since they lead us to wonder why postcolonialists have theorised the processes of reception of *English* literature in a place like India, where linguistic communities who spoke, heard, and read multiple modern Indian languages in relatively large numbers, in ways similar to those occurring in the diasporas, where the communities were far smaller and, in some senses, culturally uprooted.

These insightful caveats from scholars based in India had no impact whatsoever. Indeed, the slipshod treatment of contextual details and of *bhāṣa* literatures in the next canonical book of postcolonial studies, Homi Bhabha's *The Location of Culture* (1994), a collection of essays written between 1985 and 1992, was such that many academics from both within and outside India could not but draw attention to these shortcomings. These included Ania Loomba (1991), Suvir Kaul (1992), Philip Howell (1996), Bart Moore-Gilbert (1997), Benita Parry (2002), and Rosinka Chaudhuri (2002), with Bill Bell (2012) and

Robin Gill (2014) providing new and perceptive critiques in recent years. In 1991, Joshi wrote:

> The theoretical problem of colonial discourse seems to lie in treating the realm of discourse as autonomous, totally detached from material reality; in its tendency, through the systems of representations, to render the colonized peoples and their culture without history; and in its unwillingness to see that these representations are inextricably linked up with, indeed shaped by, the question of the political economy of colonialism and its constant negotiation with the existing pre-colonial, pre-capitalist indigenous social and economic practices.
>
> *(1991: 10)*

The following year, Suvir Kaul, then a professor of English in India, situated Bhabha's work in the linguistic turn of thinkers such as Paul de Man, whose own tendency to situate resistance at a purely linguistic level he insightfully critiqued by arguing that, in addition to locating resistance at the level of language, scholars needed to engage in an "equally rigorous and incisive examination of the contexts of reading," since it was not clear as to "why the truisms of structuralist semiotics or grammatology should provide an immediately acceptable, or even preferable, foundation" (1992: 219, 223). Poonam Trivedi's percipient observation, namely, that "Indians did not receive English literature quite as passively as it is commonly believed, and that a political critique of the colonial hegemony of English literature is not a prerogative of the postcolonial movement" (2005: 20), further underscores the dominance of the top-down model that has held sway among North American postcolonial academics. All these counter-voices, as it were, have had little collective impact, largely because the *body* of literary responses that illustrate the point about the agential colonial figure or about the complexity of colonial self-fashioning hardly gets the kind of analytical attention it deserves.[6]

Postcolonial theory also fails to give due consideration to the relationship of modern Indian-language authors and intellectuals with writings in European languages *other* than English, such as Russian, German, French, and, to a lesser extent, Spanish and Italian—indeed, it can be argued that these Western languages have been perhaps as influential (if not more) in shaping modern Indian ideas on theatre, film, and politics, than has been English. Several Indian intellectuals knew one or more of these languages, and translated directly from them. Kris Manjapra has drawn attention to the fact that, in a six-year period, the Bengali modernist journal *Kallol* (founded in 1923) devoted essays and translations "to at least thirty-one foreign modernist artists, mostly from the small or defeated nations of postwar Europe, or from Russia and Japan," of which "only three were British and only five were Nobel laureates" (2011: 345). Supriya Chaudhuri has drawn attention to the diversity of literatures, from different parts of the world, that were available in English translation in educated Bengali households in which British writing was not to be found, and has observed that "a measure of anti-colonial resistance does appear to be written into the exercise" (2021: 88). The years spent in Prague by the Hindi writer Nirmal Verma brought him in touch with European literature and sensibilities other than British, and proved to be a decisive influence on his oeuvre, while Urdu writers like Ismat Chughtai and Saadat Hasan Manto engaged productively with Russian and French literatures. Brecht has had a profound influence on modern Indian theatre, especially on Marxist playwrights. Indeed, while scholarly studies of interrelations between modern Indian literatures and those in foreign languages other than English do exist, a systematic study that enables us to determine trends or patterns has not yet been attempted. This is all the more regrettable since the use of English translations (or, in some cases, the original European texts) by Indian writers and intellectuals in order to bypass British influence reveals a degree of colonial and postcolonial agency that finds little space in the North American postcolonial theoretical paradigm, devoted as it is to the metanarrative of colonial victimhood and (we are told) post-independence decolonisation.

When critical theory is studied and "applied" to texts uncritically, both writers in modern Indian languages and those from elsewhere in the world, especially European ones, get the short shrift: the difference between assertion and proof becomes blurred, and methodological self-reflexivity, which provided the initial impetus for the flourishing of literary theory, is abandoned. A Foucault or a Bhabha takes up the same place F. R. Leavis occupied in the pre-theory days; all that is left for us to do is to "apply" their concepts with none of the kind of the rigorous attention to empirical data and methodological rigour that is abundantly present in Foucault, and is conspicuously absent from the work of Bhabha and his acolytes. Why did such a downturn come to pass, even when it is clear that, in the early 1990s, there were Indian scholars who were doing what serious literary theorists need to do, namely engage with theoretical concepts and examine their strengths and limitation, when it was especially necessary to do so?

Theory, "Vernacular" Literary Scholarship, and Interdisciplinary Studies in India

There are multiple reasons behind the eventual dominance, in India, of postcolonialism as it developed in North America, over the timely and astute objections raised by India-based academics. In order to outline an understanding of the causes, we need to consider international contexts as well as local-level ones. Elsewhere, I have argued that decolonisation "did not shift the real centre of cultural capital from the West"; consequently, "for third-world countries, to engage globally with more powerful countries was to operate under the sign of the centres of political power and cultural capital" in the postcolonial period (Sen 2020: 191). Such a condition puts pressure on Indian academics to align themselves with North American postcolonialism, despite its scant regard for contextual detail, for which there are pragmatic advantages too: doing so ensures that one is able to reach out to postcolonial theorists on shared common grounds, which is far more convenient than grappling with historical, geographical, and linguistic differences involving countless languages, peoples, and their histories. If Indian scholars do not learn, or get to learn, say, even major African languages such as Kikuyu or Swahili, they cannot expect their non-Indian counterparts to learn languages like Hindi or Tamil, unless there are compelling economic or political reasons for learning any of these languages. No knowledge is disinterested, and the hermeneutics of suspicion can be made to bear on the tacit compromises made by "radical" postcolonialists themselves. Till the time the ex-colonised regions of the world gain political, economic, and cultural capital at an international level, postcolonialists are likely to retain their Anglophone orientation, despite their professed commitment to challenging the inequalities of power relations.

Drawing attention to the neglect of contextual and historical specificities by several postcolonial scholars, Lazarus writes:

> I am sure I am not alone among scholars who read and teach "postcolonial" *literature* as well as postcolonial *theory* in deploring both the sheer opportunism of so many of the critical readings currently being produced, and also the narrowness of the research base or range of works that is typically canvassed for this production. To read across postcolonial literary studies is to find, to an extraordinary degree, the same questions being asked, the same methods, techniques, and conventions being used, the same concepts mobilised, the same conclusions drawn, about a remarkably small number of literary works (which are actually much more varied, even so, than you would ever discover from the existing critical discussion).
>
> *(2011: 22)*

Nirmala Menon has pushed this point further by arguing that "the very narrowness of the range of works invoked for the field is by itself restrictive and limits the theoretical assumptions" of postcolonial studies (2016: 3), bringing out the disconcerting implications of Robert C. Young's observation that Anglophone and Francophone postcolonial writers themselves often "explore well-known issues of postcolonial theory" (2012: 217).

One must, therefore, hope for redress at the local levels: even if literary scholars from ex-colonised countries are not able to speak with each other in as informed a fashion as one ideally hopes, there is no need for them to adopt an analytical methodology that requires them to ignore their own non-Anglophone (or non-Francophone) literary histories. I should clarify once again that there were—and are—indeed several distinguished scholars in various humanities disciplines, including literature, who are either of Indian or non-Indian backgrounds, are based in North America, and pay scrupulous attention to historical detail and larger cultural contexts, and engage with non-Anglophone literatures in their work: scholars like Partha Chatterjee, Aparna and Vinay Dhardwadker, Sudipta Kaviraj, A. K. Ramanujan, Anna Schultz, Clinton B. Seely, Audrey Truschke, and several others readily come to mind. Irrespective of wherever they are geographically situated, scholars working on literatures that are generally covered by postcolonial theory need to connect with each other in bringing responses by writers and intellectuals from the ex-colonies who did not use English as their primary medium, to the centre of analysis of the study of the cultural dimension of the colonial encounter and its long-term ramifications. Deferring that project to the future, as Viswanathan self-consciously does, will not suffice any more.

One reason for the current popularity, among Indian academics, of postcolonial theory that employs the context-free approach towards analysis that has always been popular in North America, is not just because of the current anti-empirical fad that often masquerades as anti-positivism, but also because of what Swapan Chakravorty (2021) has correctly identified as the difficulties involved in archival research among Indian scholars. There are historical reasons behind such a situation. Supriya Chaudhuri has observed that the "segregation of vocational, engineering, and medical courses in separate institutions" was a product of the Nehruvian era, and its "restrictive and utilitarian notion of knowledge and its social functions" led to the valorisation of technology and management at the cost of the neglect of the basic sciences, philosophy, and languages (2011: 17). Consequently, Indian universities, of which the Yash Pal committee noted an acute shortage in 2009, had, about ten years ago, only about 10% of its funds for research and development (S. Chaudhuri 2011: 16). With "the insufficient integration of the library and the laboratory into the learning experience," Chaudhuri observes that the result was "a highly regulated, corpus-based, examination-oriented system of education placing a high value on the paper 'degree' as a token of competence, and it is this system that has stifled the university in India to this day" (S. Chaudhuri 2011: 15, 17). As someone who has taught in both an Indian university and at an Indian Institute of Technology, I can attest to the paradox of being able to teach the humanities much more freely and meaningfully to engineering undergraduates at a technology institute than to English honours majors at a leading university, an experience for which the rigidity of the Indian university system is primarily responsible. There is no reason why the Indian university system should not be given more freedom so that a humanities education can be more meaningful; instead, what we get is increased regulation and emphasis on classroom teaching instead of time for research and discussion.

The inordinate focus on teaching at the expense of research time and opportunities that still continues to inform the regulatory policies and practices of the Indian university system makes research in multiple languages, especially modern Indian ones, all the more difficult, for which some planned state investment from the *school* level onwards is necessary if any progress is to be made on that front. If in India there are opportunities for studying some European languages at an age when human beings are able to pick up languages with facility (childhood to early teens), these are provided by foreign organisations like the Max Müller Bhavans and the Alliances françaises. In the 1990s, in Kolkata, the Ramakrishna Mission Institute of Culture (RMIC) offered courses in some of the major Indian and European languages, but the minimum age requirement was eighteen, by which time one's language acquisition capacity goes down drastically. The two major universities in Kolkata at that time, Calcutta and Jadavpur, offered language courses, but again, not for children. There are no comparable institutions for modern Indian languages, even in the larger cities, for school-going children to learn either Indian or foreign languages over multiple years. The few opportunities for training in regional languages often come from unexpected quarters, the courses in Marathi offered by the *German* department of the University of Mumbai being a case in point. As more and more Indians from diverse linguistic communities interact professionally and personally in multilingual environments, opportunities should be made, at the very least, in the more culturally cosmopolitan urban centres, for children and adults to learn whichever major Indian language they wish to learn. Such schools are necessary if we wish to have scholars who can, in the future, read multiple Indian languages and make good scholarly use of their early training. Instead, overemphasis on English or any single Indian language will create either a rootless cosmopolitanism or a myopic parochialism, neither of which is beneficial to academic research or cultural pluralism.

A third problem adversely affects vernacular-language research in India. If university professors get little time for research, whatever time they *are* able to find is often inadequate for research in Indian archives and libraries because of a host of problems, ranging from difficulties faced by libraries in making publishers submit deposit copies, poor-quality cataloguing done by ill-trained and overworked staff, and the lack of organised online databases, resulting in gaps in the archival records, poor maintenance of archives and of microfilms, and so on.[7] Furthermore, even recent, post-2000 publications by the likes of the Book Review Literary Trust are carefully preserved in several university libraries in the US and are, therefore, readily available, while many of them are available neither at the National Library of India and other deposit libraries nor through e-commerce websites such as Amazon, or even from the publishers themselves. Such a situation makes research very difficult for scholars in India, irrespective of whether he or she works in modern Indian languages or even

English. In contrast, it is not only with regard to holdings and maintenance, but also cataloguing (online) and ease of access (from anywhere in the world) that some foreign libraries score far better than Indian ones *even with regard to their holdings of Indian-language and Indian-related materials*.

Furthermore, in India, book or print holdings are kept in better condition than audiovisual materials and audio recordings. As a result, it is relatively easier to do archival research in literature vis-à-vis music or film. For instance, archival collections of print materials and letters at the Rabindra Bhavan library at Santiniketan are superbly catalogued and are handled by a team of knowledgeable, efficient, and friendly staff; in contrast, the audio section of the same library, located in a different portion of the building, is in shambles. It is impossible for any musicologist to make use of the priceless recordings that are supposed to be there. In a country with traditions as rich and diverse as India, the neglect of the non-verbal art forms needs to be set right urgently. Thankfully, ameliorative steps in archiving priceless materials are being taken by schools and centres within universities and by private organisations, such as the Archive of North Indian Classical music at Jadavpur University in Kolkata (Chakravorty 2021: 175). In recent years, the resources provided by the National Digital Library of India and by archive.org have been invaluable: digitisation has helped research in countless ways, even though several books have pages missing. With improvements in online cataloguing and access, some of the problems faced by Indian researchers can be remedied, although these also need to be supplemented by improvements in physical archives, and quick and user-friendly access to them.

Such efforts at archiving and improving library services are fruitful only when there are communities of students and researchers who are eager to capitalise on these opportunities. In the days when critical theory was beginning to make its impact upon Indian education, publishers such as Urvashi Butalia (1991) and Rukun Advani (1992) drew attention to the relationship between Indian academia and publishing. While Advani examined the reasons behind the preponderance of anthologies, annotated texts, and especially *kunji*s (i.e., guide-books) over scholarly research monographs (Advani 1992: 118–124), Butalia sought to "articulate possibilities of the reconstitution of the field of English studies through a realignment between radical academics and committed publishers" (Butalia 1991: 323). The fact that Butalia and Ritu Menon, her collaborator in the publishing field, went on to carve a prominent space for specialist academic publication shows that it can be a viable activity within India. Yet, with the possible exception of caste studies, any impetus for exploring new areas of research involving India, especially those involving Indian languages and artistic traditions, comes largely in the wake of developments in the Global North, especially the US.

Many of the issues that have been highlighted here were raised and analysed at length thirty years ago by the contributors to the essay collections edited by

Joshi (1991) and Rajeswari Sunder Rajan (1992), volumes that attest to the sophistication of Indian academic analysis of its own practices and their long-term implications, at a time when literary theory was only beginning to have its impact in Indian academia. Meenakshi Mukherjee spoke for many in the Indian professoriate when she wrote:

> When the institution is a megalith and when the individual teachers have no say in framing the syllabus, in choosing the texts to be taught, or in organizing the evaluation system, we all have to devise our personal strategies for survival, our secret devices for making life more meaningful to ourselves, if not to anyone else.
>
> *(1992: 228)*

Yet, despite her warning, Indian academia has witnessed greater centralisation of the university system, lesser emphasis given to research at the universities (as opposed to engineering institutes), and an unbridled proliferation of *kunji* culture everywhere,[8] a decline behind which neither Indian university academics not students can be held solely, or even primarily, responsible, since they have not shaped this downfall: I suggest that it has happened, among other reasons, due to the neglect of timely warnings of the Indian professoriate by non-academic policymakers. Such a decline has not only adversely affected the study of literature, English or Indian, but also of theory: Foucault and Bhabha have also been *kunji*-fied. After seventy years of independence, it is time we stopped blaming colonialism and accepted that this fall in standards has been, at least in part, of our own making.

Concluding Observations

It was perhaps inevitable that, with all the continuing challenges and frustrations involved in doing research on literatures in modern Indian languages within India itself, a kind of context-free postcolonial theorising came to hold sway, despite the critically probing responses to some of its methodological drawbacks by Indian academics in the late 1980s and early 1990s. One can understand why the reductive metanarrative of colonial guilt, rather than the plurivocal Tower of Babel of anticolonial responses, took centre stage in North America: in the culturally diverse classrooms of universities there, colonial guilt can be acknowledged in literature departments like English, based on the national history model, through the analysis of texts written in the language of the coloniser. But the knowledge of various local languages is still required for geopolitical control, and such knowledge is provided not by postcolonial theorists but by area studies specialists. This may be one reason why politically significant global languages from South Asia and elsewhere are still taught in North American universities, and libraries of universities with strong area studies programmes have excellent holdings of texts in these languages, even though they are of little use to postcolonial theorists.[9]

While the differential treatment accorded to non-European languages in North American academia has its own "logic," the constraints and lack of incentives in Indian academia, coupled with the pragmatic advantages of conforming to the methodological approach and concerns of the dominant North American version of postcolonial theory, can be said to be among the principal reasons for the inattention given to modern Indian-language writing, except to an extent in one vitally important emerging field—the study of literatures produced by marginalised communities. The upper-class backgrounds of many of the Indian-born North American postcolonial scholars perhaps have a role to play in the overemphasis on the metanarrative of colonial victimhood *without an attendant focus on issues of class*, as noted by Ahmad (1993: 68, 196). But such scholars, and many of even their Indian counterparts, increasingly use English as a first language, lacing their Indian "mother" tongues with English words. Such shifts in language use are also likely to have contributed to the marginalisation of writings in modern Indian languages in postcolonial scholarship produced in metropolitan centres in the West as well as in India. This has led to a situation in which the number of English scholars in India who also do some of their academic writing in at least one modern Indian language is steadily diminishing.

Noting the rise of the development of "Hinglish," the variety of Hindi that is increasingly interspersed with English words, Harish Trivedi has observed that "a larger and more hegemonic social fraction of the culturally deracinated elite is now using this pidgin" (2003: 983). But what Trivedi says about the pidginisation of Hindi is true in urban settings of several other Indian languages as well. It is true that living languages *always* change, but the contribution of this change in language use among the Indian elite is yet another contributory factor to the increasing marginalisation of modern Indian languages in English studies. The decline in postcolonial scholarship, in English, on Indian vernacular or *bhāṣa* literatures, needs to be situated in the context of these local developments as well as in the context of the global dominance of the methodological practices of postcolonial theory in North America. Ideally, students and scholars of English and modern Indian-language literatures should learn from each other; but with class differences remaining firmly entrenched in place and being reflected in changes in language use in modern India, the gap between an Anglophone elite producing scholarly work on colonial victimhood exclusively in English and the vast majority of Indians who have only an imperfect, functional command over the language will only increase.

Given the insufficient importance Indian policymakers attach to research in the humanities, students are expected to succeed by cracking examinations in a system in which research has far less significance than is desirable. This situation is particularly dangerous with regard to critical theory, since, as Frank

Lentriccia rightly states, "theory is not the pointlessly specialised activity of disengaged individuals; it is rather the fundamental obligation to live self-reflexively and even [...] a condition of democratic community" (quoted in Kaul 1992: 221). When theory is reduced to a set of points for regurgitation in examinations, the negative consequences of *kunji*fication become particularly notable, since it affects not just our analysis of texts, but also our understanding of the very premises of our analysis and, more importantly, of the choices we make in our daily lives and the political positions we take as citizens. The teaching of critical theory with greater self-reflexivity should, therefore, lead us to take carefully considered positions regarding our language choices, at both personal and policy levels. It should also lead to Indian postcolonial scholars paying scrupulous attention to contextual detail, and to their joining hands with their counterparts from other ex-colonies to retrieve histories of resistance and self-assertion through indigenous art forms, instead of rehashing the same narrative of colonial victimhood and postcolonial resistance. With renewed self-reflexivity about the premises of postcolonial theorising, present-day Indian academics should realise the importance of the caveats voiced by an older generation of scholars in the 1990s and, in turn, ought to give literatures in modern Indian languages a far more significant place in their research.

Notes

1 See Timothy Brennan, "What was Deconstruction?" Chronicle of Higher Education, 3 June 2022 (https://www.chronicle.com/article/what-was-deconstruction).
2 The term *bhāṣa* literature has been used increasingly in order to counter the negative connotations of the term "vernacular." It does not seem to me that replacing one term by another helps, as long as literature in modern Indian languages are accorded secondary status in English-language scholarship, whatever one calls it. Indeed, the term "vernacular" is helpful in drawing attention to the parallels between the relationship between ancient and modern European languages, on the one hand, and ancient and modern Indian languages, on the other.
3 For influential critiques of *Orientalism* along these lines, see R. Chaudhuri (2002: 8) and Kaviraj (2010: 76), among others.
4 For an excellent, well-balanced analysis of *Orientalism*'s Foucauldian orientation, and Said's gradual distancing from Foucault, see Lazarus (2011: 183–203). On Said's non-rigorous ways of drawing upon Foucault, see Ahmad (1993: 159–99) and Kaviraj (2010). For an account of some of the alternative ways in which Said, over a twenty-year period, theorised the analysis of cross-cultural exchanges in ways that are far more attentive to historical specificities and differences between media, see Sen (2018: 276–81).
5 Bagchi cites at this point Viswanathan's essay, "The Beginnings of English Literary Study in British India" (1987), in a footnote.
6 For an example of how a close reading of a vernacular-language colonial-era text yields insights that are very different from those from a top-down postcolonial approach, see Sen (2020: 151–72).
7 See Chakravorty (2021) and his interview here: https://www.telegraphindia.com/west-bengal/let-s-talk-about-the-library/cid/1279865, accessed 5 October 2022. I am

grateful to Professor Chakravorty, my teacher and mentor, for sharing the unpublished version of his essay before Routledge eventually published it in around the time of his sudden and untimely demise.

8 Anyone who remembers the kinds of books that used to be available in the College Street bookshops in Kolkata in the 1990s and compares them with what one finds in 2020s would find ample evidence of this decline.

9 One could check the accuracy of this assertion by comparing, in any given period, the number of Anglophone literary texts vis-à-vis those in modern Indian languages that are studied and cited by postcolonial scholars situated in North America. How many Indian-language texts have been examined in the original language by, say, Homi Bhabha, across the breadth of his oeuvre?

Bibliography

Advani, Rukun 1992. "Master English, Native Publisher: A Publishing Perspective on English Studies in India," *The Lie of the Land*, Rajeswari Sundar Rajan (ed), Delhi: Oxford University Press, pp 112–29.

Ahmad, Aijaz 1993. *In Theory: Classes, Nations, Literatures*, Bombay: Oxford University Press.

Bagchi, Jasodhara 1991. "Shakespeare in Loin Cloths: English Literature and the Early Nationalist Consciousness in Bengal," *Rethinking English*, Svati Joshi (ed), New Delhi: Trianka, pp 146–59.

Bell, Bill 2012. "Signs Taken for Wonders: An Anecdote Taken from History," *New Literary History*, Vol 43, No 2, pp 309–29.

Bhabha, Homi K. 1994. *The Location of Culture*, London: Routledge.

Butalia, Urvashi 1991. "English Textbook, Indian Publisher," *Rethinking English*, Svati Joshi (ed), New Delhi: Trianka, pp 321–45.

Chakravorty, Swapan K. 2021. "Silenced Archives and Archived Voices: Archival Resources for a History of Post- Independence India," *Archival Silences: Missing, Lost, and Uncreated Archives*, Michael Moss and David Thomas (eds), London: Routledge, pp 168–85.

Chaudhuri, Rosinka 2002. *Gentlemen Poets in Colonial Bengal: Emergent Nationalism and the Orientalist Project*, Kolkata: Seagull.

Chaudhuri, Supriya 2011. "What is to be done? Economies of Knowledge," *Thesis Eleven* Vol 105, No 1, pp 7–22.

——— 2021. "Which World, whose Literature?" *Thesis Eleven* Vol 162, No 1, pp 75–93.

Gill, Robin 2014. *A Textbook of Christian Ethics*, 4th ed, London: Bloomsbury.

Howell, Philip 1996. "Review of *The Location of Culture*, by Homi K. Bhabha," *Ecumene* Vol 3 No 1, pp 113–17.

Joshi, Svati 1991. "Rethinking English: An Introduction," *Rethinking English*, Svati Joshi (ed), New Delhi: Trianka, pp 1–31.

Joshi, Svati, ed. 1991. *Rethinking English: Essays in Literature, Language, History*, New Delhi: Trianka.

Kaul, Suvir 1992. "The Indian Academic and Resistance to Theory," *The Lie of the Land*, Rajeswari Sundar Rajan (ed), Delhi: Oxford University Press, pp 207–28.

Kaviraj, Sudipta 2010. "Said and the History of Ideas," *Cosmopolitan Thought Zones: South Asia and the Global Circulation of Ideas*, Sugata Bose and Kris Manjapra (eds), Houndmills, Basingstoke: Palgrave, pp 58–81.

Lazarus, Neil 2011. *The Postcolonial Unconscious*, Cambridge: Cambridge University Press.
Loomba, Ania 1991. "Overworlding the 'Third World'," *Oxford Literary Review* Vol 13, Nos 1–2, pp 164–91.
Manjapra, Kris 2011. "From Imperial to International Horizons: A Hermeneutic Study of Bengali Modernism," *Modern Intellectual History*, Vol 8, No 2, pp 327–59.
Menon, Nirmala 2016. *Remapping the Indian Postcolonial Canon: Remap, Reimagine, Retranslate*, London: Palgrave Macmillan.
Mohan, Anupama, and Sreya M. Datta 2019. "'Arriving at Writing': A Conversation with Abdulrazak Gurnah," *Postcolonial Text*, Vol 14, Nos 3 & 4, pp 1–6, https://www.postcolonial.org/index.php/pct/article/view/2548/2328
Moore-Gilbert, Bart J. 1997. *Postcolonial Theory: Contexts, Practices, Politics*, London: Verso Books.
Mukherjee, Meenakshi 1992. "Mapping a Territory: Notes on Framing a Course," *The Lie of the Land*, Rajeswari Sundar Rajan (ed), Delhi: Oxford University Press, pp 229–46.
Parry, Benita 2002. "Signs of Our Times: A Discussion of Homi Bhabha's *The Location of Culture*," *Learning Places: The Afterlives of Area Studies*, Masao Miyoshi and Harry Harootunian (eds), Durham: Duke University Press, pp 119–49.
Rajan, Rajeswari Sunder, ed. 1992. *The Lie of the Land: English Literary Studies in India*, Delhi: Oxford University Press.
Roy, Modhumita 1994. 'Englishing India: Reconstituting Class and Social Privilege.' *Social Text*, Vol. 39, pp 83–109.
Said, Edward 2001. *Power, Politics, and Culture: Interviews with Edward W. Said*, Gauri Viswanathan (ed), New York: Pantheon Books.
Sen, Suddhaseel 2018. "Orientalism and Beyond: Tagore, Foulds, and Cross-cultural Exchanges between Indian and Western Musicians," *Studies on a Global History of Music: A Balzan Musicology Project*, Reinhard Strohm (ed), New York: Routledge, pp 274–307.
——— 2020. *Shakespeare in the World: Cross-Cultural Adaptation in Europe and Colonial India*, New York: Routledge.
Trivedi, Harish 2003. "The Progress of Hindi, Part 2: Hindi and the Nation," *Literary Cultures in History: Reconstructions from South Asia*, Sheldon Pollock (ed), New Delhi: Oxford University Press, pp 958–1022.
Trivedi, Poonam 2005. "Introduction," *India's Shakespeare: Translation, Interpretation, and Performance*, Poonam Trivedi and Dennis Bartholomeusz (eds), New Delhi: Pearson, pp 13–39.
Viswanathan, Gauri 1989. *Masks of Conquest: Literary Study and British Rule in India*, New York: Columbia University Press.
Young, Robert J. C. 2012. "World Literature and Globalization," *The Routledge Companion to World Literature*, Theo D'haen, David Damrosch, and Djelal Kadir (eds), New York: Routledge, pp 213–22.

5

A VERNACULAR ARCHIVE OF SEX AND SEXUALITY

Personal Annotations

Charu Gupta

This chapter draws from my research of more than 30 years on disparate subjects to reflect on how and why the vernacular has been my constitutive archive to study sex and sexuality in colonial India. Questioning the authority and authenticity of the official archive, and inspired in part by the intellectual provocations of Dalit and feminist studies, I have been concerned about the erasures and silences in the archive, have sought to read between the lines and have attempted to reframe the archive by exploring diverse histories of sexuality in vernacular imaginative texts. In terms of its historical and literary politics, it is crucial to recognise the vernacular as a malleable concept, whose meanings are contingent on its contexts. A vernacular signifying practice has critical problems as it can offer disquieting elements that uphold dominant and normative values. At other moments, however, it can be liberatory and act as a vehicle of dissent.

There has been a rich scholarship on the meanings of the vernacular in the Indian context. Partha Chatterjee sees the vernacular as a discursive space which is less alienated from the popular, and lyrically states that the vernacular indulges 'in the fabulous and the enchanted' and mocks 'the scientific rationality [...] of the academic' (2008: 21). Sudipta Kaviraj reflects that in some ways 'vernacular critical thought' was 'more original and more intransigent towards Western reasoning than what appeared in English' (2010: 63). S. Shankar (2013) suggests that the perspectives of the vernacular and related ideas of the local and the traditional are not more worthy of automatic dismissal from theoretical discourse than are the perspectives of the transnational and related ideas of the modern. Udaya Kumar remarks that the vernacular can often be marked by innovative transactions with local and cosmopolitan idioms and languages of earlier and newer epochs (2016: 22–3, 180–2). Rashmi Sadana

DOI: 10.4324/9781003279921-7

underlines how two leading 'Indian novelists who write in English – Amitav Ghosh and Arundhati Roy – affirm their loyalty to "bhasha worlds" as a way to assert their own politics' and 'loyalty to particular causes, people, or ideas' (2012: 169). And while discussing the writing of South Indian History in early twentieth-century Tamil Nadu, A. R. Venkatachalapathy notes: 'While history writing in English was almost exclusively concerned with dynastic history and obsessed with chronology, a major strand of Tamil historiography turned towards cultural history and literary historiography' (2006: 4).

Bhāṣā archives have emerged as critical for humanities and social science research in India. The vernacular offers not just a counter-record but it helps us remake and demolish dominant archival perceptions, and make room for a more robust literary history. The vernacular is not just a linguistic category. It has no particular notion that one can claim authority over, or appropriate, as there are multiplicities residing in a seemingly unitary vernacular. It is an expansive form that encompasses not only *bhāṣā sāhitya* but is also a synonym for one's *matṛbhāṣā* (mother tongue), which questions language hegemony of any kind.

From late nineteenth century, burgeoning presses, mass print cultures, libraries and laws of marketplaces worked in tandem with increasing literacy, solitary reading practices, emerging middle classes, urbanisation and new ways of living and being in colonial India. Print connected the global with the local, while facilitating the emergence of a vibrant vernacular print-public culture in urban India (Ghosh 2006; Venkatachalapathy 2012). Vernacular materials sometimes received colonial patronage but were also often outside its gaze, creating their own social and cultural world. In spite of wavering colonial support, vernacular publications thrived in colonial India and were sustained by the substantial growth of publishing houses and presses, and the rise of multiple and distinct vernacular publics in different regions. It was the vernaculars, and not so much English, that significantly contributed to expanding and commercialising the print market and making the written word ubiquitously available at a relatively low cost.

By early twentieth century, a heterogeneous Hindi print-public sphere came to flourish in north India, as Hindi became the dominant print language of a large section of middle classes, reformers and writers (Orsini 2002; Nijhawan 2012; Gupta 2001: 30–4). However, in spite of its fragmented nature, the Hindi print world till as late as the 1920s, was still largely controlled by the Hindi literati, men and women, who belonged to Brahmin, Bhumihar, Kayasth, Agrawal, Khatri and Thakur castes (Orsini 2002: 4). The Hindi vernacular thus provides a discursive space to understand the perceptions of indigenous Hindu middle classes and dominant castes. While, on the one hand, the upper-caste Hindi-Hindu literati worked towards an imposition of a standardised and Sanskritised Hindi from above, on the other hand, there was democratisation of language and subjects through dissenters and popular texts.

The vernacular print sphere also quickly marginalised Sanskrit and Persian, and there was an explosion of prose in periodicals, newspapers, tracts, novels, travel accounts and autobiographies.

These vernacular landscapes became the troubled sites where divergent representations, transformations and contestations around gender, sex and sexuality came to be staged. Exploring possibilities within the language of representation, this chapter navigates how a contentious associational discourse around sexuality developed in the vernacular and permeated the social fabric in contradictory ways. The vernacular has been central to my work also because the non-vernacular archive, more often than not, records the extraordinary, the cataclysmic and the official. The vernacular, however, is a tactic of the everyday, the mundane and the anecdotal, where gender, sex and sexuality are often ubiquitous. The chapter posits three sites of enquiry by drawing from the vernacular of early twentieth century. I first discuss the sexual anxieties around servants and domestic workers, which were also tied to their caste and religious identities. Second, I consider religious conversions to Islam and Christianity by women on the margins as sites of desire, and their portrayals in the vernacular. Finally, I reflect on vernacular sexology from the margins by discussing the writings of a woman and a Shudra. While there are various other sources to study servants, conversions and sexology, the vernacular reveals a distinct flavour and perspective. The practice and potential of employing a feminist vernacular, not just as an object of analysis but as a critical methodology, is explored through 'records of incrimination', reflected in the Hindi writings of upper-caste Hindus.

Servants and Sexual Anxieties

A didactic manual, which retailed the appropriate behaviour for girls and women (Gaur 1927), had '*Jokhimoṃ se cetāv'nī*' (Warning from Dangers) as its last and stated to be the most significant chapter (220–8). It carried the following instruction for dominant caste, middle-class Hindu housewives regarding subordinate caste women domestic workers:

> In households various *kūṭ'nī*s (pimps) keep coming and going. We have to daily engage with the *mālin* (female flower seller and gardener), the *nāin* (female barber), the *kahārin* (female water drawer), the *camārin* (Chamar woman), the *dhobin* (washerwoman), the *baraïn* (woman betel leaf seller), the *pisan'hārin* (woman who grinds the corn), the *manihārin* (female bangle-seller) and the *dāī* (midwife) for our household work. All these women also indulge in pimping. They start fights in peaceful homes [...]. They tell tales about depraved conducts of husbands and corrupt the minds of brides. [...] These *kūṭ'nī*s work hand in glove with other wicked characters. They take money from them to trick women of decent homes [...]. Be very careful of

> these women. They are notorious for telling bad and false tales. You clearly tell them that you have no time for their dirty stories. It is *Rāmāyaṇ* and *Mahābhārat* that are only worth listening to.
>
> (*Gaur 1927: 222*)

In the same year, a thin tract *Strī śikṣā* (Education for Women) was written by Shiv Sharma Mahopdeshak (1927), a prominent pandit and member of the Arya Samaj in the United Provinces, which retailed 'proper' behaviour for Hindu women, particularly ordering them to keep away from Muslim men. Muslim workers were specifically referred to in this context. The pamphlet stated:

> Do not get your clothes stitched from Muslim tailors [...]. Do not buy toys and fruits from Muslim hands for your children. Do not buy or wear bangles from the hands of Muslim bangle-sellers [...]. Never approach a Muslim servant without purdah [veil] and never cross him.
>
> (*Mahop'deśak 1927: 5–10*)

These two quotes reflect compelling grids, as they epitomise the nature of anxieties about class, caste and religion that can be gleaned from the representations of subordinate caste women and Muslim male servants by dominant caste Hindus in popular vernacular print media of the early twentieth century. They also signify that the relationship of the domestic servant with the housewife became a trope through which caste and religious, along with spatial and bodily exclusions, were sharpened. Utilising circuits of vernacular production, this section underlines a social history of power relations and sexual anxieties between servants and dominant caste Hindus in early twentieth-century north India.

Representations of servants, to paraphrase Jacques Ranciere, are often 'embodied allegories of inequality' (2009: 12). In the early twentieth century, they not only carried power relations but also rendered dominant caste Hindu perceptions, prescriptions and desires into words and images. Material circumstances and changing dynamics of the period intersected with the vernacular print culture to shape the relations between servants and their masters-mistresses. Domestic service included a range of servants, workers and service providers like sweepers, midwives, households labourers, washers and gardeners. These domestics produced cracks in divisions between private–public, inner–outer and home–world, as they were both 'marginal insiders' and 'intimate outsiders' in dominant caste, middle-class Hindu households (Ray and Qayum 2010). While imaging 'ideal' domestic workers, the vernacular was also infused with their negative counterparts, taking its cue from quotidian life and caste–community relations of the time. Increasing assertion by Dalits and growing antagonism between Hindus and Muslims left its imprints on the portrayals of subordinate caste and Muslim domestic workers. Advice manuals, while seeking legitimisation of servant–employer relationship, also expressed anxieties around personal interactions and illicit liaisons between mistresses and Muslim-Dalit domestic servants. The vernacular straddled this contradictory domain of distance/desire and hate/love.

There have been some significant studies on servants in the context of colonial India (Sinha and Varma 2019). The contentious sociopolitical economy of north India at the turn of the twentieth century left its imprints on representations of servants (Gooptu 2001: 27–65). Census records of 1911, 1921 and 1931 of UP point to domestic service as slowly becoming an important constituent of occupation in urban UP (*Census* 1933: 216). The inter-war period in UP also witnessed the emergence of the Adi Hindu movement, which acquired huge Dalit following by the 1930s, leading to their increasing assertiveness and demands for rights (Rawat 2012: 144–74; Gooptu 2001: 152–84). There was also a meteoric growth in the politics of Hinduisation, whereby the campaign for unifying the Hindus gained new urgency and became more aggressive and influential (Freitag 1989: 208–9; Gupta 2001: 222–39). These developments helped in reinforcing dual anxieties around Muslim and Dalit male servants.

In early twentieth-century north India, there was a flooding of didactic books in Hindi, which principally addressed themselves to Hindu middle-class housewives and became an important means to refurbish respectable domesticities, patriarchy and inequality, by disseminating normative prescriptions of behaviour (Gupta 2001: 123–76; Stark 2007: 413–20). Many of these edifying tracts also helped in circulating certain ideas regarding servants, as they distinctly marked differentiations between dominant caste, middle-class Hindu housewives and their domestic women workers, often from the subordinate castes (*camārin, dhobin, bhaṅgan, dāī, mālin, nāin* and *kahārin*), by juxtaposing the former as civilised, beautiful, cultured and superior, and the latter as inferior, loud, uncultured, uncivilised and excessively sexual (Gupta 2016: 28–43). The vernacular construction of subordinate caste domestic woman worker was a constitutive footnote in the representation of the dominant caste housewife, contributing to a rhetoric that 'naturalised' inequality. These manuals differentiated between housewives and women servants in terms of social status, lifestyle, dressing and behaviour. They directed housewives to cover themselves and not to speak loudly, fight or gossip. These traits were often identified with women workers. Class and caste difference was marked in profound ways through constructions of gender difference. Consorting with subordinate caste women servants was declared as dangerous, and housewives were pronounced vulnerable to social contamination from women servants. A manual stated that the *dāī* and the *bhaṅgan* were mainly responsible for spoiling housewives, and because of them *īrṣā* (jealousy), *dveś* (fight) and *kalah* (tension) prevailed in the family (Caturvedī 1946: 68–9). Housewives were warned to be on constant vigilance against these perceived *vyabhicāriṇī* (adulterous), *patit* (degraded) and perilous women (Śarmā 1938: 235).

In tandem, many manuals expressed anxieties about sexual liaisons and illicit romances between the master and women servants. Housewives were warned to especially beware of subordinate caste women workers who could woo their husbands and to ensure that *their* men kept away from them. An advice book stated:

> The licentious tendencies of men are very much visible [...]. They will not talk with their wife at home, but will laugh and talk with the *jamādārin* (female sweeper). They will flirt with the *manihārin* (female bangle seller) and the *camārin*, completely neglecting their wife. Dear housewives, please be cautious.
>
> *(Ṭhākur 1930: 105–6)*

Negative descriptions of women workers were most visible in the cases of the midwifery, practised largely by Dalit women in UP (Briggs 1920: 24–6, 53–4; Blunt 1931: 242). With the firming up of colonial rule and establishment of western medical practices, systems of surveillance came to manifest around the midwife's reproductive technologies (Gupta 2016: 43–51). The Hindu middle-class reformers and writers carried a sharp attack on the Chamar *dāī* in the vernacular in early twentieth century. For example, a long article in *Cā̃d*, a leading reformist journal in Hindi, attempted to transform the 'morally and sexually polluting' *dāī* into a dirty, evil and dangerous witch of progressive India (Sanyāsī 1928: 650–5). Another issue of *Cā̃d* carried a coloured picture titled '*Hamārī dāiyā̃*' (Our Midwives), which not only typecast the *dāī* but also criminalised her (Figure 5.1).

> In this period of progress also, due to lack of educated midwives, thousands of children, as soon as they enter the earth, see their life end. [...] We find in many regions the detestable custom of cutting the umbilical cord by a sickle. In the picture see a very old *camārī* of sixty years, whose hands are trembling and who is using a sickle used for chopping vegetables to cut the umbilical cord. Because of her trembling hands, it has been cut much more. Blood is oozing out and the poor, innocent child has become quiet forever. The poor woman who has recently given birth is also suffering alone and silently. Who will touch the *camārī*! Readers, please also notice the torn mat, the floor bed and the burning fire on the side.
>
> *(Cā̃d, December 1924: between 144–45)*

However, constant lack of finances, an overwhelming urban, middle-class bias and much more expensive official trained midwives ensured a regular demand for Chamar *dāī*s. Many of them started refusing to do the work if not paid

FIGURE 5.1 'Our Midwives'

adequately, and began demanding wages in cash and increased fee for services performed (Briggs 1920: 54, 65). Equally, the first generation of Dalit intellectuals like U. B. S Raghuvanshi, Ramnarayan Yadvendu and Chandrika Prasad Jigyasu deployed the Hindi vernacular in early twentieth century to offer a counter-discourse that challenged *begār* (unpaid labour), servitude and bondage (Rawat 2012: 120–36). The dominant, mainstream vernacular print culture in UP, however, reveals that subordinate caste women workers and servants became a surrogate for refurbishing domestic inequality.

Simultaneously, in some of the curative impulses of reformist and didactic vernacular literature, symbols of deference came to exemplify ideal male servants. Exhibiting a domesticated and subordinated masculinity, they were embodied as asexual, emasculated and effeminate. Alongside, they were appreciated for their gentleness, childlike simplicity and affection (Gupta 2016: 114–21). At the same time, a section of vernacular literature expressed anxieties around intimate liaisons between Hindu mistresses and their servants. In spite of various controls, subordinate caste and Muslim male servants particularly embodied 'dangerous' masculinities and sexualities. In conjunction, there were patriarchal jitters and fantasies about the autonomy and potentially dangerous sexuality of the household mistress. A part of the vernacular, for example, elucidated uneasiness about women sharing moments of laughter and fun with male servants *(striyā̃ naukaroṃ se ṭhiṭholī kar'tī haiṃ)* (Poddār 1925: 25).

FIGURE 5.2 Benefits All Around for the Muslim Bangle Seller

Didactic manuals constantly ordered household mistresses to keep away from Dalit and Muslim servants, or to observe strict *purdah* when dealing with them (Tirath'rām 1924: 12; Vaiśya 1924: 285). In early twentieth-century north India, there was an intensified surveillance of Hindu women's day-to-day interactions with Muslim workers (Gupta 2001: 267–320). The vernacular deployed a whole new language for women vis-à-vis Muslim workers, telling them how to move, whom to talk to, where to go and what to do. For example, Hanuman Prasad Poddar commanded women to boycott Muslim *manihārs* (bangle-sellers) (1925: 25–6), which also involved questions of purity-pollution and touch. Cartoons w*ere* published in the vernacular to this effect (Figure 5.2).

A section of vernacular print literature thus underlined norms of seclusion for the Hindu mistress. In spite of immense vigilance, however, the home offered a turf for housewives to develop intimate bonds. I end this with this cartoon, which, on the one hand, epitomised the threats felt by middle-class household patriarchies but, on the other, also personified recalcitrant intimacies between the mistress and the servant that were indifferent to regulative structures (Figure 5.3).

Mistress: When you rub my feet with your hands, I am deeply contented.
Servant: I know your pulse.
'Body Paste'

FIGURE 5.3 'Tending the Feet'

Mistress: Rub a little more....
Servant: I might sprain you....
(Vyaṅg citrāvalī 1930: n.p.)

The vernacular provides layered representations of relationships and worries around servant–mistress relationships, which are relatively absent in other sources. This vernacular literary field is a critical device to delve into the mentalities of the times. I move in the next section to another discourse in the vernacular.

Religious Conversions as Sites of Desire

Religious conversion has been one of the common expedients resorted to by those at the bottom of caste hierarchies in India, to improve their position, reject stratification, reconfigure social boundaries and register protest as well as social assertion (Vishwanathan 1998; Clarke 1998). There have been significant works which have focused on gendered dimensions of conversions, particularly to Christianity, in colonial India (Kent 2004; Bauman 2008), with missionary archives providing a wealth of information. However, I wish to focus on conversions by women on the margins – Dalit women to Christianity and widows to Islam – and their representation in the Hindi vernacular, which intersected with anxieties among caste Hindus over the relationship between conversions, desire and intimacy. Popular missionary literature in Hindi, cartoons and some writings of dominant castes and reformers show how conversions, or the possibility thereof, produced deeply politicised representations of converted women, especially those who were on the margins – Dalits and widows. At the same time, the vernacular provides tantalising glimpses of how conversions by women were also perceived as implicit acts that embodied their desires, choices and aspirations, which aided a transformative politics of religious rights. First, I briefly look at vernacular depictions of Dalit women's conversions to Christianity, and its intersection with sartorial desires. Second, I study some representations of conversions to Islam by widows, which were often embedded in love and marriage. The vernacular became a medium for high-caste and reformist Hindus to underwrite an exclusivist grammar of difference in sexual regimes, be it clothing or inter-religious romance. At the same time, women's desires, expressed at times through highly ritualised acts of conversion, implied a language of intimate rights, creating ripples in codified definitions.

Vernacular tracts published by the missionaries became one of the chief vehicles of propagating Christianity (Clayton 1911). The North Indian Christian Tract and Book Society in UP widely disseminated vernacular painted story scrolls, books and a multitude of songs and hymns (Lucas n.d.; Church Missionary Society 1926). Their vernacular tracts launched a stringent attack on various teachings of Hinduism and the caste system, which was contrasted with an egalitarian Christianity that provided dignity, education, clean clothes and happiness (for example, *Hindū dharm ke phal* 1905; *Jāti kī chūt chāt* 1905). These created apprehension among high-caste Hindus, Arya Samaj and Hindu Mahasabha, who effectively utilised the vernacular to challenge conversions.

Certain vernacular missionary publications were specifically aimed at women. They depicted the 'positive' changes conversions brought in their everyday habits, and preached subjects like hygiene, cleanliness, nutrition and child nurturance (for example, *Caritra sudhār* 1910; *Candra Līlā sādhunī kā vṛttānt* 1910). While strong impulses towards 'disciplining' of women were discernible through conversions, it also proved to be an enabling discourse. For example, it opened limited horizons of education and training for Dalit women, many of whom refused to do unpaid midwife's work or *begār*. Conversion to Christianity also had particular implications for Dalit women's clothing as it brought to the fore questions of the body per se in relation to caste. Traditionally, Dalit women had to endure humiliating dress restrictions, which were also ways to mark their bodies as inferior and sexually promiscuous. Conversion to Christianity was a declaration of an altered relationship with the world through a transformed disposition of caste-marked bodies (Gupta 2016: 182–97). Ironically, even while lamenting conversions, reformist vernacular cultures could not help but acknowledge this change. Pictures appeared in Hindu reformist literature portraying on the one hand a naked, 'dirty' and unkempt outcaste women and on the other a fully clothed, sari-clad, 'clean' and smiling Christian Dalit woman.

Cartoons depicting the crisis of conversions through clothing entered the vernacular Hindu reformist iconography in early twentieth-century UP, putting on display their moral dilemmas, perceived insecurities and sexual unease. A series of cartoons published in *Cā̃d* and Arya Samaj publications, and many of them compiled in *Vyaṅg citrāvalī* (1930), usually depicted two outcaste women (or men) together, of which one had converted to Christianity. These images catalogued the supposedly alarming results of Dalit conversions to Christianity. However, even while lamenting conversions, they could not help but acknowledge the irony of change in demeanour and elevation of stature that it brought about in Dalit women – in their mode of dressing, walking style, gait, status and prestige. One cartoon, for example, visualised the converted outcaste woman walking ahead royally, carrying an umbrella and a purse, wearing a hat, skirt and high-heeled shoes, reflecting an elevated status. The unconverted woman walked behind head bent, barefooted and carrying the child of the converted Dalit woman.

Another had a Christian Dalit woman carefully sitting on a chair looking down while the untouchable took care of her dog, looking up (Figure 5.4).

FIGURE 5.4 Christian-Hindu Untouchable Woman

मेम साहिबा एक बनी है, और एक मछली वाली !
धन्य धर्म ईसा-मसीह का, कितना महा शक्तिशाली !!

FIGURE 5.5 Madam Lady and Fish Seller

īsāyin kutte kī mālik, hai achūt usˡkī naukar!
par donoṃ the ek jāti ke, dekho hindu ā̃kheṃ bhar!!
(The Christian woman is the master of the dog, while the outcaste woman her servant.
But they both were of the same caste, Hindus please see carefully).
(*Vyaṅg citrāvalī, 1930: n.p.*)

Yet another lamented the loss, showing the converted woman again in shoes, hat and umbrella (Figure 5.5).

mem sāhibā ek banī hai, aur ek machˡlī vālī!
dhanya dharm īsā-masīh kā, kitˡnā mahā śaktiśālī!!
(One has become a madam-lady, the other a fish seller.
Blessed be the religion of Christ, which is all powerful).
(*Cā̃d, May 1929: 77*)

These banal and popular embodied communications can function as our constitutive archives and pivotal documents in conceiving the anxieties of Hindu reformers, while also offering a counter politics of sartorial desire. The rhetoric of such repeated caricaturing was meant to manufacture Hindu public opinion against conversions and warn the caste Hindus not to treat Dalits badly. Such cartoons did not encompass the 'truths' of conversions and sartorial styles of Dalit women, as very few dressed in ways illustrated here. In fact, the dress for Dalit Christian women in missionary schools was very modest, with the sari and the blouse. Further, it was not that missionaries tried to impose Western clothes on converted outcaste women. Rather, a good deal of subtle jousting went on between missionaries and women converts, where desires and ambitions were bound up in dilemmas over what to wear (Kent 2004; Tarlo 1996: 23–61). However, the very depiction of Dalit women in such clothes signified an inversion of norms. Their powerful language made explicit caste Hindu perceptions of Dalit women's desires, while also reflecting their traumatised identities. These women literally wore their difference on their bodies, signifying an uncomfortable anomaly in the reformist-nationalist discourse.

Amidst a context of militant Hindu assertion and growing Hindu–Muslim conflict in early twentieth-century north India (Freitag 1989: 8–9, 230–41), jitters were also reflected in the vernacular around possibilities of conversion to Islam, particularly by Hindu widows, due to romance, elopement and marriage, which came to be rewritten in a language of abductions. It was emphasised in Hindi magazines and newspapers that widows were being constantly abducted, molested and forcibly converted by Muslim men. It was tied with negative portrayals of Muslims, stereotypes about widows' sexual desires and agency, fears of loss of Hindu numbers, and potential childbearing wombs (Gupta 2001: 298–320). In such circumstances, it was declared that it was necessary to support widow remarriage and control the widows' reproductivity within the bounds of Hinduism. The liberal promise of widow remarriage was overturned by a community need for better economy of potential childbearing wombs. Widow remarriage now was to be advocated because widows were entering the homes of Muslims, because they were increasing Muslim numbers, because they were producing *gau bhakṣak* (cow killers), and because Hindu religion was in danger (Siṃh 1924: 94–7).

A Hindi tract said that large numbers of widows were entering the homes of *yavanas* (foreigners, often used for Muslims) and *mlecha*s (barbarians, often used for Muslims), producing children for them and increasing their numbers (Mahārāj 1939: 170–72). Another said that Brahmin, Kshatriya and Vaishya widows particularly were walking into Muslim hands and decreasing the number of Hindus (Śarmā 1917: 9). The famous Hindi poet Ayodhyasingh Upadhyaya 'Hariaudh' penned these lines at this time:

god meṃ īsāiyat islām kī
beṭiyā̃ bahueṃ liṭā kar ham laṭe!
āh ghāṭe par hameṃ ghāṭā huā
mān bevoṃ kā ghaṭā kar ham ghaṭe!!
(Quoted in: Upādhyāy 1927: 1)

(We have made our daughters and daughters-in-law lie in the lap of Islam and Christianity. We have suffered loss after loss. By not respecting widows, we have dwindled in numbers.)

One Hindi tract stated:

> Our sexually unsatisfied widows especially are prone to Muslim hands and by producing Muslim children they increase their numbers and spell disaster for the Hindus. [...] Muslim *guṇḍās* are especially seen outside the houses that have Hindu widows. [...] You yourselves say, would you like our Aryan widows to do *nikāh* (marriage) with a Muslim?
>
> *(Dvivedī 1924: 1, 26, 35)*

Another stated that two and a half crore Hindu widows had been enticed by the Muslims through various methods (Chaudh'rī 1928: 12). Even sympathetic vernacular accounts of Hindu widows, which criticised Hindu society for its oppression, could not resist simultaneously highlighting the 'sad' state of the widows due to their conversion to Islam. To enhance their message and to make their narrative more convincing, some of the magazines and widows' organisations started speaking in the ostensible language of widows. In 1926–27, Zahurbakhsh (1897–1964), a teacher and prolific writer for children, starting writing in *Cā̃d* a series of 'first person confessions' under the heading '*Samāj kā agnikuṇḍ*'. In these, he frequently took the woman's voice and wrote pieces like 'How I Became a Muslim' or 'How I Became a Christian' (Zahur'ba<u>kh</u>ś 1926, 1927). The supposedly personalised accounts heightened the impact of the melodramatic narrative. The Vidhva Sahayak Karyalaya (Office to Help Widows) at Agra, which appears to have been one of the biggest homes for widows in UP at this time, published a series of pamphlets, adopting the language of widows, highlighting the moral contamination of Hindu society due to widows running away with Muslims and converting (Kāśyap 1927, 1929, 1931). The series had many short stories, supposedly based on true accounts narrated by the widows themselves, which broadly followed a similar pattern of their miserable plight due to conversions. Accompanying them were pictures in which on the one side was depicted the Hindu widow in 'Hindu clothes' and on the other was the same woman as a married Muslim in 'Muslim attire' (Figure 8). The stories had titles like 'Rampyari alias Shirdara Begum', 'How I Became Fatima from Champa' and 'Shahzadiya Devi, who was Rakko Before'. In the process of recitation, the widow, though ostensibly telling her own story, was denied a will of her own or her own agency. Within the narratives of widows as victims, however, were also implicit the constant fears of assertion by the widows themselves. There was a thin line between the victim forced out of her home and the apostate acting against her former community. A pamphlet said that Gulab Devi, a Hindu widow converted to Islam, had cautioned:

> Find some way to protect the reproductive and mothering capacity of Hindu community. Otherwise, these *devīs* [goddesses] of yours, who produced Ram, Krishna, Bhim, Arjun and Harishchandra will produce Khudabaksh, Rahimbaksh and Karimbaksh. They will get cows cut and temples destroyed. Then the identity of this Hindu community, which could not be wiped out even by tanks and swords, would vanish in thin air.
>
> (*Kaśyap 1929: 33*)

The Vidhva Karyalay series also made the widows potent actors and agents of their own fate. In one, a Hindu widow was seen warning Hindu males:

> *jis din ṭhan jāyegī man meṃ, kahīṃ nikal maiṃ jāū̃gī.*
> *kisī yavan kā hāth pakaṛ'kar, us'ko maiṃ ap'nāū̃gī.*
> *paidā kar'ke bacce us'se, us'ki śakti bhaṛhāū̃gī.* [...]
> *gauoṃ ko kaṭ'vāū̃gī nit, maṃdir maiṃ tuṛ'vāū̃gī.*
> *dev'sthānoṃ ko miṭ'vākar, masjid maiṃ ban'vāū̃gī.* [...]
> *dharma-granth jal'vā dū̃gī maiṃ, coṭiyoṃ ko kaṭ'vāū̃gī.*
>
> (*Kaśyap 1929: 11*)

(The day I decide, I would go somewhere. I would catch the hand of a Muslim and make him mine. I would bear his children and increase his potency. I will have cows slaughtered daily, and temples broken. I would destroy temples and construct mosques instead. I would burn religious books and get the *coṭī* cut.)

These vernacular tracts can be also read against the grain as they also implicitly draw attention to the widow's sexuality, needs and desires. The widows were 'using' the instruments of conversion and elopement as a mode of coping with, challenging and, within limits, transgressing an oppressive social order. Religious conversions for romance also suggest that sometimes identities were recast so as to disrupt the logic of communal boundaries. The vernacular is a ubiquitous site to explore these intersections between conversions, sexuality and women on the margins. Intertwining conversions with desires of clothing and love in the context of Dalit women and widows gives conversions more intimate meanings, while also bringing them in the public sphere.

Vernacular Sexology from the Margins

In this last section, I centre on the Hindi sexology writings of Santram BA, a shudra, and Yashoda Devi, a woman. I explicate how their writings moved on different registers, whereby they envisaged a heterosexual ethics that relied on utopian and dystopian descriptions of modernity. I argue that while largely operating within reformist sexology frames, these vernaculars at times punctured dominant upper-caste, male-centric authority and created frictions in normative equations. They contributed significantly in creating a vernacular archive of sexual sciences in India.

In her book *Dāmpatya prem*, Yashoda Devi stated:

> Even if the woman is in no mood and has no desire, the men torture her sexually. In other countries men cannot do anything without the woman's consent. [...] Many ill women come to me and say that what to do, our husbands just do not listen. Even if we say a firm 'no', they do not listen, even if we are ill they do not listen. [...] Out of 100, 99 men are such that as soon as they touch a woman or read a dirty book, their sperms start leaking. [...] Those sexually depraved and blind men who think that women will be thrilled if they do intercourse every day and will give them a certificate of masculinity, and desire them even more, are really stupid.
>
> *(Devī 1933: 218–23)*

And wrote Santram BA in 1931:

> Probably, like Kunti, the mother of the Pandavas, no one will regard an unmarried mother and her child as bad and dirty. [...] Social stigmas attached to pre-marital sex will gradually diminish and eventually disappear. [...] There will be much more parity between women and men [...]. It is quite natural for both women and men not to be monogamous [...]. Intelligent and thinking human beings will refuse to be tied in a lifelong miserable relationship [...]. It will be easier for a woman to live with many men and for a man to live with many women [...]. There are many women and men who feel the need and desire multiple partners [...]. The woman will not have to state the fatherhood of her child [...]. There are many amazing women who want to have sexual relations, want to have a child but do not wish to have a permanent husband or marry. They will have a right to do so [...]. The main purpose of intercourse is the fulfilment of sexual desires.
>
> *(Santʹrām 1931: 302)*

These potentially radical passages by Yashoda Devi (henceforth Devi), a woman ayurvedic specialist, and Santram BA (henceforth Santram), a Shudra anti-caste reformer, reflect a heterosexual ethics that gives women a greater place in governing sexual life. Devi questions masculine sexual privileges and Santram celebrates a utopian sexual future of man–woman relationships. The vernacular texts of these two 'minor' and marginal figures allow 'for a fuller exploration of sexology's polyvalent political potential' (Leng 2018: 34), and help retrieve a lost archive of sexology. In early twentieth-century India, sexology discourse was overwhelmingly construed as an elite, bourgeois project, dominated by upper-caste and middle-class male intellectuals. However, a look at the catalogue of Hindi books reveals that no one was writing so much as Devi and Santram on the range that sexology encompassed. These self-styled sexologists produced sexual knowledge in the vernacular which had a wide reach and appeal.

There was an unprecedented efflorescence and commoditisation of what has been termed 'global/Hindu sexology' literature in Hindi (Pande 2018), in the early twentieth century (Berger 2013; Botre and Haynes 2017). Devi and Santram too capitalised on this boom. The textual politics of sexology in the vernacular, while fracturing claims of hegemony of English and Sanskrit in the field, spread from elite medical circles and Sanskrit scholars to Hindi-speaking publics, where a diverse constituency of educated middle-class and upper-caste men were the main actors and authors. Alongside, sexology in the vernaculars often drew its prowess from Indian erotica and/or modern sexology texts, liberally reinterpreting them as and when needed. However, the conceptual offering of vernacular sexology was often not so neatly translatable as Western sexology. There was a lack of fixity in its meaning, as it could encompass a spectrum of ideological rubrics and texts, including eugenics, conjugality, marriage, home science, sexual health issues, birth control manuals, erotic, 'obscene' and pornographic material, sex advisory literature and popular writings on sex. There were also various words like *kām śāstra, kok śāstra, rīti śāstra* and *rati kriyā* that could well replace 'scientific sexology' in the Hindi vernacular. The word *kām* [Skt. *kāma*], for example, meant 'sex', 'pleasure', 'desire' and 'erotic love'. At least 30 titles published in Hindi in early twentieth century contained the words *kām*, *kok, rīti* or *rati* (Gupta 2020b). The vernacular tells us about the range, plurality and heterogeneity of the field, and a world of epistemic possibilities that could at times collude and at others defy the imperium of mainstream sexology.

To give a brief background of my two protagonists, Devi was a leading, extremely popular woman ayurvedic practitioner in early twentieth-century Allahabad, with her own Strī Auṣadhālay (Women's Dispensary) and publishing house known as Devī Pustakālay. She was a prolific writer, and wrote more than 50 books, which included household remedies, marriage manuals, health guides and medical food recipes. She sold more books than probably any other female writer of her time (Gupta 2005; Berger 2013: 95–9). Her books *Dampati ārogyatā* (1931), *Dāmpatya prem* (1933) and *Nārī śarīr* (1938) particularly offered ayurvedic remedies for sexual diseases, tips for a healthy conjugal and sex life and knowledge about women's bodies. Santram BA (1887–1998) was a learned, radical Shudra anti-caste reformer from Punjab and founder of the Jāt-Pāt Toṛak Maṇḍal (Organisation to Break Caste). He specialised in writing anti-caste literature, especially in support of inter-caste marriages, with more than 100 books and booklets and articles in leading magazines to his credit. Many of his writings folded caste into histories of intimacy and marriage, drawing inextricable connections between caste and gender (Gupta 2017). At the same time, he wrote several articles in leading Hindi magazines, and books on sex and birth control, which included translations of Mary Stopes' most celebrated books like *Married Love, Contraception*, and *Enduring Passion*, into Hindi for the first time. Besides these, he wrote his own books on sexology, which were a combination of his thoughts, select translations from Sanskrit sex classics and excerpts from Freud and Stopes (for details: Gupta 2020a). Santram took on the languages of power – Sanskrit and English – defying upper-caste and Western monopoly over knowledge, including sexual knowledge and translated-vernacularised them in a way that potentially challenged procreative monogamous renderings, restrictions on female sexuality and caste-based power.

Even while often replicating heteronormative paradigms, the texts of Devi and Santram were malleable, at times providing sites of productive disruption. In their unique ways, they created intimate spaces, opening ancillary textures of sex and sexuality and registers of love and intimacy. However, Devi urged her clients to have less sex, and asked men to control their sexual urges and to have sex only for procreation. Santram told women and men to enjoy sex and have it as much as they wanted. Their divergent advises show that vernacular sexology cut both ways, as it inhibited and emancipated at the same time. The heterogeneous nature of their writings accentuates that in spite of all, there was a certain freedom of thought and space in the vernacular to talk about gender and sex. Even though Devi and Santram were on the margins in terms of gender and caste, and written out in English, Sanskrit, Western, classical, Ayurvedic and Arya Samaj discourses, their vernacular writings appear to have attracted a large following. In order to legitimise their mastery, both of them made a bid for canonicity by laying claims to epistemic credibility and using translations as a key tool. Their 'two-way translations' between classical erotica and modern sexology, accompanied with modifications and creative synthesis, helped recontextualise the sexology code in the vernacular, to meet the different social terrain of colonial north India. Devi saw herself as an active translator and producer of vernacular sexual knowledge. She framed her ayurvedic authority by flagging herself as an 'indigenous female therapist', with 'eighteen years of experience', who combined '*rati śāstra* with *santatī śāstra*', and translated the ancient indigenous medical art of Ayurveda into a 'scientific' tool, to diagnose and cure the present-day sexual illnesses and 'perversions' of Indian society (Devī 1931: cover). She further made the most of 'biologically' being a woman, and to translate her unique privileged location to contest male control over Ayurveda, to enhance a language of sisterhood and to argue that she was epistemologically invested in chronicling women's sexual problems (Devī 1933: 257, 337; Devī 1938: 218–21). Her vernacular field constructed not just women as recipients of medicines but also their producers and disseminators (Figure 5.6). Such translations became critical for Devi to promote sex reform and to govern over the collective sexual life of the nation.

Santram considered himself to be mainly an anti-caste activist, seeped in a non-Brahmin ideology. The central vehicle of his anti-caste articulations was promotion of inter-caste marriages. At the same time, he saw himself as an educator of vernacular sexual knowledge, and his anti-caste thinking cannot

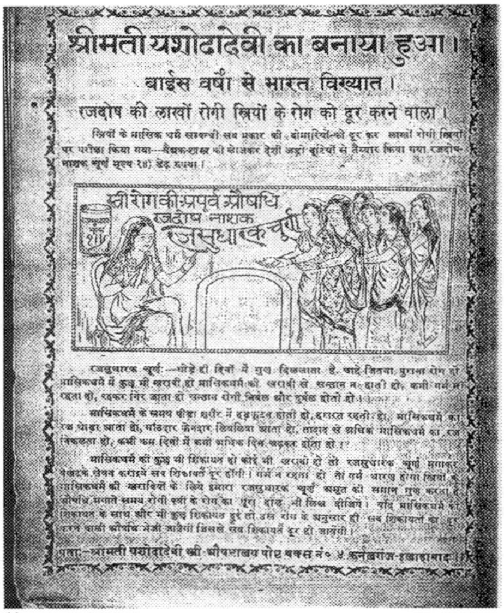

(a)

(b)

FIGURE 5.6 (a and b): Women Buying Medicines from Devi and Women Sharing Medical Knowledge

(*Devī 1931:* n.p.)

be separated from his sexology writings, as both were permeated by concerns that questioned *savarṇa* authority. Romantic love emerged as a powerful metaphor in Santram's anti-caste and sexology vernacular. Passionately endorsing inter-caste marriages, he stated: 'Love does not see any caste boundaries; hunger is indifferent to food taboos' (Sant|rām 1959: 31). While translating and interpreting Stopes, he provided further credence to her views by comparing them with classical erotica (Sant|rām 1925: footnotes on 27, 32–3, 97). At the same time, he insisted that classics were insufficient to provide all sexual answers to contemporary problems of the modern conjugal couple, which is where his vernacular writings helped. Santram's unauthorised translation of Stopes was a serious bid to translate sex without becoming complicit with its analytical regimes. Switching codes, he inserted footnotes and perspectives, thus indigenising Stopes according to local and vernacular worlds of conjugal relations in India. His translations thus built a bridge between the text and the reader, between the local and the global, as he remoulded Sanskrit classics and modern sexology texts to vernacular contexts (Gupta 2020a).

Both Santram and Devi, while interspersing their writings with Sanskrit, often wrote in colloquial Hindi, meant for a lay readership. Devi was writing mainly for women readers and often wrote in a simple, non-technical and accessible style: 'For the convenience of women, I have made this book so simple that women who are less educated can also easily understand it' (Devi 1931: 432). And in Santram's hands, Hindi itself was vernacularised and democratised as he wrested it from the casted and the dominant, and emphasised that those who did not know Sanskrit or English would greatly benefit from his Hindi translations of sexology (Sant^lrām 1923: 399, 1925: 601). Their 'unruly appropriations' (Fuechtner, Haynes and Jones 2018: 3) and translations thus became ways to make notions of sex knowable to a larger vernacular reading public.

The sensuous and the sexual were often presented by Devi and Santram within conventions of a heteronormative ethics. Yet, in oppositional ways, they interrogated male-centric beliefs about sex. They provided a scathing attack of ignorant and selfish husbands, who either imposed themselves forcefully over women's bodies, or were oblivious to women's desires. In line with social purity feminists, Devi attacked the excessive libidinal drive of husbands for an epidemic of venereal diseases, women's ill health, alienation of wives and miserable marriages (Devī 1938: 738). Alongside, she attacked masturbation, calling it *duṣkarm* (evil activity) (Devī 1931: 19–39). In Devi's discourse, modernity, which brought sources of racy entertainment, like theatre, cinema, 'dirty' novels and romances, was seen as an inciter of lustful thought. In contrast, modernity was not a curse but held the promise of liberation for Santram. He too critiqued men for their misplaced hegemonic masculinities, but from a different lens, censuring them for not having enough knowledge about 'the art of sex' (Sant^lrām 1925: preface, k), and for not contributing to household work. His main ire, however, was against *brahmacarya* as a tool of sexual self-discipline, and he bolstered his critique by declaring it unnatural, and emotionally, physically and medically harmful (Sant^lrām 1932: 77). At the same time, both Devi and Santram perceived women as active sexual partners and consumers of sex. As a woman sex reformer, catering mainly to middle-class audiences, Devi often imposed self-censorship and endorsed patriarchal stances, to appear respectable and acceptable. Her heteronormative, monogamous ethics was based on moderation, self-control and 'legitimate sex' (Devī 1933: 50). These ensured marital bliss; not doing so resulted in sexual diseases.

It is easy to dismiss Devi's vernacular writing, as the bulk of it is an unrepentant upholding of conjugal norms and procreative impulses. And yet, her trope of female sexual dissatisfaction and lack of consensuality offered different glimpses. She moved at two parallel levels, where endorsements of procreation and disciplining of bodies went hand in hand with readings of health, marriage and sex from a gendered perspective.

Santram evolved a heterosexual ethics that was grounded in love, female sexual gratification, women's rights and humanist principles. He dismissed assumptions that contraception would lead to *vyabhicār* (adultery) and increase *kām vās^lnā*, and decoupled sex from reproduction (Sant^lrām 1932: 77–9). Santram offers us an ethical utopian narrative of sexual relations in which human bodies, and their relationships, allow for different conceptions of desires and aesthetics. Devi and Santram created a name for themselves in the print-public life of the vernacular world, which also provided a space for wider diffusion of their sexology pedagogy. Yet, even while pulsating with the subject of sex, their vantage points were quite different. Devi restricted meanings of sexualities by reifying the moral sexual heteronormative monogamous marital code and framing sexology in 'negative' terms, by constructing a dystopian present world of modernity. Santram entered a more radical terrain, by embodying sexology in 'positive' terms and envisaging a utopian future that held the promise of sexual freedom. Devi's vernacularity was based on policing and prohibiting bodily functions and relied on fears and dangers of unruly impulses, promiscuity and illnesses. Santram provided a vernacular language of pleasure, cultivation and transformation of man–woman relations.

Conclusion

The world of the Hindi print-public sphere in early twentieth-century north India was deeply heterogeneous. It of course entailed standardisations and impositions from above, but these jostled with vernacular transactions and negotiations, along with a democratisation of language. This widely differentiated vernacular sphere reveals how dominant trends towards greater regulation of sexuality tangled with potential instabilities and counter-sexualities, making room for a more robust history of sex and sexuality. Equally, discussions on sex and sexuality often needed a corporeal presence and nearness of lived experience that the vernacular could offer. As a feminist historian of modern India, largely working on sexualities, the vernacular, in my case Hindi popular tracts, magazines and cartoons, have thus been my constitutive rather than supplementary archive. Histories of the vernacular also reflect a mundane texture, where women were ubiquitous, where varied meanings were imparted to sex and sexuality.

The first section of the chapter on representations of servants showed how the vernacular signified quintessential literary tropes of otherness and difference, while also at times inadvertently hinting at transgressive sites of intimacy and desire. Similarly, in the second example, I reflected on sartorial representations of Dalit women's conversions to Christianity in vernacular reformist iconography and cartoons, which recognised dress as an important terrain for contesting social relations and articulating new religious identities. Potential or actual conversions of widows to Islam, largely due to romance, on the one hand generated deep condemnation in the vernacular and, on the other, reflected the playing of their desires, generating an intimate politics, an embodied struggle, in which community agendas were reformulated and contested. Finally, in the last section I discussed vernacular sexology from the margins, which reified, constructed, destabilised and questioned sexual norms. As a woman and a Shudra, Devi and Santram were negotiating the complexities of translating sex in vernacular idioms amidst a colonial cosmopolitan sexology. The location of writers in the social hierarchies was also critical here. Santram's writings showed that there were spaces to carve a literary democracy through the idiom of the vernacular. For someone like Santram, his marginality and vernacularity was a statement of strength and protest, where he was not just writing back to the Empire, but to the elites – the coloniser and the colonised. The appropriation of Sanskrit and English through the idiom of the vernacular became a way to give words to delegitimised people and subjects, to challenge dominant social conventions, to offer a cultural critique and to create meanings of resistance.

These disparate sites and issues together show that the vernacular was a significant, if ambivalent, site for the reproduction, transformation *and* contestation around matters of sex in colonial India. In the congenial environment of the early twentieth century, sex and sexuality became an active subject of empirical knowledge in the public vernacular. Print indexed sex as an object, and the vernacular became central to histories and texts of sexual control *and* sexual pleasure. Thus, the practice and potential of employing the vernacular as a method for theorising sex and sexuality cannot be underestimated. The vernacular produced interlocking sets of power relations, while also exposing the contradictory impulses at the heart of its project. It is precisely because of its malleability and innovativeness that the vernacular holds promise.

Acknowledgement

This research was supported by the Faculty Research Programme Grant of IoE, University of Delhi.

References

Bauman, Chad M. 2008. *Christian Identity and Dalit Religion in Hindu India, 1868–1947*. Michigan: Wm. B. Eerdmans Publishing.

Berger, Rachel. 2013. *Ayurveda Made Modern: Political Histories of Indigenous Medicine in North India, 1900–1955*. New York: Palgrave.

Blunt, E. A. H. 1931. *The Caste System of Northern India: With Special Reference to United Provinces*. London: Oxford University Press.

Botre, Shrikant and Douglas E. Haynes. 2017. 'Sexual Knowledge, Sexual Anxieties: Middle-Class Males in Western Indian and the Correspondence in *Samaj Swasthya*, 1927–53'. *Modern Asian Studies*, 51(4): 991–1034.

Briggs, Geo W. 1920. *The Chamars*. Calcutta: Association Press.

Census of India, 1931: United Provinces of Agra and Oudh, Vol. XVIII, Part II: Imperial and Provincial Tables. 1933. Allahabad: The Superintendent, Printing and Stationery.

Candra Līlā Sādhunī kā vṛttānt (Biographical Account of Chandra Lila, a Lower Caste Female Convert). 1910, 2nd edn. Allahabad: Christian Literature Society for India.

Caritra sudhār (Character Improvement). 1910. Allahabad: Christian Literature Society for India.

Chatterjee, Partha. 2008. 'Introduction: History in the Vernacular'. In Raziuddin Aquil and Partha Chatterjee, eds, *History in the Vernacular*. Ranikhet: Permanent Black: 1–24.

Caturvedī, Jag'pati. 1946. *Hamārī pārivārik vyavasthā* (Our Familial Organisation). 2nd edn. Prayāg: Mātṛ Bhāṣā Mandir.

Chaudh'rī, Gauriśaṅkar Śukl. 1928. *Kyā Svāmī Śraddhānand ap'rādhī the?* (Was Swami Shraddhanand a Culprit?). Kān'pur: Publisher not mentioned.

Church Missionary Society. 1926. *The Mass Movement in the United Provinces: A Survey and Statement of Needs*. Kittayam: Church Missionary Press.

Clarke, Sathianathan. 1998. *Dalits and Christianity: Subaltern Religion and Liberation Theology in India*. Delhi: Oxford University Press.

Clayton, A. C. 1911. *Preachers in Print: An Outline of the Work of the Christian Literary Society for India*. London.

Devī, Yaśodā. 1931. *Dampati ārogyatā jīvan'śāstra arthāt· ratiśāstra-santatiśāstra aur devī anubhav prakāś* (The Science of Healthy Conjugal Life or the Science of Sexual Intercourse and Procreation and Light of Devi's Knowledge). 2nd edn. Ilāhābād: Devī Pustakālay.

Devī, Yaśodā. 1933. *Dāmpatya prem aur ratikriyā kā gupt rahasya* (Secret of Love and Sex between the Married Couple). Ilāhābād: Devī Pustakālay.

Devī, Yaśodā. 1938. *Nārī śarīr vijñān strī cikitsā sāgar: sambhog vijñān* (Women's Physiology and Women's Medical Treatment: Science of Intercourse). Ilāhābād: Devī Pustakālay.

Dvivedī, Manan. 1924. *Hamārā bhīṣaṇ hrās* (Our Severe Decline). 3rd edn. Kān'pur: Publisher not mentioned.

Freitag, Sandria B. 1989. *Collective Action and Community: Public Arenas and the Emergence of Communalism in North India*. Berkeley: University of California Press.

Fuechtner, Veronika, Douglas E. Haynes and Ryan M. Jones. 2018. 'Introduction: Toward a Global History of Sexual Science: Movements, Networks, and Developments'. In Veronika Fuechtner, Doulgas E. Haynes and Ryan M. Jones, eds, *A Global History of Sexual Science, 1880–1960*. California: University of California Press: 1–25.

Gaur, Rām'dās. 1927. *Kanyāoṃ kī pothī yā kanyā subodhinī* (Text for Girls Retailing Appropriate Behavior for them). Prayāg: Gāndhī Hindī Pustak Bhaṇḍār.

Ghosh, Anindita. 2006. *Power in Print: Popular Publishing and Politics of Language and Culture in a Colonial Society*. Delhi: Oxford University Press.

Gooptu, Nandini. 2001. *The Politics of the Urban Poor in Early Twentieth-Century India*. Cambridge: Cambridge University Press.

Gupta, Charu. 2001. *Sexuality, Obscenity, Community: Women, Muslims and the Hindu Public in Colonial India*. Delhi: Permanent Black.

Gupta, Charu. 2005. 'Procreation and Pleasure: Writings of a Woman Ayurvedic Practitioner in Colonial North India'. *Studies in History*, 21(1): 14–44.

Gupta, Charu. 2016. *The Gender of Caste: Representing Dalits in Print*. Ranikhet: Permanent Black.

Gupta, Charu. 2017. 'Speaking Self, Writing Caste: Recovering the Life of Santram BA'. *Biography: An Interdisciplinary Quarterly*, 40(1): 16–43.

Gupta, Charu. 2020a. 'Cast(e)ing and Translating Sex in the Vernacular: The Writings of Santram BA in Hindi'. *Porn Studies*, 7(1): 19–35.

Gupta, Charu. 2020b. 'Vernacular Sexology from the Margins: A Woman and a Shudra'. *South Asia: Journal of South Asian Studies*, 43(6): 1105–27.

Hindū dharm ke phal (Fruits of Hinduism). 1905. 2nd edn. Allahabad: North Indian Christian Tract and Book Society.

Jāti kī chūt chāt (Unreasonableness of Caste). 1905. Allahabad: North Indian Christian Tract and Book Society.

Kāśyap, Nārāyaṇ Datt Śarmā. 1927, 1929, 1931 respectively. *Bhār'tīya Vidh'vāoṃ kī karuṇāpūrṇ kathāyeṃ arthāt· hindū vidh'vāoṃ par atyācār Parts I, II, III* (The Moving Tales of Indian Widows, meaning the Atrocities on Hindu Widows), Āgrā: Vidh'vā Sahāyak Granth'mālā Kāryālay.

Kaviraj, Sudipta. 2010. *The Trajectories of the Indian State: Politics and Ideas*. Ranikhet: Permanent Black.

Kent, Eliza F. 2004. *Converting Women: Gender and Protestant Christianity in Colonial South India*. New York: Oxford University Press.

Kumar, Uday. 2016. *Writing the First Person: Literature, History, and Autobiography in Modern Kerala*. Ranikhet: Permanent Black.

Leng, Kirsten. 2018. *Sexual Politics and Feminist Science: Women Sexologists in Germany, 1900–1933*. Ithaca: Cornell University Press.

Lucas, J. J. n.d. *History of the North Indian Christian Tract and Book Society, 1848–1934*. Allahabad: Mission Press.

Mahārāj, Acal'rām. 1939. *Hindū dharm rahasya* (Secret of Hindu Religion). 2nd edn. Āgrā: Śānti Pres.

Mahop'deśak, Śiv Śarmā. 1927. *Strī śikṣā* (Women's Education). Barelī: King Press.

Nijhawan, Shobna. 2012. *Women and Girls in the Hindi Public Sphere: Periodical Literature in Colonial North India*. Delhi: Oxford University Press.

Orsini, Francesca. 2002. *The Hindi Public Sphere 1920–1940: Language and Literature in the Age of Nationalism*. Delhi: Oxford University Press.

Pande, Ishita. 2018. 'Time for Sex: The Education of Desire and the Conduct of Childhood in Global/Hindu Sexology'. In Fuechtner, et al., eds, *A Global History of Sexual Science*, Oakland: University of California Press, pp. 279–301.

Poddār, Hanumān Prasād. 1925. *Samāj sudhār* (Social Reform). Gorakh'pur: Geeta Press.

Ranciere, Jacques. 2009. *The Emancipated Spectator*. Trans. Gregory Elliot. London: Verso.

Rawat, Ramnarayan. 2012. *Reconsidering Untouchability: Chamars and Dalit History in North India*. Ranikhet: Permanent Black.

Ray, Raka and Seemin Qayum. 2010. *Cultures of Servitude: Modernity, Domesticity, and Class in India*. Delhi: Oxford University Press.

Sadana, Rashmi. 2012 *English Heart, Hindi Heartland: The Political Life of Literature in India*. Ranikhet: Permanent Black.

Sant'rām. 1923. 'Nāgar-sarvasvam'. *Mādhurī*, April: 396–9.

Sant'rām. 1925. *Vivāhit prem*. Lāhor: Rāj'pāl.

Sant'rām. 1931. 'Vivāh kā bhaviṣya' (The Future of Marriage). *Sudhā*, October: 302–10.

Sant'rām. 1932. 'Kām'śāstra aur dhārmik pakṣ'pāt' (Sexual Science and Religious Sectarianism). *Sudhā*, February: 76–80.

Sant'rām. 1959. *Antarjātīya vivāh hī kyū̃?* (Why Only Inter-Caste Marriages?). Hośiyār'pur: Jāt-Pāt Toṛak Maṇḍal.

Sanyāsī, Bhavānīdayāl. 1928. 'Strī aur sevā' (Women and Service). *Cā̃d*, October: 650–5.

Shankar, S. 2013. *Flesh and Fish Blood: Postcolonialism, Translation, and the Vernacular*. Hyderabad: Orient Blackswan.

Śarmā, Bhūmitra. 1917. *Niyog mardan ka vimardan* (Tract Defending the Practice of Niyoga). Meerut: Publisher not mentioned.

Śarmā, Candrikānārāyaṇ. 1938. *Mānavotpatti vijñān* (Science of Human Origin). Kāśī: Publisher not mentioned.

Siṃh, Ṭhākur Rāj'kiśor. 1924. *Hindū Saṅgaṭhan*. Baliyā: Publisher not mentioned.

Sinha, Nitin and Nitin Varma, eds. 2019. *Servants' Pasts: Late-Eighteenth to Twentieth-Century South Asia*, Vol. 2. Hyderabad: Orient Blackswan.

Stark, Ulrike. 2007. *An Empire of Books: The Naval Kishore Press and the Diffusion of the Printed Word in colonial India*. Ranikhet: Permanent Black.

Tarlo, Emma. 1996. *Clothing Matters: Dress and Identity in India*. Chicago: University of Chicago Press.

Ṭhākur, Keśav'kumār. 1930. *Vivāh aur prem* (Marriage and Love). Ilāhābād: Cā̃d.

Tirath'rām. 1924. *Striyoṃ ko cetāv'nī* (Warning to Women). Ilāhābād: Publisher not mentioned.

Upādhyāy, Gaṅgā Prasād. 1927. *Vidh'vā vivāh mīmāṃsā* (An Arya Samaj Tract Advocating Widow-Remarriage). Ilāhābād: Cā̃d.

Vaiśya, Cimman'lāl. 1924. *Nārāyaṇi śikṣā arthāt· gṛhasthāśram* (Women's Education meaning Family Life). Prayāg: Ārya Darpaṇ Pres.

Venkatachalapathy, A. R. 2006. *In Those Days There Was No Coffee: Writings in Cultural History*. New Delhi: Yoda Press.

Venkatachalapathy, A. R. 2012. *The Province of the Book: Scholars, Scribes, and Scribblers in Colonial Tamilnadu*. Ranikhet: Permanent Black.

Vishwanathan, Gauri. 1998. *Outside the Fold: Conversion, Modernity, and Belief*. Princeton: Princeton University Press.

Vyaṅg citrāvalī (Collection of Cartoons and Caricatures). 1930. Ilāhābād: 'Cā̃d' Kāryālay.

Zahur'bakhś. 1926. 'Maiṃ musal'mān kaise huī?' (How I Became a Muslim). *Cā̃d*, December: 249–54.

Zahur'bakhś. 1927. 'Maiṃ īsāī kaise huī?' (How I Became a Christian). *Cā̃d*, March: 506–12.

6

POLITICAL REFORM, TERRITORIALISING LANGUAGE

Re-casting Difference, Constitutional Categories and Developmental Goals, 1905–1950s

Veena Naregal

Introduction

The Report of the Official Languages Commission, set up by the Government of India in the 1950s, begins by noting a basic assumption that language is important "only at the level of instrumentality" and is of no "intrinsic consequence". These terms of description are not exceptional within the enunciation of language policy as it emerged post-Independence. Within post-1947 public and political debates, we know that the language question has persistently figured – in purely instrumental terms – as the 'medium of instruction' issue. Nevertheless, given the polyglot heritage of South Asia, such an instrumentalist dismissal of linguistic diversity as being unimportant is both startling and disquieting. In the light of the great linguistic munificence that it obtains on the subcontinent, attributing such instrumental significance to language ought to strike as profoundly incongruous. Yet this tragic paradox between the complexity of our linguistic heritage and its current pared-down figuring in the public domain after 1947 is rarely acknowledged or questioned. In stark contrast to the vigorous debates with respect to the Indian nation around other markers of difference such as class, caste and gender, the critical reticence around the language question stands out as peculiar. Noting this, one may even speak of a consensus among the elite that to raise the language question today remains a sign of backwardness and that it can only be a source of acrimonious social tensions.

Official documents in the 1940s and 1950s, including statements from the Indian National Congress, and reports of the Dar Commission and the JVP Committee, are replete with references to the country's linguistic diversity as a barrier to national integration and disruptive threats of 'linguism', which

DOI: 10.4324/9781003279921-8

needed to be checked at all costs. The rising tones of majoritarian assertion in the aftermath of Partition only further disabled the possibilities of recasting India's multilingualism as a core issue of Indian democracy. And so throughout this period, the question of the official/link language was posed most reductively in the Constituent Assembly debates, as an apparent choice directly between English and Hindi. From the posing of the language question as one of mere instrumental worth to the paring down of language issues within higher education as a concern with translating pedagogic materials largely into Hindi, instances abound of the reductive effects of such an instrumental framing of the language question in post-1947 Indian public discourse.

On the one hand, the long history of Indian linguistic reorganisation as it played out before and after 1947 concedes the significance of the linguistic marker for Indian political modernity and federal structure. At its core, this importance derived from the democratising excitement tapped into by the regional language mobilisations of the late nineteenth century. In contrast to caste belonging or sectarian identity, these language movements had amply highlighted the seemingly open-ended potential for an infinite extension of the political community formed along linguistic lines. How then, on the other hand, did these democratising impulses around linguistic mobilisations yield the anxiety-ridden discourses among influential political elites about 'linguism' being the most potent threat to the nascent nation-state? Such anxieties about the 'problems' posed by our linguistic diversity remain unresolved and persist to the present: it seems evident that the very political processes that yielded the federal map showcasing India's linguistic diversity as state boundaries based on the 'one state, one language' principle has simultaneously created the space for an ultra-conservative, instrumentalist discourse about linguistic diversity that effectively undercuts the democratising thrust of the momentum of the language movements. If so, does not such a simultaneity also point to a drastic containment of the democratising impulses of the late nineteenth-century language movements through subsequent decades?

To kick-start this analysis, an important question would be: How did such a privileging of the language issue within the federal imagination of the Indian nation through the reorganisation of the Congress organisational structure in 1920 *simultaneously* produce a discourse about its dangerous divisiveness and mere instrumentality within the post-1947 political order? In the decades after 1920, these linguistic mobilisations that gained visibility from the last decades of the nineteenth century mutated into territorial entities within the self-narratives of the Indian nation-state, and eventually materialised as linguistic states the decade after the Republic was born in 1950. At what stage of this process and through what steps did this instrumentalising narrative about India's linguistic diversity gain strength? Can we afford to read this paradoxical articulation of India's linguistic diversity into the organising principle of her federal-political map alongside the widely held views across many domains of contemporary Indian public life on the debilitating consequences of that very linguistic richness, as some mere coincidence? Does the apparent hesitation or failure in framing these paradoxical aspects as part of a single reality by the late 1950s suggest that linguistic reorganisation had assumed the proportions of a false step and limiting move with damaging and enduring political and intellectual outcomes? In other words, would it be right to assert that so successful has this closure been that the underlying paradoxes have remained to be posed sharply as questions to be probed, ensuring that thus far Indians and South Asianists have perhaps not even begun to connect the dots in recognising its repercussions? Having assumed proportions of a blind spot at the level of elite consensus, official moves and social scientific understanding, the lack of deep questioning around the wiring of the language question within the Indian federal imagination has resulted in a predominant tendency *not* to treat even the hierarchical divide between English and regional language spheres as a deeply divisive issue at the core of Indian democracy. These are deep concerns, made more complicated by the seeming silence around them.

To address these issues around the reductive instrumentalisation of the language question in contemporary Indian society, this chapter steps back to emphasise that the place of language within public–political life needs to be critically reframed as concern about the role of linguistic diversity in relation to deepening Indian democracy. In particular, such an analysis needs to focus on developments on the subcontinent from the decades from the end of World War I onwards until the late colonial period. Flagging our as-yet-sparse understanding of the long and staggered history of linguistic reorganisation, the argument here highlights the foundational significance of the moves to map territorial redistribution along linguistic lines in the decades between the Bengal Partition in 1905 and the 1950s. Through this phase, the radical indexing of linguistic difference as a territorial category in colonial India was nested within a complicated array of intertwined and rapid transformations that determined the fundamentals of how representative democracy was structured into constitutional categories and federal principles for the Indian context. That a lot was at stake was widely recognised through this political phase: these outcomes would define representative structures, the place of language in the public–political domain and the shape of democratic politics in the years to come. Especially in decoding the paradoxical assessments of the potential of India's linguistic diversity, two aspects of this story need to be recognised as of fundamental consequences:

(i) provincial reorganisation on linguistic lines was implicitly about determining how the several markers of social difference or hierarchies in our setting, viz. caste, religion, language and so on, would be coded into structural representational and constitutional categories; and

(ii) the extended and staggered temporality through which the logic of linguistic territorialisation was advanced meant that it intersected with the embracing of developmental agendas in the same period – our analytical reframing of the language question must give due credence to this simultaneity.

Again, as we shall see, the intertwined simultaneity of both these sets of processes was not lost on contemporary political agents and commentators.

In taking up these themes, the chapter is divided into three sections. The first section elaborates upon developments towards administrative reform and territorial redistribution around the Bengal Partition. The aim here is to show how debates on linguistic identity and territorial redistribution intersected with competing mobilisations that sought to stake alternate claims in shaping political categories and contours of the political in the inter-war period. The discussion in the second section works with two inter-weaving strands: firstly, it offers an overview of proposals towards linguistic provinces as articulated in the Report of the All Parties Conference of 1928 (widely identified after its author as the Motilal Nehru Report), considered the first draft of the Indian Constitution. The demand for a separate University for Maharashtra to be located at Pune gathered momentum in the early 1920s. Focusing on this campaign led by many prominent Marathi intellectuals, including the eminent economist D. R. Gadgil (who later emerged as the key spokesperson and ideologue of the Samyukta Maharashtra Parishad, taken up briefly in the final section), this section further considers the officially defined, circumscribed possibilities opened to regional languages through these years that saw steps towards the much-needed expansion of higher education in late colonial India. This latter discussion highlights the shifting positions of Marathi cultural elites over the role of the regional university and place of regional languages in higher education approximately between the end of World War I and 1947. These changes in the Marathi intelligentsia's opinion around 1947 point to important shifting nuances in the internal consensus between regional elites in the Bombay–Pune region and official discourse over language as a democratising/disruptive force within the region. The final section briefly dwells upon the drawn-out temporal intersections between the logic of linguistic territorialisation and simultaneous leveraging of development agendas in the decades between the 1920s and 1950s. Building on the argument in preceding sections, this section brings out the inherent tensions between the democratic stimuli in the former processes as against the centralising thrust of the latter. This is done through a brief focus on the 'battle for Bombay' at the peak of the Samyukta Maharashtra movement in the mid-1950s over the inclusion of Bombay within the monolingual Maharashtra state, which saw two apparently colliding visions of federalism, represented by the votaries of Samyukta Maharashtra and the formidable big business and industrialists' lobby based in Bombay city, pitted against each other.

Linguistic Regions, Political Reform

Since the late colonial period, language – more specifically, the Indian 'vernaculars' – were closely linked with the imagination of the region across the subcontinent. Historically, the 'regional' evolved as part of the modern political imagination in South Asia through very distinct processes tied to political shifts in the period between the Bengal Partition of 1905 and the linguistic reorganisation of Indian states through 1956–1960. It is frequently noted that the mobilisation of public opinion against the Bengal Partition contributed singularly to the growth of politically tangible regional consciousness cohering around linguistic unity. And yet, the larger story of the emergence of broader linkages between territorial reorganisation, linguistic inclusiveness and modern regional consciousness has remained largely unexplored. Further, the present understanding about linguistic reorganisation remains mostly drawn from limiting narratives produced around internal Congress viewpoints and its positions on reorganisation needed to fulfil party-political goals as a leader of the national movement. Such an identification with the self-narratives of the Congress needs urgent revisiting so that an account of the various phases from the consolidation of linguistic identities to their territorialisation and further indexing of linguistic territories as federal units can be unentangled and their coding within (progressive) Indian nationalist accounts be opened up for analytical interrogation.

Each of the three Presidencies saw a significant upsurge of political sentiment and activity through mobilisations in the regional language press and associations throughout the closing decade of the nineteenth century. It is no doubt but true that mobilisation of Bengali public opinion against the Partition served as a great impetus towards assertions of regional nationality and administrative-political autonomy within colonial India. However, the earliest campaigns along lines of regional unity were advanced by emerging nationalities that perceived themselves as neglected within the Presidency structure, namely Biharis and Oriyas within Bengal Presidency and Andhras in Madras. At least a decade before Curzon's Minute of 1903 announced the Bengal Partition,[1] there were visible signs within the Bengal Presidency of the mobilisation of Bihari and Oriya sentiment on the basis of linguistic inclusiveness. Following these patterns, assertions within the Presidencies after 1905 proceeded mainly through foregrounding the identification of distinct 'regions' with a *single* linguistic marker/identity. Within a polyglot polity characterised by immense linguistic diversity, as obtained within the subcontinent, such direct identification between the region and 'its' linguistic identity is peculiarly striking. Alongside, this aspect needs to be viewed against several discernible disparate yet criss-crossing experiments through these decades to mobilise inter-woven markers of collective identities across spatially fluid parameters. In turn, this dynamic was tied to the democratising potential of linguistic mobilisations and found resonance, as colonial authorities sought a viable rationale that enabled administrative reform and reorganisation in the three Presidencies, but one that struck the 'right' balance of promising better governance without conceding any more than the minimum necessary in terms of political control. Revisiting the political calculations that had led to the Bengal Partition in 1905 while formally announcing its revocation and the shifting of the imperial capital to Delhi, Viceroy Hardinge's address of August 1911 at the Delhi Darbar also proclaimed the shifting of the imperial capital to Delhi and the separation of the combined province of Bihar and Orissa from Bengal. Acknowledging the inevitability of gradually giving the provinces a large measure of self-government, the Viceroy expounded on provincial autonomy as follows:

> Nevertheless, it is certain that in the course of time the just demands of Indians for a larger share in the Government of the country will have to be satisfied, and the question will be how this devolution of power can be conceded without impairing the supreme authority of Governor-General-in-Council.
>
> *(Hardinge 1913: 413)*

It is worth reiterating here that the claiming of and contestations around political rights in late colonial India did not presume a prior recognition of equality and fraternity among political subjects. Especially in a scenario where the polity was marked by graded inequalities and great internal diversity, as the discussion below demonstrates, it was amply recognised by political players all around that debates around redrawing territorial boundaries were no mere administrative exercise. A lot was at stake as debates on territorial redistribution fed directly into how representational and electoral constituencies would soon be demarcated. Further, these contestations around territorial boundaries could actively impinge upon how key questions of political inclusion, provisions for franchise and minority rights would be settled.

Social Difference, Political Reform, Representation

The Montagu–Chelmsford Reforms through the Government of India Act 1919 paved the way for greater participation of Indians in the provincial government. As the first concessions towards self-government, the Montford–Chelmsford reforms of 1919 were a landmark signal for native elites. The gathering momentum in anticipation of these reforms from 1917 onwards had brought to the fore debates about the scope and basis of franchise and delimitation of political rights, particularly with respect to minorities. Keenly awaited through the war years, the signal was clearly read by regional elites as an opportunity to simultaneously leverage advantageous positions vis-à-vis their own immediate constituencies, but also in relative terms with respect to adjacent rival groupings along multiple axes. Amidst the vast scale of political malleability on evidence through the inter-war period, diverse groupings sought to assess the relative strengths and rallying potential of core markers of identity and difference. Especially the years after the revocation of the Bengal Partition were marked by manoeuvres to assess the relative mobilisational weight of alternate 'viable' configurations across key markers of collective belonging such as caste, religion, ethnicity and language. The most prominent instance of this was the Lucknow Pact of 1916.

The Congress had not met since the Surat session in 1908. Now, as a signal of their readiness for self-government and political reform, the Lucknow session of the Congress in 1916 saw the party not only reconvening for the first time after the internal split between the Moderates and Extremists in 1908 but also Tilak and Jinnah endorsing the Lucknow Pact, suggesting a new understanding between the Congress and the Muslim League. For the first time, amidst much fanfare, at this session, the Congress explicitly conceded the principle of communal representation (report of the 31st Indian National Congress). Part of the effort to determine the most advantageous and relatively durable outcomes in terms of representative possibilities, such assessments to 'fix' optimal values for an array of markers held great significance through this fluid period as these calculations would factor into ongoing negotiations that would shape constitutional categories and the spatial parameters of electoral constituencies and federal units.

The urgent decisions taken at the historic Nagpur session of the Indian National Congress to comprehensively restructure the Congress organisation and its political strategies marked the response to these reforms. Fronting linguistic identity as the marker of territoriality and the organisational structure from now on, the changes heralded in Gandhi's famous three-pronged initiative and the adoption of a new Congress Constitution at Nagpur Congress centred around a change in Congress creed: the announcement of non-cooperation and reorganisation of the Congress's provincial structure along linguistic lines. Indeed, Gandhi's announcements marked a radical turning point. However, in resisting euphoric readings that treat the 1920 moment as exemplifying the contrast between the inertia before and after Gandhi's assumption of the Congress leadership, Dr. Ambedkar's emphasis that the three moves by Gandhi as he took over the reins of the Congress need to be seen as linked and so must be read together, is useful (Ambedkar 1945:19). The discussion here has therefore sought to view the 1920 Congress decisions equally as a response to the dynamism of sub-regional nationalities newly awakened to self-consciousness in the preceding decades, while also contextualising those outcomes in relation to ensuing developments in subsequent decades.

Significantly, political commentary well into the late 1940s showed an unequivocal and realistic understanding about the rationale, basis and implications of the several positions for or against unilingual provincial entities. Highlighting the advantages of unilingual provinces as administrative units or for purposes of expanding higher education, contemporary accounts of constitutional debates were candid about their awareness that unilingual provincial entities were integrally about the need to demonstrate adequate levels of homogeneity and cross-cutting avenues of unity in the governed population. Assertions of a viable level of homogeneity, as already available or foreseeable, helped pave the ground to define constitutional categories and federal principles. Equally, however, over the medium- and the long term, homogeneity in the subject population helped bolster the representational claims of the regional leadership to govern successfully (Gadgil 1945: 7–16). Claims for separate provinces on a linguistic basis and their assessment or rebuttal typically sought to foreground the comparative access to government employment, high school and higher education or public office of major communities in relation to their demographic distribution within the existing administrative unit (Ambedkar 1948: 192–94). Similarly, official and public documents proposing administrative reorganisation and redrawing territorial boundaries were replete with demographic compilations for the relative share in total population for various religious communities, minorities and, in some cases, underprivileged/backward groups (Nehru Report 1928: 27–60, Appendices A–C). Although official documents, petitions and public debates took care to link arguments for a separate linguistic province to broadly asserted claims of economic viability, typically they rarely included any detailed exposition of revenue and expenditure figures or comparative economic and developmental advantages that would accrue to the new entity. This indicated that assertions of homogeneity enabling representational claims on the one hand, and good governance on the other, was a key 'truth' sought to be fixed through these moves.

This effort to open up questions around the coding of India's linguistic diversity into the late colonial political domain has of course drawn on the wealth of historical scholarship for these decades focusing on simultaneous mobilisations and contestations around nationalist, communal, caste, working-class and their reverberations upon the freedom struggle and politics at the local, regional and pan-Indian level. Additionally, a valuable body of work on the making of the Indian Constitution has now emerged that has explored the ways in which constitutional debates were shaped by the political imperatives of both colonialism and nationalism. Some of this work has also dwelt upon the significant record of engagement by civil society groups and ordinary citizens engagement with the Constituent Assembly, and also how ordinary people and occupational groups soon took recourse to the constitution to engage with policy, protect their livelihoods and transform their daily lives (Elangovan, 2014; De 2018; Shani 2022). Similarly, Linda Colley's work on the making of constitutions in the modern world has shown that written constitutions have never only been devices to do with the business of law and government. As she writes, "Written constitutions have also always been bound up with changing patterns of thought and cultural practices, with the histories of war, gender, race, social class, religion, literacy and literature, communications, empire and nation-making and more [...]" (Colley 2021: 88).

Next we discuss the proposals towards linguistic provinces as articulated in the Report of the All Parties Conference of 1928, considered the first draft of the Indian Constitution. The terms upon which the provisions for redistribution into linguistic provinces were legitimised in the above draft Constitution are most telling. These are placed against the provisions under which the 'vernaculars' found re-entry into university curricula after a lapse of nearly six decades as part of the reform of higher education in preparation for the first limited concessions towards self-government. Read together as they must be, these combined proposals by the nationalist leadership and the colonial state bring out how the coding of linguistic diversity into the sphere of representational politics and the late colonial public–political domain was subject to severe instrumental and circumscribed limits that effectively undercut the democratising thrust of the momentum of the preceding language movements.

Legitimising Linguistic Provinces: Nehru Report, Regional Universities

The preceding sections have focused on the close imbrication between territorial redistribution and urgent debates around political representation, franchise and political guarantees for minorities, particularly between 1905 and 1935. Following the Bengal Partition, native elites wrestled with the colonial state and other contenders to optimise control over avenues for limited political representation. Against this, the subcontinent's distinctive linguistic diversity seemed to offer unique possibilities of furthering claims for imminent political reforms to be in consonance with public opinion and popular aspirations. A historic landmark of great political significance, the All Parties Conference is particularly noteworthy for the advancement of the idea of linguistic provinces and joint electorates, while simultaneously reversing the previous support by the Congress for separate electorates for Muslims. A detailed analysis of the importance of the Nehru Report of 1928 for constitutional debates and the long history of linguistic reorganisation is taken up elsewhere (Naregal, forthcoming). Here the aim is far more specific, which is to draw attention to a single but central and telling aspect, namely the terms upon which the Nehru Report legitimises its chief recommendation that the redistribution of provinces should take place on a linguistic basis (Nehru 1928: 123–3).

No stand-alone proposal, the Report's provision for linguistic provinces was tied to its other major recommendations on communal and 'other controversial matters' placed at the very end of the report (ibid.). This contingent logic through which provisions for territorial redistribution along linguistic lines are arrived at in the text is evident in the very structure of the report: significantly, the chapter on redistribution of provinces (ibid.: 60–69) is placed after two long chapters that elaborate upon the communal aspect with respect to provisions of separate electorates as representational basis and reservation of seats for minorities (ibid.: 27–59). In line with this, chief among the recommendations that followed was the stipulation that there shall be joint mixed electorates for the Central and Provincial Legislatures. This went hand in hand with the rejection of separate electorates, which were unceremoniously debunked thus in the preceding discussion on the 'communal aspect':

> It is admitted by most people now that separate electorates are thoroughly bad and must be done away with. We find that there has been a tendency amongst the Muslims to consider them as a "valued privilege", although a considerable section are prepared to give them up in consideration for some other things. Everybody knows that separate electorates are bad for the growth of a national spirit, but everybody perhaps does not realise equally well that separate electorates are still worse for a minority community [...]. Separate electorates must therefore be discarded completely as a condition precedent to any rational system of representation. We can only have joint or mixed electorates.
>
> *(ibid.: 30)*

As previously discussed here, the agreement on separate electorates was the major plank of the much-celebrated Lucknow Pact signed between the Congress and Muslim League in 1916. To demonstrate its political conviviality in anticipation of imminent political reforms, the Congress had endorsed Muslims' claims for a fixed number of seats contested on the basis of separate electorates, thus conceding the principle of communal representation for the first (and last) time. Interestingly, soon after the Montagu–Chelmsford Report on Constitutional Reforms was available in 1918, most prominent stalwarts in the Congress who had unequivocally endorsed separate electorates at the Lucknow Congress now withdrew their support. This changed stance and opposition to the terms of the Lucknow Pact was signalled soon afterwards in their submissions between November 1918 and February 1919 to the Indian Franchise Committee (known as the Southborough Committee). The provisions towards dyarchy in the Montagu–Chelmsford Report had given indications that the situation and very structure of politics had changed. This led "many of the Congress leaders – all of the Hindus in particular – to change their positions regarding the Lucknow Pact, about which most of them had earlier displayed conspicuous enthusiasm" (Datar 2012: 65–8).

Repudiating the Lucknow Pact and the principle of separate electorates, from now on there was a clear endorsement within the Congress of joint mixed electorates as the viable basis for representational politics, along with a strong support for territorial reorganisation to be explicitly linked to the possibility of linguistic provinces. This marked a significant departure from lines of thinking on representational and federal structures endorsed hitherto by the nationalist leadership until 1918. That was the context in which the All Parties Conference was convened – also in Lucknow – in 1928. Despite the apparent lack of unanimity, the Motilal Nehru Report of the All Parties Conference formally endorsed linguistic provinces as the basis of territorialisation within the Indian federal structure:

> The redistribution of provinces must take place on a linguistic basis on the demand of the majority of the population of the area concerned, subject to financial and administrative considerations.
>
> *(Nehru 1928: 122–23)*

Alongside, in the face of bitter Hindu opposition, and as an instance of this principle of linguistic redistribution, the Report also oddly conceded the demand – on 'democratic' grounds – for the separation of a Muslim-majority Sind from the Bombay Presidency. However, demands from other regions, including Andhra, Karnataka and Orissa, were held in abeyance (Government of India Act 1935: 182–83).[2] Read in the context of the broader historical record, we thus note how the leveraging of the question of linguistic provinces within constitutional debates showed that, by 1928, linguistic redistribution was already as much about the terms upon which the Congress leadership thought it fruitful and expedient to accommodate major interests, particularly the key demand for special electorates from religious minorities and lower-caste groups. Meant to bring together nationalists of all hues with the aim of drawing up the first blueprint anticipating the Indian Constitution, the 1928 All Parties Conference instead saw the Hindu–Muslim unity fronted through the 1916 Lucknow Pact collapse. Accepted by the Congress and its allies only amidst acrimonious discussions, many Muslim groups and Jinnah's Muslim League refused to sign the Nehru Report. Notwithstanding its failure to produce a consensus, and despite being ignored by the British government, the Nehru Report was publicised actively throughout the country as part of a concerted and well-funded Congress campaign.

The following years brought forth the demand for separate electorates from the scheduled castes under the leadership of Dr. Ambedkar. He believed that separate electorates for the scheduled castes were a requirement to ensure adequate representation at the provincial and central levels to the scheduled castes in proportion to their share in the total population, and so key to social and political justice and the making of a strong democratic order. Through the first two round-table conferences (1930–32), Dr. Ambedkar held firm to his commitment towards separate electorates and representatives elected strictly from scheduled castes themselves. The MacDonald Award announced on 16 August

1932 granted a separate electorate and a specific number of reserved seats in all elected governmental bodies for the depressed classes. Almost immediately that decision led to Gandhi's fast in protest against the provisions of the MacDonald Award and the famous Poona Pact, signed on 24 September 1932 by Dr. Ambedkar (under protest), Gandhi and caste Hindu leaders, that allowed for representation of untouchables in political bodies but elected by all through joint mixed electorates.

Most striking about the above is the fact that the Nehru Report is positioned midway between the Lucknow Pact of 1916 and the Poona Pact of 1932, noted above as important landmarks in negotiations around representational arrangements endorsed by the Congress with the Muslim League and scheduled castes, respectively. In first repudiating its previous endorsement of separate electorates in the Lucknow Pact, and then through the Poona Pact successfully prevailing upon Dr. Ambedkar as the leader of the scheduled castes to accept representation for the latter to be structured around joint mixed electorates, the Congress leadership essentially closed off possibilities of constitutional and electoral arrangements and the ensuing distribution of political power between caste Hindus, Muslims and scheduled castes to being determined through separate electorates. Significantly, the formal delegitimisation of separate electorates was spearheaded by the efforts of the Congress leadership to have the principle of joint electorates inscribed in the Report of the Congress-led All Parties Conference in 1928, despite the fact that deliberations at the Conference had failed to yield a consensual agreement between the participating parties on this vital point. Recognising that the emphases placed in the Nehru Report on the rejection of separate electorates followed by the acceptance of territorial redistribution along linguistic lines *as linked* moves that are central to the constitutional architecture that the Congress saw as most desirable and advantageous is most important.

This move helps decentre the story of territorialised redistribution along linguistic lines beyond the conventional narrative built around the 1920 moment when major changes were effected in the Congress Constitution and structure. Delineating these historical contexts serves to juxtapose the simultaneity of multiple negotiations to arrive at 'permissible' trade-offs that fixed the several scales of difference and inequality into a legitimate grid. Meant to yield an accommodation of democratic aspirations and interests of regional and national elites into an appropriately 'balanced' vision of the federal nation, such calculations eventually found normative sanction within the official discourse of citizenship and minority rights as enshrined in the Constitution. Linguistic reorganisation emerges as the most legitimate among available options for manageably reconciling the divergent minority and regional interests within emerging representational structures. Viewed thus, we are able to see how an instrumentalising view of language was not an unfortunate 'by-product' of the political sanction for linguistic provinces, but rather, lay at its very core.

Regional Languages and University Network after 1917

The aftermath of the Rebellion of 1857 had seen stringent decisions to exclude the study of the vernacular languages from college and university curriculum. Referring to higher education in colonial western India, for a brief period until 1863, it had been possible for students to pursue the study of the 'Prakrits' beyond matriculation by offering two papers in Gujarati, Marathi, Kannada, Hindustani, Sindhi or Portuguese in the First Year Arts exam of Bombay University. From then on, however, students had to choose their second language of study from among offered classical options – Sanskrit, Latin, Arabic, Greek and Hebrew (Bombay University Calendar for 1923–1924, 1924: 71–74).[3] Significantly, it was only after education was transferred to provincial legislatures in the wake of the political reforms of 1919 that the reintroduction of vernaculars into university curricula was mooted after a lapse of nearly six decades, but now only as separate *literary* disciplines. In 1921, separate Boards of Studies for Marathi, Gujarati and Kanarese were instituted at the Bombay University outside of the Board of Studies of Sanskrit and allied languages. Simultaneously, the social science disciplines were instituted separately as specialised subjects studied through English and could be pursued beyond the BA level,[4] thus sowing the seeds of the divergences between 'academic', 'vernacular' and 'regional' discourse, cast as discrete, separable spheres (Bombay University Calendar 1924–1925, 1924: 648).

Demands for additional universities gained momentum through the Bombay Presidency Conference in 1917, where a resolution was adopted in favour of the establishment of separate universities, one for each of its four linguistic divisions comprising the predominantly Kannada, Marathi, Gujarati and Sindhi areas, respectively (Report of the Maharashtra University Committee 1943: 2). Such demands followed in the wake of major private initiatives towards the foundation of Aligarh Muslim University and the establishment of Benares Hindu University in 1915. In 1924, the Government of Bombay appointed a committee under Sir Chimanlal Setalvad to look into the question of university reform for the Bombay Presidency, including the feasibility of instituting other universities at mofussil centres. Among its 13 members were Barrister M. R Jayakar, Prof. K.T. and Principal M.R. Paranjpye of Fergusson College, Pune. The Committee sent out an extensive questionnaire with 54 questions to 321 persons, including Dr. Ambedkar. As official and public discourse sought to mobilise support on different aspects of this expansion, pressures to extend the university structure beyond Presidency capitals opened up debates around the category of the 'regional'.

Scrutinising a large volume of evidence, the Committee on University Reform accepted in principle the need for universities to be created for Maharashtra, Gujarat, Karnataka and Sind. Equally, however, an expansion of higher education could only bring new anxieties; yet it was maintained that the new universities were needed to develop interest in "the study of local culture, literature, history and conditions of life and feel that this could be best done by local universities" (Report of the University Reform Committee 1924:46). As a site for potential investments by regional elites, these simultaneously opened up room for tough negotiations that would determine the nature and extent of cultural, intellectual and political control exercised over this expanding realm of higher education as limited opportunities for self-government were imminent. Unsurprisingly, the top university brass officials took a conservative view of the task at hand and saw the expanded network as a site through which the larger domain of political discussion and activity could be reinscribed and regulated. Thus, Vice Chancellor Chimanal Setalvad's convocation address of 22 November 1922 referred to "the greater catastrophe of peace" unfolding after the Great War, "which had brought an undefined yearning for more freedom and transfer of more power to the hands of people". Noting it was no longer possible to cherish the delusion that universal education alone could make democracy really safe, he warned of dangers that came from "men who merely read and write but are unable to think for themselves are sometimes more likely to be swayed by the half-truths and lies disseminated by the party press and to be led into hasty and ill- considered action". Therefore, in addition to reading and writing, people must be taught to reflect and judge, to provide honest and capable leaders. Higher education was thus essential to "render inestimable service to representative government by producing men, who having acquired the habit of clear thinking, and by being inspired by liberal ideas and wide outlook, can rise over passion and prejudice and lead the masses to right path" (Bombay University Calendar for 1923–24 and 1924–1925, 1924: p. 688).

In the light of the new scenarios opened up through political reforms, the disciplines had a definite role to play in the larger political domain, which would determine the place of the regional languages in the university structure:

> The study of history, civics, politics and social economics must be largely encouraged in the University in order to supply training for social life, cultural life, political life and economic life [...] the benefits of University education should not be confined to students within the portals of the university but must be made available to larger numbers outside.
>
> *(ibid.: 689)*

And yet, the authorities did not wish to envisage that by "making instruction and examinations conducted through the medium of the vernacular languages [...] English should merely be taught as an additional language". Setalavad marshalled a long litany of difficulties and disruptions that would ensue, threatening seemingly everything from budgets, academic standards, institutions and prospects for advancement opened up to Indians, to national unity and the very university structure that had been built up through assiduous effort. Thus, any considerations of what an emphasis on addressing the 'local' or the 'regional' would need to be set aside. The Bombay University Reform Committee report concluded that currently conditions were not as yet ripe for drawing up plans for new universities at centres other than Pune and endorsed a recommendation of a second University only at Poona. However, the Committee rejected petitions submitted by influential Pune elites including the then young but eminent economist Dhananjay Gadgil that the new university ought to be *more than* a teaching university; they wanted it to be a residential institution. Further, as for the core concerns (including views expressed by its own members) of adopting Marathi as the language of study, the official report elided the issue by declaring it fit for the issue to be decided "internally" within the new University (ibid.: 53). Thus, even while it avoided engagement with measures to align higher academic pursuits through the vernaculars, the report loftily prescribed that "a University established at Poona must not have a preponderance of merely local influence but must reflect and represent the sentiments, aspirations and opinions of the whole of Maharashtra" (ibid).

It was eventually in 1948 that Poona University, only the second in the Bombay Presidency, was established. Interestingly, Maharashtra University Committee, appointed by the Bombay Government 1942–43, was headed by M. R. Jayakar, with eminent economist, Dhananjay R. Gadgil as a member of the seven-member team, of whom four were Marathi speakers. From the 1920s onwards, the latter had written extensively on the functions and a viable design of a university for Maharashtra at Poona and the imperative for it to function through Marathi so as to meaningfully sustain the redistribution of provinces into unilingual entities (Gadgil 1927). Most critically, the terms of reference contained no mention of the regional language/s as germane to the work of the proposed university (Report of the Maharashtra University Committee 1943: 2–4).[5] The Committee submitted its report in August 1943. It noted that the question of the medium of instruction was perhaps the most difficult that the Committee had to deal with, and "which has most exercised them mind of the public". However, despite having given it every serious consideration, the Committee recommended the retention of English as the language of instruction and examination at the Maharashtra University in Poona. The report noted that "a larger use of Marathi is generally desirable", but took the view that

> [...] the practical difficulties in the way of speedily attaining this end cannot be overlooked [... as] the previous preparation necessary for the immediate adoption of this step is lacking. Marathi is not yet rich enough in the majority of the subjects, especially scientific subjects that will have to be taught at the University [...]. There is a vicious circle, which can only be broken by vigorous effort. Ultimately *the result will depend on the zeal and ability of the scholars whom the University produces and their effort in the service of their mother tongue.*
>
> *(ibid.: 67–72)*

What is most striking, however, is that the jettisoned case for Marathi in favour of English had the approval of the very elite groups and individuals who had previously passionately championed the vernacular cause over previous decades. By the time Poona University was finally established in 1948, in the immediate aftermath of the Partition, the national leadership seemed even more reluctant than colonial authorities previously had been to commit to decisions on linguistic provinces, the use of regional languages in higher education or exercising political will on the official/national language question. Deemed part of the agenda of the Constituent Assembly, the tenor of discussion of these issues, post-Partition, had changed significantly. Under these circumstances, mirroring the trajectory of debate in the Constituent Assembly, the very possibility of choosing Marathi as the medium of instruction in the new regional University seemed beyond the pale; the only real contenders envisaged for the role could be Hindi and English. Given these pared-down options, when Poona University began functioning in February 1948, it was significant that English prevailed as the chosen language through which all teaching would officially occur. Significantly, M. R. Jayakar, who, as a member of the University Reform Committee of 1924, had submitted a note of dissent over the issue of the use of Marathi as the language of instruction and examination in Poona University now became the first vice chancellor of the new Poona University established in 1948. It was amply clear through this that a regionalist vision of federalism had been superceded to make room for a dominant view of federalism that was far more unitary in its vision and operating from a centralising national perspective.

'Regional' Federalists vs. Developmentalist Federalism

The foregoing analysis has pointed to the importance of acknowledging that processes of linguistic redistribution were leveraged simultaneously alongside development agendas. Even as emerging contours of the 'region/regional' within the Indian nation-space were being worked out, these envisaged spatio-political entities were already subject to the imperatives of governmental projects and economic development with their own uneven territorial mandates. Here we can only schematically highlight the intertwined but staggered way in which the logic of linguistic territorialisation and the embracing of developmental agendas proceeded. This drawn-out, extended temporality in the story of linguistic reorganisation is important: while the embracing of developmental agendas in the 1930s onwards was prefaced by a formal political acquiescence to the logic of linguistic territorialisation from 1919 onwards, actual linguistic reorganisation of states had to wait till 1960, a whole decade after economic planning became the centrepiece of the national mission.

The transformative appeal that had fueled the rise of language nationalities around the close of the nineteenth century was tied to their potential. They appeared as the harbingers of new horizontally extendable communities that held a promise of a democratic nation-state form and dissolution of caste society. The democratising energy mobilised via these regional nationalities around language had soon to contend with another nationalism and a different perspective on federalism, fuelled by aspirations of a different coalition of interests spanning merchant castes, big business interests and industry owners largely from western India, aptly termed as 'capitalist' without being 'bourgeois'. Increasingly by late 1947, the dominance of this coalition with respect to national politics and federal and economic policy was unmistakable, deriving in equal measure from their direct partnership with the national leadership and from their pan-Indian economic ambitions. In his Founder's Day lecture at the Gokhale Institute in 1939, Dr. Ambedkar had observed pertinently:

> Different people are looking at this Federation from different points of view. There is the point of view of the Princes. There is the point of view of the Hindus and the Muslims and the Congress. There is also the point of view of the Merchant and the Trader. The point of view of each one of these is of course the result of their particular interests…but there can be no doubt about it that the point of view of this community is really more decisive than the point of view of any other community. This community has been behind the Congress.
>
> *(Ambedkar 1939: 144–49)*

To capture this clash synoptically here, we may speak of the more historically rooted federal vision of the regionalists or 'regional federalists' now confronted by the unitary vision of 'non-regionalist' federalism, espoused by big business and industrialists' interests cohering around the role of planned capitalist development led by a strong centre. These rival visions of federalism assigned significantly different weightage to the cohesive potential of linguistic homogeneity and unilingual provincial units as the basis of federation. As Gadgil emphasised, the quest for homogeneity was a primary necessity for democracy and federation, for which "no consideration of finance or strategy can come in the way of this […] the process of Federation must begin with the formation of primary homogeneous unilingual federating units whose representatives must come together to form the federation" (Gadgil 1945: 14). Similarly, strongly supporting the inclusion of Bombay city in the separate state of Maharashtra, Ambedkar endorsed linguistic units whose "social composition is homogeneous and therefore more suited for the realisation of those social ends which a democratic Government must fulfil". But equally, however, he warned that

> language of the Province [… needs to] be limited to the creation of the Province, i.e., for demarcation of the boundaries of the Province. There is no categorical imperative in the scheme of Linguistic Provinces which compels us to make the language of the Province its official language. […]

> In Linguistic Provinces without the language of the Province being made its official language the Provincial culture would remain fluid with a channel open for give and take. Under no circumstances, we must allow the Linguistic Provinces to make their Provincial languages their official languages.
>
> *(Ambedkar 1948: 6–8)*

In contrast, the federalism of mercantilist interests and industrialists in Bombay claimed to 'directly' articulate a national viewpoint that did not claim the legitimacy of speaking for any particularistic regional community. Rather they asserted a disproportionately representative status for their views on the basis of their national-level economic aspirations. Indeed as Dr. Ambedkar observed of their efforts in 1948:

> A meeting was held in Bombay in the building of the Indian Merchants Chamber. The meeting was attended by no more than sixty. With the exception of one Indian-Christian it was attended by only Gujarati-speaking merchants and industrialists. Although it was small and sectional meeting, its proceedings were flashed on the front page of every important newspaper in India and the *Times of India* was so impressed by its importance that it wrote an editorial which while mildly castigating the vituperative tone which the speakers at the meeting adopted against the Maharashtrians, supported the resolutions passed at the meeting regarding the future of Bombay [...] this proves [...] that there are cases where a minority is a majority.
>
> *(ibid: 15)*

Dominated by Gujarati industrialists and businessmen, this Bombay Committee stressed that Bombay owed its development to[...] all communities, such as Parsis, Gujaratis, Cutchis, including Khojas and Memons, Maharashtrians, Canarese, Tamilians, Telugus and Chris tians, even foreign settlers. Claiming to *represent different communities in the city*, they argued that the creation of new provinces be postponed in the *wider interests of the country*. If, however, the reorganisation of provinces on a linguistic basis was to take place, Bombay ought to be constituted as a separate province 'on the strength of political, economic, strategic and cultural considerations and its cosmopolitan and multilingual character. (Isaka 2015: 146)A few years later, in their submission to the States Reorganisation Commission, this group stated that their representative claims were now stronger than in 1948:

> The representative character of the Committee has been strengthened by broadening its base through enlisting of more members [...] this Committee, as will be noted from the enclosed List of Members, is not exclusively confined to any particular communal, political or linguistic group, but is composed of enlightened representatives drawn from all walks of life and

> speaking different languages. The members are actively connected with the public life of the City of Bombay.
>
> *(Bombay Citizens' Committee 1954: iv)*

Though stationed in Bombay, the Committee claimed to have "no provincial or sectarian bias in their approach" and were bound only by "their desire to contribute towards the political solidarity and national unity of the country". Transcending particularistic interests unanimously, they believed that "unless the people are infused with the spirit of national consciousness and rise above considerations of regional or sectarian interests, it would not be possible to consolidate the forces of national unity, for economic reconstruction, essential for the maintenance of our hard-won freedom". Clearly, their views on linguistic states differed significantly from the perspective of the 'regional federalists':

> If the linguistic States are seeking to create something special and distinct in terms of loyalties apart from that which a citizen must owe to the country as a whole, it is a phase in our development which is fraught with dangerous possibilities and must be discarded as the basic test for the formation of constituent units for a Federal Union.
>
> *(ibid.: 8)*

Echoing the recent appeal made by Prime Minister Jawaharlal Nehru against the great danger of the language issue disrupting the national life and promoting a sense of disunity, they were at pains to reiterate their stance as 'leaders of public opinion' in sharing the responsibility of the Commission

> in examining the problem of Reorganisation of States which raises fundamental issues affecting unity, particularly by an undue emphasis on the linguistic principle.
>
> *(Bombay Citizens' Committee 1954: iv–v)*

Targeting the views of the impassioned votaries of Samyukta Maharashtra as particularly expressed by chief ideologue and eminent economist, Dhananjay Gadgil, the Bombay Citizens Committee spoke of their singular loyalty to national unity and the goals of economic development for the nation as a 'whole':

> There can be only one citizenship for all the people of India, owing undivided allegiance to the Indian Republic as its citizens, and if competing loyalties, by virtue of their membership of communities united by mystic linguistic ideologies and ties are allowed to be created, the same will tend to weaken the fabric of our infant State.
>
> *(ibid.: 8)*

Acutely distrustful of regional loyalties, their federal vision claimed to uphold an over-riding commitment to address the various problems of economic development in India common both in nature and in intensity to every part of the country:

> The requirements of planning emphasize that economic development should proceed, not on principles of linguism, but on principles of economic regions, such as the River Valley Project Development -areas, like the Tennesse Valley Authority in the U.S.A. or the Damodar Valley Project in India. In our view the formation of linguistic States would not only not help in any way in furthering the economic progress of the country, but is bound to adversely affect the pace of progress of planned economic development.
> *(ibid.: 17)*

Conclusion

The regional language movements in the late nineteenth century in colonial India had tapped into the seemingly open-ended potential for an infinite extension of the political community formed along linguistic lines. How then by the decade after 1947 did these democratising impulses around linguistic mobilisations yield the anxiety-ridden discourses among influential political elites about 'linguism' being the most potent threat to the nascent nation-state? If enduring anxieties about 'problems' posed by linguistic diversity to Indian nationhood and unity worked against the grain of the democratising energies unleashed by the language movements, the argument here has highlighted how processes to instrumentalise the language question and depoliticise the regional were simultaneously at work through the same time frames. This chapter has thus sought to map the long history of linguistic reorganisation of federal units in India between 1905 to the 1950s in ways that historically illuminate the seemingly paradoxical outcomes of the specific routes followed in inscribing linguistic provinces as the organising principle of the Indian federal structure.

The account begins by tracing the category of 'region' as a territorial entity around language as it emerged through developments following the revocation of the Bengal Partition. This is further linked to the new salience that language and linguistic communities acquired as demands for political reform and responsible government gained ground towards the end of the Great War. Introducing the first measures towards self-government at the provincial level, the announcement of Montford–Chelmsford reforms precipitated debates around territorial redistribution, constitutional norms and distribution of franchise. These inter-war debates to reconfigure spatial and territorial parameters of constituent units in late colonial India were as much about foundational manoeuvres to fix the place of key markers of caste, religion and language and delimit political rights for minorities within Indian democracy. Here, the significance of the Motilal Nehru Report of 1928, which first mooted territorial redistribution into linguistic provinces as a constitutional principle while rejecting separate electorates in favour of joint mixed electorates, is underlined. Recognising these linked emphases as central to the constitutional architecture that dominant Indian nationalism saw as most desirable and advantageous is a necessary step in decentring the story of linguistic states beyond conventional narratives that simply trace their origins to major changes effected in the Congress Constitution in 1920.

Further drawing on higher education policy and regional discourse between the 1920s and 1950s, the chapter has explored the shifting positions of Marathi cultural elites, particularly, with respect to the place of regional languages in higher education and in the making of regional universities. The final section has dwelt upon the conflict between two colliding visions of federalism played out through the drawn-out temporal intersections between the logic of linguistic territorialisation and simultaneous leveraging of development agendas in the decades between the 1920s and 1950s. These intersections and tensions between the democratic stimuli inherent in the vision of 'regionalist federalists' as against the centralising thrust of 'developmentalist federalism' served to further depoliticise the regional and its links with democratic considerations within the post-1947 imagination of India's federal structure.

Notes

1 The initial notification on Bengal dated 3 December 1903, outlined a plan to transfer Mymensingh and Dacca districts for inclusion in Assam province while incorporating Oriya-speaking districts into the Bengal Presidency but clearly stopped short of a full-fledged Partition of Bengal carving out a separate Muslim-majority province of East Bengal. See Home Department Public Notification 3678 (1903).

2 See the provisions in Article 289: "a) Sind shall be separated from Province of Bombay and shall forma a Governor's Province to be known as the Province of Sind. b) Orissa and such other areas in the Province of Bihar and Orissa as may be specified in the Order of his Majesty shall be separated from the Province of Madras and Central Provinces respectively, and Orissa and other areas so separated shall together form a Governor's Province to be known as the Province of Orissa; and c) the province formerly known as the Province of Bihar and Orissa shall be known as the province of Bihar."

3 Details of the courses and examinations for First Year and Final Year BA and MA students for 1866–67 in Bombay University note that these examinations in Portuguese, Marathi, Gujarati, Canarese, Hindustani or Sindhi are only meant for persons who matriculated before the close of 1863. However, even these would be discontinued after the year 1869.

4 At the University of Bombay, the first investments in this direction went into the setting up of the Bombay School of Sociology and Economics.

5 The terms were framed as follows: "(1) to consider whether a university for Maharashtra should be established and (2) if in the opinion of the Committee it should be established, to make recommendations as to what should be its form, and jurisdiction and (3) to report on the cost of its establishment and maintenance and to make

proposals for the raising of necessary funds. (4) the committee should be requested to submit its report to the Government as early as possible before the end of July 1942". However, we have mention of resolutions in successive meetings of the Marathi Sahitya Sammelan, 1926 onwards, of how the new university of Maharashtra would accord special importance to Marathi literature in the curricula of all examinations, strive for the enrichment of Marathi literature in the curricula of all examinations, strive for the enrichment of Marathi literature and keep before itself the ideal of imparting, as speedily as possible, all education through the Marathi language.

Bibliography

Ambedkar, Bhim Rao. 1939. *Federalism versus Freedom*. Pune: Gokhale Institute of Economics and Politics.

——— 1990. "On Creation of a Separate Karnatak Province", Bombay Legislative Council Debates Vol. 3 (04.04.1938) in *Dr. Babasaheb Ambedkar: Writings and Speeches*, Vol. 7. Bombay: Government of Maharashtra, 188–196.

——— 1945. *What Congress and Gandhi Have Done to the Untouchables*. Bombay: Thacker & Co.

——— 1948. *Maharashtra as a Linguistic Province: Statement Submitted to the Linguistic Provinces Commission*. Bombay: Thacker.

——— 1989. "Thoughts on Linguistic States, 1955." In *Dr. Babasaheb Ambedkar: Writings and Speeches*, Vol. 1. Bombay: Government of Maharashtra, 143–44.

Bombay Citizens' Committee. 1954. *Memorandum to the States Reorganization Commission re: Re-organisation of States*. Submitted to the Chairman, States Reorganisation Committee.

Bombay University Calendar for 1866–1867. 1866. Bombay: Thacker Vining and Co..

Bombay University Calendar for 1923–24 and 1924–1925, Vol. 1. 1924. Bombay: Bombay Government Central Press.

Colley, Linda. 2021. "What Happens When a Written Constitution is Printed?" *Transactions of the Royal Historical Society*, 31: 75–88.

Datar, Abhay. 2012. "The Lucknow Pact of 1916: A Second Look at the Congress-Muslim League Agreement." *Economic and Political Weekly* Vol. 47, Issue 10, 65–69.

De, Rohit. 2018. *A People's Constitution*. Princeton: Princeton University Press.

Elangovan, A. 2014. "The Making of the Indian Constitution: A Case for a Non-nationalist Approach." *History Compass*, 12, no. 1: 1–10.

Gadgil, Dhananjaya. 1945. *Federating India*. Pune: Gokhale Institute of Politics and Economics. (Publication No. 13).

——— 1948. *Future of Bombay City*. Poona: Samyukta Maharashtra Publication.

——— 1974. "Puṇe University kaśī asāvī?" (What Form Should Pune University Take?) *Ratnākar* 2, June 1927; reprinted in Brahme, Sulabha. *Collected Works of D.R. Gadgil*, Vol. 2. Pune: Gokhale Arthashastra Sanstha, 237–45.

Report of the Committee on University Reform, 1924–25. 1924. Bombay: Government Central Press.

Government of India Act. 1935. http://www.legislation.gov.uk/ukpga/1935/2/pdfs/ukpga_19350002_en.pdf, accessed January 7, 2020.

Hardinge, Charles. 1913. "Coronation Reforms." In *Speeches of Lord Hardinge*, Vol. 1. Madras: Ganesh and Company, 410–39.

Home Department Public Notification 3678. 1903. "From H. H. Risley, Secretary, Government of India to Chief Secretary, Government of Bengal", dated December 3 1903. *Gazette of India* No. 50, December 12, 1903, p. 10; https://ia801600.us.archive.org/21/items/in.ernet.dli.2015.91217/2015.91217.The-Gazette-Of-Indiaoctober-december1903.pdf, accessed January 23, 2020.

Isaka, Riho. 2015. "The Multilingual City of Bombay and the Formation of Linguistic States, 1947–60." In Crispin Bates, Minoro Mio et al. (eds): *Cities in South Asia*. London: Routledge, 159–74.

Naregal, Veena. Forthcoming. "Monolingual States in a Polyglot Setting: The Long History of Linguistic Territorial Reorganisation in India." In V. Naregal and M. Prasad (eds): *Language Movements and the Democratic Imagination in India*. Hyderabad: Orient Blackswan Delhi.

Nehru, Motilal. 1928. *All Parties Conference 1928: Report of the Committee Appointed by the Conference to Determine the Principles of Constitution for India*. Allahabad: All India Congress Committee.

Phadke, Yashwant D. 1979. *Politics and Language*. New Delhi: Himalaya Publishing House.

Report of the Maharashtra University Committee appointed by the Bombay Government 1942–43. 1943. Bombay: Government Central Press.

Report of the Thirty-fifth Session of the Indian National Congress held at Nagpur. 1920. Published by Dr. B. S. Moonje, Hon. General Secretary, Reception Committee, Nagpur.

Report of the Thirty-first Indian National Congress held at Lucknow. 1917. Allahabad: Leader Press.

Shani, Ornit. 2022. "The People and the Making of India's Constitution." *The Historical Journal*, 65: 1102–123. https://doi.org/10.1017/S0018246X21000856.

PART II

Lost/Found in Translation between Vernaculars and English

7

LINGUISTIC ESTRANGEMENT

When Is a Language My Own?

Sudipta Kaviraj

Estrangement

Estrangement, we know, is not just the presence of strangeness. It is, to capture the unsettling point of Marx's use, a strange form of strangeness.[1] Concisely, it is the strangeness of something that ought not to be strange. Another way of putting it is to say that when the strange and familiar exchange places, we have the problem of estrangement in this specific sense. Because there is an inversionary process involved in this – the process by which something that ought to be familiar *becomes* strange to us. It seems to me that this insight can be applied to the lingual situation that arises as a consequence of colonial cultural domination. Linguistic estrangement – if we use that idea – is a common feature of the colonial world's cultural history. Estrangement should not be confused with linguistic plurality. Before colonialism, in many contexts, a multiplicity of languages was part of social being. Intellectuals and ordinary people often used languages other than their 'own'. Cosmopolitan languages often had this character. In medieval Europe, scholars learnt Latin, in ancient and medieval India Sanskrit, and across the Islamic world Arabic and Persian: while, in their everyday, they presumably used some regional vernacular tongue. When engaging in some specific, high form of activity, they would use the cosmopolitan language. The purpose of these high cosmopolitan languages was precisely to overcome the divisions of local languages in which people lived. Colonialism, however, changed the rules of this language economy in significant ways.

Thus, in the following, I shall try to think through the problem that in colonial settings, our language of experience and language of reflecting on that experience tend to become disjunct. Can I say, for instance, that Bengali is my language? Of course, neither of the obvious paraphrases of this statement

DOI: 10.4324/9781003279921-10

makes real sense: I do not own the Bengali language: the obverse, that I belong to the Bengali language, also is not immediately meaningful. What is the sense then in which we say so unproblematically that Bengali or Tamil or Urdu is my language? I shall try to explore whether this is true, and what this means. I shall then explore what are the problems of using English as our main language of social science reflection. In the last part, I will explore the opposite proposition: that being situated between two languages instead of being immersed in one may also have some advantages; and explore this constantly 'translational' situation with a few examples of concepts of social philosophy. I think, however, that such an analysis must start with an unexpected move: not by studying social features of individual languages, but by studying a *language economy* as a whole – the complex, interactive structure that all linguistic performances form in a particular society. In India, simple accounts of single-language public spheres fail to take into account the real complexities of language use and language experience.[2] Public spheres in India – literary or political – are constituted by not the singularity, but the multiplicity of languages. Additionally, these are not flat but sloped, structured, partially open, and closed for groups with differential competences. Public spheres in India are formed in ways quite different from the shape assumed in Habermas's initial classic work. Analysis of language in India cannot follow Habermas's analytics too literally. But the linguistic economy is marked by two types of relationships – diversity and hierarchy. In North India, Urdu and Hindi exist side by side or in partial overlap. High languages, however – Sanskrit, Persian, and later English – hover over the lower status of vernaculars.

Precolonial Linguistic Economy

Present-day linguistic orbits were created by the great colonial rupture in our cultures. So, in a sense, a historically informed study of language should start with an account of the premodern linguistic economy and analyze how it changes with the impact of colonialism. Thus, it is wrong to study Sanskrit, Persian, Urdu, Hindi, and Bengali separately and ask how they related to each other in the time of the Mughals in North India. Because this starts from the wrong assumption that they normally exist separately and are then brought into interconnection. Rather, we should start with the following questions: What is the linguistic economy in North India? How many languages can we find in its composition, and what does each language do? How does an average individual from a specific social group use his own linguistic competences to navigate social relations?

Language is something peculiarly intimate to the human subject. Can we say that something as internal to us as *our* language can be estranged? Should estrangement not be about something that we acquire or something that is external to us? Why does raising the question seem so strange? Language, after all, pre-exists us. Despite the common English phrase, we do not pick up a language, we are born into it, and it surrounds us from the time before we speak. This is the sense in which a language pre-exists us: it is ever-pre-given, if you like Althusser, or always already there, if you prefer Derrida. What does that mean? As some philosophers would say, a young child, who does not yet speak, sees a color, and learns gradually that that color is called blue. Without acquisition of this language usually called the mother tongue, the child is not able to do anything expressive about his experience of color.

In our world, however, the notion of mother tongue is not unproblematic. What if the mother immigrates to the US or Germany before the child learns to speak? In that case, his mother tongue most likely will be German or US English. If the mother still speaks Turkish or Bengali, it will be an interestingly indeterminate question. Human beings are not biologically equipped to have only one single language: the result could well be that the child grows up knowing both equally well.

Our problem here is of course with language about social objects, not with terms like 'blue'. In cases like blue, or like 'rabbit' in Quine's example, the initial difficulty in intelligibility gives way to the probability of translation, because ostensive reference is possible. The only difficulty is getting the beast called rabbit in English to scamper across a field under well-lighted conditions reasonably frequently for the two interlocutors to reach a consensus in translation. But what if the linguistic reference is to an institution like caste, or an emotional organ like *manas*, or a theoretical concept like *rasa*, or a technical procedure like mandamus, internal to a large legal system, or the political judgment that an act of government is undemocratic?

Translation happens when a word is transferred between two languages – usually one of them is my own, and the other not. But 'own' here is a tricky term. When and why do we say that Bengali or Tamil is my language? The usual assumption behind this assertion is that I function socially by means of that language. Most of the social interactions I have – which constitute the totality of experience of my life – occur through the use of that language. That gives that language a priority in my social existence, and thus 'is my language'. That also involves the idea that the meanings of words in that language are easily and effortlessly intelligible to me.

How Language Opens up the World to Us

We generally assert – correctly – that the world opens up to us through language. Without language we would not have the tools by which we name things in the world, their relations, and our relations to them – which also includes our relations with ourselves (social relations). It is interesting to notice the difference between expressing this notion in English and Bengali. 'Open up' in English translates as 'খুলে দেওয়া/*khule deoẏā*' in Bengali; but the Bengali locutions is closer in its meaning to the verb 'to disclose' – preferred in the German philosophic tradition. Disclosing pre-supposes, somewhat counterintuitively, that before we use language, the world – though given to us in experience – is in some important sense closed to us: it is the function of language to *dis*-close it. After structuralism, it is a truism that each language discloses the world to us differently according to its peculiar 'system of differentiation'. Mouton in French does not have the differentiation that English carries between the animal – sheep – and its meat – mutton. In Bengali, interestingly, 'চিকেন/*ciken*' (chicken) as a Bengali loan from English will mean only the meat, not the animal. The fact that such systems of linguistic differentiation affect our understanding and judgments even of the physical world can be illustrated by words denoting physical things. The term 'summer' in English, or in any cold country, always carries a connotation of something enjoyable and pleasurable – after the end of the cold, hard winter. Autumn, or the American fall, is always associated with a splash of colors. In Bengali, because of the physical world folded into the language, summer is hardly pleasant: by contrast, rains, always unpleasant weather in English, are accompanied by a sensation of relief and pleasure after the burning endured in the previous months. Physical terms describing seasons in nature are not neutral. They carry a penumbra of associations from the nature that is given to us, and which, linguistically, we take for granted. Is this the meaning of saying that Bengali is my own language – *āmār bhāṣā*, or *āmār nijer bhāṣā*? If we assume an always pre-given connection between a language and a world – in this case, the natural world – is that the meaning of saying that this is my language, this language is *my own*? In fact, does the statement 'this is my language' incongruously suggest my ownership of the language while it is actually an inverted presentation of the truth that this language and its world own me, i.e., I am part of a pre-existing world, and this language is also pre-existingly linked inextricably to that pre-existing world? If this is true of the physical, natural world, can this be true of the social world as well?

Thinking about Social Theory in Bengali

My narrow field of research and writing is social/political theory. I would like to turn to that field and reflect about the experience of writing in English and Bengali. All my real training in thinking about social theory has been in English. I went to an excellent Bengali-medium small-town school. I was introduced to the names of Hobbes, Locke, and Rousseau at the end of my school days in utterly perfunctory Bengali books – perfunctory, because they were written with the expectation that if I happened to learn about these subjects seriously, I would do that in English in college. Those books were not really giving me any serious, if elementary, grounding. They were like names on maps from which it was not possible to acquire even a basic understanding of what the thing was like. So, the seriously intended training in thinking and writing was entirely through English books and English writing in college education.

Writing about social theory in Bengali is hard. But this difficulty can be caused by two different reasons. It can be simply because I have little or less experience in writing about social theory topics in Bengali: which means this is a relatively simple matter of technical fluency and familiarity.[3] Because I do not regularly make decisions about choosing between alternate terms, phrases, and locutions, such choices are hard for me. I think there is an important truth in this observation. Though this raises the further question: Why? Why do I usually read poetry in Bengali, but write social theory – let us say about secularism, because I shall use this as an example later – in English? A simple answer is that I was formed by an educational system that trained me to see those two languages as appropriate vehicles for poetry and social science. It is not that I did not learn English enough to read and understand poetry: but, for some reason, still my access to the poesy in reading poetry – my grasp of the quality which makes that use of language poetic – is more accessible to me in Bangla. Why did my society train me that way? Was this a result of mere imitativeness? Was it because the colonial order imposed this decision on our society? In one sense that is tritely true; but our society became politically independent nearly eight decades ago. Assuming that social theory should be done in English rather than in the vernacular may have originally been part of the colonial education system, but that system has been retained and vastly extended. Colonialism is not to blame if we decide not to eradicate its institutions.

Our Language about the Natural World

Let me make a preliminary statement – to be qualified by further thinking. In thinking about nature, Bengali is closer to me. Because there is a Bengali world present inside my English, when I say summer does not feel pleasant; autumn is unrecognizable as a distinct season in the Bengali natural world; and rain is like a celebration and renewal of the earth – so that feelings associated with the seasons are all wrong. If I have to describe the season to an interlocutor, if I say, ‘*āmi garam'kāle kal'kātāẏ yete cāẏ nā*’ (I don’t want to go to Kolkata in summer), note that the connotative effect of ‘summer’ is complex: it does a lot of linguistic work pithily and quickly in the same utterance. First, it refers, neutrally, to the season, but, second, it also indicates the unpleasantness of the heat, and, third, it offers a reason for not going there at that time. The term *garam* accomplishes all that through the complex lingual functions of a single term. In comparison, the English sentence, I do not feel like going to Kolkata in summer, would be much flatter – though Bengali interlocutors might be able to grasp all those layers of meaning because they are a Bengali and will be able to hear my Bengali within my English.

It is the same way about expressions in poetry and music. Since there is always an inseparable connection between natural surroundings, seasons, and their attunement to human emotions – like love or longing – these associations are embedded in 'our' language. In Bengali poetry, there is a deeply conventionalized or samsakarized[4] connection between rain and love. The tumult of the rains is often recorded in poetry – Tagore describes the Yamuna as restless, bursting its bounds, covered in a garment of darkness. Despite the suggestions of turmoil, the language persuades us to see this picture in our inward eye as beautiful.[5] Is this simply because of my connection of nativeness, inhabitance, with the natural world is invoked in the poetic picture? There is a connection of belongingness between the subject, the language, and the world.

Our Language about the Social World

Should we not expect a similar relation of inhabitance in the social world as well, such that it produces an impression of being *inside*, seeing social relations from the inside? What is social *description*? What is social *theory*? How does our language work in these two tasks? Social theory is a cognitive activity that seeks to examine and analyze social conduct. Social conduct occurs always *in* the language of that society. If we add another dimension to this question – the relation between ordinary commonsensical thinking about a society and social science thinking – the significance of the 'internal' language becomes reinforced. It is generally acknowledged that the relation between 'science' and 'commonsense' about social life is not disjunct to the extent natural science knowledge can be. In truth, the earth goes round the sun, though it might appear the other way round. Such inversionary relations between common sense and science are unusual in social sciences. Rather, social science or social theory must refine the perceptions and analyses of common sense to arrive at its own analyses and judgments – which are built, as hermeneutic theorists insist, at least initially from an understanding of what human agents intended to.

Here we come across a problem created by colonial modernity. In many social settings – in activities that have happened for centuries or even longer – we have prolific, highly expressive, elaborate language. In most conventional aspects of religious life, we have such language. In acts of religious worship, we possess a highly elaborate vocabulary. But when we turn to some other settings – for example, in political public life – often in everyday conversation we do not use a vernacular term but use English instead. Our everyday language about politics, for example, must appear odd to inhabitants of non-colonial societies. When Americans discuss politics among themselves, they have a full vocabulary in their own everyday language. Yet, when I speak about the last election to my Bengali relatives or friends, I shall frequently use English words. English words are used because of two reasons: in some cases, it is due to laziness – I can use *nirbācan* instead of election. Though unless I am deeply self-conscious, I shall say *ebār* election*e Mamatā Byānerjīr pārṭi jiteche*.[6] Suppose I want to say something that is also very relevant for political analysis,[7] like, 'the CPIM suppressed civil society in its thirty-four year rule'; or 'we need civil society leaders in public life to play a larger role in a democracy'. Finding Bengali words or locution will be harder: for election I could have used *nirbācan*, and for democracy I can use *gaṇatantra* – which has also become sufficiently conventionalized – but people will probably understand the connotative force more clearly with the use of democracy *as a Bengali word*. Similarly, if I want to use the word 'public', I have to use it *as a Bengali word*: we simply have not invented a usable translation. Of course, using the generative powers of Sanskrit roots, I can produce tolerable equivalents of 'private' and 'public'; but my listeners will hear them. Ironically, as *translation-words* – because they first understand the English words, which function in the background to facilitate their understanding of the Bengali terms I deploy. If 'civil society' forms an indispensable part of my argument, I shall be in difficulty: neologisms like '*suśīl samāj*', *nāgarik samāj*, etc. are hardly intelligible. Each one of them tends to deflect the meaning of the idea in a direction distinct from the English notion. If my primary purpose is to produce intelligibility, these words will not convey my intended meaning to the hearer. If he already knows English and has read Gramsci, using Bengali words is redundant. He is understanding it, bypassing Bengali. If he does not know English, he will not have a clear idea.

Why is this so? Of course, it is certainly partly due to the fact of the historical newness of these ways of conducting ourselves in public. Democracy was introduced as a formal legal institution in 1950, and ordinary people – used to living in a society of deep hierarchy – took another 30 years to understand not merely how democracy worked, but, crucially, how critically it depended on their own acts like voting, attending meetings, running for election, and becoming a minister, etc. Civil society is not such a term. It is an implicit but cardinal requirement for the functioning of democracy, but it is not the name of a formal institutional institution like the Supreme Court or a procedure like election. In that sense, it can be called a second-order, analytical category – essential for understanding the proper functioning of institutions, but it does not belong logically to the same class of word concepts. Not surprisingly, societies that have had a longer historical experience of functioning democracy are likely to be richer in their vocabulary – both first-order institutional words and second-order analytical words of this kind.

Sometimes, however, there is a generative quality to popular language that intellectuals tend to disdain. Popular language is for obvious reasons more instantly sensitive to experiential change: it has to invent expressions to communicate. It has no time to wait. Usually, it takes longer for such experiential change to filter into the encrusted vocabularies of academic 'normal science'. Constant repetitive use in educational practice makes them both authoritative and inert. I have noticed a linguistic alteration in the language that describes the relationship between political leaders and their supporters. Initially, this shift was tentative and comic; but gradually it settled into a more standard vocabulary. Academic political science is wedded to an unrealistic high-minded notion of the relationhip between political leaders and their followers. The coupled words – leader-followers – reflect two rather different origins – first, an abstract, idealistic theoretical picture of deliberative democracy in which individual voters, endowed with sovereign powers of reasoning, deliberate and decide to 'follow' a particular party or its leader because of the rational persuasiveness of their ideas or policies. The verb 'follow' here is invested with unrealistically elevated associations of rationality. But this vocabulary is also influenced by a second, more sociological model of party functioning – which assumes that sociological groups would support parties which advance their calculations of collective self-interest. Workers will support Labor, while middle classes and entrepreneurs will support Conservatives. Actually, following can be a far more complex affair; but there was a background assumption that the relationship between parties and their followers was mediated by such considerations of interests or more inchoate 'demands'. Parties funneled aggregated interests into the political system: that is reflected in saying that a leader has followers.

Rajni Kothari sensed in the late 1970s that even this more inchoate process of articulation of interest or aggregated demand was changing in Indian democracy, and parties were changing their character. He observed two features of this change – the infusion of violence and calculations of criminal 'ability' into political leadership – reflected in the alarmingly large number of party candidates with criminal records. Secondly, followers tended to show a form of unconditional attachment or outright dependence on these leaders which could not be fitted into the decorous models of interest articulation of political science textbooks. This new political reality fundamentally contravened the assumptions behind the rational interest-bearing individual and group models of conventional comparative politics. Kothari, after all a political scientist, initially registered this as 'anomalous', and did not immediately look for a conceptual vocabulary to capture this item of 'historical difference'.[8]

Ordinary language cannot wait for academics to think and invent a vocabulary to capture palpable experiential change. In most north Indian languages – I know of Bengali, Hindi, and Marathi – this slow but significant change was captured with a subtle alteration of terms. Leader–follower are antonymic counter-concepts: their meanings depend on each other. In Bengali, the older terms would have been translated as a *netā* and his *anugāmī* (followers, going after) or *samarthak* (supporters, giving support). In slang, which is the advance guard of popular language, the second term was supplanted by *cām'cā* (spoon, or dependent, adherent, sidekick, abettor of crimes – all of these negative qualities mixed together). But of course, counter-concepts carry their meanings together, so that, a change in the meaning of one side inevitably alters the inflection of the other. Introducing the word *cām̐cā* thus alters the meaning of *netā* as well – it comes to have an association with crime, violence, extortion, and intimidation, forcing both ordinary people, but also small bureaucrats to 'do things' – all contributing to the new *netās'* malignant mystique. While in the 1940s B. C. Roy would have been called a *netā*, in the 1980s and 1990s local politicians – halfway between legislative manipulator and local muscleman – would be called by that name. Popular everyday language absorbs historical changes more sensitively and instantly and evaluates a displacement and degradation in this crucial relationship, than the ponderous movement of academic language does – if at all.

Clearly, affect is a vital part of the life of politics. Politics is a world of love and hate, of enthusiasm and despair. And the question of language must also touch on the language of affect as it works through political action.

Language of Experience and the Language of Reflection

Experience and analysis, it would be readily admitted, are not only closely linked to each other but also profoundly different. Analysis cannot happen, at least not successfully, if the analyst is too close to his experience: to analyze we need a critical distance, i.e., a distance deliberately created so that it allows a critical stance toward the experienced reality. Consequently, at times, this critical distance is reflected in a deliberate, sometimes carefully, painstakingly constructed separate language.[9]

But this creates an interesting problem in a hierarchically dirempted social world like ours. Take the example of religion. If we are religious, and religion is a part of the conduct of our everyday life – i.e., if we take part in personal and collective worship, observe sacred calendars and festivals, join rituals and festivities – we are doing all that in the vernacular language *internal* to that act. No Indian is religiously Hindu or Muslim in English. Yet, when the same person goes into the university seminar room to participate in a conference analyzing their society, they must take part in analytical conduct – because that is as much a social conduct as circling a lamp in *ārati* – in English, though the first act is the analytical object of the second act. Just as the first act has rules to follow, so does the second. One could say that one of the rules of the second act – conferencing – is to distance oneself from, or not take seriously the first act of worshipping. Does this create a dissonance? I shall stick to the example of the academic analysis of religious life and thought, and explore such hardships through three examples.

Sociological Settings of Language Use

We give little attention sociologically to the fact of living between two languages. Most of the time, the analysis simply keeps the two language orbits discreet, and only occasionally does our analysis allow us to reflect on what happens when the two overlap. But we need to reflect more on focusing on an individual subject and her location in a language – sometimes entirely immersed inside one, sometimes the other, rarely thinking about what happens to the nature and structure of the subjectivity which has to function in the two languages, or sometimes more than two, in different settings. This also involves the question of how elites and ordinary people live their lingual lives. Let me focus on the elite situation alone. Elite Indians who are involved in intellectual roles – academics, bureaucrats, managers, entrepreneurs, and some politicians (not all) – use bilinguality in four distinct ways and in four distinct settings. Some social activities are held in sociological settings which impose a rule of monolinguality. Formal speech settings in the vernacular require a highly self-conscious and disciplined monolinguality. If I am asked to speak at a Bengali literary society, I shall be constrained to speak without uttering a single English word. Contrarily, when in an academic seminar (unless it is formally in a vernacular), I shall be constrained equally to speak monolingually in English. Writing an academic paper or for a newspaper will impose equally stringent conventions of monolingual language use. Consider, however, what happens the moment such sociological and institutional constraints are removed. In our spontaneous conversations about academic social theory – among Bengalis at least – the lingual practice will instantly fall into bilinguality. Quite often, if we are attentive, we shall find that we use two types of high terms – 'literary' and 'conceptual' – very differently: conceptual terms like 'democracy', 'civil society', 'development', or 'postcolonial', 'postmodern', and 'deconstructive' are likely to be used in English, but, by contrast, these are terms of literary enhancement in Bengali. We shall start using words like 'deconstruction', or 'modes of production', or 'contradiction', or 'structure' repeatedly and systematically in English in the middle of a predominantly Bengali conversation.

It is important to consider the effect of this speech form. Our arguments are formed in informal thinking – either in explicit conversational settings or even inside our own minds. The effects of this bilinguality – which is also a technique of compartmentalization – can be seen when we read serious vernacular writing. Inserting English terms in Bengali writing seems ugly and inappropriate. Transliterating the term in Bengali script is not much better, because the purpose of writing in Bengali is to make the idea accessible to someone who is fluent in Bengali, but not in English. A third solution we often use is to draw upon the vast generative capacities of Sanskrit to produce a vernacular equivalent – say, *binirmāṇ* or *abhinirmāṇ* for deconstruction. Initially, this translation is merely a shift of words, not necessarily of meaning. Simply by grasping the conventionalized meanings of the prefixes *abhi* and *bi* (Sanskrit *vi*), a Bengali reader will not be able to grasp what Derrida's concept means. Normally, the process of understanding is accomplished by phrasal strategies of various kinds: not by an etymological transfer, but by a discursive, interpretative conveyance of the conceptual content of the idea. Even this, however, is clearly a statement of the lingual problem in the narrowest sense. It does nothing to answer the sociological problem – erasing or reducing the disadvantage in discursive exchanges of individuals who are either monolingual in the vernacular or asymmetrically bilingual.

Can we make this argument, systematically, about our language of reflection? Could we say, perhaps, that we have to accept that the structure of our lived existence is marked by this diremption between a quotidian existence in the vernacular and an epistemic existence in English? Our education, from the start, assumes that serious cognitive work will have to be undertaken in English, and, therefore, through persistent training turns it into our 'natural' or standard epistemic language. Therefore, we could say that just as our natural language in doing religion is Bengali, our equally 'natural' language in doing thinking is English. But it is still an irreducible fact that English cannot be learnt by an ordinary Indian in the unmindful but efficient way in which the local vernacular can.

Some analysts of language say that we should consider English as one of the Indian languages: that the English/vernacular binary is false. Usually, they adduce the argument that the only language they learnt from their lived environment, for no fault of theirs, was English. There are two clear problems in advancing this 'second "natural" language' argument. The first is that a language can be called natural only if, like a 'mother tongue', a subject can pick it up from her surroundings through everyday interactions – without special effort or instruction. That is the sense in which Bengali is my language. I did not have to go to school to learn Bengali, though, of course, going to school helps me to use Bengali in many ways that are barred to someone who has not learnt it formally. But who have not been to school can still have Bengali as 'their language'. For an average Indian, English learning cannot ordinarily happen that way. We cannot learn English except through special instruction – against the tides and ripples of the surrounding lingual world. This immediately divides those who learn English into three groups: those who can use it with fluency and confidence, those who can use it but with difficulty, and those who simply do not get enough English to use it. As long as English remains our main language of academic reflection, this immediately cuts off the last segment and produces a relationship of deep inequality between the first two.

This lingual order, so deeply entrenched in postcolonial India, impoverishes our intellectual culture on both sides. The elite English sphere of discourse cannot draw from the experience of the masses of its own society. The vernacular spheres, which have lost their easy epistemic connection with the Sanskrit and Persian knowledge systems, and cannot fluently draw from English, are not fertilized by the vitality of modern thought systems. Because of the easy access of the elites to English, and English translation to other Western traditions, our translation tradition is meager. Iranians have translations of Hegel, Heidegger, and Derrida; we do not. Our added trouble is that even if Derrida is translated in Bangla, and Hegel into Marathi, and Heidegger in Punjabi, these will remain trapped inside regional vernaculars.

Leaving aside these sociological issues, let us return to our main problem of language and social cognition. What are the conditions under which a language facilitates or obstructs knowledge about a certain class of objects or questions? If simple familiarity is the critical issue, then it is possible to make a case that there is no problem in making English our first language of academic thinking about society. As individual subjects will be trained from the start in acquiring skills in English with the expectation that she will use it for her analytical reflection in later life if she is given a proper education – as upper-class Indians generally are – why should this be an obstacle in unimpeded cognitive use of her language? That few Indians are given a good education in English is a sociological, empirical question of training deficit, not an epistemic difficulty. This is not a question to which we return a single general answer. We need to distinguish between different sciences – i.e., systematic knowledge systems within which an individual cognitive subject has to operate – because their subject-fields are quite differently constituted; and, we need to take into account the evident difference in social sciences that the observer is part of what he observes, which completely alters the nature of the act of observation itself.[10] Natural sciences and technology clearly fall into one distinctive category where the dominant conceptual language of contemporary science is universally used. Some social sciences, like economics, or statistically driven empirical sciences like criminology, partake of this character to a large extent – not merely because formal analytical techniques are to an extent prose-independent but also because the objects about which information is gathered, and then subjected to analysis – quantitative or qualitative – are invariant across societies and times. Calories required for basic nutrition, per capita consumption of energy, or the gross national product are not intrinsically context-dependent ideas. Clearly, this leaves aside social sciences and other systematic studies which are historical in a deep sense – or to put it in a more explicitly Hegelian or hermeneutic fashion, where the object of understanding involves some element of self-understanding. Here the question of language and the cognitive subject is internal to the enquiry: there is a language that performs an indispensable role in constituting this object itself, and therefore there is a big difference between a study that uses the same language as the 'native' language of the subject-object, and another language which bears an external relation to its self-constituting social activities.

I shall try to work through three examples in the study of Indian religion and literature – because at times, the main medium through which religious movements make their arguments is through literary texts.

EXAMPLE 1 SANSKRIT/BENGALI > ENGLISH

In both my academic roles – as an intellectual historian and a social theorist (note that there are no good terms for describing these epistemic roles indigenously in our languages; the terms we use, '*bauddhik itihās*' and '*sāmājik tattva*', are translation terms: a person who has no prior acquaintance with the English phrases would be unable to understand the meaning of the Bengali or Hindi ones) – I might want to explore and analyze how Hindus thought about human life and society in the medieval period, and become interested in Vaishnava theology and poetry. Let us assume I am trying to follow the careful and loving philosophical construction of the figure of Krishna in Vrindavan, as opposed to the heroic Krishna of the *Mahābhārata*. Since Krishna's narratological character is transformed unrecognizably from the incomparable warrior to the incomparable lover, from the irresistible conqueror in battles he is changed into an irresistible conqueror of particularly feminine hearts – think of the telling phrase *madhurādhipati* (the sovereign of everything that is beautiful) – writers are engaged in a constant search for expressive words. In one place, Krishna's main quality of beauty – *mādhurya* – is expressed by a comparison with Madana or Manmatha – the traditional god of love with his five arrows (*pañcaśara*). To express Krishna's irresistible erotic charm, he is called *sākṣat-manmatha-manmatha*. Literally, this means he is veritably (*sākṣat*, or standing right in front of us) a *manmatha* to Manmatha himself. Embedded in the etymology of the word *manmatha* itself, which works as the name of the god, there is an intimation of his function: *manmatha* is a person who agitates or charms (the adjective/noun *mathana*) the mind (*manas*). Krishna's description now is that he can do to Manmatha himself what Manmatha is known to do to all human beings. Even with all this glossing, it is doubtful if I shall be able to convey to someone with a different language the lingual operation inside the term in Bengali or Sanskrit. A Sanskrit word that can be used directly in Bengali is called a *tatsama* word ('same as that') – which means that the semantic and connotative operation in Bangla will be the same as in Sanskrit.[11] To return to our terminology, there is no strangeness to the Sanskrit term. I do not have to wait for a glossing act to mediate my understanding of the words. There is no distance; I do not have to wait to access the meaning, and when the mediation happens, I do not have to suffer any deficit in the semantic conveyance – for instance in the repetitive occurrence of the term *manmatha* in two senses, and the alliterative use of the compound 'nm' twice. None of this is surprising.

But the underlying question raises the implicit oddity in all this. After all, if I am seeking to understand Vaishnava theology as part of an attempt to understand how my society's thinking about itself evolved, why should I do this in English – certainly not an internal language of South Asia – and not in Bengali? Particularly, if I did this examination in Bengali, much of the awkwardness and lack of easy translatability would not have arisen at all. But more significantly, why do I have to approach an item of my own society's intellectual history *as if I am an alien*, and as if it had to be rendered intelligible to me in exactly the same way as it would have to be to a lingual stranger?[12] Clearly, this raises a question similar to one that has been debated in anthropology for a long time: Can one do an anthropology of one's own society? When we study Indian music, should we, like Western scholars, do it under the banner of *ethno*musicology? To put it more provocatively, what does it mean to treat oneself as a barbarian?

EXAMPLE 2 ENGLISH > BENGALI/HINDI NATION

Let me turn now to an example of where the translation goes in the opposite direction: of an English term – 'nation' – to Bengali. This happens to be one of the most intriguing instances of the translation problem in modern politics. By the mid-nineteenth century, all serious Bengali thinkers noted an incipient translation problem centered on the crucial concept of the nation.[13] Three sides to the growing debate concurred that Indians did not have a collective sense of being what Europeans called a 'nation'. Colonial writers were never tired of stressing that Indians did not evince, because they did not possess, a collective identity as a 'nation'. Without the steel frame of imperial rule, they would instantly fall apart.[14]

Authors like Bankimchandra were impressed by the evident power of nationalist patriotism amongst Europeans, but acknowledged that Indians lacked this powerful adhesive sentiment, shown by the fact that they also lacked a word for it. In his Bengali writings, Bankim initiated the use of the Bengali term *jāti* to designate a nationalist collectivity,[15] but often felt obliged to explain that here *jāti* meant what is meant by the English word 'nation'. Tagore, who was philosophically opposed to both the idea of the nation and the materiality of the nation-state, concurred that we did not have terms for either of these two ideas and were better for it.[16] But underlying all three positions is a common linguistic judgment that vernaculars did not have a word for the nation concept.

Gradually, through political debates of the late nineteenth century two opposing positions emerged, represented by the lines of thought followed by Bankim and Tagore. Bankim's thinking tended to deplore the absence of European-style nationalism, and called for its institution in India. The Bengali word for nation in this European sense became '*jāti*'. But to do this successfully users had to overcome three prior meanings of the term – as a logical class (e.g., *go-jāti* meaning the class of cows), *brāhmaṇ jāti* (the Brahmin caste), or the commonly used *bāṅgālī jāti* (the Bengali people).[17] In ordinary Bengali writing, its distinction from caste was indicated by the use of the more colloquial *jāt* for the latter but the distinction between *bāṅgālī jāti* and *bhāratīya jāti* – because Bengali authors constantly used *jāti* to designate the collectivity of both Bengalis and Indians – had to be gleaned from the sentential context. Conventionally, the distinction was so clear that it hardly ever gave rise to any semantic ambiguity. Eventually, both using and overriding this tripartite distinction – *jāti* for caste, language, and nation – *jātīyatā*, particularly *jātīyatābād*[18] came to connote nationalism.

Tagore remained opposed to the sentiment of Western-style nationalism. Peoples who belonged to the world of 'no-nation' – like the Japanese and the Indians – he thought, should not fall for the meretricious appeal of singularity implicit in the nation, which was unsuited to our conditions (Tagore 1917: 31–32). If the entire Indian *people* were to be conceived as a single entity, Bengali authors often suggested, it should be called a *mahājāti*.[19] If this neologism is a deliberately intended political coinage, as I suspect it was, this would create a translation problem. Translating the term into English presents a serious problem of indetermination between two meanings. *Mahājāti* could simply mean a mighty nation, unlike ordinary instances. But it is more likely that thinkers like Tagore used *mahājāti* in the more complex conceptual sense to indicate that the political patriotism that all Indians felt encompassed and transcended all linguistic collectivities: it was indeed a *jāti* – but of a pluralistic and not of a European-style singular character – an internally diverse people, rather than a homogeneous nation. Here we encounter the same phenomenon: the 'natural' movement of vernacular conceptual thought innovated a new concept. Approaching the difference between the two terms – *jāti* and *mahājāti* – in the vernacular would immediately present a conceptual distinction. Grasping this distinction in English is harder, the connotative function of the qualifier '*mahā*' suggests not a conceptual difference, but an adjectival stress.

Is There Family Resemblance in Language?

Often it is argued that Sanskrit and English are both cosmopolitan high languages used by intellectual elites. As in premodern times specialized and systematic knowledge was accumulated in a Sanskrit zone, similarly, now, it is stored in English. Abstractly, this is correct; but the relation between these two high languages and the vernaculars are very different.

Obviously, there is something like family resemblance in languages that are linked genealogically. Entire segments of vocabularies from Sanskrit are transferred into vernacular languages that develop subsequently. Bengali has a massive overlap of vocabulary – called *tatsama* terms – with Sanskrit, like the filial relation between Latin and European vernaculars. Since connotative associations often remain constant through such transfers, 'translation' between such genealogically related languages is easier. Paradoxically, translation is easy because it is not required. Therefore, the structure of communicative difficulty is of quite a different order when ideas are passed on from Sanskrit to Bengali compared to their transfer from English. In the first case, often, no word change is required. *Rasa* – a technical term in Indic aesthetics – can also work connotatively successfully in Bangla. To transfer the meaning of 'secular' into Bangla is a much harder exercise. The seeming parallel between Sanskrit and English as cosmopolitan languages is thus quite misleading. The problem is not with cosmopolitan languages, but whether the vernacular language bears any filial connection with the cosmopolitan.[20]

On the Relation between Natural and Conceptual Languages

We exist in a highly complex lingual scene. If learning means absorbing linguistic skills from our immediate and intimate social settings, our situation is marked by a strange contradiction. Our inhabitance in the world consists of every socially reproductive activity in which we participate. Family, religious life, economic occupational activity, and commercial exchanges like going to the market are all instances of social life – all these, taken together, constitute our inhabitance in society. Evidently, when I grew up in Nabadwip and Kolkata, the language of social life was Bengali. Yet, schooling was based on the expectation that I would have to use English in my professional, particularly intellectual, life, and therefore I was taught English from primary school. Ideas and sentences in Bengali and English were quite asymmetrically intelligible to us, until we went to college. Here a strange contraposition took place. English became the primary language of *analysis* of the family, the political system, the economy, and of religious life. The language of habitation in society remains Bengali, but the language of intellectual analysis is transferred to English – not accidentally, occasionally, but systematically. Because we are trained in analysis in English for long years in school and college, we come thus to have two native languages – a language native to our social living and another native to our analysis, and this is further compounded by the fact that the conceptual language housed inside each natural language is distinct. Analytical language seeks signs of secularity, while the language of lived experience would find it hard to express it felicitously if it actually found it. Our languages of inhabitance and cognitive practice are systematically separated and played off against each other.

Estrangement or Cosmopolitanism?

An interesting counterargument to the worry about lingually induced cognitive estrangement can also be constructed. Could it be said that this form of thinking is wrongheaded and excessively nationalistic? Is it a form of cosmopolitanism that we misperceive as estrangement?

EXAMPLE 3 ENGLISH > BENGALI SECULARISM

My final example is drawn from the contemporary discussion on secularism. This captures some intriguing quirks of language use in Indian political discourse. For nearly half a century before independence, the tradition of pluralistic nationalism engaged in a rich and complex discussion about the prospects of a secular state, and institutional arrangements to secure it. As Ashis Nandy (1988) has forcefully argued, during the tense decades before independence arguments in favor of religious accommodation drew ideas from the tradition of religious toleration of the precolonial past. Premodern religious languages contained ideas like *ṣulḥ-i-kul* (peace to all) from the Islamic reflections on statecraft and religious rulership from Akbar and Dara Shukoh,[21] or *sarvadharmasamabhāva* (treating every religion the same way) from Hindu *bhakti* thinking. These did not conceive of a political arrangement in which the state remained generally distanced from religious questions – a political disposition invented by European traditions of state secularism, e.g. in Spinoza and Locke.

After independence, the Indian constitution devised its own highly specific provisions of juridical secularism. Legal-juridical structures, in order to be effective, required discursive analysis and justification. Writing in English faced no problem in this regard – as authors could draw upon an already-existing vocabulary of state secularism from Europe and America learnt through our colonial education.[22] Arguing in favor of the new constitution in the vernaculars though presented linguistic difficulties. First, *sarvadharmasamabhāva* was a term internal to religious discourse, hardly suited to the description of juridical provisions. It could also mean a state immersed in the public ritualism of all religions rather than one relatively independent of all. Finding adequate terms for 'secular' in this sense proved hard.[23] A simple term like *adhārmika* in our deeply religious culture was unpromising, because it would mean religiously improper, close to sinful. The term preferred by the first generation of leaders was often *dharmanirapekṣa(tā)*. Technically, this was an excellent choice. Though not in common use in premodern religious vocabulary – because this kind of conduct was not part of that social world – it was a felicitous use of the term '*nirapekṣa*' after the word *dharma*. But the exact meaning of this compound word could also tend in two distinct directions. *Nirapekṣa* can mean 'neutral between' two sides – as a judge should be impartial between two contending parties. Users of this term certainly intended the compound to have this meaning.

However, this could lead to lingual problems. As Bhargava has shown, the Indian juridical arrangement is not like the American 'wall of separation' and strict neutrality. Semantic inventors of this term must have also intended a second meaning pointing to a different direction. *Apekṣa* in Sanskrit bears another meaning – regularly used in technical philosophical discussion – denoting (logical) dependency, or more minimally, bearing a relation to. *Dharma-nirapekṣa* in this sense means 'not dependent on or bearing any relation to' religion, religion-independent. This second sense of the compound – not unrelated but inflectionally distinct – also captures an indispensable feature of modern juridical secularism. But neither of these inflections encapsulates the English meaning of secular in another setting – that Bhargava has designated 'ethical secularism' – linked to atheist or agnostic foundations of moral beliefs. To describe the position of a Marxist, *dharmanirapekṣa* will be inadequate and misleading. A religious person might characterize that position as *adhārmika* – irreligious, which is not inaccurate, except that the Bengali term also carries a suggestion of 'immoral' or amoral. An ethical secularist can legitimately protest that not to believe in religion is not to lack all ethical principles. Like using the English word for the receptacle object *glass* (a tumbler made of glass), we can directly transfer 'secular' to Bengali – like the word *pāblik* - commonly and successfully used in daily conversation. A twist in this linguistic situation is that, meanwhile, during the heated debates about secularity and religiosity since the 1970s, the word 'secular' in North Indian tongues has been adapted to a caricatured form '*sikulār*'[24] – though this has not happened in Bengali.

Worlds – historically constructed – are implicitly present inside languages. It is not surprising that Bengali does not have an easy word for secular, and none for secularization. Because the world in which the Bengali language is experientially fashioned/manufactured has not gone through significant secularization – at least as a dramatic change that Bengalis felt happening to themselves. By contrast, English, particularly the academic dialect of social science through which we think, is not merely comfortable with the process; it could be said to contain an implied structure of expectation that it is an inevitable process. The language itself could give rise to the idea that in the modern world, what requires 'explanation' is not the occurrence of the secularization process, but its absence.

Problems become more intractable if we begin with the sociological notion of secularization – the historical process through which religion loses dominance over cultural and social life. Clearly, religion has not lost dominance over Indian social life in any significant sense. If we use a simple distinction between the four spheres of existence – family life, social life more broadly, economic life, and political life – in neither of these spheres is there any evidence of a real decline of the force of religious beliefs and practices. Family and social life, if anything, require religious practice. Marriages are overwhelmingly solemnized in religious ceremonies. Working in factories or in modern educational, commercial, or entrepreneurial institutions does little to obstruct or undermine religious ideas. Some might claim that political life is an exception to this general dominance, but it is not. Using secularism in the Indian context simply means a

Lockean arrangement of state secularism. Through a constitutional fiction, the state pretends that citizens do not have religious affiliations. Actually, only in societies marked by deep religious sentiments does the state have to implement such constitutional techniques. State secularism, therefore, does not indicate secularization of society, but its absence. Secularization is thus not a concept that is seeking to describe an actually continuing process in Indian social life. It is the name – given after the event – to a process that happened in the European history of modernity. The differential difficulty between these two invocations of the idea of the secular – state secularism and the sociological process of secularization – is immediately reflected in vernacular linguistic expression. In Bangla, saying 'আমরা একটা ধর্মনিরপেক্ষ রাষ্ট্র চাই / *ā m'rā ek'ṭā dharmanirapekṣa rā ṣṭra cā i*' is relatively easy; that will simply mean: 'we want/seek/desire/posit/imagine a secular state'. To express a sentence like 'I think a process of secularization is going on in India' is much harder. We could rummage in our vocabulary for 'secularization as something like 'ধর্মক্ষয় / *dharmakṣaẏ*' or 'লৌকিকীকরণ / *laukikī karaṇ*' – the first meaning religion-depleted, the second, this-worldly making – neither a felicitous capture of the meaning of the English term. We discover that the language of analysis – however well practiced – stumbles or stutters when it gets ahead of the language of experience.

I want to end by pressing a bit more on the logical status of the last sentence: 'a secularization process is going on in India'. This is a contradictory idea in the following sense: nothing is more ordinary in Indian academic discussion than this sentence. A large part of Indian sociology believes that its main task is to ask and answer precisely this question. Yet, nothing is more counterintuitive in terms of our actual social experience. Devout Hindus in their millions brave potential death by Covid for a dip in the crowded river at Haridwar. Unmasked, the country's home minister rubs shoulders with the chief minister of the largest state in the crowded waters.

Yet, the way standard academic analysis proceeds, the first move, the move of the initial question, lies with Weber: Why is Indian society not undergoing a process of secularization? Rarely, if ever, would academics turn around and ask themselves, given the nature of our society, why and how do we start by asking such a question? Is not social science a study of extant facts? Of features of societies that exist? After enumerating the existing features of an existing society, social science moves into the explanatory stratum of its work and asks: Why does society work as it does? What makes it work in this particular way and no other? Empirics and explanations should constitute much of the body of social science thinking. The question 'why is religion not declining in Indian society?' starts our analytical enterprise off on the wrong foot. It implants an example of a process from a different society as if it were the experience of our own; and because it is not, it forces us to ask the explanatory question the wrong way around. Instead of asking, 'why is this happening in Indian society?', we are subtly maneuvered into asking, 'why is this not happening in Indian society?' The logical function of the word 'this' – which contains an ostensive reference to something experientially near/immediate – is displaced. Europe becomes the referent of this use of the word 'this', rather than Indian society.

Such arrangements of linguistic alienation in cognitive analysis, it can be argued, are not unprecedented in history. For long periods, precolonial societies used a system of cosmopolitan languages. Latin was the language of cosmopolitan elite intellectual culture in premodern Europe, just as Sanskrit was in India and Arabic across the Islamic world. Intellectuals could access a standardized, stable cognitive corpus to which elites of all internal regions contributed, whatever their local dialect or regional language. All these cultures prospered cognitively through cosmopolitan high languages. The Islamic world later successfully juxtaposed the Persian lingual world with the Arabic. Had Indian education not been utterly suborned to English by the colonial cultural dispensation, still, an aspiring intellectual would have spoken Bengali in ordinary quotidian exchanges and would have had to learn a hard esoteric language – Sanskrit – if they intended to participate in the circles of elite cognitive exchange. If they aspired to administrative employment, they would have added Persian. The case of Rammohan Roy shows that this was not uncommon.

The difficulty of acquiring an additional esoteric language – English – is not different in principle from that of learning Sanskrit. A student of logic coming from Andhra or Tamil country in the fifteenth century, learning Navyanyāya in Varanasi or Mithila, would be in a roughly similar linguistic situation. It can be claimed additionally that, since the cognitive sciences in the modern world carry on their operations in European languages, and now mainly in English, this arrangement of the cognition-language complex is in fact advantageous to Indians. They can access the treasures of world knowledge in every field. A non-negligible advantage is that Indian academics can work in universities worldwide. The modern knowledge system, it could be argued, simply replicates on a much larger global scale a logic of linguistic operation already implicit in premodern cultures of knowledge. The requirement of acquisition of an esoteric, technical language is simply a function of any knowledge system that is cosmopolitan, and therefore straddles a vast number of smaller local cultural worlds. This is a price paid – not for colonialism, but for cognitive cosmopolitanism. So what are we complaining about? Esoteric languages are the 'native' languages of cognitive specialization.

These arguments cannot be dismissed easily. But they pass over in silence a major peculiarity in the *colonial* configuration of knowledge and language. The last argument is interesting because it touches on an essential feature of the study of human acts. Hermeneutic theorists of the historicist school would claim, in my view quite rightly, that the first, most elementary stratum of historical understanding is the intention behind an act – what an agent, irrespective of the results, intended to do. If reconstruction of an intention requires linguistic understanding, then a grasp of the language 'internal' to the intention is essential. At the start of the enquiries in all *Geisteswissenschaften*, the basic act is to grasp that intention in its *original* language – the language in which that intention was formed.

Do We Actually Have an Advantage?

Has colonialism then given us a form of cosmopolitanism free of charge? That is what the English-restricted usually assume. The English educated in India are not merely educated in English: we must make the description stronger in order to make it accurate. Their educatedness – that is, all that they can do as educated people – is entirely confined to English. That is, by implication, when they use vernaculars, they cannot act as sophisticated cognitive subjects. Supporters of colonialism will urge us to think about what would have happened if British rulers had ignored Macaulay and decided that Indians should be educated in Sanskrit/Persian. Indian elites would have been highly skilled in Navyanyāya in our universities, and when emerging from our historically and intellectually sequestered *gurukul*s, they would have faced a wholly unfamiliar world utterly dominated by structures of finance capitalism. We would not even have had a term like 'an economy', not to speak of 'capitalism' – even to describe the world in which we lived. By giving us an education in modernity, even before modernity had broken upon us, colonialism prepared us for history.

It is not entirely untrue that colonialism also offers us an inverted, complicated, and heavily restricted version of cosmopolitanism. Indigenous languages and intellectual cultures were not obliterated; rather, with the rise of nationalism, these cultures were in some ways invigorated. But the institutional structure of education superimposed a cognitive culture functioning primarily in English. Colonialism underestimated the resourcefulness and ingenuity of people in lingual matters. If human beings can completely forget a language, then the new language they have learnt becomes their own. In Latin America, colonized people have made Spanish and Portuguese their own – without residue or embarrassment. Blacks in America have been reborn into the colonial language. Du Bois or C. L. R. James did not leave in nostalgic search for the language their ancestors had left behind. English has become their own. The effect of colonialism on our thinking culture is in-between these instances. Colonialism displaced the high languages with epistemic functions – Sanskrit and Persian – and substituted them with English. But Indian vernaculars did not fade and become entirely defunct. They remained vibrant and creative in many high functions – primarily in literature – the major implement for the self-interpretation of a society. Yet, as the formal institutional structure of education expanded during the colonial and the postcolonial periods, the primary language for cognitive intellection remained English – to which a majority of ordinary people have little access.

Time Inside a Language

There is, as it were, a time internal to languages. Languages exist in, and contain within themselves, a particular historical time – consisting of two parts: the time of its effective past and the moment it exists in in the present. Effective past refers to only those elements of the past which are still active and intelligible and deployed in the present. For a modern, educated Bengali, Kadambari or Mitravinda are not parts of its effective past. They are not likely to know of the story from Banabhatta or the puranic lore that Mitravinda was one of Krishna's main spouses. By contrast, Radha is part of this effective past: no Bengali needs to consult an encyclopedia to know who she is. My point is that the 'inside' of the Bengali language contains a lot of the usable premodern literary past. In contrast, the English language contains familiar terms which are parts of the moment contained inside the historicity of English – as a European language – but not present in Bengali's historical moment. 'Secular' is a term of this kind. It is impossible for the educated Bengali not to know this concept: but it is hard to find a semantically adequate equivalent. The 'translation problem' can also be divided into two parts – one part consists of rational or logical intelligibility. Can I intellectually (rationally) understand what it is saying? The second part is a more experiential recognizability. Can I understand, i.e., convert into an equivalent in my experience, what living in a secular society means? My argument is that we cannot. This implies that when we say we 'understand', we are conflating the first meaning of translatability with the second.

But we patently live in a historical condition – lingually, in terms of our linguistic experience – that is quite different from the linguistically more singular, or homogeneous experience of societies that are unmarked by colonial history. If we continue to treat bilingualism in the first model – the parallel existence of two lingual spheres which exist side by side and between which there is exchange – we would not grasp its full complexity and its real predicaments. Instead of that model, we must use a more complex and untidy one in which besides existence as parallel spheres, the two languages interrupt each other's internal work, intercept, facilitate, obstruct, unexpectedly modify communication, and one in which linguality is constitutive of the cognitive processes at every step.

Notes

1 In earlier stages of German philosophy, the term 'estrangement' is used with increasing subtlety and complexity – in Hegel and in Feuerbach, but Marx's use imparts to it an unprecedented sharpness and subtlety, See Karl Marx, 'Estranged Labour', in Marx (1967).

2 Some studies of Indian linguistic public spheres take this approach, e.g. Orsini (2012), or Naregal (2001).
3 There are two groups of authors who write extensively in Bengali: some renowned academic scholars also write regularly in Bengali; but there are a substantial group of academics who write on politics, political science, and political/social theory entirely in the vernacular.
4 The effect of what premodern philosophy would call *saṃskāra*.
5 '*adhīrā yamunā taraṅga-ākūlā akūlā re, timiradukūlā re.*' Ṭhākur (1973: 439).
6 Mamata Banerjee's party has won in this election.
7 As opposed to the description.
8 In the works of early social scientists, we find examples of such observations which they saw as exceptions, but we would now view them as historical differences (cf. Kothari 1970).
9 For a well-known example of analysis of this question, see McIntyre (1964).
10 This is now so widely accepted as to be platitudinous.
11 I am indebted to Hans Harder for pointing out, however, that this is not always the case: though externally the word is the same, the conveyance of meaning cannot always be taken for granted.
12 I realize that there is a separate question about the communicability of these ideas across the vernaculars. That can also raise significant difficulties, though the occurrence of the same *tatsama* words might facilitate the communication.
13 Two of the earliest Bengali thinkers to reflect on political modernity and its historical challenges – Bankimchandra Chattopadhyay and Bhudev Mukhopadhyay – clearly noted the huge significance of this concept.
14 This is a deeply paradoxical argument: that Indians can seem or act like a nation only as long as they are collectively colonized by the British. Actually, there is no internal adhesion among Indians, what held them together and gave rise to the illusion that they were one people was their common subjection.
15 Cf. particularly his essays in the collection 'Bibidha prabandha (dvitīẏa khaṇḍa)' (Caṭṭopādhyāẏ 1994: 257–380), many of which focus on issues connected with the *bāṅgālī jāti*.
16 Cf. Tagore's *Nationalism* (Tagore 1917). Tagore's thinking about the nation has been analyzed at length in Partha Chatterjee, 'Rābīndrik neśan kī?' (2018), and in his Lineages of Political Society (2011).
17 Interestingly, in Bangla, the term proposed for a translation of the English word class was never *jāti*, but *śreṇī* or less frequently *barga*.
18 The *-bād* at the end translating 'ism'.
19 For instance, a popular patriotic song by Atulprasad Sen contained the uplifting line: *dekhiẏā bhārate mahājātir utthān, jagajan mānibe bismaẏ*. 'The people of the world will wonder at the rise of a *mahājāti* in India' (Sen 1931: 91, song no. 75).
20 Though this observation should not be overgeneralized. The highly technical language of philosophical discussion in Sanskrit – found for instance, the technical terms for philosophic debate in the *Nyāyasūtra* – is not meaningful to an educated Bengali – without specialized training.
21 Cf. Makhanlal Roychoudhury (1941) and Supriya Gandhi (2021).
22 Though the work of political theorists like Rajeev Bhargava has shown that even this was not devoid of problems. Use of the term 'secular' often caused problems because the juridical devices used by constitutional systems in France, the US, and the UK were very distinct. Use of the term 'secular' indeterminately meant that which juridical provision was meant was not always clear.
23 There is a different conceptual question in this field about the significant difference between the original German meaning of some Weberian concepts, and their subsequent conventionalised meanings in English.
24 See Rita Kothari's excellent work on this question (Kothari 2006).

References

Caṭṭopādhyāy̐, Baṅkim'candra. 1994. *Baṅkim'candra racanābalī*, Vol. 1. Kalikātā: Sāhitya Saṃsad.
Caṭṭopādhyāy̐, Pārtha. 2018. 'Rābīndrik *nation* kī?'. In: idem: *Prajā o tantra*. Kal'kātā: Anuṣṭup, 67–102.
Chatterjee, Partha. 2011. *Lineages of Political Society*. New York: Columbia University Press.
Gandhi, Supriya. 2021. *The Emperor Who Never Was: Dara Shukoh in Mughal India*. Cambridge, MA and London, England: Harvard University Press.
Kothari, Rajni. 1970. *Politics in India*. Delhi, Hyderabad: Orient Longman.
Kothari, Rita. 2006. *Translating India: The Cultural Politics of English*. New Delhi: Foundation Books.
McIntyre, A. 1964. 'Is Understanding Religion Compatible with Believing?'. In: Hick, J. (ed.): *Faith and the Philosophers*. London: Palgrave Macmillan.
Marx, Karl. 1967. 'Estranged Labour'. In: Karl Marx: *Economic and Philosophical Manuscripts of 1844*. Moscow: Progress Publishers.
Nandy, Ashis. 1988. 'The Politics of Secularism and the Recovery of Religious Tolerance'. *Alternatives* 13, 1988, 177–194.
Naregal, Veena. 2001. *Language, Politics, Elites and the Public Sphere: Western India under Colonialism*. New Delhi: Permanent Black.
Orsini, Francesca. 2012. *The Hindi Public Sphere 1920`1940*. New Delhi: Oxford University Press.
Roychoudhury, Makhanlal. 1941. *Din-i-Ilahi*. Calcutta: University of Calcutta.
Sen, Atul Prasād. 1931. *Gītiguñja*. Kalikātā: Sādhāraṇ Brāhmasamāj.
Tagore, Rabindranath. 1917. *Nationalism*. New York: Macmillan.
Ṭhākur, Rabīndranāth. 1973 (1380 BE). *Gītabitān*. Kalikātā: Biśvabhārati Granthan'bibhāg.

8

BRITISH TRANSLATORS, BHAGAT SINGH, AND 'ATHEISM'

How 'Reverse Translation' Alters the Meaning of Philosophical Concepts

Ruth Vanita

This chapter is a preliminary enquiry into a process for which I have invented the term 'reverse translation' since there seems to be no specific term available for it. Reverse translation is the process by which the meaning of a Hindu philosophical concept changes in Indian languages because of a process of incorrect translation to and from English.

At the outset, I must distinguish my work from that of Paul Hacker, who uses the term 'Neo-Hinduism' to criticise modern Hindu thinkers' 're-interpretation' of Hindu concepts such as *dharma*, and also to argue that modern Hinduism has nothing in common with earlier Hindu thought and that Hinduism as a unified tradition has never existed.[1] I disagree completely with Hacker; where Hacker sees modern Hindu thinkers, such as Bankimchandra Chattopadhyay and Vivekananda, as actively borrowing Christian concepts in order to make Hinduism competitive with Christianity, I argue that European Christian lexicographers and scholars, many of whom were missionaries, mistranslated words like *āstika* and *nāstika*, with the result that many Indians ended up partly or wholly misunderstanding the meanings of these words.

Reverse Translation and Intercultural Mimesis

Reverse translation is one dimension of what Hallisey terms 'intercultural mimesis' (Hallisey 1995: 33). Nicholson describes intercultural mimesis as a process whereby nineteenth-century European thinkers 'appropriate certain concepts or symbols that they find in non-Western traditions and then recontextualize these concepts or symbols for ideological reasons specific to the European cultural sphere' (Nicholson 2010: 126).

DOI: 10.4324/9781003279921-11

What I am calling reverse translation is the next stage, whereby European scholars retranslate these appropriated concepts into Indian languages, thus altering their meaning in the Indian cultural sphere, both popular and scholarly.

The first stage, then, is the translation of philosophical terms from a Christian lexicon into Indian classical and vernacular languages, using non-equivalent Indian philosophical terms. In the second stage, those Indian philosophical terms are retranslated into English, using the Christian terms from the first stage. In the third and final stage, which completes reverse translation, the new, altered meaning of the retranslated Indian concept becomes its primary meaning in Indian languages, such as Hindi and Marathi, and to some extent (at the popular rather than scholarly level) even in the classical language Sanskrit. In this chapter, I examine some examples of concepts whose meaning has changed in this way.

I am concerned here not primarily with translation from Sanskrit to English but with 'reverse translation' that changes meanings in Indian languages. My focus is not on non-Indian readers but on Indian readers who are bilingual to different degrees and for whom English has become the primary language of thinking, even if not the language of feeling or dreaming.

'Atheists'?

My primary example of the way reverse translation works is the word *nāstika*. In most Indian languages, the word *nāstika* (and its variants, such as *nāttikar* in Tamil) has come to mean 'atheist' and *āstika* 'theist'. Nicholson speculates that scholars, such as Wendy Doniger, who incorrectly translate these terms as 'atheist' and 'theist', may be influenced 'by the modern Hindi words *āstik* and *nāstik*' (Nicholson 2010: 166). This explanation, though, puts the cart before the horse. Hindi, Bengali, Marathi, Punjabi and Gujarati obtain the word *nāstika* from Sanskrit. In these languages, these words acquire the new meanings 'theist' and 'atheist' not from Sanskrit but from incorrect Sanskrit-English translation followed by reverse translation from English into these languages.

Āstika derives from *asti*, which means 'is'. An *āstika* is one who says, 'is'. A *nāstika* is one who says, 'is not'. An *āstika* asserts the existence of something that is not matter. Crucially, however, this 'something' need not be a personal God. Three to four *āstika* schools of Hindu philosophy do not require positing a personal God. *Sāṅkhya* was an extremely influential school of Hindu philosophy; its concepts, such as *guṇa*s and *prakṛti*, undergird the *Bhagavad Gītā*. Some *Sāṅkhya* philosophers assume the existence of some kind of God; others do not.

Mimāṃsa is another important school of Hindu philosophy which argues that there is no need to posit God as creator. Early *Nyāya* philosophers write very little about God. Later *Nyāya* philosophers offer arguments both for and against God's existence. *Vaiśeṣika* philosophers are also divided on the matter.

Thus, *Sāṅkhya*, *Mimāṃsa*, *Vaiśeṣika* and *Nyāya* are Hindu schools of philosophy which could be classified as *nāstika* if this word meant 'atheist'. But from antiquity onwards, these schools have consistently been classified as *āstika*.

Some ancient Indian thinkers termed any school of thought *nāstika* that did not accept the Vedas. By this definition, Buddhism, Jainism and Cārvāka could be considered *nāstika*. However, other ancient thinkers contested this classification. Nicholson demonstrates that *āstika* meant one who accepts the premises of *dharma*, and that neither Buddhists not Jains considered themselves *nāstika* (173–75). Nicholson, who neatly translates *āstika* and *nāstika*, respectively, as 'affirmer' and 'denier', provides a detailed account of ancient, Hindu, Buddhist and Jain definitions of these terms, arguing that they refer more to ethics than to logic, and that a focus on liberation, the next life and the nature of truth or reality is crucial to an *āstika* thinker or school of thought.

Atheists deny the existence of both God and the soul (or spirit or any non-material existent), while *āstika* Hindu philosophers may or may not posit God but they do posit consciousness. Consciousness is not the same as God or even the same as 'soul'. Therefore, neither 'theist' nor 'atheist' has an exact equivalent in Sanskrit because Hindu thought operates on different premises.

To sum up, then, the primary difference between an atheist and a *nāstika* is that an atheist in a monotheistic religion, such as Christianity and Islam, denies the existence of God, which is the foundational premise of these religions. An atheist's denial of soul, an afterlife and, conceivably, *dharma*, follows from the basic denial of God. On the other hand, a *nāstika* does not accept the Vedas, from which may (or may not) follow a denial of the existence of Gods, Goddesses, Self or consciousness. However, as stated above, *Mimāṃsa* philosophers also deny the need to posit a creator God; nevertheless, they are *āstika*, not *nāstika*.

Dictionaries Invent Meaning

What is the process, then, by which *āstika* and *nāstika* (or *āstik* and *nāstik*) come to mean 'theist' and 'atheist' in Indian languages? Dictionaries are crucial to the process. The first Sanskrit-English dictionary is H. H. Wilson's in 1832. This dictionary defines 'nāstika m. (-kaḥ)' thus: 'An atheist, but applied by the orthodox *Hindūs*, to any one who denies the divine authority of the *Vedas*, or doubts the legends of the *Purāṇas*. E. nāsti there is not (a god, &c.)' (463).

Wilson first unequivocally states that the meaning of *nāstika* is 'atheist'. Then he modifies this: 'but applied by the orthodox Hindus [...]'. By implication, this indicates that for 'unorthodox Hindus' *nāstika* means atheist but orthodox Hindus have twisted it to apply to disbelievers in legends. Wilson cites no evidence for either assertion.

Fourteen years later, Yates's 1846 Sanskrit-English dictionary, which is expressly described on the title page as designed for Indian schools and colleges, picks up Wilson's definition without his modification, and simply states: 'nāstika (kaḥ) 1. *m.* An atheist' (413b). The process of reverse translation is complete, with the original meanings erased.

The process of reverse translation that is implicit in Wilson becomes explicit in Monier-Williams's influential dictionaries. First, in his 1851 English-Sanskrit dictionary, Monier-Williams translates 'atheist' into Sanskrit as 'nāstikaḥ, devanindakaḥ, anīśvaravādī *m.* (n)' (852b).

Next, in his 1872 Sanskrit-English dictionary, Monier-Williams performs what I call a reverse translation. To do this, he repeats and expands Wilson's statement:

> *Nāstika, as, ī, am*, atheistical, unbelieving, infidel, an unbeliever, applied by the orthodox Hindūs to any one who denies the divine authority of the Vedas and a future life, or doubts the legends of the Purāṇas; [cf. *āstika.*]—*Nāstika-tā*, f. or *nāstika-tva, am*, n. or *nāstikya, am*, n. infidelity, disbelief, atheism, denial of the deity, of a future state, of the authority of the Vedas, &c.; Buddhism, heresy, &c.—*Nāstika-mata, am*, n. an atheistical opinion.
> *(0481-a)*

Here, Monier-Williams adds disbelief in a 'future state', and a 'future life' to his definition, which Nicholson shows to be part of the ancient Hindu philosophers' definition. But Monier-Williams adds to his definition the terms 'infidel' (literally, unfaithful) and 'heresy', which are Christian theological terms and have no equivalents in Sanskrit.[2]

It is important to note here that both H. H. Wilson and Monier-Williams were committed to the Christian evangelisation of India. After his appointment to the Boden Chair of Sanskrit at Oxford, Monier-Williams wrote a book, *Hinduism* (Monier-Williams 1878) which concluded with the statement that thanks to Western education, Hinduism (which he terms a 'Hydra', a many-headed monstrous serpent, 227) was 'everywhere tottering and ready to fall' (184), and that Christians should take advantage of this and proceed to convert all Hindus, Muslims and Jains (184–86).

Twelve years later, Apte's *Practical Sanskrit-English Dictionary*, the first such dictionary compiled by an Indian, reasserts Wilson's and Monier-Williams's definition of *nāstika* as 'atheist' but omits the inaccurate reference to disbelief in 'Puranic legends'. Apte writes: 'nāstika nāstika. [...] An atheist, unbeliever, one who denies the authority of the Vedas and a future life or the existence of a supreme ruler or creator of the universe; Śi. 16. 7; Ms. 2. 11; 8. 22' (0617-a). Here, Apte defines *nāstika* somewhat correctly but incorrectly translates it as 'atheist' even though the word 'atheist' has nothing to do with the Vedas and an atheist's denial of an afterlife follows from the denial of God, while *nāstika*s do not necessarily deny an afterlife and rebirth.

Apte is the first to cite sources for his definition. He cites *nāstiko vedanindakaḥ (Manusmṛti 2.11)*, which means that a *nāstika* is one who denies the authority of the Vedas. He mentions *Manusmṛti* 8.22, but that verse simply states that a land full of *nāstika*s quickly perishes and does not offer any explanation of the word. Likewise, the verse (16.7) that Apte cites from Magha's seventh-century epic, *Śiśupāla vadha*, does not define the term *nāstika*. The term there occurs in a list of qualities: *ahitādanapatrapastrasannatimātrojjhitabhīranāstikaḥ* (*Śiśupāla vadha* 16.7; Dundas 2017: 6526).

Apte acknowledges in his preface that he is 'greatly indebted' to Monier-Williams's dictionary. The *Shabda Sagara Sanskrit-English Dictionary*, 1900, reproduces Wilson's definition verbatim (Bhattacharya 1900: 386b).

In this progression, then, British lexicographers first translate the English word 'atheist' into Sanskrit as *nāstika*, cursorily semi-acknowledging that Hindus interpret it differently and then reverse-translate *nāstika* into English as 'atheist'. Indian lexicographers follow suit, citing sources that do not provide evidence for the new meaning.

Finally, Hindi-English dictionaries repeat what Sanskrit-English dictionaries have cemented. Platts, in his 1884 Urdu, Hindi and English dictionary, is the first to actually translate the word *nāstik* accurately, before going on to repeat the statements of Sanskrit lexicographers:

> '*nāstik*, adj. & s.m. (f. – *ī*), "Saying (or one who says) *nāstī*, 'it is not'"; denying, atheistical, unbelieving; – one who denies the authority of the Vedas, or who expresses doubts as to the authenticity of the Purāṇas; – one who denies a future state; – an atheist, unbeliever, infidel: – nāstik-mat, s.m. An atheistical opinion; atheism'... *nāstikatā* 'Heterodoxy (esp. in reference to the authority of the Vedas &c.); atheism, unbelief, impiety'.
>
> *(1114)*

No surprise that the Oxford Hindi-English dictionary pares this down to a simple equivalence: '*nāstik* [S.], adj. & m. 1.adj. saying *nāsti* "it is not": atheistic. 2. m. an atheist; an unbeliever. – *nāstikvad*, m. atheism. *Nāstikatā* [S.], f. 1. Atheism; non-belief. 2. Heterodoxy (as in denial of the authority of the Vedas)' (555).

Significantly, Bopp's 1847 *Glossarium Sanscritum*, which is a Sanskrit-Latin dictionary, is somewhat more accurate: 'nāstika *m.* [...] qui vitam futuram esse negat, qui *brahmanicae* religioni non addictus est. RAM. I. 52. 15.: nāstiko jāyate janaḥ' (194b). This translates roughly as, 'one who denies a future life, and is not attached to the brahmins' religion'. Bopp does not use the Latin word *atheus*, which means atheist, to translate *nāstika*. This suggests that translating from one classical language to another may produce less distortion than translating from a classical language (Sanskrit) into a vernacular, whether the vernacular is English or Hindi.

The effects of these incorrect translations in dictionaries become evident in English translations of the Ramayana. In the 1870s, Griffith's translation of the Valmiki Ramayana renders the word *nāstikam* (in some most likely interpellated verses in the Rama-Jabali dialogue) as 'cursed infidel' (Griffith 1880–84: 219). Rao and Murthy's translation changes this to 'atheist', and they remark in their gloss: 'Rama refutes the atheistic arguments of Jabali' (2.109.33-34).

Modern Usage: Bhagat Singh's Essay

Let us take a well-known example of *nāstik* – in translations of Bhagat Singh's essay, 'Why I am an Atheist' into modern Indian languages. It is predictably translated into Hindi as '*Maiṃ nāstik kyoṃ hū̃?*' Reformers and nationalists of all stripes, from Periyar to Savarkar, had already used the word *nāstik* and its equivalents like *nāttikar* to mean 'atheist'.

This is not just a matter of a word that changes in meaning or acquires a new meaning. It is a matter of contested meaning. This can be seen in Bhagat Singh's essay, where the Western concept of atheism or disbelief in a personal God who creates, supervises and punishes living beings, sits uneasily alongside Indian philosophical world views that do not require such a God.

Bhagat Singh received the word 'atheist' in the context of reverse translation. But he also received other concepts from the Arya Samaj and from an Advaita Vedanta thinker who was a contemporary of his. Although he was only 23 when he was executed, he wisely notes in his essay that tearing down blind faith creates a space to construct 'a new philosophy' and that 'sometimes some material of the old faith may be used for the purpose of reconstruction' (Singh 1931: 198). He then frankly states, 'Let me admit at the very outset that I have not been able to study much on this point. I had a great desire to study the Oriental philosophy but I could not get any chance or opportunity to do the same' (Singh 1931:198). Bhagat Singh had interesting ideas about how to blend schools of thought and develop what he calls 'a new philosophy'.[3] A parallel example is that of Percy Shelley, who at the age of 18 wrote a pamphlet, 'The Necessity of Atheism', which got him expelled from Oxford, but having lived on to the advanced age of 29, he did manage to develop a new pantheistic philosophy.

Scholars now agree that Bhagat Singh did not write his essay in Punjabi or in Urdu but in English. This makes sense as the framework of his argument is primarily drawn from Western thinkers. He writes that he studied Bakunin, Marx, Lenin and Trotsky. The only work by any of these writers that he names is Bakunin's 'God and State' (Singh 1931: 196). In this work, Bakunin adduces the four main arguments for atheism that several Western thinkers had adduced before him, and that Bhagat Singh also puts forward: first, that an omnipotent and benevolent God would not create an imperfect and unjust world; second, that the universality of a belief does not prove its correctness; third, that religion exists to delude people, especially oppressed people; and fourth, that science explains the world and humans as being made of matter alone.

The difference between Bakunin and Bhagat Singh is that Bakunin engages in detail with Christian theology. Bhagat Singh does not do this but he does state that Christianity and Islam believe that good people will be rewarded in heaven and bad people punished in hell, which, he argues, is poor consolation for injustice. He mentions Sikhism only once in the essay: 'I had begun to preserve the unshorn and unclipped long hair but I could never believe in the mythology and doctrines of Sikhism or any other religion' (Singh 1931: 196). He mentions Buddhism and Jainism only once but does not engage with them.

He does, however, engage with the concept of rebirth, which he names as Hindu: 'A God-believing Hindu might be expecting to be reborn as a king'. He addresses rebirth not as a law of actions and consequences but instead places it in the Christian framework of a personal God meting out punishments to sinners:

> Well, you Hindus, you say that all the present sufferers belonged to the class of sinners of the previous births. [...] But, what is the nature of punishment inflicted by God upon men, even if we suppose them to be offenders? You say he sends them to be born as a cow, a cat, a tree [...].'
>
> *(Singh 1931: 199)*

Singh asks with regard to his imminent execution, 'What is the consolation? [...] A God-believing Hindu might be expecting to be reborn as a king, a Muslim or a Christian might dream of the luxuries to be enjoyed in paradise' (Singh 1931: 197). Despite having been raised, as he states, under the influence of his grandfather, who, he says, was 'an orthodox Arya Samajist' and having recited the *gāyatrī mantra* every day as a schoolboy (*ibid.*: 195–96), Singh nowhere mentions the Upanishadic concept of *mokṣa* or even the Buddhist and Hindu concept of *nirvāṇa*.

Bhagat Singh's Only Indian Source

The closest Singh comes to the concept of self-realisation or liberation is his citation of the book *Common Sense* by Soham Swami (1858–1918). This is the only Indian source that Singh cites for his idea of atheism.[4] Soham, the name taken by the author, whose given name was Shyama Kanta Bandyopadhyaya, means 'I am that' (*saḥ* + *aham*). In his writings, Soham refers to *ātman* as non-different from every being. This is an entirely different concept from that of

God as an omnipotent person-like being creating the world and punishing or rewarding its inhabitants. Upanishadic schools of philosophy are not based on belief or faith but on premises about the nature of existence.

The book *Common Sense* is an exposition of Advaita Vedānta. Singh does not mention the term *vedānta* but instead refers to Soham Swami and his student Niralamba Swami's Advaita Vedanta philosophy as 'only a sort of mystic atheism' (Singh 1931: 196).

The full title of Soham Swami's book is *Common Sense or Ekatma Vijnana. Ekātma vijñāna* means knowledge of the one Self. Bhagat Singh does not mention the Sanskrit title. In this book, Swami tries to prove that all religions and ideas of a personal creator – God – are full of inconsistencies and that realising the divinity in all beings is the only goal of life.

Soham Swami wrote both in English and in Bengali. In English, he wrote a book-length poem entitled *Truth* in 1913, which may be the first exposition of Vedanta in English verse by an Indian. In his introduction to the book, Soham Swami's student, Swami Nirbikalpa, states that Soham Swami has put the 'abstruse thoughts of Vedanta' in English verse just as ancient sages expressed these thoughts in Sanskrit verse (Swami 2018: iv). Nirbikalpa writes that Soham instructs the reader to destroy 'the irrational belief in an imaginary Personal God' and to eradicate 'superstitions, rituals and cults' fostered by it since these 'suppress the growth of *truth*' (Swami 2018: ii, italics original).

In the poem itself, Soham Swami makes statements that sound very much like Bhagat Singh's statements: 'The God whom East and West alike acclaim/I found imposture and an empty name' (Swami 2018: 1). He advances standard arguments against the idea of God as omnipotent, unlimited and benevolent creator, asking why such a God would allow suffering, unrequited love, injustice, natural disasters and death: 'His frequent failure, loss and waste/Prove Him an inexpert/A novice without skill or taste/And not in work alert!' (Swami 2018: 7). Section 6 of the poem is titled 'Myth of Personal God with Attributes' (Swami 2018: 22).

Having demolished Jewish, Christian and Muslim ideas of God in Section 3 and Hindu ideas of God in Section 4, he interprets Kapila, Vyasa and Patanjali in Section 5 as using the term 'Iswar' not for a personal God but for a self-realised sage (Swami 2018: 18) and attacks Hindu 'idolatry' in Section 7. He argues in favour of meat-eating as well as science, discusses 'Brahm and Maya' (*ibid.*: 42–44, 75–78), reaches a standard Advaita Vedānta conclusion: 'But Brahm thou art, nor portion, nor apart/Realise, restraining mind, that "That thou art"' and then provides instructions for how to attain self-realisation (*ibid.*: 78, 79–93): 'Unless this memory and mind do part,/From such diversions [desire and attachment] thou shalt surely smart;/ That memory, thou must eradicate,/To culminate sublime Samadhi state' (*ibid.*: 92–93).

The primary meaning of *nāstik* in Hindi as well as variants in Marathi, Gujarati, Punjabi, Bengali, Telugu and Tamil has now come to be 'atheist'. Wikipedia, fount of all knowledge, defines *nāstiktā* thus:

नास्तिकता अथवा नास्तिकवाद या अनीश्वरवाद (English: Atheism), वह सिद्धांत है जो जगत् की सृष्टि करने वाले, इसका संचालन और नियंत्रण करनेवाले किसी भी ईश्वर के अस्तित्व को सर्वमान्य प्रमाण के न होने के आधार पर स्वीकार नहीं करता। (नास्ति = न + अस्ति = नहीं है, अर्थात ईश्वर नहीं है।) नास्तिक लोग ईश्वर (भगवान) के अस्तित्व का स्पष्ट प्रमाण न होने के कारण झूठ करार देते हैं।.

(Accessed 12 March 2021)[5]

My translation: '*nāstikˈtā* or *nāstikˈvād* or *anīśvarˈvād* (English atheism) is that principle which, on account of the absence of evidence accepted by everyone, does not accept the existence of a God who creates, runs and controls the world. Nāsti=na+asti=is not, which means God is not). *Nāstik* people term the existence of God a lie because of the lack of clear evidence'.

Only after providing this incorrect definition and etymology does Wikipedia go on to give a garbled account of earlier definitions.[6] It then proceeds to reverse the ancient and accepted meaning of *nāstika* in Hindu philosophy:

वास्तव में न्याय और वेदांत दर्शनों को छोड़कर भारत के अन्य दर्शन सांख्य, योग, वैशेषिक, बौद्ध और जैन नास्तिक दर्शन कहे जा सकते हैं क्योंकि इनमें ईश्वर को सर्जक, पालक और विनाशक नहीं माना गया है। ऐसे नास्तिकों को ही अनीश्वरवादी कहते हैं।.

(Accessed March 12, 2021)

My translation: 'Actually, with the exception of Nyaya and Vedanta philosophies, all other philosophies of India, including Sankhya, Yoga, Vaisheshika, Buddhism and Jainism can be called *nāstik* philosophies because none of them accepts God as creator, preserver and destroyer. Such *nāstik*s are called *anīśvarvādīs'*.

Thus, a combination of ignorant presentism and a sequence of reverse translations (English to Sanskrit; Sanskrit to English; English to Hindi; English and Hindi to Sanskrit) changes the ancient classifications of *āstika* / *nāstika* philosophies. The incorrect equivalence here established between *nāstikˈtā* and *anīśvarˈvād* is significant, betraying a determination to equate two terms that are different. As Nicholson points out, some later twentieth-century scholars writing in English about Sanskrit texts, such as Wendy Doniger and Krishna Sharma, incorrectly translate the Sanskrit terms *āstika* and *nāstika* as 'theist' and 'atheist' (Doniger 1991: 18; Sharma 1987: 63–64).

Why It Matters

One may ask, why does this change in meaning matter? Words in every language morph and accumulate new meanings. The reason it matters is that this is not a case of words organically changing meaning. For example, the word 'awe', as in 'awe-struck', has increasingly come to mean 'excellent' or 'enjoyable' as in 'awesome coffee' (a phrase commonly used, and also a brand of coffee sold on Amazon). This is an organic change, arising from a dwindling of the sense of sublimity and of reverence in the Anglophone world.

But when meanings change due to reverse translation, and primarily due to Western colonial lexicographers and scholars, non-Western philosophical frameworks are refitted into the Procrustean bed of Western thought. The shift in philosophical framework gradually occurs with those Indians who may be bilingual but who read and think primarily in English and are also the primary makers of public opinion.

Thus, modern Indian commentators on the *Gita* and on Hinduism in general, such as Gandhi, Sri Aurobindo and Radhakrishnan, who studied and wrote in English, inevitably used reverse translations that had become part of the English language, incorporating ideas of theism, atheism, evil, sin and religion into their analyses of Hindu thought; however, these thinkers also drew on their direct knowledge of Indian languages and Hindu scriptures and popular devotional literature.[7] Thus, their thinking was not, as Hacker claims, based on borrowing Christian concepts. At the popular level, for example, in films and television, but also in everyday language, as discussed above in the case of Bhagat Singh and the non-scholarly editors of Wikipedia, the effects of reverse translation are sometimes more sweeping.

It is significant that the reverse does not happen. When philosophical concepts are translated both ways, English concepts do not change their meaning. It is well known that the word and concept *dharma* has been reduced to 'duty', 'righteousness' or 'virtue' and to the entirely different concept of 'religion', as when one has to fill out a form and put down one's *dharma* as Muslim or Christian. But the word 'religion' has not radically changed its meaning even though *dharma* is now an English word.

Let us briefly consider the mistranslation of *dharma* and *adharma* as good and evil in twentieth-century translations of *Bhagavad-Gītā* 4.7: *yadā yadā hi dharmasya glānir bhavati bhārata* / *abhyutthānam adharmasya tadātmānam sṛjāmy aham*. In 1944, Isherwood and Prabhavananda, translating the text for the Vedanta Society, render *dharma* and *adharma* in this verse as 'goodness' and 'evil' (50), and in 4.8 as 'righteousness'.

Nikhilananda's translation of *Gītā* 4:7-8, in the same year, 1944, is much more accurate: 'Whenever there is a decline of dharma, O Bhārata, and a rise of adharma, I incarnate Myself. For the protection of the good, for the destruction of the wicked, and for the establishment of dharma, I am born in every age' (48–49). Note his retention of dharma and his use of 'wicked', not 'evil'. I will return to these two words.

Despite this early accurate translation, later translators revert to earlier terminology. Juan Mascaro's 1962 translation again has 'righteousness' and 'unrighteousness' in 4.7 and 'evil in men' for *duṣkṛtām* in 4.8 (23). Barbara

Stoler Miller's 1986 translation, has 'sacred duty' for *dharma*, 'chaos' for *adharma* and 'men who do evil' for *duṣkṛtām* (50). These have been the two translations most widely used in U.S. classrooms.

The Gita Press version by unnamed translators (purporting to be based on Jayalal Goyandka's Hindi translation of the *Gītā*), first published in 2002, reverts to 'righteousness', 'unrighteousness' and 'evil-doers' (56). The Norton critical edition's translation by Flood and Martin, published as late as 2012, repeats these three words (Flood and Martin 2012: 7–8).

However, Hindus are now becoming increasingly aware of the effects of this type of reverse translation.[8] Graham Schweig's 2007 translation follows Nikhilananda in retaining *dharma* and *adharma* (Schweig 2007: 71).

What is at stake in these choices of words? 'Evil' is a Christian concept, not a Hindu one. The Latin word *malum*, which is translated as 'evil', refers to inherent sinfulness (connected to the doctrine of original sin) and is closely associated with the Devil and his acts. The Germanic or old English word *yfel*, from which comes the word 'evil', means 'bad' or 'wicked' but, over time, it comes to mean something much stronger than that. *Duṣṭa*, from the root *duh* (harm, distress, pain or sorrow), is related to *duḥkha*. The difference between *duṣṭa* (bad) and evil is evident in common usage. A bilingual parent may call a naughty child *duṣṭ* in Hindi but would never call the child evil in English. There is also a clear difference between 'bad' and 'evil' in English. Bad behaviour is not the same as evil.

Even within Christianity, the concept of 'evil' is problematic, as Augustine points out. Despite being one of the two main developers of the doctrine of original sin (the first being Paul), Augustine argues that Christianity as a monotheistic religion cannot accommodate the concept of innate evil. In his *Confessions*, Augustine narrates how he kept searching for an answer to the question of evil and finally realised that there is no such thing as evil because everything that God created is good:

> [...] all things that are, are good, and as to that evil, the origin of which I was seeking for, it is not a substance ... you [God] have made all things good, nor are there any substances at all which you have not made. ... To you, then, there is no such thing at all as evil. [...] If it were a substance, it would be good.
>
> *(Warner, VII: 13, 140–141)*

He distinguishes wickedness from evil, and writes that wickedness is just a turning away of the will from God (VII: 14, 143).

Though Augustine's logic is irrefutable, most Christians, it is safe to say, are unaware of this and consider evil to be real. This is because Christianity is strongly influenced by the binary thinking of good versus evil, God versus Devil. Augustine belonged for nine years to the Manichean religion. Manicheanism was a thoroughgoing dualistic religion, founded in Iran by the prophet Mani. From the third to the seventh centuries, it was one of the most widespread religions in the world, and it lingered on until the fourteenth century. Even though the church declared it heretical and stamped it out, Manicheanism's idea that the forces of good and evil, God and the devil, are constantly battling one another both inside each living being, and also out in the world, leaves a strong imprint on Augustine's thinking as well as on Christianity.

The morphing of the meaning of 'evil' in Latin can be seen in the 1486 book *Malleus Maleficarum* (often translated as The Hammer of Witches). Even though several theologians of the Inquisition criticised the book, it sold more copies in Europe until 1678 than any other book besides the Bible. This book recommends the extermination of witches, not their reformation. Before 1400, prosecutions for witchcraft were rare, and witchcraft was viewed as a type of delusion or hallucination. After the publication of this book came the great Renaissance witch-hunts of the sixteenth and seventeenth centuries. The book helped change the meaning of the word *malum* from harmful acts to evil acts, done mostly by women in association with the devil. The book argues for the inherently evil nature of women which makes them vulnerable to the devil.

Hindu philosophies are forms of radical monism. Monism is the principle that all things are ultimately one. It is therefore even less possible to accommodate the idea of evil in a Hindu framework than in a monotheistic one. Hindu demons or *asura*s are cousins of the Gods and are not irredeemably damned as Satan is in Christianity and Islam. Dualism in Hindu philosophy is not a dualism of good and evil but of two forces, *puruṣa* and *prakṛti*, neither of which is evil.

Demons are not the same as devils. Demons, as analysed in *Bhagavadgītā* chapter 16, are nothing but greedy and egotistical tyrants. There are almost no poor demons in Hindu narrative; almost all of them are rich and seek more wealth and power.[9] *Bhagavadgītā* chapter 16 describes demonic beings as those who try to accumulate wealth by unjust means (*anyāyenārtha*). They boast of their wealth and high birth, think that they can control everyone and plan to kill others. They are therefore consumed by anxiety.

Greedy kings like Duryodhana are termed 'demons'. However, demons have the potential to become good; they are not inherently bad and they are certainly not eternally damned as devils are in Christianity. Vibhishana is from a demon family but is good. Even Duryodhana ends up in the same celestial world as the Pandavas and Krishna.

Fortunately, many Hindus, both at the scholarly and the popular level, are now becoming more aware of the effects of incorrect translation and at the popular level also of different branches of Hindu philosophy. I notice this on online forums where earlier the question 'Can a Hindu be an atheist?' was often indignantly answered in the negative but now receives much more nuanced and accurate answers.

Notes

1 My work builds on that of Bagchee and Adluri (2013), who demonstrate that Hacker's scholarly enterprise was a 'barely disguised form of religious evangelism' (215). Halbfass, who, although critical of Hacker, tries to save some of his work as legitimate, acknowledges that the use of terms like 'neo-Hinduism 'by Western scholars reflects Christian and European claims and perspectives which continue to be an irritant to Indians today' (Halbfass 2007: 587–88). Brian K. Smith notes that not just Hinduism but '*All* religions [...] have adapted to the modern world. [...] The study of religion is the study of traditions in constant change' (Smith 1998: 325) and he regrets that 'One of the principal ramifications of the trend in Indology to deny the existence of a unified religion called "Hinduism" is to delegitimize those in India who, in varying ways, have represented themselves as "Hindus" and their religion as "Hinduism"' (Smith 1998: 332–33).

2 Some scholars and dictionaries translate Sanskrit *pāṣaṇḍa* (from which derives Hindi *pākhaṇḍ*) as 'heresy'. This is another example of reverse translation, whereby a word that means 'deceit' or 'hypocrisy' with regard to false argumentation, is equated with an English word that is inseparable from a lengthy history of burning numerous 'heretics' and 'infidels', including some Indian ones in Goa, at the stake.

3 Chris Moffat points out that many groups, from Maoists, Marxists, Sikh separatists, Hindu nationalists, the Congress party and even pacifists imagine that had Bhagat Singh lived longer, he would have gone on to subscribe to their ideologies (Moffat 2019: 3). My point here is based on his own statements about a 'new philosophy'.

4 Daniel Elam, in a 2020 article that dwells more on ideas of atheism circulating outside India in Singh's time rather than on Singh's own essay, states that Singh cites Nanak and Krishna. In fact, Singh's essay does not cite or even mention these two figures.

5 Hi.wikipedia.org/wiki/ नास्तिकता. Accessed March 12, 2021.

6 Accessed March 2021. Since then, the definitions in this Wikipedia entry have become more nuanced, which indicates growing awareness of incorrect translations among ordinary Indians. I discovered from experience that Wikipedia, while claiming to be open to anyone to edit, in fact explicitly prohibits one from editing an entry on any topic on which one is an expert. One is also prohibited from adding facts to or correcting one's own page or those of one's friends and colleagues. No wonder, then, that Wikipedia is riddled with errors. My quotations here do, however, indicate the way false definitions have percolated down to non-experts.

7 For example, as I show in my 2002 essay, 'Gandhi's Tiger: Multilingual Elites, the Battle for Minds, and English Romantic Literature in Colonial India', thinkers like Gandhi and Rajagopalachari drew both on English and Indian literature to develop their arguments. In a similar vein, I built on other historians' work to argue that after the defeat of the 1857 rebellion, colonial rule brings about a shift in world view that results in the relabelling of much earlier literature as obscene or decadent (Vanita 2012: 20–27).

8 There are now ongoing discussions among Hindus regarding the way these translations affect the understanding of Hindu concepts. While I am encouraged by these endeavours and agree with Malhotra and Dass (2020) that words such as *dharma, yoga* and *yajña* should be retained in translations of texts like the *Gita*, I do not agree with their argument that a whole slew of Sanskrit terms should be retained in the original in English translations. For example, I do not think *mūrti* needs to be retained in English nor does it have to be translated as 'idol'. These are not the only two alternatives available. It could be translated in a less pejorative way as 'icon' or 'image'. All languages have untranslatable words; overloading an English translation of a Sanskrit text with non-English words may work for scholarly readers, but is likely to put off general readers, especially non-Indian ones. In my view, a smooth

and pleasurable reading experience is crucial to drawing in non-Indian readers, such as students of my *Bhagavad-Gītā* class in the US. Once engaged, some of these readers proceed to study and incorporate more Sanskrit terms into their vocabulary.

9 I elaborate this point in *The Dharma of Justice* (2022).

Bibliography

Apte, V.S. 1890. *The Practical Sanskrit-English Dictionary, Containing Appendices on Sanskrit Prosody and Important Literary & Geographical Names in the Ancient History of India, for the Use of Schools and Colleges*. Poona: Shiralkar.

Bagchee, Joydeep and Adluri, Vishwa. 2013. 'The Passion of Paul Hacker: Indology, Orientalism, and Evangelism'. In: Joanne Miyang Cho, Eric Kurlander and Douglas T. McGetchin (eds): *Transcultural Encounters between Germany and India: Kindred Spirits in the 19th and 20th Centuries*, 215–229. London, UK: Routledge.

Bhattacharya, J.V. 1900. *A Comprehensive Sanskrit-English Lexicon: Chiefly Based on Professor Horace Hayman Wilson's Sanskrit-English Dictionary and Compiled from Various Recent Authorities for the Use of Schools and Colleges*. Calcutta: Calcutta Press.

Bopp, Francisco. 1847. *Glossarium Sanscritum in quo omnes radices et vocabula usitatissima explicantur et cum vocabulis Graecis, Latinis, Germanicis, Lithuanicis, Slavicis, Celticis comparantur*. Berolini: Dümmler.

Doniger, Wendy, edited and translated. 1991. *The Laws of Manu*. New York: Penguin.

Dundas, Paul, edited and translated. 2017. *Magha, The Killing of Shishupala*. Cambridge, MA: Harvard University Press.

Elam, Daniel. 2020. 'Bhagat Singh's Atheism'. *History Workshop Journal* 2020, 1–13.

Flood, Gavin, and Martin, Charles, translated. 2012. *The Bhagavad Gita*. New York: W.W. Norton.

Griffith, Ralph T.H., translated. 1870–74. *Ramayan of Valmiki*. London: Trübner & Co.; Benares: E.J. Lazarus & Co.

Halbfass, Wilhelm. 2007. 'Research and Reflection: Responses to my Respondents'. In: Eli Franco and Karin Preisendanz (eds): *Beyond Orientalism: the Work of Wilhelm Halbfass and its Impact on Indian and Cross-Cultural Studies*, 297–314. Delhi: Motilal Banarsidass.

Hallisey, Charles. 1995. 'Roads Taken and Not Taken in the Study of Theravāda Buddhism'. In: Donald S. Lopez (ed.): *Curators of the Buddha*, 31–62. Chicago: University of Chicago Press.

Malhotra, Rajiv, and Dass, Babaji Satyanarayan. 2020. *Sanskrit Non-Translatables: The Importance of Sanskritizing English*. Delhi: Amaryllis.

Mascaro, Juan translated. 1962. *The Bhagavad Gita*. London: Penguin.

McGregor, R.S. 1993. *The Oxford Hindi-English Dictionary*. Oxford: Oxford University Press.

Miller, Barbara Stoler translated. 1986. *The Bhagavad-Gita*. New York: Bantam Books.

Moffat, Chris. 2019. *India's Revolutionary Inheritance: Politics and the Promise of Bhagat Singh*. Cambridge: Cambridge University Press.

Monier-Williams, M.A. 1851. *A Dictionary, English and Sanscrit*. London: W.H. Allen and Co.

Monier-Williams, M.A. 1872. *A Sanskrit-English Dictionary Etymologically and Philologically Arranged with Special Reference to Greek, Latin, Gothic, German, Anglo-Saxon, and other Cognate Indo-European Languages*. Oxford: The Clarendon Press.

Monier-Williams, Monier. 1878 *Hinduism*. London: Society for Promoting Christian Knowledge.

Nicholson, Andrew J. 2010. *Unifying Hinduism: Philosophy and Identity in Indian Intellectual Hist*ory. New York: Columbia University Press.

Nikhilananda, Swami, translated. 1944; 1987. *The Bhagavad Gita*. New York: Ramakrishna-Vivekananda Center.

Platts, John T. 1997. *A Dictionary of Urdū, Classical Hindī and Englis* [1884]. Delhi: Munshiram Manoharlal.

Prabhavananda, Swami, and Christopher, Isherwood, translated. 1944. *The Song of God: Bhagavad-Gita*. New York: New American Library.

Rao, Desiraju Hanumanta, and Murthy, K.M.K. *Valmiki's Ramayana*, 2.109.33–34. http://www.valmikiramayan.net/utf8/ayodhya/sarga109/ayodhya_109_frame.htm. Accessed December 6, 2022.

Schweig, Graham M., translated. 2007. *Bhagavad Gita*. New York: HarperCollins.

Sharma, Krishna. 1987. *Bhakti and the Bhakti Movement: A New Perspective*. New Delhi: Munshiram Manoharlal.

Singh, Bhagat. 1931. 'Why I am an Atheist'. *The People*, September 27, 1931, 195–201. https://www.marxists.org/archive/bhagat-singh/1930/10/05-files/why-i-am-an-atheist.pdf. Accessed December 6, 2022.

Singh, Bhagat, translated unknown. 'Main Nastik Kyon Hoon'. https://www.marxists.org/hindi/bhagat-singh/1931/main-nastik-kyon-hoon.htm. Accessed March 3, 2021.

Smith, Brian K. 1998. 'Questioning Authority: Constructions and Deconstructions of Hinduism'. *International Journal of Hindu Studies* 2(3), 313–329.

Swami, Paramhangsa Soham. 2018. *Truth: The Advaita Philosophy Simplified in Verses* [1913]. Kolkata: Sayambhati Publication.

Swami, Soham. 1928. *Common Sense*. Dacca: Surja Kanta Banerjee, Gandharia Press.

Thomas, Terence. 1988. *The British: Their Religious Beliefs and Practices, 1800–1986*. New York: Routledge.

Vanita, Ruth. 2002. 'Gandhi's Tiger: Multilingual Elites, the Battle for Minds, and English Romantic Literature in Colonial India'. *Postcolonial Studies* 5(1), 95–112. Republished in Vanita, Ruth. 2005. *Gandhi's Tiger and Sita's Smile: Essays on Gender, Sexuality and Culture*. New Delhi: Yoda Press.

Vanita, Ruth. 2012. *Gender, Sex and the City: Urdu Rekhti Poetry in India, 1780–1870*. New York/New Delhi: Palgrave-Macmillan/Orient Blackswan.

Vanita, Ruth. 2022. *The Dharma of Justice: Debates on Gender, Varna and Species in the Sanskrit Epics*. New Delhi: Oxford University Press.

Warner, Rex, translated. 1963. *The Confessions of Saint Augustine*. New York: Signet Classics.

Wilson, H.H. 1832. *A Dictionary in Sanscrit and English: Translated, Amended, and Enlarged from an Original Compilation*. Calcutta: The Education Press.

Yates, W. 1864. *A Dictionary in Sanscrit and English: Designed for the Use of Private Students and of Indian Colleges and Schools*. Calcutta: Baptist Mission Press.

9

TELLING LIVES IN FORKED TONGUES

Reading Shanta Gokhale's and Nabaneeta Dev Sen's Autobiographical Writings

Dhrupadi Chattopadhyay

Autobiography as a genre is a relatively recent import in the literary cultures of the Indian subcontinent. Although hagiographies were integral to the development of literary practices in India, it is only in the nineteenth century that we see the development of autobiography as a flourishing genre (David Arnold and Stuart Blackburn 2004). For the most part, its popularity has to do with the proliferation of print and a growing appetite for consuming 'lives' that came in with a colonial 'western' individual sensibility (Udaya Kumar 2009: 300). What this form meant to do in the Indian context is under continuous discussion but what it seems to have accomplished, nevertheless, is catapult otherwise marginal speaking subjects into prominence.

By Nabaneeta Dev Sen's own admission, in the introduction to her translation of *Chandrabati's Ramayan*, the work of Chandrabati, the first Bangla poet of the sixteenth century, only received attention as part of Dinesh Chandra Sen's archive and was soon forgotten. Dev Sen's work in finding 'literary foremothers' drew the text out of 'oblivion', and the oral text finally found a pride of place (Dev Sen 2020: vii). However marginal their voices were in the larger literary canon, women's life-writing seems to have found a steady purchase by the end of the nineteenth century. Often written in the confessional mode, these life-writings frequently challenged received notions of the 'text' and 'subjectivity' (Chakravarti and Gill 2001).

As Shanta Gokhale would note in her translation of Lakshmibai Tilak's autobiography, *Smritichitre: The Memoirs of a Spirited Wife*, "[o]riginally begun at her son's request and published in four parts between 1931 and 1936, Smritichitre gave Lakshmibai a visibility that her poetry alone may not have done" (Shanta Gokhale 2017a: 35). At this juncture, the life-writings, whether

DOI: 10.4324/9781003279921-12

in the form of autobiographies or memoirs, took over other forms of writings and appeared in the form of journals, diaries and autobiographies, and serialized in magazines, etc.[1] Often written from locations of privilege and backed primarily by the reform movement, this proliferation of life-writings ran its course by Independence.

However, this form found a new lease of life with the Dalit feminist movement which chose life-writing as their primary tool of political expression. Contrary to the course of discussions of women's life-writing that have obfuscated linguistic practices, in search of critiquing hegemonic discursive practices and subjective agency, I argue that a certain kind of bilingualism has been central to the presence of counter-discourses. The rise of marginalized feminisms that emerged in response to a hegemonic 'savarṇa' feminism, foregrounded 'testimonios' (to borrow Sharmila Rege's term) written in the vernacular. I argue that this left the upper-caste privileged woman to reinvent the genre to articulate their urge for a subjective agency. As writers of fiction, translators and academicians, Shanta Gokhale (2017b) and Nabaneeta Dev Sen's (1938–2019) choice of the language of articulation of their life-writings becomes as important as their selection and organization of experiences.

In terms of profile, Gokhale and Dev Sen seem to have uncannily similar trajectories. They were born in privilege (in terms of class, caste and geographical locations) and brought up in decidedly unconventional households with parents keen to invest in the English education of their girl child/children. Robust literary cultures (Marathi and Bengali) and their modernities framed through the reform movements were key to their essentially bilingual upbringing. Travels between languages were also a result of their locations in the urban colonial metropolises of Kolkata, Pune and Bombay (Gokhale 2017c). However, their parents' bilinguality was divided not merely along class but, importantly, also gender lines. While the women were comfortable in the vernacular, English was the prerogative of the menfolk.[2] It was only with the next generation that the travels between the worlds of English and vernacular would become more fluid and thus also tentative. The clear divide between these linguistic spheres would give way to conscious literary choices. Dev Sen in her essay 'Mātṛbhaṣā', addressed to her mother as a kid, asks why the mother tongue is equated with mother's milk even when one can potentially grow up with bottled milk, to which she says that all answers to our understanding of languages emanate from the languages of our mothers and grandmothers to which is tied our closeness. Fractured in terms of *rāj'bhāṣā, dev'bhāṣā* and *rāṣṭrabhāṣā*, our subjectivities come to life only in the mother tongue.[3]

Crucial to this was the role of their mothers: Radharani Devi, Dev Sen's mother was a prominent Bengali poet who wrote under the pseudonym Aparajita, and Gokhale's mother was a feisty woman who ran her father's business and "was a story-teller (and a story writer and versifier too)".[4] However, these genealogies are not always even and continuous. Dev Sen, for instance, would construct a biography of her maternal grandmother out of her personal experience and through written accounts of her maternal uncle. Narayani, her grandmother, content in her domesticity and her adherence to patriarchal norms plays the perfect counterfoil to her mother's resistance (Dev Sen 1999). Although they were encouraged to think beyond the confines of the modern education system, they seem to have done exceptionally well within the system. Both were students of English Studies in India and England at a time when the discipline was looking to test its scope in terms of form, methodologies, textualities and content. While Dev Sen argued for comparative frameworks within the domain of Indian Literature to address questions of marginality, Gokhale's seminal contributions to the world of Marathi translations into English and vice versa upset set narratives about Marathi literary historiographies. Critiques of the earlier academic order can be found in their writings along with a call to re-estimate what constitutes literary studies in India. As critics, prolific translators and creators of original literary content, they were situated tantalizingly both inside and outside of academic practices; both were acutely aware of the possibilities for comparative frameworks that would emerge from translations into English. This made their writings acutely self-reflexive and in particular, aware of the possibilities of the afterlives of their works. Working through the bilingual poetic influences in her life, Dev Sen in fact attempts at critiquing her own work. Akin to racial prejudice, where all Chinese men seem to look alike, all writing by women seemed to appear alike. To distinguish her writing from others, she dismisses the notion of influence as an operative category and instead works through the internal mechanics of the poetry (Dev Sen 1999: 488).

Faced with the breakdown of their respective marriages, both Dev Sen and Gokhale shouldered the responsibility of bringing up their children in a household helmed by their strong mothers. Divorce brought them back to their parental homes. Their new 'homes' carry the burden of their personal struggles as single women leaving them to reinvent their associations with the familiar. Both reinvent their 'dysfunctional' homes anew, seeking to constitute a continuum that does not dismiss the rupture. These renewed homes and identity negotiations routinely challenge ways in which upper-caste idealized versions of ever-sacrificing mothers were imagined (Gokhale 1990: WS 101). This coming back not only firmly situates them in their linguistic context but also becomes a site of their future negotiations with their identities. Incidentally, both would also have daughters (Renuka Sahane and Nandana Sen) who would go on to become moderately successful commercial film actors. Both Gokhale and Dev Sen battled cancer. While Dev Sen succumbed to it in November 2019, Gokhale is still fighting the disease.

When it comes to literary productions, both Dev Sen and Gokhale choose their mother-tongues[5] and English remains their language of academic engagements. Dev Sen tried writing poetry in English while she was in England, and

Gokhale famously took to Marathi prose as Nissim Ezekiel dismissed her poetic efforts in English. For their life-writings, however, Dev Sen chooses Bengali and Gokhale writes in English. "In English, I could express anger, my thirst, far more openly and powerfully, irrespective of a reader's sentiment, because I was facing a faceless reading public" and use "language without social-sexual inhibition", says Dev Sen, even as she elects to exclusively write her life in Bengali. Dev Sen writes in a primarily non-linear episodic style, often scripting sketches in garb of an informal 'āḍḍā', while Gokhale follows in the manner of memoirs, including photographic evidence. Looking for means to legitimize their self-representational practice, they heavily rely on self-deprecating humour.[6] Importantly, for both, this humour emerges when their otherwise privileged selves are compromised, they admit to the existence of unspoken realities and their vulnerabilities are exposed. Reliance on humour not only deflects from emphasizing a stable subjectivity but also locates the narrative authority away from within the text. These overriding similarities between their writings allow these complex negotiations to be read in between languages and not despite them. Taking cue from Gokhale and Dev Sen, I further argue that these 'new' subjectivities in an attempt to accommodate novel frameworks of experience, cautiously choose the in-between spaces of the vernacular and English as their preferred site of identity production.

Gendering Bilinguality: Women's Life-Writing and the Vernacular

Sisir Kumar Das terms the condition of postcoloniality as a 'historical predicament' where it compels the Indian writer to look for a wider audience beyond the scope of the vernacular. It is not difficult to understand this 'historical predicament' in terms of the complex relationship that the colonial writer shared with English. What has remained relatively less explored is the relation of this predicament with the material conditions of literary production that constituted the print culture of the time. Guglielmo Cavallo and Roger Chartier tell us that "No text exists outside of the physical support that offers it for reading (or hearing) or outside of the circumstance in which it is read (or heard)" (1999: 5).

Ever since the academic world opened to the possibility of reading the proliferation of 'print capitalism' and the 'nation' as coterminal, we have seen many discussions in and around the politics of print (Benedict Anderson 2006). However, studies in the Indian subcontinent have shown that the project of imagining the nation was neither as consistent nor as homogenous as in the proverbial West, one of the primary reasons being the ways and means by which print was produced, regulated and disseminated in India. Print came to India via the missionaries, primarily through the Portuguese and then the Danish (tertiary colonial powers) (M. Siddiq Khan 1962), proliferated through proselytization and later through the colonial education system (Mondal

2013), and was later regulated by the colonial powers (Darnton 2001). Therefore, Indian print never had its 'innocent' moment, as it were, as it negotiated fractious interplay between transposed, regulated and received imaginaries. Often, this has resulted in the reading of the printing practices being split across linguistic lines.

Studies pertaining to the analysis of this complex network of print in colonial India have concentrated either on evaluating the outcomes of the print in English or their counterparts in the 'vernacular'. The study of the vernacular press has not only concentrated on the mainstream press but also investigated the subversive potential of the 'cheap' press. The first printing press set up by an Indian in Calcutta came in 1807, established in the Kidderpore area by one Baburam. The first illustrated book in Bengali, *Annadā maṅgal*, was published in 1816 (Ashit Paul 1983). By the mid-nineteenth century, printing and publishing Bengali books was financially lucrative enough to set up a network of printing presses in the Battala area of Sutanuti, at the heart of the old Calcutta town. The books published in this area were once seen in stark opposition to the Bhadralok morality; but the economics and aesthetics of Battala suggest a symbiotic relationship between the two. Studies on cheap vernacular print, most notably by Sumanto Banerjee (1987 and 2008) and Anindita Ghosh (2003), have shown how they can be mined to look for spaces of resistance instead of being dismissed.

Given that the print culture arrived in India as a result of the colonial encounter, it has often been closely read alongside the emergence of national identity/ies with close ties to the public sphere (Bhattacharya 2005b, Gupta 2008). However, unlike Europe, as has been noted, the public sphere and its related print cultures were never homogenous in their aspirations. They were rather layered and divided not only across caste, class and often gender but most importantly across languages. These hierarchies were defined in terms of how these cultures were produced, consumed, disseminated and censured. They often gave rise to definitive models of societal and political discourses in their production of gender, caste, class and national identities (Bannerji 2002, Sarkar 1992, Bhattacharya 2005b) Both Sumanto Banerjee and Anindita Ghosh have ably demonstrated how low-brow popular print cultures in the vernacular, which escaped the censure of both the colonial powers and the Bhadralok elite, were sites of production of successful critiques of the colonial powers and the comprador elite. These spaces allow for movements within languages, permitting the interpellation of discourses that are not always evident and direct. These work through the conversations between the polite and the bawdy, the genteel and the masses, and emphasize the need to evaluate literary choices. That become most evident in the choices that women make to articulate their subjectivities. It has been noted that "gendered literary spaces and women's writing are 'a major stakeholder in Indian imaginative capital'" (Gupta, Brueck, Harder and Nijhawan 2020: 803) as it emerged in the vernacular.

Patterns of evaluating literary cultures in India pertaining to the print revolution have been organized largely on linguistic lines. Even contemporary revisionist studies of Indian Writing in the nineteenth century have largely constrained themselves within a certain language culture to draw out debates in literary historiographies. A case in point is in the way that Indian English writing in the nineteenth century has been studied. In the early nationalist imagination of Indian Writing in English, the nineteenth century was dismissed as a passing phase of colonial complicity which manifested itself in the way that the authors imitated their contemporaries in the West. Indian Writing in English would find its mojo much later as it overtly tried to shed its apologetics for using English as a medium to find 'Indianness' in the colonizer's tongue (Iyengar 1985: 5).

Missing in these rather partisan understandings of colonial India is the space that bilingual identities occupy. Veena Naregal has aptly pointed out that a schizophrenic language identity promoted by colonialism is an important link to reading print cultures in India (Naregal 1999). I would like to suggest that colonial knowledge practices and in particular those that pertain to the understanding of print cultures cannot be read in contained and compartmentalized categories. Like the writers of the time who functioned in both the languages, albeit with contradictions, the literary cultures were in fact a product of a certain kind of bilinguality (Mukherjee 2000: 11). It is in these excesses that we would find linkages to our bilingual present that is spread across caste, class and gender lines. Issues around print in colonial India, though fairly unresolved, continue to be debated. Language has never been without its politics and hierarchies and pre-modern India had its fair share of linguistic pluralities. Sheldon Pollock, for instance, has aptly demonstrated how a linguistic circuit dominated by Sanskrit gave rise to a certain kind of linguistic cosmopolitanism in pre-modern India. However, it needs to be noted that colonial powers with their control over print reorganized these language maps differently, thereby reorienting their imaginaries (Mitchell 2009: 24).

Reading across contemporary perceptions of colonial print and its perception of linguistic identities, one is exposed to a range of open debates that have framed our postcolonial bilingual identities. However, in all these readings lies an overwhelming lack of reading of the excesses that define these discourses. The excesses lie in the discourses not only horizontally within a linguistic culture as it travels from high to low brow but most importantly across linguistic barriers. The print culture of colonial India was a highly bilingual space with many bilingual writers, and it is this spilling over of discourses across language that offers a fresh perspective on the way we conceive our postcolonial predicament.

The discussions on the colonial public and its material base, as I have just discussed, assess the reading/writing public and their movement between languages as essentially gender-neutral. One cursory glance at the literary production by women in the colonial times shows that a large number of texts written by women are in the vernaculars and some in English (Vyas and Sharma 2013). Feminist historiographies in the recent past have mined autobiographies written by women to essentially locate the Bhadramahilā as an actor in the otherwise Bhadralok discourse of anti-colonial struggles (Burton 2003: 5). To this end, the home and the hearth have been mined for locations of narrating the nation. Tanika Sarkar notes that this postcolonial lens is commensurate with the growth of the vernacular prose and the interest in everyday life between the 1870s and the 1890s (Sen 2008: 28, Sarkar 2001: 548). As the masculinities of the colonized Indians get increasingly compromised, the home turns into one of the few possible sites of resistance (Chaudhary 2001: Nandy 1989: 7). Autobiographies tend to get more and more self-reflexive, driven intensely inwards. As men, emasculated by colonialism, turn to the 'home' to assert authority, women as actors and agents reinvent this conceptualization of home and in turn the 'everyday' (Sarkar 1993: 36). Be it their changing mores of keeping the house, the changing dynamics of the family unit under colonial modernity or the new entries in the kitchen, all helped to define the reorganization of the 'home'. Even the life-writings of women reformers saw their resistance emerging from their kitchens with the likes of Pandita Ramabai, Savitribai Phule, Nistarini Debi, Sarala Debi, Kailashbashini Debi etc. (Banerji 1991, Moitra 2020, Karlekar 1995). My contention here is not necessarily to homogenize their conceptualizations of home, as indeed in these articulations home appears in many avatars; instead, it is the politics of 'home' even in its steady denial which becomes significant.

The quotidian with its insistence on the repetitive and with a possibility of endless reproductions worked against the normative injunctions proposed by colonial patriarchy. An apt example is perhaps Rassundari Debi's account of teaching herself how to learn in the confines of her kitchen as she continued to fulfil her household duties. Her organic resistance is born out of the incremental progress she makes, as she painstakingly teaches herself to read and write using torn pages of the Chaitanya Bhagawat. She not only uses God as a way of legitimizing her subterfuge but most importantly chooses to enter language through a rupture. Her conquering the alphabet, therefore, animates the quotidian with the possibilities of hosting endless resistances.[7] Women's travel narratives seemingly challenging the tropes of home and confinement, as evidenced in the writings of Svarnakumari Devi and Krishnabhabini Das, also take the 'everyday' as a point of departure to construe their modernities (cf. Harder 2020: 818).[8] Under constant stress from their male counterparts, these articulations often underplay their agency or couch it in uncertain terms (Mukherjee 2000).

Although there are instances of 'lowly women' such as prostitutes and actresses writing their lives, a large section of these narratives came from locations of entitlement through privileged class and caste backgrounds. As Singh observes:

> Similar to genetic engineering, the colonial intervention removed progressive and challenging linguistic elements by using force and shaped a new breed of women in Bhadralok homes who, in their writings and so-called cultivated patterns of behaviour, replaced women's popular culture in Indian middle-class society. The women of the upper strata discarded the old popular culture, which had rested on the social ties that bound women from different classes.
>
> (*Singh 2013: 63*)

The upper-caste or '*savarṇa*' women's autobiographies came under serious critique as the Dalit consciousness grew at the wake of the Dalit Panther movement in the 1970s. Life-writings became the mainstay of their political consciousness where intense suffering and oppression reimagined the everyday in Indian Literature.[9] The accepted humdrum of everyday life was jolted out of its stupor to acknowledge the forces of erasure that it fostered. As Limbale points out, "[t]he reality of Dalit literature is the language of this reality. It is uncouth-impolite language of the Dalits. It is the spoken language of the dalits" (Limbale 2004: 33). An entire literary movement rooted in the vernacular took shape with life-writing as its chosen form.[10]

In the 1980s and the 1990s, when Black and Third World women began speaking up, a pluriform imagination of the feminist consciousness was born. In India, the feminist movement began to recognize caste as an operative category and eventually was born the acknowledgement that "Dalit women talk differently" (Guru 1995). However, as Sharmila Rege notes, the onus of engaging with this 'difference' remains the only prerogative of Dalit women (Rege 1998: WS 39). The tone and tenor and positions of their voices have been debated largely, considering the fixity of their discourses as they present themselves in the vernacular textual. The politics of their entry into a largely structured literary medium and the dismantling of the expectations surrounding the literary have been eventually read through the lens of the testimonios (Rege 2014: 9). These readings throw light on life-writings as critiques of "brahminical class-based heteropatriachies" (Rege 2000: 492). By focusing on the 'unspoken' horrors of oppression in the 'everyday', it forced the reader to politicize the 'familiar' of the everyday. Unlike the incremental resistances of the *savarṇa* women, this everyday was a deliberate assault on the comforts of the familiar.

Given that Marathi proved to be the most potent receptacle for the Dalit literary movement and then soon found a larger purchase in the academic circuits of the country, it is obvious that both Gokhale and Dev Sen were part of a culture that consumed it.[11] This engagement was neither distant nor cosmetic. Gokhale, for instance, details the effect of Dalit writing in the imagination of contemporary Marathi literary practices (Shanta Gokhale 2013). In the foreword to the recent translation of Baburao Bagul's stories, she studies the scholarship around Dalit writing within the Marathi literary discourse, to point out how their imageries promoted a kind of iconoclasm that spilt beyond the Marathi literary.[12] Dev Sen's women's poetry collective SOI was instrumental in initiating a conversation between the Marathi Dalit poets and their Bengali counterparts.[13]

Gokhale has been instrumental in translating a number of autobiographies (Laksmibai Tilak and Durga Khote being the most widely received). Dev Sen has worked towards providing a community of women's readership through SOI (Gokhale 2019: 188). The Bengali word 'Soi' (*saī*) denotes at least three meanings – signature, friend and the first-person present form of to bear – was born out of a series of negotiations around creating a space for women to share their literary output outside the framework designed by men or what is called the 'guarded tongue' (*Bhālabāsār bārāndā*; Deb Sen 2016a: 214). Through their literary foremothers, both of them also have a significant investment in the first generation of women writers that we have briefly discussed. I argue that Gokhale's and Dev Sen's choice of form and language displays a deep understanding of both waves of life-writing by women.[14] They place their writings in contradistinction to these strong literary predecessors and present their subjectivities by firmly locating themselves in the familiar but distancing the everyday to create pockets of absurdity. In their idiosyncrasies are born the familiar/familial as distant. This crucial distance is measured in their ability to draw humour.

Reading Humour in the Everyday

One of the first things that Shanta Gokhale notes about Lakshmibai Tilak's autobiography is the power of the "literary storytelling that existed in my language, Marathi", that bolsters the "unfailing comical touch" (Gokhale 2017a: x). This comical touch is something that Gokhale and Dev Sen both carefully cultivate in their life-writings. However, their methods of drawing out humour differ, creating distinct vantage points. Gokhale draws humour more from the context leaving the readers to imagine its potentially amplified impact in Marathi, creating a consciously crafted gap. Dev Sen, on the other hand, skilfully employs the writerly persona which hinges on topical references, puns and intertextual references both textual and cultural, typical to the Bengali intelligentsia to elicit laughter. I contend that their humour and irony present themselves in contradistinction to their literary foremothers by foregrounding irony as a legitimizing device. The two contexts that I explore in this section, sense of place and the notion of the body, will allude to their subjectivities that exploit the humour born out of legitimizing uncertainties. Dev Sen shuns the prescriptive critical distance between the reader and the author for a persona of the next-door neighbourhood aunty. In this, she deliberately frames a subjectivity that she wants us to see: a voice that is so familiar and couched in tropes of domesticity is all but invisible. These are voices that remain unheard, ignored as it is not deemed worthy of political discourses. This persona therefore literally allows Dev Sen to make the personal as the political. The conversational frame moves from the domestic to the workings of the state, the judiciary, and the literary establishments with relative ease. Her private spaces, such as the bathroom, bedroom, kitchen, all sites of routine conversation, are transformed into sites of feminist enquiry. She uses this frame to devise a uniquely female subjectivity that navigates easily between kitchens, classrooms, cinema theatres, public parks, boardrooms, museums and art galleries across continents. Through the breadth of this geography, Dev Sen's literary ego – like her predecessors – is able to sustain a dialogue with the contemporary social and political currents while bypassing the gatekeepers of knowledge networks. This is sustained in all her writings where she couches her erudite, political commentary within a language filled with affable inflections common to the 'ghaṭīs' (natives of the state as opposed to the 'bāṅāl', refugees of the partition) in Bengal. This earns her immediate emotive effects. This in part had to do with what she believed as the woman's writer's prerogative:

> A woman writer is constantly watched, like prisoners in a jail who are made to parade before the warden every morning. Her name becomes an essential part of the text that she produces, along with her whole personal life and her body. […] I stopped writing poetry and shifted to humorous prose because my readership had started finding deep personal messages about my private life in my poems, which bothered me. Inevitably, the woman writer's personal life becomes an integral part of her writing, to be analyzed and approved by the reader, which is not something the male writer experiences or suffers.

She continuously harps on these otherwise ignored modes of very personalized acts of writing. In fact, she attempts to theorize on marginalized forms of writing that remain outside the framework of academic practice. Her book, *Nabanītār noṭ'baï* (Nabineeta's Notebook), which is a collection of columns, begins with her talking about the act of writing like a notebook.

A notebook, she argues,

> is somewhere between the public and the private and allows for partial disclosure. She aligns it with Hanuman exposing his bosom to let the world know what lies inside, a Ram Mandir or a Babri Masjid. She quips that her persona does not allow for a complete disclosure. In this she moves to her diasporic experience as a student and things that were incidentally left out of her academic notebooks.
>
> *(233)*

Her series of writings on various subjects that formed a four-part anthologized volume called Bhālabāsār bārāndā' (Verandah of love) frames this familiarity within the walls of domesticity. In the fourth volume of this series, she deliberates on what constitutes an autobiography and astutely challenges its received conventions. When asked to write 'a serious' autobiography, she quips, "yes, I write small pieces, but I invest a lot while writing these columns, I write seriously, words of my mind, soul, life – can't small pieces of writing be serious too?" (Deb Sen 1999: 160). Using humour, she critiques the literary establishment as it values certain kinds of 'serious' writings that involve a book that is shaped like a brick and is of the jungle-printed saree variety: only a book which is voluminous and has a narrative is acceptable to a serious reader. A fragmented text that resembles a fallen leaf that doesn't subscribe to neat unities can also qualify as an autobiography. She goes on to elaborate how her literary persona of a cantankerous gossipy aunt is framed as a resistance against masculinist ways of relating high literature as serious. In this, she also brings in the crucial aspect of the prioritization of English as the only medium of serious discourse at the cost of the disappearance of voices. Here one must examine both the tone of the writing and the medium that she carefully uses to critique ways of masculinist discourse that constrains voices. The masculinist expectations of formalness and 'seriousness' of subject and a singularity of form are seriously challenged as she presents the reader with diversity of forms, expressions and tones. In a short essay titled 'I am in No Hurry' (*Āmār kono tāṛā nei*), she expands on the notion of her distinct female voice which is multiplicitous. She asks the reader, "Am I a man that you can restrict me within the four dimensions of a 'workplace'? What am I?" (Dev Sen 1999: 493). She goes on to record the multiple roles that she plays that frame her subjectivity: master, driver, poet, washerwoman, cook, thinker, daughter, mother, lady of the house and someone who is always on the move. The multiple roles that she plays allow her to question the notions of certain kinds of labour as productive. Notions of writing, or more accurately contexts of writing, that lie outside the framework of 'productive labour' legitimize her take on self-narrativization.

Gokhale and Dev Sen's identities are rooted in their 'sense of place'. Dev Sen's writings are secured at the veranda of her paternal house in Kolkata, the space where the inner and outer worlds meet. In a city that has otherwise seen many comings and goings, Gokhale finds her space in a historically Marathi-speaking locality of Shivaji Park, or Dadar 28 in Bombay (Dev Sen 2006: 23). An innocuous morning walk is used by both writers to set their territory of negotiating this sense of place. In a section titled "Morning Walk: 18 February 2019", Gokhale takes the reader along as she traverses the length of Shivaji Park. She introduces each tree in the process, giving both a personal and institutional history of the park. "As varied are the people I pass, I know them all by face and by habit. Some people I understand. Others I do not" (Gokhale 2020: 163). She settles into her familiarity including meeting her 82-year-old stalker, which reminds her of "Surekha Punekar lavni: 'The leaf is ready to fall but the stalk is still green'" (Gokhale 2020: 164). The park finds its mooring in the popular culture in the form of the lavni, which accords it its sense of place. The other familiarity that makes her 'sense of place' is the language that frames it:

> There are other pleasures of the ear in Shivaji Park – the sound of many tongues. I count them today. I hear Marathi, Gujarati, Kutchi, Sindhi, Kannada, Konkani and Bomabaiyya Hindi. Not so pleasant is Minglish. Today's line was 'Mi recently aikla, to continuous bolar hota'.
>
> *(I heard him recently. He was talking continuously)*

It is in this setting that she finds her creative voice, her space and her body after her divorce. A profound liberating realization follows which illuminates the blind spots and almost establishes a historical continuity with her literary foremothers. This embodiment is expressed as the maturity of her creative idiom in Marathi:

> I wrote *Tya Varshi* seventeen years later, sitting in my own room unoccupied by any other body but mine. Rarely are women blessed with such blissful singlehood. The pleasure is not confined only to having my own space, my own work table and my own bookshelves. [...] A body by itself, no move makes it arousing thoughts of possession in another. The independence to be yourself, complete in yourself, is very heaven.
>
> *(Gokhale 2019: 169)*

Dev Sen uses the benign trope of morning walks to disrupt her 'sense of place' and 'home'. in a series of humorous snippets that recount her crisis of identity as Amartya Sen (her ex-husband and father to her daughters) wins the Nobel Prize (Dev Sen 2006). Her identity as a writer and a feminist scholar is suddenly overshadowed by her identification as the first wife of Amartya Sen. She wakes up to an uncomfortable stardom: "'Hey look! That's Nabaneeta Dev Sen! Know who that is? You don't? She's Amartya Sen's first wife!' Both boys turned to look. The Paanwala too. And the person drinking Coke lowered his bottle. The boys bought their cigarettes with their faces turned in my direction—towards Chintamani shop" (Dev Sen 2006: 40).

The familiarity of the everyday marked by routine is seen as a rupture here:

> A wintry morning. The roads, clear of traffic but not of people. Hordes of humans speeding towards the Lakes. Each one giving me a sidelong glance as they pass. On the first-floor balcony of a two-storied house, a nighty-clad woman jumped out of her skin on seeing me as if she'd seen a ghost and ran inside. What could the matter be? I turned to look at the balcony as I passed—she had summoned a shawl-wrapped sleepy gentleman; they were

> both gaping at me. This has happened before. Even a few days ago, I used to be really thrilled, I used to think they are looking at me—'Nabaneeta'! And tingle with delight. Now, I shuddered in dread. They must be looking at the first wife of the Nobel Laureate. ["She shared house with such a great man for sixteen-seventeen years. Too bad she never managed to make it last!"]

Her displacement is complete as the police force erases her identity and overwrites her 'sense of place':

> Police? Why? What's the matter? I walked out into the balcony like a defiant Amazon. The policeman looked up at me from the street—arms akimbo, and jerked his upturned thumb. 'Move this car. Is this Maruti yours?' 'Yes. Why should I move it?' 'Amartya Sen is visiting this house at five this evening.' 'So? Why do I have to move the car?' 'Security!' 'Look! My car is always parked in front of my house. That's where it will remain. You can move it if you can!'. Surmising that I hadn't heard him, the policeman announced in a thundering voice to the entire neighbourhood.
>
> *(Dev Sen 2007: 27)*

Interestingly enough, Dev Sen reclaims her identity when she decides to travel incognito on a metro train. Here someone finally recognizes her as a writer, not the ex-wife of a Nobel Prize winner: and it turns out to be a wrong strategy. The woman shuddered:'You even smile like her. How strange! It's uncanny.' 'You know what? Actually, I am a great fan of her writings. I love Echo of a Song by Rabindranath Tagore "Kena ceẏe ācha go mā?"; literally, 'Why are you looking at me, O mother?' The woman almost spoke to herself. 'I buy her books as soon as they come out. Even my mother loves Nabaneeta Dev Sen's writings. I have often thought of meeting her, but I've never found the courage. When I saw you today, it was like being handed the moon!' The woman fell silent for a while. 'And I thought to myself, "Oh my god—how lucky I am today! My favourite writer is sitting right next to me!"' (Dev Sen 1999: 307).

Gokhale in the opening section of her memoir *One Foot on the Ground: A life told Through the Body* of 2019 declares, "there is a purely writerly reason for telling the story through the events of the body. It gives me ready-made structure, a spine around which to build the narrative" (Gokhale 2019: 6) While it follows the general structure of the bildungsroman, it casts it in its most 'bare' form. True to her claims, her somatic experiences make way to accommodate the critical unease surrounding her rather unconventional life choices. From a robust body used to dance and exercise that experiences sexual awakening to a diseased postmenopausal one, her body becomes the site of enunciations. In a familiar conversational mode, she invokes laughter as she struggles to come to terms with her body from her dark skin and flat nose to the discrepancy between her buttocks and breasts. For instance: "The shape of my nose is described among the Marathi speaking brethren as a bhaja (fritter). A bhaja like nose is large where it should be small, and flat where it should be high. This is quite opposite of the ideal nose that my Marathi brethren refer to as chafe-kali – champak bud" (Gokhale 2019: 88).

Although Dev Sen in the opening paragraphs of *Bhālabāsār bārāndā* says that she would self-censor episodes that deal with her sexuality, she offers some veiled discussions on sexuality that come from her understanding of linguistic coordinates. In the opening lines of her short essay titled 'Bedroom' (Dev Sen 2016a [1996]: 193–195), she talks of how she belongs to the veranda and therefore is not qualified to speak about the bedroom. She figuratively places herself in an in-between space, someone who is privy to the discourses of the inside as well as the outside. 'Bedroom' as opposed to its Bangla equivalent, 'śobār ghar' (literally a room to sleep), carries the onus of maintaining privacy. Whereas a 'room to sleep' is quite versatile and could easily transform itself into spaces of commercial transactions, familial gatherings, accounting and myriad other things. This idea of fluidity with regard to these spaces is widespread in Bengali culture. The latter part of the essay recounts how a Bengali couple came uninvited to her apartment at Cambridge and enjoyed her hospitality only to convert her living space into their 'bedroom' aka honeymoon suite.

Dev Sen and Gokhale both reserve the same unsentimental irreverence for the diseased body. After being diagnosed with cancer, Dev Sen wrote, "I don't care kānākaṛi—jānis āmi syāṇḍo kari"?; and when people started visiting her from far and wide as her health started failing, she insisted that she would first contest an election, then organize a feast and only afterwards start her 'śubhayātrā', or her final auspicious journey. We find an analogous loud announcement of a detailed disease catalogue in Gokhale. Glaucoma, cancer, fibroids, and fractures, all find a pride of place in Gokhale's memoirs. The senile diseased body is treated with as much attention as the youthful one:

> The pink liquid begins to course through my veins. The nurses hover, the doctor hovers, each in turning asking me if there is any pain, any burning. There ain't none. How can there be when pink drugs meet pink comrade? We just meet on our side of the boxing ring, shake hands and sock it to the unruly lumpen element trying to take over this true Marathi breast.
>
> *(Gokhale 2019: 210)*

Be it the contexts of their marriage, their diseased bodies, their loves lost or the life-writings of both the writers firmly raise the question of literary choice. Life-writings seem to travel across these spaces where women were traditionally silenced. In the case of Gokhale, who firmly locates herself in the contexts of Marathi linguistic practice, she writes her first novel, *Rita Welinker* (1995, translated by the author), which is a fictionalized memoir in Marathi. Despite her celebrated forays in creative writing in Marathi, she wrote her memoirs in

English. On the other hand, Dev Sen reserves English as the language only of academic discourse and writes in Bengali. From the tropes that they borrow to the sense of cultural anxiety that they experience, both firmly present their vulnerable selves in excess of the language in which their life-writings are located. Their forms of engagement in the languages of their choice are so designed to arouse greater suspicion: Gokhale's crisp English prose, which is sought to create a critical distance between the writer and reader, in effect explores the possibilities of what the audience might know about her. On the other hand, Dev Sen uses familiarity and the homely vernacular to admit the existence of discourses that might seem alien in the everyday spoken conversational language. The carefully constructed linguistic spheres collide and animate each other. These movements within and without bring to focus their fractured consciousness that affects their literary choices. Far from being a decorative ploy, linguistic choices in life-writings become crucial to understanding the excesses that these discourses produce. As the authors negotiate the forms of subjective agency that a particular language ecosystem offers, their autobiographical literary personas critically process subjectivities that often exceed the possibilities that might restrict their functioning within either English or the vernacular.

Notes

1 Here, I rely on the account of Usha Chakrabarty, who claims that in the latter half of the nineteenth-century autobiographies became a very important mode of self-expression in Bengal. Out of the 400 recorded published works by women including short stories and poems, 50 were autobiographies. This is notwithstanding the numerous journals, letters and diaries that women wrote (Chakrabarty 1963).

2 "His letters were always in English and characteristically concise. Mother's were in Marathi and, equally characteristically, descriptive and chatty. Mine would be in English to him and Marathi to her. Once in a while she would write a secret letter in English. Secret because Father was always dismissive of her attempts to master the language. As far as he was concerned, she spoke well enough to get along, and that was as good as it needed to be. The letters Mother wrote in English were exercises. I was expected to correct them and return them to her. But since this was a secret transaction between us, I was not to send them to Lalit Estate but address them to Antu Mama who lived right behind our house and was the most discreet of Mother's ten siblings" (Gokhale 2017).

3 This is a paraphrase of her rather long argument on the spaces that English and the mother tongues occupy. These compartmentalizing draws from the language of academic practice versus a language of emotions dichotomy (Deb Sen 2016: 38).

4 While Nabanita Dev Sen has written extensively on the role of her mother in shaping her literary consciousness in her memoirs *Bhālabāsār bārāndā*, Gokhale promises to publish a full-length memoir of her mother soon.

5 Dev Sen wrote some poetry in English while she was in London, some of which has been recently published in a collection drawn up by her daughter Nandana Sen.

6 Dev Sen has argued that humour in women's writing is rare as it almost always serves as a scathing critique for hegemonic patriarchal discourses (Dev Sen 1990: 137).

7 As Moitra (2017) has eloquently argued, these spaces were not untouched by the printed world, in fact they were often centres of community readership as opposed to a singular individuated reader that one imagines in colonial modernity.

8 The other kind of travel that was permitted for women and often encouraged was pilgrimage, which, though very different from leisure travel, proposes similar tropes. See, for example, Swarupa Gupta (2017).

9 Here I take cue from Gayatri Prabhu's mapping of the life-writing in India as a literary form. She identifies the Dalit autobiographical writings as the second wave of autobiographical writings in India. https://scroll.in/article/928563/indian-literature-keeps-waiting-for-the-literary-memoir-as-a-form-distinct-from-the-autobiography.

10 One must assert that Dalit ideologues such as Kancha Illaiah (2010: xii) encouraged writings in English to challenge the caste–class nexus that kept Dalits out of the English-speaking arena.

11 Dalit writing in Bengali has come into prominence only in the past decade or so and is now frequently debated in the literature classrooms.

12 "Even more iconoclastically, Trymbak Sapkale rejected God outright in a deliberately hybrid mix of marathi and English: 'we godmakers/serve notice on you/for negligence of duty/ your services are not required'" (Bagul Baburao 2018; trans. Jerry Pinto).

13 http://www.soicreativewomen.org/events/event-reports/29-miscellaneous-events/36-soi-mela-the-festival-of-creative-women.html?highlight=WyJkYWxpdCJd

14 In this I rely partially on the work of Anindita Pan (2020) which expands the scope of Dalit feminism.

Bibliography

Anderson, Benedict. 2006. *Imagined Communities: Reflections on the Origin and Spread of Nationalism*. London: Verso Books.

Arnold, David, and Stuart Blackburn (eds). 2004. *Telling Lives in India: Biography, Autobiography, and Life History*. Bloomington: Indiana University Press.

Bagul, Baburao. 2018. *When I Hid my Caste*. Trans. Jerry Pinto. New Delhi: Speaking Tiger, xi.

Bannerji, Himani. 2002. *Inventing Subjects: Studies in Hegemony, Patriarchy and Colonialism*. London: Anthem Press.

Bhattacharya, Neeladri. 2005a. "Notes towards a Conception of the Colonial Public." In *Civil Society, Public Sphere, and Citizenship: Dialogues and Perceptions*. Eds Rajeev Bhargava and Helmut Reifeld. New Delhi: Sage, 130–158.

Bhattacharya, Tithi. 2005b. *The Sentinels of Culture: Class, Education, and the Colonial Intellectual in Bengal*. New Delhi: Oxford University Press.

Burton, Antoinette M. 2003. *Dwelling in the Archive: Women Writing House, Home, and History in Late Colonial India*. New York: Oxford University Press.

Byapari, Manoranjan, and Meenakshi Mukherjee. 2007. "Is There Dalit Writing in Bangla?" *Economic and Political Weekly*, Vol. 42, No. 41, Oct. 13–19, 4116–4120.

Cavallo, Guglielmo and Roger Chartier. 1999. "Introduction." In *idem* (eds): *A History of Reading in the West*. Cambridge MA: Polity Press.

Chakravarti, Uma, and Preeti Gill, eds. 2001. *Shadow Lives: Writings on Widowhood*. New Delhi: Zubaan.

Chakrabarty, Usha. 1963. *Condition of Bengali Women Around the Second Half of the Nineteenth Century*. Calcutta: Author's publication.

Charu Gupta, Laura Brueck, Hans Harder & Shobna Nijhawan. 2020. "Literary Sentiments in the Vernacular: Gender and Genre in Modern South Asia, South Asia." *Journal of South Asian Studies*, 43(5), 803–816, DOI: 10.1080/00856401.2020.1786788.
Darnton, Robert. 2001. "Literary surveillance in the British Raj: The contradictions of liberal imperialism." *Book History*, 4, 133–176.
Dev Sen, Nabaneeta (= Deb Sen, Nabanītā). 2018. *Nabanītā Deb Sen racanābalī*, Volume 1. Ed. Śrīkumār Caṭṭopādhyāẏ. Kal'kātā: De's Publishing.
——— 2016a. *Bhālabāsār bārāndā*. Volumes I-IV. Kal'kātā: Dey's Publishing (De'j Pāb'liśiṃ).
——— 2016b. *Nabanītā*. Kal'kātā: Mitra o Ghoṣ.
——— 2020. *Nabanītār Noṭ'baï*. Kal'kātā: Dey's Publishing.
——— 1999. "The Wind beneath My Wings." *Indian Journal of Gender Studies*, 6(2), 221–239.
——— 2021a. *Acrobat. Poems by Nabaneeta Dev Sen*. Trans. Nandana Dev Sen. New Delhi: Juggernaut Books.
——— with Indira Chowdhury. 2006. "Stand Back Please it's the Nobel." *Indian Literature*, 50(6), 23–49.
——— 1990. "The Literary Muse: Humour – Where Women Writers Fear to Tread." *Naari: A Tribute to the Women of Calcutta*, 1690–1990.
Dev Sen, Nandana. 2021b. "A Lifetime of Luminous Poetry: Nandana Dev Sen on translating the work of her mother." *Literary Hub*, May 13, 2021. https://lithub.com/a-lifetime-of-luminous-poetry-nandana-dev-sen-on-translating-the-work-of-her-mother-nabaneeta/, accessed December 11, 2022.
Gokhale, Shanta. 2019. *One Foot on the Ground: A Life Told Through the Body*. New Delhi: Speaking Tiger Books.
——— 2013. "Inextinguishable Fires: Looking Back on Half a Century of Marathi Dalit Writing." *The Caravan*, 1 August, 2013. https://caravanmagazine.in/reviews-essays/inextinguishable-fires, accessed December 11, 2022.
——— 2020. *Shivaji Park, Dadar 28: History, Places, People*. New Delhi: Speaking Tiger Books
——— (trans.). 2017a. *Smritichitre: The Memoirs of a Spirited Wife*. Originally in Marathi by Lakshmibai Tilak. New Delhi: Speaking Tiger.
——— 2017b. "The Bombay Modern in Four Languages." *Journal of Postcolonial Writing*, 53(1–2), 162–175.
——— 2017c. "Bilingual Home." In *Living with Father: A Memoir*. Online publication. https://shantagokhale.com/pages/living_with_father, accessed December 15, 2022.
——— 1990. "Mother in Sane Guruji's Shyamchi Ai." *Economic and Political Weekly*, Vol. 25, No. 42/43, Oct. 20–27, WS95–WS102.
——— 1995. *Rita Welinker*. Hyderabad: Orient Blackswan. https://shantagokhale.com/pages/living_with_father, accessed March 14, 2020.
Gupta, Charu. 2008. *Sexuality, Obscenity, Community: Women, Muslims, and the Hindu Public in Colonial India*. Hyderabad: Orient Blackswan.
Gupta, Swarupa. 2017. "Religious Travel, Place-Making and Social Collectivity: Connected Spaces in Bengal, India and Beyond, c. 1850–19271." Brill, 2017.
Guru, G. 1995. "Dalit Women Talk Differently." *Economic and Political Weekly*, Vol. 30, No. 41/42, Oct. 14–21, 2548–2550.
Harder, Hans. 2020. "Female Mobility and Bengali Women's Travelogues in the Nineteenth and Early Twentieth Centuries." *South Asia: Journal of South Asian Studies*, 43(5),

817–835. http://www.soicreativewomen.org/events/event-reports/29-miscellaneous-events/36-soi-mela-the-festival-of-creative-women.html?highlight=WyJkYWxpd

Iyengar, K. R. Srinivasa. 1985. *Indian Writing in English*. New Delhi: Sterling.

Ilaiah, Kancha. 2010. *The Weapon of the Other: Dalitbahujan Writings and the Remaking of Indian Nationalist Thought*. Delhi: Pearson India Education.

Karlekar, Malavika. 1995. "Reflections on Kulin Polygamy—Nistarini Debi's Sekeley Katha." *Contributions to Indian Sociology*, 29(1–2), 135–155.

Kumar, Udaya. 2009. 'Subjects of New Lives: Reform, Self-Making and the Discourse of Autobiography in Kerala', in Bharati Ray (ed), *Different Types of History, History of Science, Philosophy and Culture in Indian Civilization*, Vol. XIV, Part 4, 299–331.

Khan, M. Siddiq. 1962. "The Early History of Bengali Printing." *The Library Quarterly*, 32(1), 51–61.

Limbale, Sharankumar. 2004. *Towards an Aesthetics of Dalit Literature*. Trans. Alok Mukherjee. Hyderabad: Orient Balckswan.

Lisa, Mitchell. 2004. *Language, Emotion and Politics in South India: The Making of a Mother Tongue*. Bloomington: Indiana University Press.

Moitra, Swati. 2020. "A Nineteenth-Century Bengali Housewife and her Robinson Crusoe Days: Travel and Intimacy in Kailashbashini Debi's the Diary of a Certain Housewife." *Feminismo/s*, 36, 49–76.

——— 2017. "Reading Together: 'Communitarian Reading' and Women Readers in Colonial Bengal." *Hypatia*, 32(3), 627–643.

Mondal, A. 2013. *Cultural Aspects of Printing Press in Bengal: A Case Study of Serampore Mission and Indigenous Responses*. Colombo: International Association for Asian Heritage Centre for Asian Studies, University of Kelaniya.

Nandy, Ashis. 1989. *The Intimate Enemy*. Oxford: Oxford University Press.

Naregal, Veena. 1999. "Colonial Bilingualism and Hierarchies of Language and Power: Making of a Vernacular Sphere in Western India." *Economic and Political Weekly*, Vol. 34, No. 49, Dec. 4–10, 3446–3456.

Pan, Anindita. 2020. *Mapping Dalit Feminism: Towards an Intersectional Standpoint*. New Delhi: Sage.

Paul, Ashit. 1983. "Calcutta Woodcuts: Aspects of a Popular Art." In *idem* (ed.): *Woodcut Prints of Nineteenth Century Calcutta*. Kolkata: Seagull Books.

Rege, S. 1998. "Dalit Women Talk Differently: A Critique of 'Difference' and Towards a Dalit Feminist Standpoint Position." *Economic and Political Weekly*, Vol. 33, No. 44, Oct. 31–Nov. 6, WS39–WS46.

——— 2000. "'Real Feminism' and Dalit Women: Scripts of Denial and Accusation." *Economic and Political Weekly*, Vol. 35, No. 6, Feb. 5–11, 492–495.

Sarkar, Tanika. 1993. "A Book of her Own. A Life of her Own: Autobiography of a Nineteenth-century Woman." *History Workshop*, 36, 35–65.

——— 1992. "The Hindu Wife and the Hindu Nation: Domesticity and Nationalism in Nineteenth Century Bengal." *Studies in History*, 8(2), 213–235.

——— 2001. *Hindu Wife, Hindu Nation: Community, Religion, and Cultural Nationalism*. Bloomington: Indiana University Press.

Singh, Jai. 2013. "The Colonial Machinery's Marginalisation of Indian Women's Discourses by the Mutation of Socio-Linguistic Genes." *KEMANUSIAAN: The Asian Journal of Humanities*, 20(2), 61–80.

10

VERNACULARIZING SCIENCE IN COLONIAL BENGAL

A Translational Site of 'Other' Archives

Indrani Das Gupta

The introductory lines (quoted below) taken from Sukumar Ray's classic Bangla science fiction tale *Heśorām hũśiẏārer ḍāẏʹri* (1922), translated into English in 2012 as 'The Diary of Professor Heshoram Hunshiyar' by Nilanjana Chakrabarty, highlight a few key points that form the backdrop to this chapter.[1] One of the distinctive facets which we are impressed upon by the fictional editor, publisher, or embedded narrator of this tale, as elucidated in the below-quoted lines, is that the eponymous protagonist of this short story, Professor Heshoram, is angry because his stories have not yet been published. The very mention of publishing draws us into the vortex of print culture that was, as Anindita Ghosh (2002) argues, central to the restructuring of the public imagination in nineteenth-century colonial Bengal. According to Ghosh, print language and literature "played a vital role in shaping ideas and identities in Bengal from 18th century onwards" (2002: 4329). This tale's positioning within the publishing culture points towards the politics of mass production, circulation, and consumption of texts in vogue during the first half of the twentieth century in colonial Bengal. Most importantly, the articulation of publishing conceptualizes readers in conversation and in negotiation with authors, texts, and multiple social registers. Heshoram's insistence on getting his work published and the frame narrative foregrounding the fictional editor/publisher's actions to distance his establishment from any libels, blame game, and impending ruckus obliquely shift the focus onto the reader.

> Professor Heshoram is very upset with us. We have published many articles about prehistoric animals, but we have failed to acknowledge his strange hunting experiences. We agree this has been most unfair on our part. In fact,

DOI: 10.4324/9781003279921-13

we did not know of hunting stories but now Prof. Hunshiyar has sent us some extracts from his hunting diaries. We have published some of these accounts. It is up to you to decide whether they are true or false.

(Ray [1922], translated by Nilanjana Chakrabarty 2012: 135)

These two distinct characteristics: the need to be documented and the reader's importance, outline this story's basic framework. The first aspect involving Heshoram's urgency to publish his work shows the wide recognition and appeal amongst the reading public for speculative stories such as Heshoram's. Additionally, Heshoram's resolve to document his strange expedition can be read as an instance of travel narratives and expedition or exploration histories, which were widely popular in the colonial literary sphere from the late nineteenth to the early twentieth century in Britain and India. The dramatization of the reader which informs the second aspect of this story encases this text within a heterogeneous reading network. Comprised of varied interpretative strategies which were in fashion during the last three decades of the nineteenth century to the first half of the twentieth century, Ray's tale documents the presence of active readers. The embedded narrative's prominence given to the veracity angle and pieces of evidence put the reader of Heshoram's strange tale in conversation with 'current' scientific discourses and epistemologies. These scientific discourses were primarily defined by their truth-telling propensities, which makes us construe Heshoram's reader as the central authority in defining and constituting truth.

Anwesha Maity (2016: 459) notes that the early science fiction narratives in colonial Bengal functioned as a rejoinder to the Western scientific mindset introduced through the vectors of colonialism. Maity's explanation raises a few questions: Were these Western scientific attributes and technocentric features universally acknowledged and thus assimilated in various vernacular quotidian practices? Or, were other variegated responses also available? Do we read the rise and popularity of fantastical, speculative, and expedition narratives amongst the reading public from the late nineteenth to twentieth century as an illustration of a vernacular literary sphere constituted in 'response' to colonial science's epistemologies? How and in what ways is Professor Heshoram's tale located in the interstices of vernacular literary imagination and western scientific technologies?

Sukumar Ray's brilliant tale offers a self-reflexive assessment of science and the modernity that underpins it. Ray's Professor Heshoram invites us to look at the relationship between vernacular science and Western science as represented in the early Bangla science fiction narratives. Science, usually identifiable with Western ethos and construed as inseparable from the project of imperialism, is 'read' via Ray's short story as an instance of the vernacular Bengali literary sphere. Thus, in its 'response' to Western science, espoused in Heshoram's bizarre tale, this chapter draws our attention to *vernacularizing* science practices in the aesthetic and cultural productions of colonial Bengal from the 1880s until the early 1920s.

The following close reading of Ray's short story, 'The Diary of Heshoram Hunshiyar', analyzed via the image of the explorer, one of the central colonial practitioners of scientific imaginary and also a maverick storyteller, espouses 'scientific modernity' as a shifting, pluralistic term. Through its use and borrowings of generic and vernacular linguistic improvisations, and its references to popular nonsense and children's literature of the day, this tale, I argue, opens up a translational space that challenges the boundaries of colonial scientific modernity.

Theorizing Science in Colonial India

The very idea of science that continued to play a significant role in postcolonial politics was found closely connected to the project of colonialism (Baber 1996, Prakash 1999, Arnold 2000, Philip 1964, Kumar 2004). Like modernity has always been understood as a distinct characteristic of the West and mapped by a notion of development (Mitchell 2000, Dube 2002), the history of science in India has often been read as being inextricably linked with Western forms, institutions, and progressive practices. As one of the "manifest embodiments of modernity" (Ganeri 2013: 349), science has often been regarded as emanating first in the West and then in the rest of the world.[2]

The ill-famous tripartite diffusionist model of George Basalla (1967) articulated that the diffusion and transmission of science from the European metropolitan centres to the peripheries of the empire constituted the core understanding of science's history. Basalla (1967) stated that science's transmission from centre to margin ensued in multiple phases, and this scientific diffusion continued until the far-flung colonies could manifest their native scientific institutions and technological possibilities as already found in the metropolitan imperial centres. This perspective of construing science in terms of diffusion, and consequently inferring the non-West as a 'tabula rasa', led Basalla (1967) to neglect indigenous science practices.[3] However, the traffic of scientific ideas, tools, technological epistemologies, and the varied responses to scientific enquiries and experimentations by natives tell a different story. In these responses to 'modern' Western scientific epistemologies' tensions and contradictions, the politics between metropole and margin was continually being redefined and vernacularized.

Deliberation surrounding science[4] and its cognates (rationality, objectivity, and truth) emerged into prominence in the middle of the nineteenth century. This scientific discourse was materially experienced by the native subjects of the British Empire as being intrinsically associated with state power. The practices and institutions of the colonial state, which Rabindranath Tagore identified as "an applied science" ([1921] cited in Kumar 2004: 3893), in daily lived experiences came to be indissolubly associated with the transformations underlining the spatial contours of Calcutta. The mid-nineteenth century emerged as the era of momentous changes with unprecedented growth and expansion of industrialized forces entwined with transformations in, as Debjani Sengupta argues, "colonial Bengal's cultural, social and political life" (2002: 149). This spatial reordering of Calcutta, the imperial centre of the East, was succinctly expressed by the nineteenth-century poet Rupchand Pakshi.

The poem describes various factories established in the vicinity of Calcutta, which have dynamically changed the spatial contours and boundaries of the city. These industrial transformations have blurred the boundaries between small towns and cities, evident in the lines where towns and cities emerge as mirror images of each other. Simultaneously, the spatial redesigning initiated by the establishment of various industries ('flour mills, jute mills, cloth and brick mills') emphasizes the muted role of nature within the space of the mechanical city. Here, the character of 'natural' light has also undergone a mutation, with connotations of romance and mystery now being linked to 'mechanical' light. Science functions as an instrumental tool with specific functional values felt and experienced by the colonized both within the public and private spheres. While underscored as a salutation to scientific energies, the poem's use of '*praṇām*', 'reverence', plays to multiple tunes and registers. At one level, it suggests veneration for scientific apparatuses and their features of rationality and thereby inaugurates science as the new 'nature'. At another level, the multiple scientific developments initiated in Calcutta invoke a kind of crisis where the speaker finds himself at odds with the changes taking place around him. In its very adoration, the speaker finds himself distanced and alienated from the seductive and enchanting charms of science.[5] Thus, the vernacular linguistic inflection of '*praṇām*' asserts an ironic stance towards the icons of progress epitomized by factories, machines, and electricity.

Pakshi's poem firmly asserts science and technology's visibility in Calcutta's urban environs – a particularly noticeable fact post-1857. In the aftermath of the First War of Independence, known also as the Mutiny of 1857, the violence which destabilized the very foundations of the colonial regime led science and technology to become one of the 'tools' of empire that "civilize[d] the masses". In addition, these scientific tools, Manu Goswami (2004: 103) argues, "distill[ed] and communicate[d] the ideology of colonial state space". These Western scientific epistemologies were found ensconced in icons of growth and modernity like the "printing press, the steamships, vaccination-inoculation, the telegraph, the railway and in the last decade of that century electrification" (Sarkar 2010: 38). These various modernizing scientific-technological icons inaugurated the discourse of *colonial state* in natives' quotidian lives.

Science became far more entrenched in local imaginaries, with the British colonial administration expanding India's pedagogical institutions and 'reforming' natives' instructive modes and practices. As early as 1784, the institutionalization of Western science in Bengal was initiated by establishing the Asiatic Society.[6] The dissemination of colonial education in institutions like Hindu College (1817; Presidency University of today) focused on teaching English literature and on training in subjects like trigonometry and mathematics. The Calcutta School Book Society, established in the same year as Hindu College, also began publishing books on mathematics, chemistry, anatomy, and geography. Universities were opened up in Calcutta, Bombay, and Madras in 1857 and, subsequently, in Punjab and Allahabad in 1882 and 1887. Many informal places of learning were brought under the ambit of colonial state power, like Thomason Civil Engineering College in Roorkee in 1847 (Dionne and McLeod 1979: 60), to underline the instrumental basis of technical education endorsed by the British colonial administration.

The establishment of these varied educational centres marks the confluence of the dissemination of Western science and English literature in colonial India, inaugurated in the aftermath of the English Education Act 1835.[7] This confluence of teaching of science alongside English literature articulates, I argue, *science as a new language*, where "idioms, genres, and styles of a colonial vernacular moment" materialized as the outcomes of a "creative translation" (Hatcher 2017: 108). It is this 'creative translation', I claim, which informs and shapes Bengali science fiction and magazine cultures. Additionally, these institutional centres of education surfaced as key sites to reorganize the public and private domains of colonized spaces, and, thus, invest narratives of science with values both material and metaphorical.[8] These colonial pedagogical institutions and curriculums enabled the popularization of science amongst the masses while also lubricating the mechanisms of 'colonial governmentality' (Seth 2007: 110).[9] However, even as colonial science propagated "cultural technologies of rule" (Topdar 2010: 6; Headrick 1981) defined by the idiom of power, authority, and Western cultural hegemony, its *vernacularism* entailed a narrative of contesting nodes of engagement, deliberations, and reformulations. Thus, in the teaching of colonial science as a constituent element of colonial pedagogy to the natives, divergent contestations to this orientation surfaced. Dissemination of colonial science via pedagogical curriculum opened up new transformative "space[s] for multiple mobilities" (Topdar 2010: 14). These spaces of mobilities in their dynamic orientations highlighted a cross-cultural, inter-cultural exchange, which rejected colonial pedagogical science's consolidation of identities and significations (Goswami 2004; Topdar 2010).

Within the ambit of reading practices inaugurated through the growth of Bengali magazine cultures and the vernacular literary sphere, colonial science was gradually being read in alternate ways. Among these divergent ways, two widely popular schools of thought came into prominence. These schools of thought, Young Bengal led by Henry Louis Derozio (1809–1831) and Brahmo Samaj led by Raja Rammohun Roy (1774–1833),[10] espoused science and scientific enquiry in terms of the colonial science's rationalizing principle whose power and influence allowed the public to discard the moribund, superstitious, and dead thoughts of earlier times (Sengupta 2010: 42). Even as these schools of thought opposed superstitious native knowledge, they also re-signified Western scientific epistemologies by marking new technological subjectivities, recognizable with a "modern 'national' culture" which was 'neither' identical "with the precolonial indigenous nor with the modern Western" (Mitra 2013: 206).[11]

These responses and counteracting forces utilized colonial science to 'circulate' newer modes of imaginaries that intersected with local, vernacular practices. Akshay Kumar Dutta (1820–1886), one of the students of Hindu College, emerged as a key figure to popularize and disseminate science in his first book *Bhūgol* (Geography) published in 1841 under the patronage of the *Tattvabodhinī Sabhā* (Sengupta 2010: 116). The establishment of the *Indian Association for the Cultivation of Science* in 1876 by Mahendralal Sircar (1833–1904) popularized science as expressive of modernizing impulses as defined by the imperial forces while also reading science as a means to access power and gain freedom for the natives. These books and indigenous institutions enacted, I argue, a 'translation' of colonial science in conversation with local forms, practices, and other indigenous knowledge systems. Many other Indian scientists like Ashutosh Mukherjee (1864–1924), Jagdish Chandra Bose (1858–1937), Jagadananda Ray (1869–1933), and Praphulla Chandra Ray (1861–1944) popularized science amongst the masses in their various scientific writings. Conversely, many of their creative writings were marked by an ambiguous and tenuous relationship to colonial science.

In many instances, Western science was challenged by juxtaposing it with ancient Hindu traditions. This instantiation of the ancient Hindu practices inaugurated the revivalist tradition,[12] premised on an essentialized binary differentiation between the East and the West. Thus, the reading of scientific thought espoused through the collaboration of colonial and natives' expressions of science enabled the emergence of new subjectivities. This refashioning of subjectivities empowered the natives to "weave [their] way through the complexities of local settings and the exchanges they housed" (Roberts 2009: 20).

In these instances of "enchantments of Western science",[13] we see that science's assimilation and accommodation by the colonized intelligentsia becomes well-nigh impossible to be mapped in a monolithic framework. While pedagogical institutions facilitated science to be brought closer to the interpreters (*bhadralok*), who were integral to running the colonial machinery, it also assisted these 'interpreters' in creating newer expressions for further dissemination of scientific thought to the hinterlands. This 'circulation' of scientific epistemologies by the interpreters became vital for the growth of anti-colonial and nationalist sentiments. Thus, the movement, right from the formal, institutionalized sectors of knowledge production to informal sectors controlled by the colonized, enabled scientific modernity to be ensconced as an instance of popular consciousness.

Emergence of Popular Consciousness in Colonial Bengal

The rise of popular consciousness in colonial Bengal appeared as a product of scientific experimentations that manifest in the growth of print technology alongside science's reading, translation, adaptation, and reconstitution by the natives. This *pāṭhak'samāj* ([*readers society*], Mitra 2013: 207) emerges as a vital mode to unpack the rise of the various Bangla periodicals and the numerous science fiction texts that emerged in the last two decades of the nineteenth century until the mid-twentieth century. Most popular Bengali periodicals ranged from disseminating knowledge about science and technology in tandem to offering moral instructions to children of all classes. These periodicals became the key site, as Samarpita Mitra (2013: 207) remarks, of reshaping the inner and outer domains of nationalistic space. Additionally, these periodicals confronted science as the central mechanism of imperialism, which made reading of these magazines direct us to the imagining of collective social consciousness (Mitra 2013: 205). Defining the publication of periodicals as politically engaged and motivated acts of reading, Mitra states:

> Reading modern literature (and therefore literary magazines) was very much a solitary quotidian practice. At the same time it constituted a significant mode of public and collective engagement with profound implications for new visions of social change. [...] This literary sphere came to constitute a notionally autonomous domain that provided ways of thinking out a new form of solidarity.
>
> (*Mitra 2013: 208–209*)

Mitra's reading of Bengali periodicals locates them in the vortex of change and transformations. At once political and personal, collective, and individual, Mitra's investigation of reading culture demonstrates the enunciations of multiple and heterogeneous forms of scientific modernity. These widely read magazines[14] popularized science and other forms of knowledge in vernacular languages. Not only did these periodicals assimilate science and other colonial pedagogical practices in their everyday world, but in their translation of scientific thought in familiar modes of expression they "provide[d] a distinctive archive of science in translation for non-English readers in colonial South Asia" (Singh 2022: 2).

Furthermore, most popular Bengali periodicals targeted children (from early childhood to young adults) as their primary readers, enabling the Indian 'child' to function as the central node in comprehending the vectors of colonization and in participating in the nationalist reformulation of subjectivities (Topdar 2010; Sen 2005). And it is this dual orientation of the Indian child visualized both as an agent exercising control and as a subverting colonial power that informs the early science fiction narratives of colonial Bengal.

Debjani Sengupta rightly claims that early science fiction in Bengal primarily addressed children "but not necessarily with childish concerns" (2010: 40). Thus, vernacular science is not simply science rendered in a regional, local language. Instead, it presupposes a cross-connection and translation, which together constitute the vital element in the framework of early Bengali science fiction texts.

The rise and growth of science fiction, as John Reider's seminal study *Colonialism and the Emergence of Science Fiction* (2008) and Patricia Kerslake's *Science and the Empire* (2010) examined, is closely aligned with colonialism. But what exactly constitutes and frames these early Bengali science fictions? Bodhisattva Chattopadhyay in his article "On the Mythologerm: Kalpavigyan and the Question of Imperial Science" (2016) classifies Bengali science fiction as 'kalpavigyan' (*kalpabijñān*).[15] 'Kalpavigyan', as a term, refers to science fiction and speculative narratives that became widely popular in the early 1960s in Bengal and incorporated the whole Indian science fiction tradition spanning from antiquity to contemporary times (Chattopadhyay 2016). Used for the first time in the 1960s in the Bengali science fiction journal *Āścarya* (meaning wonderous, fantastic, and unimaginable) under the editorship of Adrish Bardhan, Chattopodhyay reads 'kalpavigyan' as a complex neologism made up of – 'kalpa' and 'vigyan'. Chattopadhyay reads 'gyan' (*jñān*) as referring to a comprehensive general knowledge, which includes both the spiritual and the material world. 'Vigyan' (*bijñān*) is understood by Chattopadhyay as a more specialized form of knowledge influenced by the discipline and practice of science. According to Chattopadhyay, 'kalpavigyan' evolves through the "linkages and intersections between diverse kinds of knowledge" (2016: 431–34). For Chattopadhyay, these diverse kinds of knowledge identify science in terms of the confluence of global and local motifs, a "particularity of the historico-cultural core of the imaginary transformations of a specific sf tradition" (2016: 438).

Borrowing from Chattopadhyay, I read 'kalpavigyan' as suggesting a wider understanding of scientific imagination. Here, science is not merely imaginatively recreated; instead, I argue, science functions as imagination. This polysemic nature of science fiction effectuates a rupture, a break, from the familiar and known epistemological native traditions, and, simultaneously, it shows a continuity of patterns drawn from folkloric, oral, and local traditions to redraw the polysemic terrain imbricated by the scientific consciousness as continually evolving and shifting.

Bengali science fiction is a less-defined cultural product than its popular and more recognized counterpart of the Anglocentric tradition. Recalling both the philosophical and the religious strains of our ancient traditions and the material, rational features of Western science fiction imaginaries, Bengali science fiction published in colonial Bengal, as Hans Harder asserts, "represents an instance of intercultural semantics" (2001: 105). Harder rightly states that though these terms were initiated as equivalents to Western conceptualization, nevertheless, the idea of science/imagination, as the poem by Pakshi also describes, is projected as something alien enunciated in the very topography of Calcutta. And it is this strangeness, the uncanny element, that undergirds these vernacular science fiction texts.[16] These early science fiction stories combine scientific knowledge with other non-canonical literary traditions, such as mystery, romance, ghost stories, fairy tales, and folklore.[17]

Science and scientific epistemologies that figure in these science fiction tales are, I argue, a translation of science taught in colonial schools and experienced in the urban spaces of the colonies. The act of translation enacted in the plethora of Bengali periodicals and Bengali pieces of science fiction literature comprised of, in the words of Bishnupriya Ghosh, "a re-codification of the subaltern subject and her acts in accordance with the desires of specific populations or publics" (2005: 459). It is in the 're-codification' that Sukumar Ray's Professor Heshoram will be examined.

'The Diary of Professor Heshoram Hunshiyar' and Vernacularized Science

Sukumar Ray's delectable tale, 'The Diary of Professor Heshoram Hunshiyar' was published in 1922 in the journal, *Sandeś*, which was started by his father, Upendrakishore Roy Chowdhuri (1863–1915). The name *Sandeś* has a double meaning in that it suggests simultaneously a sweet delicacy, which is intrinsic to Bengali culture and imagination, and news (majorly news of public importance). This journal then offered 'delectable news' or 'news told in a delectable manner',[18] and primarily targeted young readers. *Sandeś* played a crucial role in vernacularizing the literary scene and advanced articulated diverse interpretations of the Bengal renaissance. Most of the stories published in this journal under the editorship of Upendrakishore and Sukumar engaged in inspiring the children to become adept political and intellectual actors and, thus, deftly navigated the terrains of family, community, and public spaces.

Professor Heshoram Hunshiyar's (roughly translated as Cautious Chuckleonymous) strange tale, in the interplay of multiple genres like diary narratives, adventure stories, hunting expeditions, exploration, travel narratives, nonsense literature, children's literature, and comprising of embedded narratives and interviews, refuses the boundaries of any literary genres. This automatically opens up the heterogeneous perspectives that inform science and scientific imagination defined by boundaries, classifications, and categorizations. The story begins ironically as the editor apologizes for not having published Heshoram's expedition tales earlier and seeks to make amends to the 'angry' Professor by publishing the 'strange' story in the current issue of the periodical. However, this frame narrator inserts an editorial observation that if the story is being published, it is only because Professor Heshoram has forwarded a few extracts from his diary, which is what shall comprise the major content of the story. Nevertheless, the editor is quick to lay the onus of responsibility on the reader regarding the veracity of Professor Heshoram's expedition stories. The tripartite organization of the story raises questions regarding science as the site of truth and objectivity. However, from the very first section of the story, one which comprises the frame narrative functioning as an embedded commentary, a shadow is cast over the truth claims of Professor Heshoram's narrative. The second section with its random, fragmentary, and strange adventures documented in Heshoram's diary adds to our woes of ever extracting the truth of Professor's travelling tales. These diary extracts include the adventure stories of Professor Heshoram and his crew while exploring the Karakoram Range, 10–25 miles of Mt. Bandukush (a parody on Hindukush mountains), and the fictional Kankramati River. The extracts span 72 days of exploration/expedition, but provide incomplete descriptions of the multiple fantastic adventures and exploration to distant lands undertaken by Professor Heshoram and his crew. Heshoram's exploration crew consists of his nephew, Chandrakhai ("Swallowmoon"), two brothers known for their hunting and fighting skills, Lakkar Singh and Chakkar Singh, six coolies, and a dog that vanishes without a trace at the end of the tale. These fantastical disappearances of the dog and other related stuff are ultimately mocked by the embedded narrator/publisher as an instance of 'Tall-tale-therium' (Ray [1922] 2012: 146), which eventually mocks the colonial authority of the state underpinned by scientific epistemologies.

As an element of travel narratives and expedition tales about strange and dangerous adventures, describing intrepid travelers' and explorers' voyages into the unknown, Ray's Professor Heshoram underpins the popular terrain which constituted the vexed colonial encounter of the late nineteenth and the first half of the twentieth century. Along with the setting up of cultural institutions and the visible tools of industrial progress, Debjani Sengupta states, "European surveyors, plant collectors, mineralogists, doctors and engineers were an important part of the Company personnel who carried out surveys, created maps, established printing presses and steam railways, used the telegraph and the steam vessel" (2010: 41). In fact, these surveys, censuses, and "official statistics on agriculture, trade, education, births, and deaths", as per Sanjay Seth, did more than just "count" (2007: 109). They were crucial links engaged in empire building. These "scientific soldiers" (Dionne and McLeod 1979: 163) based their authority on the knowledge disseminated by the colonial pedagogical institutes, and emerged as important agents of colonial sovereignty and institutionalized knowledge "to feed the rapidly expanding colonial administration" (Bhattacharya and Hiradhar 2014: 282). The professor's diary, in describing the empty terrain – "[t]his is a no man's land, devoid of the slightest human civilization anywhere" (2012: 138) – recalls Daniel Defoe's *Robinson Crusoe* (1719) and Shakespeare's Prospero's (from *The Tempest* 1610–1611) continual attempts to refashion such 'no man's land' into imperial spaces.

However, the idea of constituting the imperial terrain as natural, inevitable, and empty, is, as J. G. Cons states, framed in "silencing the natives" (read Caliban) (2005: 2).

In this hunting expedition, Heshoram and his crew encounter several animals that are named according to their physical characteristics understood and defined by the Bengali language, and subsequently the naming process is rendered complete by adding Latin prefixes. So, the first animal Heshoram's crew encounter is named 'Hanglatherium' (continually hungry) because of his perpetual hunger, then 'Gomratherium' because of the animals' sullen expression, 'Lyangratherium' for the animals' lame disposition, 'Chillanosauraus' for the animals' shouting/screaming propensities, and 'Becharatherium' for the wretchedness and lost soul-like qualities of the animal. The act of naming, classifying unknown people, and flora and fauna, which constitutes Professor Heshoram's scientific enterprise, was an integral part of British administration. These technological conceptions of naming, as Deane Heath spelled out, not only embodied "new conceptions of space and time and new understanding of economy, society, history and progress" but also "set about enumerating, demarcating and classifying colonized people' (2010: 9). Professor Heshoram's absurd mapping strategies, I argue, inaugurate what Ian Hacking calls a 'dynamic nominalism' (1986). Hacking writes,

> The claim of dynamic nominalism is not that there was a kind of person who came increasingly to be recognized by bureaucrats or students of human nature but rather that a kind of person came into being at the same time that the kind itself was being invented. In some cases, that is, our classifications and our classes conspire to emerge hand in hand, each egging the other on.
>
> *(Hacking 1986: 228)*

Sukumar's Heshoram's exploratory act of classification fails to give us any information apart from the physical characteristics. The Professor's ordering, mapping, and naming strategies render colonial science's power not only as arbitrary but also ludicrous. Baidik Bhattacharya asserts:

> by mimicking the protocols of the original and by transferring its codes and practices to a trivialized and derisive organization, parody disputes the fixity of the original. Parody, in other words, through its retelling of the source and target texts reveals a complex notion of representation and connotation beyond any simplistic reading of either.
>
> *(2006: 279–80)*

What is subverted in the upside-down adventures of Professor Heshoram's expedition is the authority identifiable with the colonial state. Apart from the explorers, scientists, and surveyors, i.e., the central agents of the empire being mocked and their services debunked, there's another fascinating innovation initiated by Sukumar Ray's mind-boggling inventiveness. This inventiveness and creativity are projected in the juxtaposition of Bengali and Latin registers. In the juxtaposition of Bengali and Latin adjectives for the animals, we see a 'counterchallenge' develop that refutes the silencing of the voice and histories of the natives.

Borrowing from Mary Louis Pratt's explanation of the "contact zone" (1992), I shall read Ray's absurdist neologisms as facilitating a new anti-colonial politics to read the colonial encounter. Pratt writes:

> "[C]ontact zone" is an attempt to invoke the spatial and temporal co-presence of subjects previously separated by geographic and historical disjunctures, and whose trajectories now intersect. By using the term "contact", I aim to foreground the interactive, improvisational dimensions of colonial encounters so easily ignored or suppressed by diffusionist accounts of conquest and domination. A "contact" perspective emphasises how subjects are constituted in and by their relations to each other. It treats the relations among colonisers and colonised, or travellers and "travellees", not in terms of separateness or apartheid, but in terms of co-presence, interaction, interlocking understandings and practices, often within radically asymmetrical relations of power.
>
> *(1992: 7)*

Heshoram's convoluted expressions of vernacular Bengali and Latinate expressions with unprecedented vocabulary and idioms are cast in a series of displacements whose meanings are always deferred. What 'gomratherium', 'becharatherium' and other neologisms suggests is that the diffusionist model of science and the linear modernity framework from West to non-West is wholly absurd and, worse, factually incorrect. The drawing up of boundaries and hardening of erstwhile fluid identities in the colonial regime is now shown in these neologisms as being accommodative of non-scientific thought where neither indigenous nor the Western modes of knowledge offer a complete truth. If linkages or circulation of science are to be understood, then one needs to read the 'polycentric' networks espoused by Susan Friedman. She writes:

> *Polycentric* and *multimodal* suggest power linkages differently. The globe, these adjectives suggest, has multiple centers or nodes of power, not one. Positing different cores existing synchronically within a single time period fundamentally rewrites the diffusionist metanarrative of Western modernity.
>
> *(2015: 153)*

While Friedman's model of polycentricity define multiple locations of power and modernity is construed as not solely concentrated in Eurocentric imagination, Ray's Bengali–Latinate combinations suggest how circulatory power of science refashions polycentricity and multimodality as offering "science as being co-produced through the encounter and interaction of heterogenous specialist communities of diverse origins" (Raj 2013: 345). The neologisms do not suggest a linear diffusion and transmission of scientific modernity. Instead, the interconnections and the intersections, divisions, and ruptures, demonstrate networks and nodal linkages of relationality. The logic that operates in these usages of neologisms follows the circularity trajectories. Circularity is "different from simple mobility". Instead, it "implies an incremental aspect and not the simple reproduction across space of already formed structures and notions" (Markovits et al., 2003: 2–3).

This circularity can be further clarified by reading Heshoram's peculiar tale, in terms of how reading communities brought to the fore local meanings and value systems to what was hailed as universal forms of knowledge, effectuated by the operations of translation or *anubād* or *rūpāntar*. However, this translation is not a faithful rendition of the original or even marked by what Lawrence Venuti (1995) defined in terms of the methods of domestication or foreignization. These neologisms are neither a seamless nor a smooth rendition of the original nor an absolute innovation. What these neologisms contain are forms of interpretative strategies that are invariably multiple, heterogenous, plural, and circular. The act of translation in Bengal, as Brian A. Hatcher defined it, created a site of contradictions, "of significant tension and intellectual negotiation in nineteenth-century Bengal" (2017: 108). Science that is depicted in Ray's text refuses to be merely a translation of colonial science in indigenous or revivalist terms, nor does it extol the superiority of western forms of knowledge. The neologism suggests a 'recodification', a 'grafting' of civilizational ethos encoded in linguistic terms.

Ray's tale of Heshoram's wonderous naming ability occasions the rise of the forgotten histories and forgotten trajectories of connections and calibrations. The creative translation that characterizes these neologisms functions to nominate vernacular science as 'other archives'. Drawing from Bishnupriya Ghosh's reading of vernacularity as 'other archives', these neologisms are read as "'supplemental' in the Derridean sense", dramatizing reading as "multiple levels of lost epistemologies" (2004: 202). These 'lost epistemologies' become apparent in the animals and human encounters etched in Heshoram's diary extracts. The classification of the animals epitomizes multiple semantic registers drawn from homely endearments to absurdist references, and identifies the animals–humans discourse as paradoxical and ambiguous. Heshoram's endearments and familiar representations take on board the discourse of cruelty to animals during the colonial period, which were underscored as defining the relationship of humans and non-humans, British and natives: "[w]e didn't know what was going on, [...] a large creature that was neither a crocodile, nor a snake, not even a fish, though it bore a resemblance to all three" (2012: 143). Samiparna

Samanta's (2012) study of this vexed relationship between humans and animals postulates the class, race, and gender anxieties of empire, and she discusses how they were deliberated in terms of governmental rationality. In Sukumar Ray's text, the boundaries between humans and non-humans/animals are redrawn to project a local, contested, contingent, collaborative matrix where boundaries denote an authoritarian and arbitrary power.

Also, the fact that the stories are left open-ended with no single evidence to substantiate the claims of Heshoram is a direct response to the transformations being wrought on the cityscape of Calcutta. At the end of the diary extracts, the embedded narrator/publisher/editor seeks clarification about the stories by demanding evidence from the professor. Heshoram sends his nephew, who offers truth in the form of his and his uncle's physical presence. The lines concerning the veracity of Heshoram's strange narrative also postulate that Heshoram's story is illustrative of the genre of 'tall-tale'—a classification that is used by the editor/publisher/frame narrator of Heshoram's bizarre tale to Chandrakhai, Heshoram's nephew: '[h]e's a Tall-tale-therium, sitting around telling tales' (Ray 2012: 146). Tall tales are illustrations of nonsense literature where the mechanistic world pushes 'the boundary of the possible' but, in doing so, renders it as an excess of reality, in short fantastic.

Conclusion

Centred in the Western discourses of science that were inaugurated in Bengal and other parts of the Indian subcontinent and occasioned by colonial politics, this chapter, via its 'reading' of Ray's short story, navigates the terrain of colonial modernity and enunciates how Western 'science' was vernacularized. In its reproduction, appropriation, figuration, and articulation of vernacularized science underlined in Heshoram's (mis)adventures, we see multiple ways of reading and a "certain practice of 'doing' science in India" surface (Bhattacharya and Hiradhar 2014: 278).

Ray's short story postulates in its absurdist inflections and linguistic experimentations the initiation of a vernacular science. What Ray's story reflects is a kind of interface and intercultural exchange, a connection between "two seemingly different orientations: the specifically local character of individual encounters and the increasingly global networks that both afforded and attributed meaning to the conditions and outcomes of these local exchanges" (Roberts 2009: 10).

Sukumar Ray's 'The Diary of Professor Heshoram' along with other Bangla science fiction tales and children's magazines in the colonial period can be read as 'public narratives' (Chakrabarty 1997: 376), and also as a key site offering a nuanced knowledge about consumption, reception, and subversion of colonial scientific epistemologies. If these technological and co-related administrative changes facilitated communication by bringing many disparate communities together and led to the shrinking of spaces (towns and cities as twins, neologisms bringing Latin and Bangla cultures together), it simultaneously paved the way for the rise of nationalist consciousness. Maybe, the pun on Hindukush as Bandukush is no longer merely an aspect of parody but implies an oblique political gesture of rejecting Lord Curzon's division of Bengal. Bandukush is an Urdu term, referring to 'banda', a person close to God, or simply being human. Whether one reads Bandukush as a parody or as enunciating solidarity between communities in the backdrop of the First Bengal Partition (1905), Ray's tale refuses a singular meaning.

Thus, vernacularizing scientific practices configure and redraw the contours of modernity to imagine national solidarities, so as to redefine democratic participation outside of traditional communities based on caste, class, and religion. This vernacular science involves a multidirectional, contrapuntal approach to reading and translating scientific epistemologies. It is as if the neologisms comprising the Bengali and Latin idiom showcase one idiom being perpetually haunted by the other. Ray's story invites us to read science as not merely defined by an imperialist framework. Instead, this funny tale prompts us to read in the absurd depictions and linguistic mutations a long-refracted political and cultural struggle over science and modernity's meanings, values, and effects.

Notes

1 In this chapter, the English translation of Ray's text has been selected instead of the Bengali original, although it is widely available on the net. The translated version has been used to include more readers who are unacquainted with the Bengali language and to draw attention to the idea of translation itself.

2 Historians like Roy MacLeod (1982) have suggested that the science which flourished in the colonies of the Empire, like India, was different from the science that shaped the metropolitan centre's politics. The science that affected and directed the course of the state and its colonized subjects was identified as 'colonial' science, while the ones developed at imperial centres were defined as 'metropolitan' science. Scholars have suggested that 'colonial' science was primarily concerned with fact-gathering and was more instrumental in nature. Metropolitan science was considered superior to colonial science and majorly dealt with philosophical theorization and research-oriented scientific theorization. However, in both the cases, colonized subjects responded to science's narratives from the margins. This chapter explores the enactment of 'colonial' science as it was enforced, imposed, regulated, and translated in the peripheries of the empire.

3 See Rajesh Kochchar's article for the Indian version of the diffusionist model of science (2008).

4 The history of science discussed and analysed in this chapter focuses on the period from the 1880s to the 1920s. The studies by David Arnold (2000) and Atanu Bhattacharya and Preet Hiradhar (2014) focus on science dating from the ancient Vedic times to Mughal systems to the flourishing of science under the East India Company. For science's political and cultural influence during the sixteenth and seventeenth centuries, read Debjani Sengupta (2010).

5 Amitav Ghosh's reading of Rabindranath Tagore's short story "Kṣudhita pāṣāṇ" ("The Hungry Stones") depicts this 'crisis' in terms of self-fashioning of a divided subject underlined in the figure of Tagore himself (B. Ghosh 2004: 200). The story of a "man in 'crisis' is replayed in the continual exchange of identities and clothes of the protagonist, which dramatizes the paradoxical relationship of this individual with the modernizing forces. The individual is aware of the seductive enchantments of 'Enlightenment legacies' while 'anguished' over his imbrication as a colonial subject" (ibid.).

6 The Asiatic Society, concerned with promoting Oriental literature and research primarily through translations, in the words of Shiv Visvanathan (1985: 85), established "the institutionalization of Western science in India [...] for all practical purposes".

7 The English Education Act of 1835 introduced by Lord Macaulay was a major political move initiated by the British colonial administration. This act introduced English literature in higher education leading to the fashioning of anglicized Indians, who became known pejoratively as 'Macaulay's Children'.

8 In Partha Chatterjee's book *The Nation and Its Fragments* (1993), science emerges as identifiable with the rational, material, and public domain in contradistinction to religion and spirituality which defined the private domain. However, while science inevitably drew up the public domain, the domestic sector was not impervious to events and discourses occurring in public spaces. Chatterjee claimed that the domestic/private sector was being realigned in tune with issues concerning nationalism, science, the women's question, etc.

9 Governmentality, a practice elaborated by Michel Foucault, refers to the disciplining and control of a population as per the ideas of the state. Borrowing this idea, Sanjay Seth uses governmentality to refer to the regulating and disciplining of Indian natives as per the will of the colonial British administration. Governmentality finds a unique expression within the colonial pedagogical system where the study of English literature and science sought to govern, civilize, and rule the natives.

10 The Young Bengal Movement, or Derozians, included scholars from Hindu College who followed their charismatic leader-cum teacher, Henry Louis Derozio, to reject Hinduism's fossilized beliefs and frameworks. Among the Derozians, the most famous members included Reverend Lal Behari Dey and Reverend Alexander Duff. The Brahmo Samaj, a monotheistic sect of Hinduism, was led by the great reformer Raja Rammohun Roy. The Brahmo Samaj shaped the *bhadraloks*' middle-class identity in tune with the scientific principles of rationalism and objective knowledge. Among its famous members was Rabindranath Tagore's father, Debendranath Tagore.

11 See Partha Chatterjee 1993: 1–13.

12 Bhattacharya and Hiradhar state that *bhadraloks* – Radhakanta Deb and Nundcomar Mukherjee – sought to establish an ancient Hindu scientific practice equivalent to western epistemologies (2014: 285).

13 I borrow the term from Shruti Kapila's article where science appears as the mode of enchantment for Indian modernity and emerges as pivotal to redefining cultural and public discourses (2010).

14 Few of the well-known Bengali magazines that were published in the mid-half of the nineteenth century included: Pramadasaran Sen's *Sakhā* (*The Friend*, 1884), *Bālak* (*The Child*, 1885), *Sandeś* (meaning both *"News"* and a popular Bengali sweet, started in 1913), *Maucāk* (*The Beehive*, 1920), and *Āmār deś* (*My Country*, 1920).

15 Chattopadhyay (2016) refers to the whole Indian science fiction tradition from the colonial times to the present day as an example of 'kalpavigyan'. In this chapter, I prefer to use this term primarily for Bengali science fiction from the 1880s to the

1970s. While this neologism is useful for Hindi and in Maratha SF contexts as well with a few variations, my understanding of science fiction refuses the classificatory mode outlined by Chattopadhyay in his use of mythologerm as the defining characteristic of Indian science fiction.

16 The few eminent science fiction texts produced in colonial Bengal from the 1880s to 1920s include the first science fiction written in India, "Rahasya" ("Mystery" 1882) by Hemlal Dutta. Other popular science fiction narratives written by colonized natives include "Śukrabhramaṇ" ("Travels to Venus" 1892) by Jagadananda Roy, Jagdish Chandra Bose's "Niruddeśer kāhinī" ("Story of Disappearance" 1896), republished as "Palātak tuphān" ("Runaway Cyclone" 1921), Rokeya Sekhawat Hossain's *Sultana's Dream* (1905), written in English.

17 The fantastic, the improbable, the scientific, the gothic, and the fairy tales were widely read during the last quarter of the nineteenth century till the mid-twentieth-century colonial India. It continued to be popular even after the 1940s. During its heyday from the 1870s–1940s, an increasing readership was observed for these 'minor' works of literature. See Priya Joshi's study of readership patterns in the case of British novels and how book culture that evolved in Bengal under the aegis of colonial policies of the nineteenth century went against the imperial pedagogy (2002).

18 I prefer to read *Sandeś* as the news was told in a delectable manner which allows the idea of *Pāṭhak samāj* to be more materially visible.

Bibliography

Arnold, D. 2000. *The New Cambridge History of India*, Vol. 3, Pt.5. Cambridge: Cambridge University Press.

Baber, Z. 1996. *The Science of Empire: Scientific Knowledge, Civilization, and Colonial Rule in India*. Albany: State University New York Press.

Basalla, G 1967. "The Spread of Western Science [online]." *Science* 156(3775): 611–622. https://science.sciencemag.org/content/sci/156/3775/611.full.pdf.

Bhattacharya, A. and Preet Hiradhar. 2014. "Own Maps/Imagined Terrain: The Emergence of Science Fiction in India." *Extrapolation* 55(3): 277–297.

Bhattacharya, B. 2006. "Jokes Apart: Orientalism, (Post)Colonialism Parody and the Moment of Laughter." *Interventions: International Journal of Postcolonial Studies* 8(2): 276–294. https://doi.org/10.1080/13698010600782030.

Chakrabarty, D. 1997. "The Difference—Deferral of a Colonial Modernity: Public Debates on —Domesticity in British Bengal." In *Tensions of Empire: Colonial Cultures in a Bourgeois World*, edited by F. Cooper and A.N. Stoler, 373–405. Berkeley: California University Press.

Chatterjee, P. 1993. *The Nation and its Fragments: Colonial and Postcolonial Histories*. Princeton: Princeton University Press.

Chattopadhyay, B. 2016. "On the Mythologerm: Kalpavigyan and the Question of Imperial Science." *Science Fiction Studies* 43(3): 435–458. https://www.jstor.org/stable/10.5621/sciefictstud.43.3.0435.

Cons, J.G. 2005. "Claiming Territory: Colonial State Space and the Making of British India's North-West Frontier." Thesis (MS), New York: Cornell University.

Dionne, R., and Roy McLeod. 1979. "Science and Policy in British India, 1858–1914: Perspectives on a Persistent Belief." In Gaborieau, Marc (ed.), *Asie du Sud: Traditions et Changements*, 59–77. Paris: Centre National de la Recherche Scientifique.

Dube, S. 2002. "Introduction: Enchantments of Modernity." [online]. *The South Atlantic Quarterly* 101(4): 729–755. [Accessed 25 April 2015].

Friedman, S.S. 2015. *Planetary Modernisms: Provocations on Modernity across Time*. New York: Columbia University Press.

Ganeri, J. 2013. "Well-Ordered Science and Indian Epistemic Cultures: Toward a Polycentered History of Science." *Isis* 104(2): 348–359. https://www.jstor.org/stable/10.1086/670953.

Ghosh, A. 2002. "Revisiting the 'Bengal Renaissance': Literary Bengali and Low-Life Print in Colonial Calcutta." *Economic and Political Weekly* 37(42): 4329–4338, http://www.jstor.org/stable/4412747.

Ghosh, B. 2004. "On Grafting the Vernacular: The Consequences of Postcolonial Spectrology." *Boundary 2* 31(2): 197–218.

——— 2005. "The Subaltern at the Edge of the Popular." *Postcolonial Studies* 8(4): 459–474. http://dx.doi.org/10.1080/13688790500375124

——— 2020. "In Difference: The Vernacular Then and Now." *South Asian Review*, 1–4. DOI: 10.1080/02759527.2020.1725226.

Goswami, M. 2004. *Producing India: From Colonial Economy to Nationalist Space*. Chicago: University of Chicago Press.

Hacking, I. 1986. "Making Up People." In *Reconstructing Individualism*, edited by T. Heller et al. Stanford: Stanford University Press.

Harder, H. 2001. "Indian and International: Some Examples of Marathi Science Fiction Writing." *South Asia Research* 21(1): 105–119.

Hatcher, B.A. 2017. "Translation in the Zone of the Dubash: Colonial Mediations of 'Anuvāda.'" *The Journal of Asian Studies* 76(1): 107–134. https://www.jstor.org/stable/44506826.

Headrick, D.R. 1981. *The Tools of Empire: Technology and European Imperialism in the Nineteenth Century*. New York: Oxford University Press.

Heath, D. 2010. *Purifying Empire: Obscenity and the Politics of Moral Regulation in Britain, India and Australia*. Cambridge: Cambridge University Press.

Joshi, P. 2002. *In Another Country: Colonialism, Culture, and the English Novel in India*. New York: Columbia University Press.

Kapila, S. 2010. "The Enchantment of Science in India." *Isis* 101 (1): 120–132. JSTOR. http://www.jstor.org/stable/10.1086/652700.

Kochchar, R. 2008. "Cultivation of Science in 19th Century Bengal." *Indian J. Phy*. 82(3): 1003–1082.

Kumar, D. 2004. "Emergence of "Scientocracy": Snippets from Colonial India." *Economic and Political Weekly* 39(35): 3893–3898. https://www.jstor.org/stable/4415469.

MacLeod, R. 1982. "On Visiting the 'Moving Metropolis': Reflections on the Architecture of Imperial Science." *Historical Records of Australian Science* 5(3): 1–16.

Maity, A. 2016. "Estrangement, History, and Aesthetic Relish: A Reading of Premendra Mitra's Manu Dwadosh." *Science Fiction Studies* 43(3): 459–478. https://www.jstor.org/stable/10.5621/sciefictstud.43.3.0459.

Markovits, C., Pouchepadass, J., and Subrahmanyam, S. 2003. "Introduction: Circulation and Society under Colonial Rule." In *Society and Circulation: Mobile People and Itinerant Cultures in South Asia 1750–1950*, edited by C. Markovits et al. Delhi: Permanent Black.

Mitchell, T. 2000. "The Stage of Modernity." *Questions of Modernity* [online], 1(34). http://www.ram-wan.net [Accessed 1 May 2015].

Mitra, S. 2012. "Cruelty Contested: The British, Bengalis, and Animals in Colonial Bengal, 1850–1920." Thesis, Florida: The Florida State University.

——— 2013. "Periodical Readership in Early Twentieth Century Bengal: Ramananda Chattopadhyay's Prabāsī." *Modern Asian Studies* 47(1): 204–249. DOI: 10.1017/S0026749X12000819.

Philip, K. 1964. *Civilizing Natures: Race, Resources, and Modernity in Colonial South India*. Brunswick: Rutgers University Press.

Prakash, G. 1999. *Another Reason: Science and the Imagination of Modern India*, Princeton: Princeton University Press.

Pratt, M.L. 1992. *Imperial Eyes: Travel Writing and Transculturation*. London: Routledge.

Raj, K. 2013. "Beyond Postcolonialism… and Postpositivism: Circulation and the Global History of Science." *Isis* 104(2): 337–347.

Ray, S. 2012. "The Diary of Professor Heshoram Hunshiyar" (1922). In *The Crazy Tales of Pagla Dashu and Co.*, translated by Nabaneeta Dev Sen, 135–46. Gurgaon: Hatchette Book Publishing.

Roberts, L. 2009. "Situating Science in Global History: Local Exchanges and Networks of Circulation." *Itinerario* 33: 9–30. doi: 10.1017/S0165115300002680.

Samanta, S. 2012, "Cruelty Contested: The British, Bengalis, and Animals in Colonial Bengal, 1850–1920." Thesis (Ph.D.). Florida: The Florida State University.

Sarkar, S. 2010. "Technical Content and Colonial Context: Situating Technical Knowledge in Nineteenth Century Bengal." *Social Scientist* 38(1/2): 37–52, http://www.jstor.org/stable/25621955.

Sen, S. 2005. *Colonial Childhoods: The Juvenile Periphery of India, 1850–1945*. London: Anthem Press.

Sengupta, D. 2002. *Mechanicalcutta: Industrializations, New Media in the 19th Century*, 149–158. Sarai Reader 02. New Delhi: Centre for the Study of Developing Societies.

——— 2010. "The Wondrous Traveler: Leela Majumdar and Science Fiction in Bengal." *Extrapolation* 51(1): 40–52.

Seth, S. 2007. *Subject Lessons: The Western Education of Colonial India*. Durham: Duke University Press.

Singh, C. 2022. "The shastri and the air-pump: Experimental fictions and fictions of experiment for Hindi readers in colonial north India." *History of Science* 60(2): 232–254. DOI: 10.1177/0073275320987421.

Topdar, S. 2010. "Knowledge and Governance: Political Socialization of the Indian Child within Colonial Schooling and Nationalist Contestations in India (1870–1925)." Thesis (Ph.D.), Michigan: University of Michigan.

Venuti, L. 1995. *The Translator's Invisibility: A History of Translation*. London: Routledge.

Visvanathan, S. 1985. *Organizing for Science: The Making of an Industrial Laboratory*. Delhi: Oxford University Press.

11

MULTILINGUAL LOCALS IN TRANSNATIONAL GEOGRAPHIES

Vaijñānik Upanyās and the Cosmopolitanisation of Hindi in Late Colonial North India

Ishita Singh

The development of the Hindi novel from the 1880s onwards has been seen as a direct response to the colonial encounter and vernacular education in North India (Kalsi 1992; McGregor 1967). From the 1890s onwards and particularly from 1901, there was a proliferation of Hindi novels, original and translated, in the region. The Hindi Literary Canon, defined and constructed by Ramchandra Shukla, is centred around three personalities that influenced the writing of Hindi prose in the late nineteenth and early twentieth centuries—Bhartendu Harishchandra, Mahavir Prasad Dwivedi, and Premchand.[1] In the late nineteenth century, Harishchandra attempted to cleanse the Hindi language of Urdu influences and make Sanskrit loan words the norm, and in the early twentieth, Dwivedi played a vital role in formalising the Hindi public sphere as the editor of the leading Hindi literary journal *Sarasvatī*. Dwivedi aimed at standardising Hindi, which would be a language for public discourse, representing and serving the various purposes of a modern nation. In a 1901 editorial of *Sarasvatī*, Dwivedi wrote:

> I also wish to write that these days the storehouse of Hindi is full of plays and novels of magic, fantasy, detective works and love stories. This is not at all beneficial for literature. Instead, lovers of Hindi should have the courage to lift their pens to write on business, technology, chemistry, the history of Europe and India, the nature and means of European progress, etc. This would benefit Hindi and lead to the elevation of the character of its readers.
>
> (*Gupta 2002: 57*)

DOI: 10.4324/9781003279921-14

Dwivedi's definition of literature is based on the exclusion of 'novels of magic, fantasy, detective works and love stories' and the inclusion of writings on science and technology. It is beyond the margins of such canonical corpus planning that SF came to be located, not because of its connection with hard science, of course, but due to the fantasy aspects it also embodied. *vaijñānik upanyās* in Hindi has not been a subject of serious academic inquiry despite its widespread publishing and readership since the early twentieth century. This creates a lacuna in our understanding of the vernacular public sphere and vernacular identities. This chapter surveys the complex relationship between Hindi novels, Western science and technoscientific modernity in late colonial North India. By mapping the non-realist conventions of storytelling onto a complex terrain of competing linguistic nationalisms, this chapter will examine how writers of *vaijñānik upanyās* in the early twentieth century, in negotiating that which is alien and unfamiliar, make claims to a cosmopolitan identity for the 'vernacular' Hindi by embracing the 'other', English, Sanskrit and Urdu, within its fold. This exploration of the cosmopolitan demands made of and through Hindi recontextualises the vernacular public sphere and its translocal geographies and multilingual locals.

Vijñān: Translating Science into the Vernacular

The process of translating Western science into the vernaculars had begun in North India from the mid-nineteenth century onwards as a part of the colonial mission of educating and civilising the native subjects. The colonial government and British educators had reservations regarding the vernaculars' fitness as vehicles of Western knowledge due to linguistic incommensurability and perceived it as a lack.[2] The Superintendent of Delhi College, Felix Boutros, had begun the programme for vernacular textbook production in 1842 with Hindustani, that is Urdu, as he felt that despite its deficiencies, its widespread usage made it the "most appropriate language to use for educational translations in NWP" (Dodson 2005: 821). Where a linguistic equivalent could not be found, he recommended the usage of transliterated English-language scientific terms. In the mid-1840s, Urdu became the primary vernacular medium for the publication and teaching of scientific knowledge, with Delhi and Agra as central locations of the production, publication and distribution of translated textbooks.

By the late 1840s, translational activity and textbook production had shifted to Benaras, where James Robert Ballantyne was the superintendent of Benares College. This shift led to a move away from Urdu to Sanskrit as the language of translating Western scientific and philosophical texts. He believed that "the translation of Western scientific and 'useful knowledge' into Indian vernacular languages for use in mass education required that it first be rendered into Sanskrit", as presenting it in Sanskrit would earn it legitimacy from Brahmins (Dodson 2005: 824). There was also a difference in methodology. Unlike

Boutros, Ballantyne did not endorse engraftment or transliteraton of English words as that would lead to a 'barbarisation' of the language. Instead, Ballantyne proposed an appropriately coined Sanskrit terminology. Following this, Ballantyne supervised the translation of these texts into Hindi and other vernaculars, and for these, he recommended the engraftment of Sanskrit technical and scientific vocabulary directly into the text.

Over the next few decades, Hindi dictionaries would be prepared and published that provided the scientific lexicon in Sanskrit as several Indian elites, which included Sanskrit scholars, university teachers and Hindi writers, began to translate scientific terminologies into their vernacular languages (Singh 2021b: 2). This new scientific lexicon was useful for the writing and proliferation of the new genre of writing in Hindi, i.e. popular science writing, which was particularly energised from the 1880s onwards when the movement for Hindi and Nagari script gathered steam. The Hindi print media became an important site of the vernacularisation of Western science as it was disseminated in the Hindi-language magazine of Northern and Central India from the late nineteenth century onwards. The establishment of Indian-owned printing presses like Indian Press and Munshi Naval Kishore Press in the 1870s and the 1880s played a contributing factor in the consolidation and strengthening of the Hindi movement. The most important actor in the advocacy of Hindi as a national (and modern) language, the Nagari Pracharini Sabha, established in 1893, also took up the task of producing glossaries and dictionaries of scientific terms in Hindi. The *Hindī vijñān koś*, first published in 1906, provided the vocabulary needed for scientific discourse in the 'vernacular' Hindi.

In 1900, the Nagari Pracharini Sabha began publishing *Sarasvatī*, which regularly carried articles on science with illustrations promoting science journalism in Hindi (Mishra 2017, 480). Magazines like *Sarasvatī* and *Vijñān*, which began to be published from 1915 onwards, were vital in building a science-literate public in Hindi. Two factors intersected at the production of this science-literate public: emergence of Hindi as a site of nationalistic assertions and the creation of Hindi as an effective medium of mass scientific education needed for the building of a modern nation. In foregrounding the nation in the study of vernacular assertions and sensibilities, literary historiographies have focused almost entirely on the serious reformist literature. The centrality given to Dwivedi and the Nagari Pracharini Sabha in the story of the making of the vernacular public sphere seems to suggest the transformation of a multilingual region into a monolingual and linguistically discrete world. However, when we shift our gaze to the literature on the margins of Hindi literature, the boundaries of the linguistically defined world seem to blur as do the boundaries of the nation. The vernacular, then, as I will show in this chapter, displays a 'malleability' of form and use as it emerges to be more than just a 'linguistic category' but rather a critical site for the contestation between nationalism and cosmopolitanism; translation and transformation; and home and Europe.[3]

The Novel of the New Mechanical Age

In a 1911 article titled, "Hindī kī vartamān avasthā", Dwivedi wrote, "Novels should contain only those depictions of society that promote good behaviour, not bad behaviour. We should keep in mind that stories should seem neither artificial nor excessively real" (Mody 2018: 113). Dwivedi, in his editorial, asserts that the primary function of literature is to be a disseminator of useful positive instruction, and that would be possible if the representation were neither excessively real nor excessively artificial. Dwivedi thus formalises his concept of *'ādarś svabhāvik'tā'* that Sujata Mody translates as 'exemplary naturalism'. A reflective shift towards the mundane can be seen in the publication of Hindi novels in the early twentieth century, which led to the development of the social novel from 1917 onwards, pioneered by Premchand. Gopal Rai divides this development of the Hindi Novel into two phases: 1901–1917 and 1918–1930, the pre-Premchand and the Premchand era, respectively (Rāi 1968: 72). While the number of novels published in the two periods is comparable, Rai observes that there is a visible shift in genres of the Hindi novels being published. The 1901–1917 period, which he calls the Experimental Period, on account of flooding of the print mark with experimental genres like *tilismī* Romances ("talismanic"), Historical Romances, Detective and Crime Novels and *manaḥkalpanā* ("fantastika"; Rai includes *vaijñānik upanyās* as its subgenre). The period 1918–1936, the Premchand era, is marked by the prominence of the Social Novel. Table 11.1 provides some information regarding the number of novels printed in the two periods according to the various sub-genres.[4]

Dwivedi, therefore, rejects 'novels of magic, fantasy, detective works and love stories' at a time when thousands of readers were learning the Devanagari script to read the most commercially successful Hindi novels at the turn of the century: Devakinandan Khatri's *Candrakāntā* (1888–1891) and *Candrakāntā santatī* (1894–1905). Dwivedi's conceptualisation and demands for *'ādarś svabhāvik'tā'* and Shukla's historiography of Hindi literature exclude modes of storytelling that disrupt realist conventions. They are relegated to the pulp

TABLE 11.1

Genre	1901–1917	1918–1936
Social Novel	180	351
Historical Novel	78	46
Tilism-Aiyārī	45*	15
Crime and Detective Novel	132	74
Novels in Translation** (from Bengali, Marathi & Gujarati)	175	115

* Some of these had more than 20 and up to 50 parts in the series

** The number of novels being translated from English remained more or less the same.

industry of *qissa* and *tilismī* romances and *jasūsī upanyās* (detective mystery novels). This exclusion of 'paraliterature' reveals significant cleavages in our understanding of the making of Hindi and the formation of the Hindi public sphere.

Devakinandan Khatri's use of the everyday language of the market, Hindustani, made the novels popular amongst "low-brow groups of readers and their illiterate listeners" and produced a readership for Hindi novels and widened the habit of reading for pleasure (Gaeffke 1978: 26; Śukla 1942: 489). Khatri thus created a habit of Hindi novel reading amongst a larger public and thereby also performed the critical role of "educating the reader to the new novelistic conventions" (Orsini 2009a: 272). In creating the "first bestseller in modern India", he successfully capitalised on the possibilities of print entertainment (Gaeffke 1978: 25). The commercial success of the novels allowed Khatri to start his literary magazine, *Upanyās laharī*, in 1894, which serialised the *Candrakāntā* novels, followed by establishing his printing press, the Lahari Press, in 1898. Various young men took to writing novels after reading *Candrakāntā* as there was a burgeoning market for "Chandrakanta-like books" (Śukla 1942: 499). However, this new genre of *tilismī* romances and adventures was not entirely imitative of Persian and Urdu *dāstān*s but instead showed imprints of the "new mechanical age" (Orsini 2009a: 198).

In the introductions to *Candrakāntā* and *Candrakāntā santatī*, Khatri argued for the scientificity of the skills of the *aiyār*s, explained in technical terms as opposed to magical. Scientific reasoning orients the fantastical and *tilism* world of Chunar as his *aiyār*s use mechanical devices like latch doors, wheels, buttons and wires that produce the effect of *tilismī* marvel as characters and objects magically disappear or appear (Orsini 2009a: 187–198; Yadav 2013: 189). Khatri thus naturalises the enchanted world of a *dāstān* to reconcile it with modernity and the modern form of the novel. By providing scientific explanations, Khatri fulfils the novel's new expectations of providing accountability, and also the expectation of and fidelity to Western science as a novel of the new mechanical age. The naturalisation of the marvellous through scientific explanations and the dissemination of scientific knowledge and lexicon in the vernacular produced a vernacular sensibility that facilitated the writing and reading of the *jasūsī upanyās* and the *vaijñānik upanyās*. It is the latter that is the object of inquiry in this chapter.

Vaijñānik Upanyās: *Svarg'purī* and *Bāīs'vīṃ Sadī*

The most popular term for science fiction (hereafter SF) in Hindi used by publishers and writers is *vaijñānik upanyās* or *vijñān-kathā*.[5] In Hindi, it refers to a type of literary production that draws upon science or the scientific method as a framing device of the story.[6] In this chapter, I examine two *vaijñānik upanyās* published in the 1930s, Durgaprasad Khatri's *Svarg'purī* and Rahul

Sankrityayan's *Bais'vīṃ sadī*. Khatri's *vaijñānik upanyās*, *Svarg'purī*, is divided into three parts: 'Lohe kā ād'mī', 'Svarg'purī' and 'Māyā'. The first part introduces the protagonist of the novel, Professor Gamut, and his unique invention, Steelman, a robot who was "built like a human [...] walked like a human, shook hands like a human, took off his hat like a human and spoke like him too [...] but under his gloves were hands made of iron" and the antagonist of the novel, Framji (Khatrī 1938, 5). Through various twists and turns in fast-paced action sequences, Khatri tells a thrilling story of the mysterious disappearance of Steelman and Professor and the failure of the various policemen and detectives that were meant to protect them. This takes Professor Gamut and the reader on an adventurous journey on first a ship, then a submarine, to the utopian city of Svargpuri (*svarg'purī*), literally 'heaven town'. Aboard this ship, Framji engages in a long conversation with his prisoner Professor Gamut. He declares his ambitions of building a perfect world devoid of unhappiness and suffering. Framji argues:

> [...] if gentlemen of good character were to be resettled in a new place away from this sinful world and its poisonous air, then will we not be creating a new world based on truth and good manners? If we can establish a world whose citizens are well-mannered, truthful, strong, healthy, hard-working, thoughtful, intelligent, and selfless [...] then in that world, won't there be happiness, peace and prosperity?
>
> *(Khatrī 1938: 67)*

This dream of Framji had led him to search the planet far and wide, looking for people who would be the perfect citizens of this perfect world. Built underground, near the icy peaks of the South Pole, the route to Svargpuri was intentionally difficult so that its existence could remain unknown. In this part, we see Svargpuri through the eyes of the visitor Professor Gamut, who anticipates and asks questions about this new world and how it works. Here, Khatri shifts the reader's perspective to this utopia that is possible only because of the marvels and wonders of modern science. Framji is no longer framed as the antagonist but as the chief architect of this utopia. We also learn that he had kidnapped Professor Gamut to not use Steelman for destructive purposes but to protect Svargpuri from dangers that are both human and non-human. In the third part, 'Māyā', Svargpuri is under attack, and Professor Gamut, the scientist-hero, is engrossed in experimentation and research to find a solution to defeat the various monstrous animals that reside in the warm waters of this utopian kingdom. This part returns to the espionage motifs and the fast-paced action similar to the first part where we see that Svargpuri is under attack not only from genetically mutated animals but also from humans who are trying to infiltrate its boundaries. The book ends with a cliffhanger encouraging the reader to pick up the next instalment *Sāgar samrāṭ*—just like the volume begins where the action of another work (*Svarṇ-rekhā*) by Khatri ended. From serialising the story over several parts to using familiar motifs from *jasūsī upanyās*, complete with several scientific mysteries solved by the detective-scientist hero, Khatri further manoeuvres commercial publishing and entertainment in the idiom of the vernacular.

Rahul Sankrityayan, too, constructs a utopian world in *Bāīs'vīṃ sadī*, but unlike Khatri, he does not explicitly refer to the novel as *vaijñānik upanyās* and nor does he use any of the tropes and formulas used by him. Explained as a vision that came to him in a state between wakefulness and sleep, Sankrityayan, on the title page, describes it as "a portrayal of a socialist world and its varied village-towns, factories, hospitals, schools, dress and language customs etc.". In *Bāīs'vīṃ sadī*, the protagonist, Professor Vishvabandhu, awakens from a long sleep in a cave in Nepal to find himself in the twenty-second century. The circumstances of his travel 200 years into the future are not made intelligible. Instead, the professor embarks to record the changes that have taken place in society since 1924. Sankrityayan's novel takes on the form of a fictional travelogue as he performs the task of observing and documenting the work, leisure, food cultures, domestic spaces and relations, public sphere, linguistic practices, education, child-rearing and technologies of this socialist utopia. This twenty-second-century society has also found national borders obsolete, unifying the world's continents under a single government. The smaller units in this globalised living are not the nation but village communities centred around one trade; entire villages are dedicated to growing and packing apples, manufacturing railway parts, etc. In this society, private property and wealth have been discarded, and all resources and wealth are state-owned. This has done away with the disparities between the rich and the poor as everyone now lives in state-built and owned houses. Doing away with the accumulation of wealth and capital has eliminated greed, which has led to an elimination of crime, prisons and similar institutions of disciplining and punishing.

This society has also found religion obsolete and useless as a moral and ethical framework and instead relies on science and scientific temperament. Rejection of religion has also gotten rid of caste-based practices, instilled respect for all and infused dignity in labour and work. In this society, everyone, man or woman, works the same number of hours, eats the same kind of food, speaks the same language and also lives in the same kind of house and wears the same kind of clothes as a way of unifying under a universal brotherhood.

Much scholarship exists on Gandhi's utopian dream of a future India glorified and perfected based on the presumed former glory of ancient Hindu culture or the Arcadian pastoral paradise (Fox 1989; Mohan 2012; Srinivas 2015). While like Gandhi, Sankrityayan locates the utopia in a village community, unlike him and more like Khatri, he believes machines to be a means of liberation and sees railroads, trams, automobiles and flying machines as signs of a progressive cosmopolitan modernity. For Sankrityayan, technology offered a path to workers' and women's emancipation and the transformation of society and governmentality.

Vaijñānik Upanyās: Domesticating the 'Alien' and Cosmopolitanising the Self

By the late nineteenth century, "Indian subjects lived conscripted to a world increasingly reshaped under the sign and influence of science", and this public was primarily a multilingual one (Singh 2021a: 222). With the increasing visibility of new technologies in North India from bridges and railroads to sewing machines; with the opening of schools and colleges; the proliferation of science writing and scientific education in the vernacular; and the development of the Hindi movement, North Indians were exposed to the material culture of 'alien' science. By the second decade of the twentieth century, the new novel of the mechanical age, written in response to this strange and wondrous encounter, had begun to develop a new set of generic expectations that had at its centre scientific and technological innovation. That product would come to be recognised as a wholly new genre of the Hindi novel, the *vaijñānik upanyās*. Until the second and third decade of the twentieth century, Hindi novels that bear a resemblance to what was identified as *vaijñānik upanyās* had been translations of French, English or Bengal scientific novels.[7] It is only with Durgaprasad Khatri that we see the production of an original body of work that fashions and fulfils certain new generic expectations and comes to refer to itself as *vaijñānik upanyās*. The son of Devakinandan Khatri, Durgaprasad Khatri, has been written into history only in a filial capacity. As the son, he succeeded the father at the helm of the Lahari Press. The junior Khatri also inherited from his father the *Bhūtǀnāth* series, of which he wrote five parts of the seven parts from 1915 to 1935. The prose style of the *Bhūtǀnāth* books published posthumously is so similar that their authorship continues to be accorded to the senior Khatri. The literary legacy of the Khatris is thus intertwined in the production of novels that not only broke away from conventions of realism but also relied on the everydayness of vernacular sensibility to produce not mundane or 'exemplary naturalism' as advocated by Dwivedi but the *ajāyab* (*'ajā'ib*), and the *āścaryajanak*, the strange and the wondrous.

In the early twentieth century, often referred to as the Golden Age of the genre, the 'alien' genre of SF was a global phenomenon influencing cultural productions in the Americas, Asia and Europe (Banerjee 2012; Ginway and Brown 2012; Smith 2012; Banerjee 2020). The writers of *vaijñānik upanyās* in Hindi also incorporate within their novels tropes from other popular modern genres like the *tilismī* romance, *jasūsī upanyās* and the travelogue. The hybridity of tropes, often used for purposes of scientific education and pedagogy, also allowed the writers to domesticate a globalising culture.[8] Science fiction relies upon 'cognitive estrangement' to defamiliarise its readers from the scientific principle and its consequences that are at the centre of the story.[9] In using tropes from the *jasūsī upanyās*, the scientific is translated and explained through clues, exhibition and ratiocination. The *vaijñānik upanyās*, I argue, therefore, does not estrange the reader to produce *āścarya* or wonder. Instead, it uses *āścarya* (wonder) and *kautuhal* (curiosity) to explain the scientific principle and to cultivate a scientific temperament using the vernacular idiom. In both Khatri's *Svarg'purī* and Sankrityayan's *Bāīs'vīṃ sadī*, the aesthetic of technology and Western science governs the storytelling, but this technology and science are not made strange. Instead, scientific innovations (nova) and scientificity (the culture of scientific temperament and experimentation) are explained and made familiar. This native elite who is the intermediary between the coloniser and native, we and they, performs the role of intermediating, exploring, seeing, explaining and translating the Western other as well as the colonised other. They do so in two ways: explaining and exhibiting the other by making it a part of the everyday. Much like spaces like museums, exhibitions, schools, colleges, railways, post-office, etc. in the nineteenth century, the *vaijñānik upanyās* became one of the sites of acculturation of 'alien' science, as science-learners in schools and readers of literary and scientific periodicals and newspapers filled with advertisements of these products became "consumers of technoscientific modernity" (Prakash 1999: 25; Singh 2021a: 223). Therefore, it is telling that Khatri should, in the opening chapter of *Svarg'purī*, have Professor Gamut exhibit and explain his invention of Steelman on stage. This incident is framed by another sign of vernacular modernity and colonial power—the newspaper. The narrative takes the form of a newspaper report that has appeared in the *Karachi Times*:

> [...] but the most amazing feat this statue of iron can perform, the Professor told us, was his ability to converse with others. Certainly, the Professor had already informed us a little earlier that 'he can utter only those sentences and phrases that have been fed into him beforehand'. However, it is wondrous that he should have the intelligence to decipher which words to use as an appropriate response. [...] A few people present asked him how a man built of iron could perform all of these tasks. Professor Gamut gave a short lecture to explain his handiwork. [...] In brief, in his lecture, Professor explained that there is an artificial brain within this iron man that operates through wireless technology using radio waves and electricity. For speech, a phonograph-like device has been implemented, and his ears are constructed so that different sounds collide with them to produce vibrations. Accordingly, he performs the actions commanded of him. Several technologies have been put to use to produce movement and motor skills. On request from the audience, Professor removed the clothes from Steelman's back to display the various gears and machines installed inside his chest. He, however did not elaborate upon what energy is used to operate him, deliberately

hiding that information as to his 'secret' as letting it out would help others build a similar statue."

(Khatrī 1938: 9–10)

The 'alien' machine is introduced as a mesmerising spectacle that initially estranges the public and the reader before the wonder or *āścarya* it produces translates into understanding through demonstration, exhibition and newspaper reports. In *Bāīs'vīṃ sadī*, the initial wonder that the protagonist experiences upon waking up 200 years into the future is framed within a structure of feeling similar to wonder, curiosity or *kautuhal*. Both wonder and curiosity as structures of feeling are seen as essential for a modern scientific temperament possessed by a scientist or science professor, i.e., the scientist-hero in the pages of the *vaijñānik upanyās*. This wonder and curiosity are articulated in the opening chapters when Professor Vishvabandhu says, "My curiosity has no bounds. While where I am travelling is not far from here, but it certainly is distant from this time" (Sāṅkrityāyan 1934: 7). Professor Vishvabandhu declares early in the novel, "I heard Devmitra with amazement and wonder as I began to understand that all these were the miracles of science" (Sāṅkrityāyan 1934: 16). The novel uses this curiosity to drive the plot forward and to explicate the various aspects that structure the twenty-second-century society. It also progresses to reveal the various technologies used by this society. These aspects are explained and rationalised by the members of this society as Professor Vishvabandhu encounters them on this journey to another time. The initial estrangement from the world and its technology is naturalised through exposition as Sankrityayan utilises several sub-genres like travel writing, ethnography, pastoral and dialogue in the novel.

By naturalising the technoscientific, writers of *vaijñānik upanyās* not only recontextualise the Hindi public vis-à-vis Western science but also reposition the Hindi public sphere to embody multilingual locals and translocal geographies. *Vaijñānik upanyās* is further domesticated by localising it within a particular geocultural space. Both Khatri and Sankrityayan have chosen to use Hindi, a vernacular, which, unlike cosmopolitan languages like English in the colonial world and Sanskrit or Persian in the past, does not travel.[10] Writers of the *vaijñānik upanyās* not only use the vernacular to imagine the "local" but also expand their geocultural imagination to the transregional so as to include the planetary and intergalactic. The language and imagination of science allow writers to construct these new worlds. This geocultural imagination becomes the site of cosmopolitan assertions by Hindi writers.

In *Svarg'purī*, Khatri imagines Karachi as an urban fantasy. It exists in the interstices of the doubleness of here/there, everywhere/nowhere, then/now, metropolitan/colony and home/alien. The port city in the colonial Bombay Presidency is infused with signs of technoscientific modernity and in the novel becomes an imagined Europe, so much so that this modernity is universalised by erasing all signs of the colonial encounter and the native response. While these ubiquitous signs have been made possible only due to the colonial encounter, there is no reference to it. The coloniser has wholly disappeared from this landscape, but the signs of colonial institutions and influence remain. Most visible is the police and, more particularly, the figure of the detective; educational institutions where young scientific-minded young men invent technological marvels; and laboratories and scientific journals that were often used to identify and fashion the figure of the scientist-professor-detective. The city and its people have embodied this colonial power by subsuming this doubleness of metropole and colony. By writing Karachi as an imagined Europe, Khatri provides the modern scientific tools to Framji and Professor Gamut to colonise new lands and create a utopian society, employing the new technologies of colonial governance to articulate several 'ideological fantasies'.[11]

Similarly, Sankritayan, too, recontextualises contemporary colonial North India and articulates several 'ideological fantasies' by incorporating within the genre idioms and tropes of travel writing. Sankrityayan frames the spectacle of the everyday and mundane of the twenty-second century to the twentieth-century traveller with the structures of feeling arising from wonder and curiosity. *Bāīs'vīṃ sadī* directly responds to the material, extra-fictional world; the visitor, Professor Vishvabandhu, becomes the site of this comparison. *Bāīs'vīṃ sadī* is a didactic text written with the belief in the perfectibility of twentieth-century colonial North Indian society. Civil society is organised in the twenty-second century; the cities and towns are clean and planned; public distributions systems work smoothly; wealth and resources are not hoarded; there is no famine, scarcity or crime. *Bāīs'vīṃ sadī* thus addresses the problems faced by the twentieth-century society. This comparison within the novel's narrative leads to the collision of two realities; the reality of the twenty-second-century society that we enter and the reality of the twentieth century to which the visitor-narrator-reader belongs.[12] The collision and collusion of two realities within the world of the novel mirrors the two realities, East and West, of the twentieth-century reader. In that respect, the framing of this utopian narrative through wonder reflects the elements of discovery, wonder and exoticisation present in vernacular travel writings in colonial North India.[13]

This imagined future South Asia that needs to be discovered and made known is the geocultural space across which the *vaijñānik upanyās* writer forges the cosmopolitan identity of the vernacular. The *vaijñānik upanyās* asserts the supraregionality of Hindi and its literary value by mapping it onto a translocal imaginary, and through this, a cosmopolitan vernacular comes to be produced as a new epistemological tool. By choosing to write in Hindi, Khatri and Sankrityayan communicated and created a Hindi-reading public that could dream and aspire to travel abroad with Hindi and still be cosmopolitan in their attitudes. Hindi was thus formed into a language that could travel, and Hindiwallahs experienced unfettered mobility not only across space but also across time.

At Home with the World: Multilingual Locals in Transnational Geographies

The scholarship on modern Indian literary history locates the vernacular in a position of subalternity and locality in relation to the more cosmopolitan or classical language like Sanskrit or colonising language like English (Pollock 2009; Guha 1992). The lack of commensurability in technical and scientific terms, already discussed earlier, defined and embodied this powerlessness of the vernacular in the colonial episteme. But it also allowed the vernacular the malleability to imitate and appropriate the style and sensibility of another language, i.e., it could make itself into an image of another. In the translation of Western science into the vernacular, the terrain of the Hindi language becomes a multilingual one, containing within it technical terms in Sanskrit, Urdu and English.

This was reflective of the very formation of Hindi from a multilingual terrain and of the desire to create a vernacular that could perform a number of functions—in this case that of technoscientific modernity (Rai 2001; Orsini 2009b). Its idiom becomes malleable based on the function expected of it. In the hands of the *vaijñānik upanyās* writers, the use and function of Hindi in their imagination extends beyond the regional and national borders and beyond. Hindi can be deployed for all modern purposes—quotidian, administrative, legal, literary, scientific and imaginative. In such a context, the vernacular sensibility is local and translocal at the same time. As a language of a technoscientific utopia or uchronia, it makes claims to be a language that is both multilingual and cosmopolitan.[14] Through *vaijñānik upanyās*, writers like Khatri and Sankrityayan attempted to fashion Hindi as a language of the contemporary world and its futures. Therefore, it is especially significant that both Khatri and Sankrityayan attempt to cosmopolitanise the Hindi language and the Hindi-speaking identity by incorporating and appropriating multiple linguistic codes and thereby producing a hybrid register. This linguistic hybridity is motivated by the language of the bazaar, i.e., *bol cāl kī bhāṣā* and the language of commercial publishing, Hindustani. This hybridity in its usage remains haphazard and inconsistent, as Khatri and Sankrityayan casually shift from one register to another, Hindi, Urdu, English and Sanskrit to produce a hyperglossic text representative of the multilingual public sphere it is being produced in.

Hindi was not just posited as a language of anti-colonial discourse competing with cosmopolitan English, but as a product of post-colonial and post-nation society; a language in a bid to not just replace but also make space within itself for other cosmopolitan and vernacular languages, i.e., to be worldly. Sankrityayan in *Bāīs'vīṃ sadī* imagines a post-nation, transregional community that is linguistically hybrid but unified. "And language? The mother tongue of Bharat is Bharati. One could say it is representative of the

Hindi-Urdu of your time. This is the language that is spoken everywhere, and the script that is used is Nagari" (Sāṅkrityāyan 1934: 49). He imagines a world that has rejected national borders to build a cosmopolitan world with a universal language. The easy movement of people in a world without borders and boundaries has created a world in which race, caste and class no longer matter, and there is no place for linguistic nationalism. The people of the twenty-second century have a functionalist approach towards language. For more local and regional purposes, they use Bharati across the Subcontinent, and *sārv'bhaum bhāṣā*, universal language, for international use and purposes, leaving no use or need for other vernaculars. One of the characters argues that "just for the protection of languages, we cannot sacrifice the unity of the human race", which is only possible with the universalising of Bharati in Devanagari script across the subcontinent (Sāṅkrityāyan 1934, 211). Bharati or Hindustani, then, for Sankrityayan, in all its hybridity, is the mother tongue of the modern uchronia that can transcend regional, local and national boundaries.[15]

The process of language formation for both Khatri and Sankrityayan was an ongoing and incomplete one. Thus, the very attempts to standardise the language, spearheaded by Harishchandra, Dwivedi etc., were counterintuitive to those who tried to cosmopolitanise it. This chapter has shown that Khatri and Sankrityayan rejected the use of chaste Hindi to carve a cosmopolitan sensibility in the vernacular idiom. Choosing to write in Hindi literarily is an act of political and ideological will of the native elite. In their writings, Hindi is used as a tool to construct a colonial elite in the vernacular imagination that is modern, progressive, cosmopolitan and multilingual, all the while choosing to use Hindi. Thus emerges a new category of Hindiwallah in the pages of these vernacular utopias that is multilingual, cosmopolitan and participates in translocal networks and socialities.

Notes

1 Shukla in his *Hindī sāhitya kā itihās* maps the influence of Harishchandra, Dwivedi and Premchand on the development of *gadya sāhitya*, Hindi prose. For more see, Śukla, *Hindī sāhitya kā itihās*, 1942.

2 Lydia Liu argues that this linguistic commensurability was founded upon the premise that "a word in language A must equal a word or phrase in language B; otherwise, one of the languages is lacking" (Liu 1995: 4). Lisa Mitchell traces this emergence of the emphasis on commensurability of languages at a lexical level, i.e., "a word in any language must have a ready equivalent in each and every other language" to the nineteenth century (Mitchell 2009: 176).

3 For this chapter, I am borrowing 'malleability' as a concept from Charu Gupta's essay "Malleability of the Vernacular" in which she argues that "it is crucial to recognize the vernacular as a malleable concept, whose meanings and uses are contingent on its contexts" (Gupta 2020a: 198). I find this concept particularly useful to understand and expand the meanings of the vernacular imaginary.

4 This table is based on the numbers as provided in Gopāl Rāi, *Hindī upanyās koś Khaṇḍ 2* (1969: 132–244).

5 Rai recognises this as a sub-genre of *Manaḥkalpanā* that takes place underground, in unknown lands or on other planets. In his *Hindī upanyās koś Khaṇḍ 1*, Rai makes a distinction between *tilismī* Romances and *Manaḥkalpanā* but in his *Hindī upanyās Khaṇḍ 2* the subgenre is not mentioned. Instead, he focuses briefly on *Vaijñānik upanyās*. Within this, he only categorises scientific novels in translation and not those written originally in Hindi. For more, see Rai, *Hindī upanyās koś Khaṇḍ 1* (1968: 218).

6 *Vijñān-kathā* is a seemingly simple neologism used for the genre from the 1950s onwards. The first word, *vijñān*, with *vi-* prefixed to *jñān* or knowledge, transforms its meaning by association as a diminished or specialised knowledge, signifying something material as opposed to *jñān* that refereed to all-encompassing knowledge, the knowledge of the material as well as transcendental. And *kathā* is story, tale or narration. It interesting that *kathā* should be used to signify the genre when *kahānī* and *qissa* were more popular terms used at the time to refer to prose narratives. And while they all are the standard modern Hindi words for story, kathā has the connotation of religious tales due to its long association with *vrat-kathā* in popular imagination (Pritchett 1985: 321). From the mid-20th century, more and more editors and writers began prefacing works of the genre as '*vijñān-kathā*'.

7 Pratapnarayan Tandon in "Hindī kahānī kalā" argues that while the writing of *vijñān-kathā* in Hindi began in the Bhartendu period, they were imitations of European writers (Mevārī 2011: 26).

8 Charu Singh, in her essay "The Shastri and the air-pump: Experimental fictions and fictions of experiment for Hindi readers in colonial North India", discusses the writings of Prem Vallabh Joshi published in the popular science journal, *Vigyan*. In his writings, Joshi relied on the framework of popular genres like detective mysteries to embed clues, make observations, teach scientific concepts and provide scientific explanations for natural phenomena that had hitherto been considered supernatural. These stories were prefaced with subtitles that proclaimed them to be a "scientific mystery" or "scientific story" (Singh 2021c: 14). Similarly, Hans Harder in his examination of Marathi SF argues that the writers of these novels were concerned not only with imagining dislocations in time or space but also with science and its dissemination. The genre plays a significant role in scientific pedagogy and fiction "is not a necessary ingredient of *vijñān sāhitya*" (Harder 2001: 108–9).

9 Darko Suvin has argued that estrangement is a critical concept to designate, delineate and understand the genre of SF as he argues that "the attitude of estrangement [...] has grown into the formal framework of the genre" (Suvin 1979: 7). Suvin further combines estrangement with cognition to set SF apart from other genres like fantasy, fairy tales etc. that also rely on estrangement. He thus sees the presence and interaction of cognition and estrangement as sufficient and necessary conditions of the genre. By doing so, Suvin delimits SF or, in his opinion, 'real SF' to a small set of texts that fulfil these conditions. It, therefore, becomes essential to examine this understanding not only to open up the boundaries that limit SF but also to understand how this definition pertains to non-Anglophonic SF. Conceptually, estrangement carries within it several meanings relating to defamiliarisation and alienation. These meanings are embedded within estrangement also because Suvin in his conceptualisation is influenced by Victor Schlovky's concept of *ostranenie* and Bertolt Brecht's V-effect, V standing for *Verfremdung*, meaning estrangement, defamiliarisation and alienation. While both Brecht and Schlovsky use this technique to defamiliarise the known world or make this world other-worldly, SF does the opposite. In Suvin's conceptualisation, SF is "a realistic irreality", that is, it renders otherworlds this-worldly (Suvin 1979: vii). Spiegel, on the other hand, argues that the

formal framework of SF is not estrangement but naturalisation as "SF does not estrange the familiar, but rather makes the strange familiar" (Spiegel 2008: 372). By re-theorising the formal framework of SF texts, he opens up the limits of the genre.

10 I have borrowed Pollock's conception of a vernacular language as one that does not travel. I find it particularly useful to understand the vernacular imaginary of the genre of *vaijñānik upanyās* that recontextualises the geocultural space. For more see, Pollock, "The Cosmopolitan Vernacular," 1998.

11 For Rieder, the otherworldliness of colonies provides the material for the imagining and writing of the 'alien' in SF. Therefore, for him, colonialism becomes part of the genre's texture and its ideological fantasies in the construction of the possible and imaginable. For more on "ideological fantasies," see John Rieder, *Colonialism and the Emergence of Science Fiction* (2012).

12 Typically, in utopias the "visitor" is the single character whose accidental entry sets off the action in the utopia and who becomes the "registering apparatus" and provides the narrative vehicle through which the utopia is described and its harmony opened to the gaze of the reader (Burwell 1997: 58).

13 For more on travel writings in colonial North India, see Gupta, "Masculine Vernacular Histories of Travel in Colonial India" (2020b).

14 Various linguistic nationalisms aimed to overcome this status of vernacularity and claim a 'natural' status of the linguistic repertoire and community. For more, see Mitchell, *Language, Emotion, and Politics in South India* (2009).

15 This insistence on making a claim for Hindi as the national language distanced Sankrityayan from the Communist Party, because by the 1940s the espousal of Hindi was often perceived as communal and parochial. A polyglot who knew around 34 languages and wrote in 3 (mostly Hindi, apart from Bhojpuri and Tibetan), Sankrityayan chose not to write in English. For more see, Joshi's "Rahula Sankrityayan's Journeys of the Self" (2009: 123).

Bibliography

Banerjee, Anindita. 2012. *We Modern People: Science Fiction and the Making of Russian Modernity*. Middletown: Wesleyan University Press.

Banerjee, Suparno. 2020. *Indian Science Fiction: Patterns, History and Hybridity*. Cardiff: University of Wales Press.

Burwell, Jennifer. 1997. *Notes on Nowhere: Feminism, Utopian Logic, and Social Transformation*. Minneapolis: University of Minnesota Press.

Dodson, Michael S. 2005. "Translating Science, Translating Empire: The Power of Language in Colonial North India." *Comparative Studies in Society and History* 47, no. 4 (October): 809–835.

Fox, Richard G. 1989. *Gandhian Utopia: Experiments with Culture*. Boston: Beacon Press.

Gaeffke, Peter. 1978. *Hindi Literature in the Twentieth Century*. Wiesbaden: Otto Harrassowitz.

Guha, Ranajit. 1992. "The Authority of the Vernacular Pasts." *Meanjin* 51, no. 2: 299–302.

Gupta, Charu. 2020a. "Malleability of the Vernacular: Personal Anecdotes." *South Asian Review* 41, no. 2: 197–199.

———. 2020b. "Masculine Vernacular Histories of Travel in Colonial India: The Writings of Satyadev 'Parivrajak'." *South Asia: Journal of South Asian Studies* 43, no. 5: 836–859.

———. 2002. *Sexuality, Obscenity, Community: Women, Muslims, and the Hindu Public in Colonial India*. New York: Palgrave.
Ginway, Elizabeth M. and J. Andrew Brown. 2012. *Latin American Science Fiction: Theory and Practice*. New York: Palgrave Macmillan.
Harder, Hans. 2001. "Indian and International: Some Examples of Marathi Science Fiction Writing." *South Asia Research* 21, no. 1: 105–119.
Joshi, Maya. 2009. "Rahula Sankrityayan's Journeys of the Self: Nation, Culture, Identity." *Journal of the Inter-University Centre for Humanities and Social Sciences* 16, no. 1&2: 119–146.
Kalsi, A.S. 1992. "Parīkṣāguru (1882): The First Hindi Novel and the Hindu Elite." *Modern Asian Studies* 26, no. 4 (October): 763–790.
Khatrī, Durgāprasād. 1938. *Svarg'purī*. Vārāṇasī: Lahari Book Depot.
Liu, Lydia He. 1995. *Translingual Practice: Literature, National Culture, and Translated Modernity-China, 1900–1937*. Stanford, California: Stanford University Press.
McGregor, R.S. 1967. "The Rise of Standard Hindi and Early Hindi Prose Fiction." *The Journal of the Royal Asiatic Society of Great Britain and Ireland*, 99, no. 3/4 (October 1967): 114–132.
Mevārī, Devendra. 2011. *Merī priya vijñān kathāeṃ*. Pañc'kulā: Ādhār Prakāśan.
Mishra, Pooja. 2017. "Science Education and Science Writing in Hindi in the North West Provinces (1860–1900)." *Indian Journal of History of Science* 52, no. 4: 463–483.
Mitchell, Lisa. 2009. *Language, Emotion, and Politics in South India: The Making of a Mother Tongue*. Bloomington: Indiana University Press.
Mody, Sujata S. 2018. *The Making of Modern Hindi: Literary Authority in Colonial North India*. New Delhi: OUP India.
Mohan, Anupama. 2012. *Utopia and the Village in South Asian Literatures*. Hampshire: Palgrave Macmillan.
Orsini, Francesca. 2009a. *Print and Pleasure: Popular Literature and Entertaining Fictions in Colonial North India*. Ranikhet: Permanent Black.
———. 2009b. *The Hindi Public Sphere 1920–1940: Language and Literature in the Age of Nationalism*. New Delhi: OUP India.
Phondke, Bal (ed.). 2012. *It Happened Tomorrow*. New Delhi: National Book Trust.
Pollock, Sheldon. 1998. "The Cosmopolitan Vernacular." *The Journal of Asian Studies* 57, no. 1 (February 1998): 6–37.
———. 2009. *The Language of the Gods in the World of Men: Sanskrit, Culture, and Power in Premodern India*. Berkeley, CA: University of California Press.
Prakash, Gyan. 1999. *Another Reason: Science and the Imagination of Modern India*. Princeton: Princeton University Press.
Pritchett, Frances W. 1985. *Marvelous Encounters: Folk Romance in Urdu and Hindi*. Bloomington: Indiana University.
Rai, Alok. 2001. *Hindi Nationalism*. Hyderabad: Orient Longman.
Rāi, Gopāl. 1968. *Hindī Sāhitya Koś, Khaṇḍ 1: 1870–1917*. Paṭ'nā: Granth Niketan.
———. 1969. *Hindī Sāhitya Koś Khaṇḍ 2: 1918–1936*. Paṭ'nā: Granth Niketan.
Rieder, John. 2012. *Colonialism and the Emergence of Science Fiction*. Middletown: Wesleyan University Press.
Sāṅkrityāyan, Rāhul. 1934. *Bāīs'vīṃ sadī* (2nd edition). Chap'rā: Sāhitya Sevak Saṅgh.
Śukla, Rām'candra. 1942. *Hindī sāhitya kā itihās*. Vārāṇasī: Nāgarī Pracāriṇī Sabhā.

Singh, Charu. 2021a. "Science and Its Publics in British India." In *The Routledge Handbook of Science and Empire*. London: Routledge, 218–227.

———. 2021b. "Science in the Vernacular? Translation, Terminology and Lexicography in the Hindi Scientific Glossary (1906)." *South Asian History and Culture*, 13, 1, 63–86. DOI: 10.1080/19472498.2021.2001200.

———. 2021c. "The Shastri and the Air-pump: Experimental Fictions and Fictions of Experiment for Hindi Readers in Colonial North India." *History of Science: Cultures of Scientific Publishing*, 60, 2, 1–23.

Smith, Eric D. 2012. *Globalization, Utopia and Postcolonial Science Fiction: New Maps of Hope*. Basingstoke: Palgrave Macmillan.

Spiegel, Simon. 2008. "Things Made Strange: On the Concept of "Estrangement" in Science Fiction Theory". *Science Fiction Studies* 35, no. 3 (November 2008): 369–385.

Srinivas, Smriti. 2015. *A Place for Utopia: Urban Designs from South Asia*. Seattle and London: University of Washington Press.

Suvin, Darko. 1979. *Metamorphoses of Science Fiction: On the Poetics and History of a Literary Genre*. New Haven/London: Yale University Press.

Werbner, Pnina. 2006. "Vernacular Cosmopolitanism." *Theory, Culture and Society*, May, 496–498.

Yadav, Rajendra. 2013. "An Interesting Account of a Pitiable Greatness: "Chandrakanta Santati"". Tr. by Rajul Bhargava. *Indian Literatures* 57, no. 2 (March/April): 180–201.

PART III

Language Ideology, Literature and the Vernacular Public Spheres

12

VERNACULARIZING EMOTIONS

Mohammed Ali's *Comrade* and *Hamdard*

Margrit Pernau

Introduction

Historians of emotions have underlined the profound link that exists between emotions and language, and rightly so.[1] Instead of assuming that emotions emerge fully formed in an interior space and only get translated into language as a second step, they point out that language shapes emotions on three levels. Firstly, language (here held to encompass also visual and audiovisual modes of representation) is central to the expression of emotions. Secondly, the investigation of emotion-concepts and emotion-metaphors provides us with indications of how subjects conceive emotions. The fact that *jaẕbāt* has become the central concept for talking about emotions in Hindi and Urdu since the late nineteenth century already indicates a specific understanding of emotions as a force that comes to the subject from outside and draws him or her along (Pernau 2019a). Lastly, the language of emotions feeds back into the possibilities of experiencing emotions. We only have to look at Francesca Orsini's (2006) careful analysis of the subtle differences between *ʿishq*, *muḥabbat, prem*, and love, to realize how these different concepts open up a way to not only describe emotions at the point of time in which they are already fully formed. More than that: they allow the subjects to align their expectations what to feel in a specific situation and their recognition of their own experiences with the models provided by a linguistic tradition, the many stories, images, and even sounds evoked by a concept like *ʿishq* or *śṛṅgāra*.[2]

The question I propose to address in this chapter is what happens to feelings once subjects start moving between languages. Outstanding work has investigated the transition from a cosmopolitan language to the vernaculars in South Asia, be it the move from Sanskrit to locally bounded languages (Pollock 1998,

DOI: 10.4324/9781003279921-16

2006), the increasing replacement of Persian by Urdu (Faruqi 2001), or the role that English has taken on in the colonial context and beyond as a new cosmopolitan language (Viswanathan 1989). These studies have often been read as histories of replacement of one language by another, instead of focusing on the subtle details of how one situation of multilingualism was replaced by another, with changes happening differently and at varied speeds depending on literary genre and social space. The Mughal court retained Persian as a language of administration right until 1857, while some (not all) poetic recitals were already conducted in Urdu since the mid-eighteenth century, and Urdu, English, and Hindi overlapped as a medium of the public sphere in North India in the nineteenth and twentieth centuries. Instead of a transition from one language to another, we find a situation in which many languages were co-present, forming what Sudipta Kaviraj has called a linguistic economy.[3] Moreover, every language carried the traces of its encounters with other languages, encounters that were constitutive to the formation of each of them (Orsini, Marzagora, & Laachir 2019; Orsini 2020).

What I suggest investigating is the question as to what happens to emotions in a multilingual situation in which there is no functional division between languages (as in the early modern allocation of Arabic for prayer, Persian for administration and poetry, and Urdu in its different registers for everyday communication).[4] What happens to emotions if the same situations can be – and are – interpreted and voiced in different languages? Does this question our assumption of a strong link between language and emotion, forcing us to revert to a position that minimizes the constitutive relationship between emotions and language, with language adding but the icing on the cake of fully fledged emotions? Or can we, alternatively, develop models for translating multilingualism into emotions? This would need to be based on a conception of subjectivity that allows for multiple and shifting emotions; at the same time, it would also need to avoid essentializing languages and their attributes.[5]

The case study I wish to use to reflect on these questions is a familiar one. Mohammed Ali [Muḥammad ʿAlī] is a well-known political figure. Born in Rampur in 1878 into an Urdu-speaking family of the *ashrāf*, he received an English-medium education, before proceeding to Aligarh and then to Oxford. After a short stint in the administration, he discovered his vocation in journalism, "the only avenue through which I could hope to reach a place in which I could prove of any appreciable use to [my community], while still earning a livelihood" (Hasan 1999: 73).[6] He founded the English weekly *Comrade* in Calcutta in 1911, taking up the roles of editor, proprietor, and printer in one. With the move of the capital to Delhi, *Comrade* also moved, in order to remain close to the center of politics. The newspaper was instantly popular, mainly among younger, Anglophone Muslims, many of them with links to the Aligarh movement. However, it also received patronage from colonial officers, right up to the Viceroy, Lord Hardinge, at least in its first phase. In 1913, he added an Urdu daily, *Hamdard*. This move allowed Mohammed Ali to reach out beyond the circle of those familiar with the English language and Western knowledge. After some initial problems, the newspaper rapidly grew, generating not only political influence but also income.[7] The period between April 1913, when *Hamdard* started to appear regularly, and November 1914, when *Comrade* was shut down by the colonial authorities for articles sympathizing with the Ottoman Government, allows us to compare, first, how the same events were variously depicted and interpreted in English and in Urdu and, second, which emotional registers were used.

For this chapter, the focus will be on 1913. Mohammed Ali stands at the center of attention because he not only decided on the strategies for both newspapers but also wrote most of their editorials and opinion pieces. However, this is not an exercise in individual psychology. If we situate emotions not in some hidden interiority, but in the space between subjects (Scheer 2014), the attention shifts to communication: we ask how emotions arise in interaction, how they create a common interpretation and a shared view of the world, and how multiple languages play a role in this communication (Pernau & Rajamani 2016). Moreover, from Mohammad Ali's generation onward, an increasing portion of the elite was bilingual. While we need to bring vernacular sources into history writing to a much greater extent than has been hitherto done, we also have to consider the effects of bi- or multilingualism. We cannot write the history of Urdu concepts in the twentieth century based only on Urdu, not even by including translations into it (nor can we assume that English can be interpreted in the Indian context without referring to the vernaculars with which it was in constant interaction). If language affects emotions, we need to find tools to consider multiple languages and their inherent heterogeneity and bid farewell to the assumption of monolingualism, which still lies at the foundation of much of emotion history.

Two contexts need to be briefly introduced to facilitate the reading of the source materials. First, Urdu journalism. While the Indian subcontinent knew a long tradition of handwritten newsletters in Persian, its first printed newspapers came out in English. From 1824, a number of Persian printed newspapers also appeared, followed by the *Delhi Urdū Akh̲bār* in 1837 (Fisher 1993; Pernau & Jaffery 2009; Pernau 2003). The Urdu press can thus be situated at the crossroad of a double vernacularization, taking inspiration from both Persian and English models for printed news media. Sir Saiyid Ahmad Khan founded the flagship journal of the Aligarh movement, *Tahẕīb ul-Akh̲lāq*, modeled on the eighteenth-century British journals *Spectator* and *Tatler*. Together with his speeches, Saiyid Ahmad Khan considered journalism as the most effective means for transforming the Muslim community. Through his articles and those of his collaborators, he aimed at convincing his readerships of the merits of the Aligarh project: opening up the community to new forms of knowledge, in cooperation with the colonial government, in order to progress toward his vision of the future. Emotions were central to this project because what was at stake for him was nothing less than the (honorable) survival of the Muslim community, and also because the reform of the community needed the transformative power of *josh*, of intensely felt, hot emotions, especially by young men (Pernau 2019a, chapters 3 and 4).

Both *Comrade* and *Hamdard* took up the legacy of Aligarh and of *Tahẕīb ul-Akhlāq*. Judging from the present-day language situation, *Hamdard* may indeed appear as a vernacular newspaper, given its choice of Urdu as the medium, when juxtaposed to the English language newspapers. However, if the vernacular carries with it the notion of spatial boundedness, Urdu hardly comes under this category: at the turn of the century, Urdu was a lingua franca used and understood across the Indian Ocean no less than in Afghanistan and beyond. Looking at the content and the regions covered by the news, both newspapers were equally cosmopolitan, looking out to the world beyond Delhi, beyond India, and even beyond Islam. Urdu was not only much more "wordly," as has been acknowledged for a long time (Datla 2009, 2013), but also more cosmopolitan (Green 2011, 2018).

The other context we have to take into consideration is political. In the first decade of the twentieth century, it looked as if Aligarh's loyalist politics had paid off. Separate electorates and the partition of Bengal favored the interests of the educated and landed Muslim elite, who kept their distance from the Congress and the Swadeshi movement. Things began to change with the revocation of the partition of Bengal in 1911, and change picked up speed in 1912 with the (failed) campaign to grant university status to Aligarh College. The mobilization of Muslims reached a fever pitch in 1913 with the Balkan wars and the destruction of a part of a mosque in Kanpur. New newspapers and journals accompanied these political developments: in 1911, Zafar Ali Khan's *Zamīndār*; in 1912, Abul Kalam Azad's al-Ḥilāl; and finally, in 1913, *Hamdard.*

Mohammed Ali on English and Urdu

One of the advantages of using Mohammed Ali's newspapers as a case study for the vernacularization of emotions is that he wrote explicitly about how the difference in language affected his aims for each newspaper. However, his own writings were often out of tune with the goals he had set himself –allowing us in turn to juxtapose the ideology of language with its actual practice. In accordance with the expectation that trustworthiness and personal character would depend on the consistency of the self, a movement between languages could be imagined as taking up different roles, but without changing authentic emotions. This expectation, nevertheless, was still quite recent in the North Indian context, which until the end of the nineteenth century and even beyond it stressed the need to stay in tune emotionally with particular situations (Pernau

2019a). Mohammad Ali's movement between languages thus affected not only the emotions themselves and the perception of the languages and their relationship but also the rules for navigating between changing emotions.

Surprising for those whose knowledge about Mohammed Ali focuses on his later life, during which colonial officers over and again called him a firebrand and a rabble-rouser, the Mohammed Ali who founded *Comrade* in 1911 was a declared loyalist in the tradition of the Simla Deputation and the early Muslim League. In tune with the Aligarh tradition, he saw his and his newspaper's task in building bridges between the Muslims and the colonial government. *Comrade* saw itself as a speaker for the Muslim community, addressing colonial officers no less than Indians and catering to their tastes (Hasan 1999: 93–97). At the core of this endeavor was the belief that an understanding would be possible if the Indian side were to curb their passions, renounce excessive language and emotions, and thus present themselves as reasonable interlocutors, and if the British, in turn, entered into the spirit of this relationship and cure disaffection with affection: "The English have hitherto captivated our reason. I would have them ensnare our heart also. They command our respect. Let them also ask for a little of our love" (ʿAlī 1907: xv).[8] As this quote already makes clear, the sweet reasonableness at which he aimed was expressed in an emotional language, while the emotions themselves partook of this reasonableness. At least for that moment, this strategy seemed to have worked, and Mohammed Ali was satisfied with his position as a translator between the government and the community, a critical, but esteemed and indispensable friend to both.

What is even more surprising is the extent to which Mohammed Ali, in his English writings, adopted the colonial perspective on vernacular emotions. The interpretation of the causes and events of 1857 had reinforced and systematized the discourse on the danger of oriental emotions, marked at the same time by excess and by lack, by their dangerous uncontrollability and their perfidious insincerity. This, in the colonial eyes, made the vernacular press so much more dangerous than newspapers in English, necessitating close supervision. Already in the 1860s, the Vernacular Newspaper Reports provided an insight into vernacular daily and weekly writings in translation; this was followed by the Vernacular Press Act in 1878, which facilitated the demand for securities and the closing down of presses. This perception of the distinct attributes of the two languages by the historical subjects is important and needs to be taken into consideration, without, of course, taking it at face value and in turn subscribing to a vision of English as the language of rationality and Urdu, of sentiments and passions.

Comparing the two newspapers, Mohammed Ali claimed that

> the *Hamdard* was intended to educate the people whereas the *Comrade* had to be their spokesman as well [...]. I was anxious to exclude from the former all exciting topics such as could not be avoided from the latter in the heat of

> advocacy. [...] The readers of the *Hamdard* were not permitted to overhear what passed between the *Comrade* and the Government in power in England.
>
> (*Hasan 1999: 97*)

The same emotions, Mohammed Ali seems to agree with the colonial officers, that could be voiced without danger in English became threatening when translated into the emotional language of Urdu. This was not only because the vernaculars evoked colonial anxieties of disaffection arising without the British noticing them until too late but also because the British interpreted Urdu as a language given to hyperbole and exaggeration of emotions. We cannot exclude the possibility that Mohammed Ali was consciously playing up to colonial prejudices here. It might also be a question not only of language but of class as well, as Urdu newspapers were accessible to a non-elite (or rather less-elite) audience. We simply do not know enough about the readership of *Hamdard*. Judging by the topics discussed, their interests do not seem far apart from the readers of *Comrade* – here, too, we find long discussions about transforming Aligarh into an (English medium!) university and about the reform of the Service Commission, which might have been of primary interest to an audience that was bilingual, or at least closely affected by the fate of the anglicized group, even if they were more comfortable with Urdu in their daily interactions. Still, the aim of using a different degree of emotional intensity, if not altogether different emotions, in each language needs to be followed up by a close reading of the newspapers themselves.

The article that introduced *Comrade* to its readers, beginning with the famous words, "we are partisans of none, comrades of all," was a journalistic masterpiece. The political objective was clear: *Comrade* wanted to bridge the gaps between races, the rulers and the ruled, and between creeds, the Hindus and the Muslims. From the very first line, this was as much an emotional agenda as a political one, even though the author claimed for himself "sobriety of judgment and temperate expression." The demarcation between the rulers and the ruled was already growing fainter, Mohammad Ali asserted, and would soon disappear. This can be read as a political claim for an expansion of civil society and its ability to influence the government, leading to more Indian members in Parliament, more Indian advisors, and the introduction of Indian members to the Government. Mohammed Ali, however, took the obliteration of difference far beyond this. It pointed toward a future in which "the dream of the poet would [... be] realized – 'I became Thou and Thou becamest I, I became Life and Thou becamest Body / That none may henceforth say, I am different and Thou art different.'" Mohammed Ali draws here on the mystical poetry of Amir Khusro, describing the desire for union with God, the Divine Friend. After the quotation of this verse has established the atmosphere, Mohammed Ali reverts to the role of the newspaper as the voice of the Muslim community. The government is right, he affirms, to put down not only all criticism that "encouraged disobedience to the law of the land" but also "every insinuation about the good faith of the government," every depiction of the "fault of the administrators" that went beyond the desire to see it rectified, by aiming at "exciting popular disaffection" and suggesting that it was "removable only with the removal of the Government itself." Journalists need to be aware "that India is not Europe," and that there is "a vast quantity of inflammable material spread all over the country, which a chance spark might at any moment kindle into an ungovernable flame." This paragraph might as well have been taken from *The Pioneer*, the mouthpiece of the most conservative and imperialistic section of the Anglo-Indian public. However, Mohammed Ali made it clear that his sense of responsibility and his loyalty to the government never foreclosed effective criticism, aimed at closing the "gulf between the races." In the end, it was only emotions that could make the vision of a common future come true: "Remove pride and suspicion on one side, and prejudice and suspicion on the other, and it will not be difficult to throw a cantilever bridge across the yawning chasm" (*Comrade* 1911a: 2).

For Sir Saiyid, the future had been a trope of anxiety; future generations are crying out to the present one to fight for them in a rapidly closing window of opportunity, as otherwise they will be denied a life of honor and prosperity (Pernau 2019b). Mohammed Ali's emotions for the future were no less intense. However, unlike Sir Saiyid, he was driven by an almost chiliastic hope for the days in which the rulers and the ruled would become one, linked by a bond of mystical love that would bridge all differences. His confidence in his ability to play a crucial, if not *the* crucial, role in this history was unbounded in these early days. His claims to balance and sobriety were not mere claims, but central to his mission. At the same time, they were passionately felt – there was *josh* in his striving for balance, and drunkenness in his pursuit of sobriety.

The tone of the introductory article to *Hamdard* is very different. This is not only a difference in language. By mid-1913, the bright hopes at the beginning of 1911 had gone through severe disappointments, including the revocation of the partition of Bengal, the problems in the campaign for the Aligarh Muslim University, and most painful of all, the Balkan Wars, which raised the question whether the last Muslim empire, home to the *khalīfa*, would survive the onslaught of the imperial powers. *Hamdard*'s beginnings, too, were anything but smooth. More than two years passed between the initial plan and the first issue of the newspaper, and even then it could not be fully printed at its planned length because the types ordered from Beirut did not arrived on time. So, while the first short issue came out already in April, it was not until June 1 that the article "*Bismillah*" announced the official birth of the paper and set out its agenda (*Hamdard* 1913a).

Mohammed Ali used the traditional tropes of modesty, playing down his efforts and foregrounding his anxiety that *Hamdard* might not have an honorable existence (*nang-e wujūd*). Even the warm, if not passionate, welcome he had received could not hide the ocean of difference between European newspapers and the Urdu journalists that followed their example. It was too early for applause, only once the courageous and adventurous fighter would return home after the battle and his achievements become visible, might praise be in order. At present, all the passionate longing (*ishtiyāq*) for *Hamdard* that its future readers had expressed in their interactions with Mohammed Ali, nudging him to finally start the newspaper, did nothing but increase the editor's sense of responsibility out of anxieties that the reality of *Hamdard* might not be worthy of these anticipations. Foregrounding these anxieties and the support Mohammed Ali claimed he needed from his readers sounded quite different from the self-confident civilizing mission toward the Urdu-reading community that he promised to take up when writing in English. Not the reader, but the editor was the one who walked in darkness: "If we get lost, we will never reach our goal. Having exposed our goal, readers can become our guides [...], and when we go astray, they can stop us." Though, as a true sympathizer (*hamdard*), he felt the pain of the Muslims and had compassion (*hamdardi*) for them, he would not simply indulge in cries of sorrow (*nohā-e ġam*). He would not promise to create a new heaven and a new earth (*ek nayā asmān aur ek naʾī zamīn tayyār karnā*) no one had ever imagined, but would continue advancing in hope (*umīd par qadam āge baṛhānā*), trusting that the readers of *Hamdard*, in turn, would remain its sympathizers (*hamdardān*).

Mohammed Ali continued by explaining that *Hamdard*'s duty is to bring daily news, verified for their veracity, and to provide the background knowledge needed for their understanding. It would not become a "*masjid kā mullā*" and tell people what they should think.

> *Hamdard* wants to learn from you and teach you. It will cry and make you cry [...]. Sometimes it will make those who laugh cry, and those who cry laugh. Today is the beginning of the journey, [...] and *Hamdard* has become so tired already that it will not be able to proceed without the encouragement (*himmat afzāʾī*) of the readers.
>
> (*Hamdard 1913a*)

This display of emotions is not easy to decipher. Neither is the use of poetic tropes a direct pointer to emotions nor can we assume that conventional words – even if they did not express existing emotions – had no impact on the emotions of the editor and his readers. We also cannot discard the possibility that Mohammed Ali took up these tropes in a playful manner. At least the beginning of the article can be read for the distancing smile with which he displayed tropes of modesty belonging to a tradition that was both his and not his at the same time. However, this distancing from the language seems to disappear as the article moves on; the author glides between dressing up as an

Oriental and the disguise catching up with him and transforming his emotions – he might well have started to feel and to become what at the start he only wanted to pretend to be. The vernacular, we might argue, and specifically the emotional experiences it both expressed and brought forth, kept a space open that was not so much pre- or even paracolonial, but interwoven with, yet distinct from colonial languages and emotions (Orsini 2015).

The Future of Islam

As hinted earlier, the distinctions that Mohammed Ali so carefully established between the aims of his two newspapers reveal themselves as more complex once we look at his actual writings. In the remainder of the chapter, I shall look in some detail, first, at the articles in which he voiced his emotions with regard to the future and to time more generally, and then at the coverage of the events surrounding the mosque in Kanpur.

The first eighteen months of *Comrade* were marked by the proclamation of a "calm certitude" with regard to the future (*Comrade* 1911c). Though Mohammed Ali admitted his love for the "impatient idealist" – who was and was not himself – he also feared him and did not trust him (*Comrade* 1911a: 2). Evolution required steady progress (*Comrade* 1911b). The time of the Muslims would come if they steadfastly held on to hope and continued their work. In this, they could put their trust in the help and benevolence of the colonial power (*Comrade* 1911c, 1911e). Education remained as important as it had been in Sir Saiyid's time, and Mohammed Ali acknowledged that this was going to be a labor of many years. This may partly be read as strategic: if he aimed at becoming the builder of bridges between his community and the colonial power, he needed to prove himself trustworthy and avoid the image of the young firebrand; if the Muslim community was to hope for official support, they had to be perceived as progressive, but patient. At the same time, there is no reason to doubt these statements as insincere. Indeed, in the first decade of the twentieth century, the strategy of Aligarh and the Simla Deputation seemed to bear fruit, and Mohammed Ali and his readers seemed to have every reason for their calm certitude.

An important difference from the old Aligarh school can be found in the notion of progress. For Mohammed Ali, "the full realization of the ideal of Islam is in the womb of futurity" (*Comrade* 1911d: 451), and not in some past golden age, not even the time of the Prophetic commonwealth in Medina. "The ideals of progress are always before, not behind us" (*Comrade* 1912a: 3). Unlike what Sir Saiyid or Altaf Hussain Hali had claimed, progress was not to be the re-enactment of a progressive past that had been lost to the Muslims (Pernau 2019b), but the reaching out for an unknown future. This future was awaited with some excitement, but mainly with the willingness to proceed patiently, one step at a time. The pace might be slow, much work and some sacrifices might be needed, but the march of time would be steady and the future good. Overall, the affective mood was one of profound hope and confidence.

The Italian attack on Ottoman Libya in autumn 1911 led to the first surge of feelings of solidarity with Muslims in other parts of the world, and even more so with the Ottomans. However, it was the British policy in the Balkan Wars (1912–1913), its support of the Ottoman provinces fighting for independence, and the rhetoric of a crusade against Islam that went with it, that completely shattered this vision of the future. Mohammed Ali's feelings of devastation were so profound that he even contemplated suicide – his interpretation of the world, of the place of the present in history and time, and of his own role in bringing about the future unity between creeds and races all lay in shambles (Hasan 1999: 75). Again, this was not an individual psychological moment, but the experience of a whole generation. Over the next months, the articles in *Comrade* repeatedly bemoaned the Muslims' lost "child-like trust in the goodwill of Europe." Instead, the Muslims, "who had dreamed of justice and fairplay in a world of international brotherhood and peace, had been rudely awakened to the naked reality" (*Comrade* 1912b: 395). It became clear to him that, if there were to be a future, any future, for the Muslims in India and in the world, they would have to rely on their own strength. Neither the colonial government nor "prayers and pious aspirations" would help them (*Comrade* 1913a). Instead, the requirement of the hour was to organize the community. Even if they could not go and fight and sacrifice their lives, they could at least contribute financially to help those who did. This was the time of Dr. Ansari's medical mission to the battlefields of the Balkan, his letters providing firsthand information to *Comrade*'s readers and further kindling their pan-Islamic fervor. A little later, Shaukat Ali founded the *Anjuman-e Khuddam-e Kaʿaba*, the details of whose activities also found their place in *Comrade* (Robinson n.d.).

Unlike *Comrade*, *Hamdard* only entered the fray once the Balkan wars were over, making a direct comparison difficult, as we cannot tell for sure which changes were due to language and which to the passing of time. The world of Islam remained a focus in reporting, very often occupying the first or the second page of the newspaper. In *Comrade*, Mohammed Ali was both vocal and emotional with reference to Islam, but what he emphasized was not so much its religious aspects (which disappeared behind a vague "spiritual idea" of unity) (*Comrade* 1913b) as its social ethic. The tone in *Hamdard* was notably different. The authorship of the articles on the regeneration of the Muslims still needs investigating, but even if Mohammed Ali did not write them himself, he must have approved of them. *Dīn* and *dunyā*, religion and the world, could not be separated. Any deterioration in the worldly position of the Muslims also involved a religious decline, and vice versa. Accordingly, the reform of the Muslim community could not be limited to changing their material circumstances and providing them with new enthusiasm, but entailed a return to observing the five pillars of Islam. Religion was more than the conviction that the social ethics of Islam was superior to all others and more than the identification with the global Muslim community, pride in its history, and anxiety for its future. Here, God and the worship to which he was entitled were no longer diffused into the community, but seen as the center toward which the life of Muslims was oriented. Working for the advancement of the Muslims was certainly required, but it was no substitute for *ʿibādat*, for religious worship (Hamdard 1913b).

Kanpur

After the Balkan wars and the campaign for turning the Aligarh College into a full-fledged university, the events surrounding the mosque in Kanpur in 1913 were the third event that shook the Indian Muslim community within a short time period. Together, they resulted in a profound transformation. The facts of Kanpur are well known: as part of sanitation and improvement works in the old city, the municipality decided to pave a new road through a densely populated area. This required the demolition of the washing house (*wuzūʿ khāna*) of a mosque in the Macchli bazaar. Compensation was offered, and the caretakers of the mosque gave their consent. However, it quickly became a nationwide issue and a test case for the relationship between the government and the Muslims. Passions rose and, in August 1913, led to a clash between the local Muslims and the police, in which a number of people were killed and many more wounded or thrown into prison.[9]

In spite of his bitter disappointment with the British after the Balkan wars, Mohammed Ali once again tried to take up the position of a mediator behind the scenes. Building on his prior acquaintance with James Meston, the lieutenant governor of the United Provinces, Mohammed Ali, attempted to convince him through an exchange of letters of the need to intervene and revoke the local decision. While this matter was still under deliberation, neither *Comrade* nor *Hamdard* reported anything on the events in Kanpur, once again trying to prove their sobriety and their trustworthiness by avoiding exciting the emotions of the Islamic public (*Hamdard* 1913c). Once again, Mohammed Ali was disappointed – it became clear that the plan for unity between ruler and ruled, brought about by the good offices of a young Muslim journalist, was much less attractive to the authorities than he had thought.

The first long articles on Kanpur appeared in *Comrade* on July 5, 1913, and in *Hamdard* three days later, joining the campaign that had already been ongoing in the Urdu press for several weeks. In the interstice between the destruction of the mosque and the deadly clashes between the Kanpur Muslims and the police, *Comrade* limited itself to describing the outraged feelings of the community. Its own criticism was expressed in a sarcastic voice. It mocked the way the chairman of the Kanpur Municipality and his Public Works Department had suddenly discovered their aesthetic sensitivities when it came to a decision between the symmetrical plan of a street and the religious feelings of a large part of the population (*Comrade* 1913c: 7), and asked who had turned local officers into muftis, qualified to pass judgment on whether or not a *wuzūʿ khāna* was an unalienable part of a mosque according to Islamic law (*Comrade* 1913d). As a leader of the Muslim community, Mohammed Ali exhorted his co-religionists to stop crying:

> Let us [...] request them, for God's sake, not to play the woman. A great blow has been dealt to their religious feelings, but they are expected to bear themselves manfully. Let them prove for once that they can act with courage, determination, sustained energy in time of need.
>
> (*Comrade 1913c: 7*)

At this stage, he still kept his distance – at stake were "their" religious feelings, not "ours," and it was "they" who needed the appeal to act manfully, while Mohammad Ali's own manliness remained beyond question. The expression of emotions and the feeling-rules here drew more from the colonial discourse than from the Urdu tradition. Mohammed Ali was willing to fight for the Muslim community, and he was indignant on their behalf, but he kept his emotional distance, at least in English.

This distancing started to fade once the reports on police violence came in, "a tragedy that is being mourned in every Moslem home throughout India." Here, the reports on "children mangled to death or crying in agony, venerable old men hunted out of their places of hiding in the mosque and gored with spears" acquired an immediacy that was lacking earlier, thus narrowing the gap between reporting in English and Urdu, at least to some extent.

From the start, *Hamdard* had used emotional and religious language to report and interpret the events in Kanpur. Whereas *Comrade* consistently spoke of the sacrilege of Kanpur, *Hamdard* called it *shahādat*, the martyrdom of the mosque, invoking the battle of Karbala, which led to the martyrdom of the Prophet's grandson Husain. This allusion ran through most of the sermons, speeches, and articles in the Urdu public sphere (accounting for the tears that Mohammed Ali so contemptuously dismissed in his English article). Already in its very first article, *Hamdard* gave voice to the pain of the subjects and placed their hearts at the center of its discourse:

> These events tell us clearly, that local self-government is the name for a deception. It is not democracy, but a cult of personality (*shakhsīyat pasandī*) and autocracy (*khūd mukhtārī*). The rulers, with great calm, can turn the hearts of their subjects into the target of their muskets.
>
> (*Hamdard 1913c: 3*)

Much earlier than *Comrade*, *Hamdard* gave voice to the religious leaders. It reported *al-Ḥilāl*'s indictment of the dishonoring (*be-hurmatī*) of the mosque, the resulting feeling of *josh* among the Muslims, and its reopening of the question of what the legal status of India might be under these circumstances. This was a dangerous question, as a claim that India had been converted from an abode of peace (*dar ul-aman*) to an abode of war (*dar ul-ḥarb*) only left in theory the options to either fight or migrate (*Hamdard* 1913d). *Hamdard*'s printing of the telegram Khwaja Hasan Nizami had addressed to the viceroy, in the name of the Sufi shaikhs he claimed to represent (*Hamdard* 1913e), laid the seeds of an alliance that was further developed by the appointment of Nizami as *Comrade*'s and *Hamdard*'s special correspondent in Kanpur (*Comrade* 1913e).[10] After the violent clashes, the emotions in both newspapers came close in their level of intensity, but *Hamdard* foregrounded the vocabulary of insulted honor, implicit in the colonial denial of the authenticity of Muslim *josh*, and once again brought religious sentiments more directly into play (though they were no longer absent in *Comrade* as well) (*Hamdard* 1913f).

Conclusion

One of the well-known topoi of Orientalism was the assumption that something was wrong with Oriental emotions. However, European authors never quite decided whether the Orientals were childlike in their inability to control their emotions, thus needing colonial rule to guide and discipline them, or whether they suffered from the coldness coming from the excessive control typical of old civilizations and cunningly disguised their true feelings, manipulated others, and therefore were not to be trusted.[11] In the years before the First World War, the younger generation of the national movement, especially the journalists among them, shared both these attributes in the eyes of the colonial administration: a bunch of firebrands constantly overwhelmed by their emotions, and cunning agitators, who used the emotions they evoked in others to mobilize them against the government. We have seen how Mohammed Ali initially subscribed to these assumptions of the Urdu public sphere and used his mastery of the English language and its emotional codes to distance himself from the excited Urdu-speaking Orientals by pointing to his calmness and trustworthiness and offering to build bridges and civilize the emotions of his co-religionists.

The argument that civilization is the disciplining of emotions, however, is only one part of the narrative. In my previous work, I have argued that the nineteenth century in North India had seen a movement from *e'tidal* to *josh*, from an emotional ideal of balance to a desire for strong and passionate feelings, as a precondition for the survival of the community. Unlike what the Orientalists sought to claim, this was neither an emotional condition inherent to the Orient (its actual beginnings can be dated to the 1870s), nor was it by any means specific to India or its emotional languages, but could be found, in different shapes and hues, also in many European countries and languages

(Pernau 2019a).[12] The present chapter has shown that this movement toward *josh* and *jazbāt* continued to gain in intensity in the years prior to the First World War and became the dominant mood in the Urdu public sphere immediately before it – what we have seen for *Hamdard* seems to have been also true for *Zamīndār* and *al-Ḥilāl*.

So what does this tell us about the correspondence of moving between languages and moving between emotions? English and Urdu form part of the linguistic economy of the Muslim reading public in the years before the war. Irrespective of the command they exercised over one or both of these languages, authors and readers moved in a multilingual environment, in which languages did not exist in watertight compartments. Nor were languages endowed with quasi-natural characteristics, making one more "emotional" than the other, unlike what the colonial discourse assumed. However, as the comparison between *Comrade* and *Hamdard* has shown, both Urdu and English came with certain expectations (always in need of historicization) concerning appropriate styles of writing, be it self-presentation or the voicing of emotions. If Mohammed Ali had thought that he could use both languages strategically, without himself being affected by this choice, he was to discover that language had at least as much power over him as vice versa. Rather than his Urdu writings conforming to the plan he had developed in English, it was the emotions he expressed in Urdu that started to shape his English writings and finally took over. The conventional model of vernacularization as the transition from a cosmopolitan language to a locally bounded one does not appropriately describe this process. If we can trace such vernacularization at all, it happened within the English language itself, when its cosmopolitan and colonial version was transformed under the impact of Urdu. Urdu, however, was not conceived as a local mother tongue (at least not in this context), but shared its authors' outward-looking gaze.

Finally, we have to reflect on what the convergence of emotional styles in English and Urdu, with Urdu taking the lead, meant for the vernacularization of politics.[13] The joining of forces between Aligarh and Deoband, the Western-educated and the ulama, is usually seen as the hallmark of the Khilafat movement after the end of the war.[14] Here, we can show that this not only happened earlier – Mohammed Ali's reconversion in jail was the result of these developments, rather than their pre-condition – but that it also went deeper than the mere strategic alliance many have taken it to be. Since 1913, whether they wrote in Urdu or English, both increasingly shared not only political goals but also emotional styles anchored in Urdu.

Acknowledgement

A huge thank you to Eve Tignol, with whom I compared notes of my readings of *Comrade* and *Hamdard*. Her attentive reading of my draft chapter allowed me to correct a number of errors. Farha Noor helped with the grammar of a particularly tricky sentence, for which I am grateful. My former students, Frederik Schröer, Soheb Niazi, and Sébastien Tremblay, once again, commented on the text carefully and in detail and pushed me to clarify my ideas. No one could wish for better students, transitioned into intelligent and kind colleagues. A big thank you to them as well!

Notes

1 For the European context, see Dixon 2003; Frevert *et al.* 2014. For an introduction to emotions in South Asia, see Pernau 2021.
2 For an attempt to show the interplay between different registers of a single emotion in different periods and different media, see Rajamani, Pernau, & Schofield 2018.
3 Cf. Kaviraj's contribution to this volume.
4 For the reconfiguration of the relationship between languages through the introduction of the concept of a mother tongue, see Mitchell 2009; Yildiz 2012.
5 So far, investigations of emotions and multilingualism focused mostly on the emotions of either translators or pupils acquiring a second language in the present (see the excellent study of Aneta Pavlenko [2005]). While inspiring for the present work, they cannot be directly translated into it, due to the assumption here that both emotions and multilingualism have to be historicized in order to grasp their specific relationship at a certain time and place.
6 For biographical information on Mohammed Ali, see Hasan 1981; Chatterji 2013.
7 Beyond the literature mentioned in the previous footnote, see also Zaman 2014; Tignol forthcoming, chapter 3. I am grateful to Eve for sharing the manuscript with me. The Urdu literature on *Hamdard* is extensive. Besides the older work of Ṣābrī (1974), see Shāhjāhānpūrī 1983; ʿUmar 1988.
8 I have not found corresponding statements in Urdu – that the Indian Muslims would be ready to respond with love, once they were asked for it, does not seem a question for Mohammed Ali.
9 For more details and references to previous literature, see Pernau 2019a, chapter 10.
10 Nizami is not mentioned by name here, but the text is identical to the report he printed in his pamphlet *Kānpur kī khūnī dāstān*, 1913.
11 For details on this argument and further literature, see Pernau 2009.
12 For a larger picture of the changes in the civilization discourse, bringing together European and Asian perspectives, see Pernau *et al.* 2015.
13 For the concept of the vernacularization of politics, see Hansen 1996; Michelutti 2008.
14 Still unsurpassed: Minault 1982; Robinson 1974.

References

ʿAlī, M. 1907. *Thoughts on the Present Discontent: Reprinted from the "Times of India" and the "Indian Spectator"*. Bombay: Bombay Gazette Steam Press.

Chatterji, R. 2013. *Gandhi and the Ali Brothers: Biography of a Friendship*. Delhi: Sage Publishing.

Comrade. 1911a. "We." *The Comrade*, 1–3, 14 January.

Comrade. 1911b. "Nation-making." *The Comrade*, 305, 29 April.

Comrade. 1911c. "The Dawn of Hope." *The Comrade*, n.p., 1 July.

Comrade. 1911d. "Lest we forget." *The Comrade*, 451–452, 25 November.

Comrade. 1911e. "Illusions." *The Comrade*, 452–453, 25 November.
Comrade. 1912a. "Ring in the New." *The Comrade*, 3–4, 6 January.
Comrade. 1912b. "The Crescent and the Cross." *The Comrade*, 395–396, 16 November.
Comrade. 1913a. "The Indian Moslems and their 'Friends'." *The Comrade*, 266, 5 April.
Comrade. 1913b. "The Future of Islam." *The Comrade*, 497–499, 21 June.
Comrade. 1913c. "The Cawnpor Sacrilege." *The Comrade*, 6–8, 5 July.
Comrade. 1913d. "The Cawnpor Sacrilege, III." *The Comrade*, 75, 2 August.
Comrade. 1913e. "The Cawnpore Tragedy." *The Comrade*, 95–97, 9 August.
Datla, K. 2009. "A Wordly Vernacular: Urdu at the Osmania University." *Modern Asian Studies* 43(5): 1117–1148. doi:10.1017/S0026749X08003715.
Datla, K. 2013. *The Language of Secular Islam: Urdu Nationalism and Colonial India*. Honolulu: University of Hawaii Press.
Dixon, T. 2003. *From Passions to Emotions: The Creation of a Secular Psychological Category*. Cambridge: Cambridge University Press.
Faruqi, S.R. 2001. *Early Urdu Literary Culture and History*. Delhi: Oxford University Press.
Fisher, M.H. 1993. "The Office of Akhbār Nawīs: The Transition from Mughal to British Forms." *Modern Asian Studies* 27(1): 45–82. https://www.jstor.org/stable/312878.
Frevert, U., Bailey, C., Eitler, P., Gammerl, B., Hitzer, B., Pernau, M., Scheer, M., Schmidt, A., and Verheyen, N. 2014. *Emotional Lexicons: Continuity and Change in the Vocabulary of Feeling 1700–2000*. Oxford: Oxford University Press.
Green, N. 2011. "The Trans-Border Traffic of Afghan Modernism: Afghanistan and the Indian 'Urdusphere'." *Comparative Studies in Society and History* 53(3): 479–508. doi: 10.1017/S0010417511000223.
Green, N. 2018. "The Waves of Heterotopia: Towards a Vernacular Intellectual History of the Indian Ocean." *The American Historical Review* 123(3): 846–874. https://doi.org/10.1093/ahr/123.3.846.
Hamdard. 1913a. "Bismillah." *Hamdard*, n.p., 1 June.
Hamdard. 1913b. "Musalmānon kī taraqqi aur tanazzul." *Hamdard*, n.p, 6 July.
Hamdard. 1913c. "Masjid kī shahādat." *Hamdard*, 3–5, 8 July.
Hamdard. 1913d. "Kānpur ki masjid." *Hamdard*, 5, 11 July.
Hamdard. 1913e. "Ḥalqa-e nizām ul mashai<u>kh</u>-e delhi aur masjid-e kānpur kī be-hurmati." *Hamdard*, 6, 11 July.
Hamdard. 1913f. "Kānpur ki waqeʾat apni aṣli roshnī men." *Hamdard*, 4, 8 August.
Hansen, T.B. 1996. "The Vernacularization of Hindutva: The BJP and Shiv Sena in Rural Maharashtra." *Contributions to Indian Sociology* 30(2): 177–214. https://doi.org/10.1177/006996679603000201.
Hasan, M. 1981. *Mohamed Ali: Ideology and Politics*. Delhi: Manohar Publishers.
Hasan, M. 1999. *My Life, a Fragment: An Autobiographical Sketch of Maulana Mohamed Ali*. Delhi: Manohar Publishers.
Michelutti, L. 2008. *The Vernacularization of Democracy: Politics, Caste and Religion in India*. Delhi: Routledge.
Minault, G. 1982. *The Khilafat Movement: Religious Symbolism and Political Mobilization in India*. Delhi: Oxford University Press.
Mitchell, L. 2009. *Language, Emotions and Politics in South India*. Bloomington: Indiana University Press.
Orsini, F. 2006. "Introduction." In *Love in South Asia: A Cultural History*, edited by Orsini, F., 1–43. Delhi: Oxford University Press.

Orsini, F. 2015. "Whose Amnesia? Literary Modernity in Multilingual South Asia." *Cambridge Journal of Postcolonial Literary Inquiry* 2(2): 266–272. https://doi.org/10.1080/02759527.2020.1725227.

Orsini, F. 2020. "Vernacular, Flawed but Necessary?" *South Asian Review* 41(2): 204–206.

Orsini, F., Marzagora, S., and Laachir, K. 2019. "Introduction: Multilingual Locals and Textual Circulation before Colonialism." *Comparative Studies of South Asia, Africa and the Middle East* 39(1): 63–67. https://doi.org/10.1215/1089201X-7493777.

Pavlenko, A. 2005. *Emotions and Multilingualism*. New York: Cambridge University Press.

Pernau, M. 2003. "The *Delhi Urdu Akhbar*: Between Persian Akhbarat and English newspapers." *Annual of Urdu Studies* 18: 105–131.

Pernau, M. 2009. "Rationalizing the world: British Detective Stories and the Orient." In *Empires and Boundaries: Rethinking Race, Class, and Gender in Colonial Settings*, edited by Fischer-Tiné, H., and Gehrmann, S., 179–194. London: Routledge.

Pernau, M. 2019a. *Emotions and Modernity in Colonial India: From Balance to Fervor*. Delhi: Oxford University Press.

Pernau, M. 2019b. "Fluid Temporalities: Saiyid Ahmad Khan and the Concept of Modernity." *History and Theory* 58(4): 107–131. https://doi.org/10.1111/hith.12138.

Pernau, M. 2021. "Introduction: Studying Emotions in South Asia." *South Asian History and Culture*, Special Issue: Emotions in South Asia, edited by Pernau, M. https://doi.org/10.1080/19472498.2021.1878788.

Pernau, M., and Jaffery, Y. (eds). 2009. *Information and the Public Sphere: Persian Newsletters from Mughal Delhi*. Delhi: Oxford University Press.

Pernau, M., Jordheim, H., Bashkin, O., Bailey, C., Benesch, O., Ifversen, J., Kia, M., Majumdar, R., Messner, A.C., Park, M., Saada, E., Singh, M., and Wigen, E. 2015. *Civilizing Emotions: Concepts in Nineteenth-century Asia and Europe*. Oxford: Oxford University Press.

Pernau, M., and Rajamani, I. 2016. "Emotional Translations: Conceptual History beyond Language." *History and Theory* 55(1): 46–65. https://doi.org/10.1111/hith.10787.

Pollock, S. 1998. "The Cosmopolitan Vernacular." *Journal of Asian Studies* 57(1): 6–37. https://doi.org/10.2307/2659022.

Pollock, S. 2006. *The Language of the Gods in the World of Men: Sanskrit, Culture, and Power in Premodern India*. Berkeley: University of California Press.

Rajamani, I., Pernau, M., and Schofield, K.B. (eds). 2018. *Monsoon Feelings: A History of Emotions in the Rain*. Delhi: Niyogi Books.

Robinson, F. n.d. "Anjuman-i Khuddām-i Kaʿba." In *In Encyclopaedia of Islam, THREE*, edited by Fleet, K., Krämer, G., Matringe, D., Nawas, J., and Rowson, E. doi: http://dx.doi.org/10.1163/1573-3912_ei3_COM_26345.

Robinson, F. 1974. *Separatism among Indian Muslims: The Politics of the United Provinces' Muslims, 1860–1923*. Cambridge: Cambridge University Press.

Ṣābrī, I. 1974. *Tārikh-e Ṣaḥāfat-e Urdū*, vol. 4. Delhi: Jadīd Printing Press.

Scheer, M. 2014. "Topographies of Emotions." In Ute Frevert, et al., *Emotional Lexicons. Continuity and Change in the Vocabulary of Feeling 1700-2000*. New York: Oxford University Press, 32–62.

Shāhjāhānpūrī, A.S. 1983. *Maulānā Muḥammad ʿAlī aur unkī ṣaḥāfat*. Karachi: Idāra-e taṣnīf o taḥqīq.

Tignol, E. (forthcoming). *Revolutions in the Garden: Sadness and the Making of a Muslim Community in Colonial North India.*
ʿUmar, S. 1988. "Muqaddamah." In *Intikhāb-e Hamdard.* Delhi: Anjuman-e taraqqī-e Urdū (Hind).
Viswanathan, G. 1989. *Masks of Conquest: Literary Study and British Rule in India.* New York: Columbia University Press.
Yildiz, Y. 2012. *Beyond the Mother Tongue: The Postmonolingual Condition.* New York: Fordham University Press.
Zaman, F. 2014. "Futurity and the Political Thought of North Indian Muslims, c. 1900–1925." PhD diss., Corpus Christi College, University of Cambridge.

13

IN DEFENCE OF THE *PREM'SĀGAR*

Re-evaluating the Narrative of the Hindi–Urdu Split

Gautam Liu

Introduction

The year 2010 marked the 200th anniversary of a defining moment in the history of Hindi literature: the publication of the first printed book in Modern Standard Hindi, the *Prem'sāgar*. I am not aware of any festivities or conferences to commemorate this event. In academic discourse, this work is almost exclusively mentioned in the context of the Hindi–Urdu split. Book titles such as *A House Divided* (Rai 1984) or the more recent anthology *Before the Divide* (Orsini 2010) inevitably suggest that a linguistic bifurcation took place in a once-common house of Hindi–Urdu.

I Beg to Differ and Question This Narrative

My observation is that the common house of Hindi–Urdu was never divided as there always existed with regard to written prose two semi-detached houses. The foundation they share I would refer to as Khaṛī bolī or Dehlavī, two terms denoting the dialect of Delhi on which Modern Standard Hindi and Urdu are based. It goes without saying that over time there have been many interactions between the dwellers of these two living quarters. Some residents were even comfortable with living in both houses. There is no doubt that there have also been altercations between some members of those two camps, especially in the last quarter of the nineteenth century and the decades before partition in 1947, and numerous books and articles have been written on the political and social aspects of the Hindi–Urdu controversy in the colonial era. However, it would not be correct to superimpose this bipartisan rivalry on the linguistic origins of both literary traditions.

DOI: 10.4324/9781003279921-17

The nineteenth century is generally portrayed as the crucial period of the bifurcation of the common linguistic house of Khaṛī bolī with British rule functioning as the catalyst of this dividing process. The central piece of evidence put forward to corroborate this supposition is Lalluji Lal's *Prem|sāgar* (1810), as the language of this book published from Fort William college is often referred to as the starting point of linguistic cleansing in Hindi prose. My argument is that in view of the absence of a respective substantial literary corpus it is wrong to assume a common Hindi–Urdu prose tradition in the eighteenth century from which the *Prem|sāgar* could have broken off. By contrast, I will demonstrate that the language of the *Prem|sāgar* is not an artificial Sanskritised construct but an organic development of a vibrant literary and oral prose tradition in the Hindi heartland. Claims of a lexical purge in the *Prem|sāgar* tend to reflect a modern discourse that idealises a linguistic middle path called Hindustani against the backdrop of the strive for national unity in the first half of the twentieth century.

Sanskritised versus Sanskrit-Oriented

What is meant by the term 'Sanskritised Hindi' that we read all the time? Alok Rai in his tract *Hindi Nationalism* even speaks of a "Sanskritic usurper" which, in his view, has overshadowed the people's vernacular Hindi (Rai 2001: 122). But the complex relationship between Sanskrit and Hindi needs some more calibration. After all, for a New Indo-Aryan language such as Hindi that has derived from Old Indo-Aryan, having Sanskrit words in its vocabulary should not come as a surprise. In my definition, the term 'Sanskritised' refers to the outcome of a deliberate procedure to substitute *tadbhav* words as well as words of foreign origin with corresponding *tatsam* words and Sanskrit neologisms (i.e., Sanskritisms) by default: for example, the *tadbhav* word *dūdh* ('milk') with the *tatsam* word *dugdh* and widespread foreign loanwords such as Persian *caśmā* ('glasses') and Japanese *rikśā* with uncommon Sanskritisms like *upanetra* ('a second pair of eyes') and *nar|yān* ('man-vehicle'). This style can definitely be called artificial. It is important to add though that Sanskritisation is not limited to a purist agenda driven by religious nationalism, but that it has also served secular purposes in literature.[1] To illustrate the Sanskritised Hindi style, Rai quotes from a letter of the Hindi poet and writer Shridhar Pathak (1860–1928):

> *priyavarya śrī padmasiṁh: nati nivedam. āp|kā suślāghyaśālīn|tā śobhit śubh patra yathāsamay samāgat huā. asvasthatāvaś uttar vilambit ho gayā, etadarth kṣamā prārthit hai.*
>
> *(Rai 2001: 80)*[2]

This Sanskritised style wherein all *tadbhav* and foreign words are purged played virtually no role in the development of modern Hindi prose. The style that the vast majority of Hindi authors, including Lalluji Lal, preferred was not

Sanskritised, but Sanskrit-oriented, i.e., a language that generously borrows words from its natural source Sanskrit, but is also open with varying degrees to words of foreign origin.

Hindi and Urdu Prose Literature before 1800

Amrit Rai's postulate that there was an "old unified Hindi/Hindavi" and that linguistic purists "split Hindavi into modern Hindi and modern Urdu as two separate and mutually exclusive languages" (Rai 1984: 285) is merely an assumption with regard to Khaṛī bolī prose literature that still waits to be substantiated by significant texts. The examples Rai presents in his book *A House Divided* to premise a common literary idiom before the so-called divide are predominantly verses from Dakhini poems of the seventeenth century. It is certainly true that in that era poetic compositions with secular themes in Dakhini had a fairly balanced vocabulary as they incorporated a good number of Sanskrit words, which were for the most part discarded in Urdu poetry over the course of the eighteenth century (cf. Rahman 2011: 109–135). But for prose literature in North India, which is the main focus of this chapter, we can safely state that a unified language was, with the possible exception of some writings in syncretistic movements, never the literary norm before the colonial period.

One of the oldest prose texts of Hindi in its Braj form, *Caurāsī Vaiṣṇavan kī vārtā* (1640), a hagiographical account of 84 saints devoted to Krishna, and of Urdu in its Dakhini form *Sab ras* (1635), a Sufi allegory, clearly differ in their choice of words, as can be seen by a comparison of the following paragraphs from these two works[3]:

Braj Hindi (*Vārtā*):

> *tā samay Śrīācāryajī Mahāprabhūn ne pūcho jo Damˈlā te kuch sunyā? tab Dāmodarˈdās ne bīnˈtī kīnī jo mahārāj Śrīṭhākurjī ke vacan sunau to sahī parantu kuch samjhau nahīṃ. tab Śrīācāryajī Mahāprabhūn neṃ kahī jo moko Śrīṭhākurjī neṃ ājñā kīnī hai jo tum jīvan kauṃ brahmˈsaṃbaṃdh karāvoge tinˈkauṃ hoṃ aṃgikār karūṁgo tinˈke sakal doṣ nivṛtt hoṃyge tāte brahmˈsaṃbaṃdh avaśya karno.*[4]
>
> *(Gokulnāth 2008: 2)*

Dakhini Urdu (*Sab ras*):

> *ek śahar thā is śahar kā nāʾoṉ sīstāṉ. us sīstāṉ ke bādśāh kī nāʾoṉ aql, dīn o duniyā kā tamām kām us te caltā. us ke ḥukm bāj ẕarrā kīṉ nīṉ hiltā. us ke farmāʾe par jinoṉ cale har do jahāṉ meṉ hūʾe bhale. duniyā meṉ xūb kahvāʾe, cār lokāṉ meṉ ʿizzat pāʾe, jahāṉ rahe khaṛe, vahāṉ qabūl paṛe, na āfat dekhe na zalzalā. ape bhalā to ʿālam bhalā. kisī koṉ burā bolnā yo vasvās hai, bhalāʾī burāʾī sab apne pās hai.*[5]
>
> *(Vajhī 1964: 13f.)*

The specimens quoted above show that though the language in both texts is close to colloquial speech, the vocabulary differs considerably.[6] Based on these textual sources we cannot assume that a unified literary Hindi–Urdu prose tradition was prevalent in the seventeenth century.

It is only in the first decades of the eighteenth century that Khaṛī bolī appears prominently as a literary language in North India, written in its Hindi and Urdu styles. My theory why this did not occur earlier is that, on the one hand, the dominant literary medium in the Mughal capital Shahjahanabad, i.e., Delhi, was Indo-Persian. We should not forget that Persian until the beginning of the eighteenth century was not limited to literary use only but also a commonly spoken language by a considerable part of the capital's Ashraf elite. On the other hand, Braj Bhāṣā, based on a Hindi dialect spoken in an area stretching from south of Delhi to Gwalior, developed from 1450 to 1750 under the patronage of nearby Rajput courts into a transregional literary medium in North India.[7] With the decline of the Mughal empire and the destruction of Delhi in the first half of the eighteenth century, most inhabitants of the former metropolis, such as clerks, traders, bankers, scholars, poets, artisans, soldiers, courtesans, etc., sought refuge in provincial towns along the Grand Trunk Road, stretching from Kabul to Kolkata (cf. also Dvivedī 2000: 197). This new urban elite helped to make Khaṛī bolī or Zabān-e Urdū, i.e., the language of Delhi,[8] the dominant lingua franca in North India. The template available for the written form of Delhi's common language, spoken by Hindus and Muslims alike, was either Sanskrit-oriented Braj bhāṣā or Persian.[9] Thus, it should come as no surprise that the oldest available Khaṛī bolī prose texts from North India, the *Bhāṣā Yogˡvāśiṣṭh* (1741), composed by Ramprasad Niranjani in the court of Patiala,[10] and *Karbal Kathā* (1733), an Urdu translation of a Persian work by Fazl Ali Fazl, have two completely separate registers, a Sanskrit-oriented one for Hindi and a Persian-oriented one for Urdu, as we can see in the following two specimens:

Khaṛī bolī Hindi (*Bhāṣā Yogˡvāśiṣṭh*):

Agastˡjī ke śiṣya Sutīkṣaṇ ke man meṃ ek saṃdeh paidā huā tab vah usˡke dūr karˡne ke kāraṇ Agast muni ke āśram ko jā vidhisahit praṇām karˡke baiṭhe aur binˡtī kar praśn kiyā ki he bhagˡvān! āp sab tattvoṃ aur śāstroṃ ke jānanˡhāre hau, mere ek saṃdeh ko dūr karo. mokṣ kā kāraṇ karm hai ki jñān hai athavā donoṃ haiṃ, samˡjhāy ke kaho.[11]

(Śukla 2002: 283)

Khaṛī bolī Urdu (*Karbal Kathā*):

ahl-e siyar muʿtabir śahādat amīr-ul-muʾminīn ḥaidar ko̠n yū̠n rivāyat karte hai̠n ki jab haz̤rat amīr jang-e nihirvān se fāriġ hūʾe, farmāʾe kaun hai ki xabar fatah merī kūfe men̲ pahūn̲cāve. Ibn Muljam la'īn ne kahā, yā amīr-ul-mu'minīn ḥukm hū'e main̲ jā'ūn̲ aur xuśxabrī-e fataḥ ahl-e kūfe ko pahun̲cāūn̲.[12]

(Faẕlī 1965: 81)

Both passages, which are fairly understandable for readers familiar with Hindi and Urdu literature respectively, follow evidently two very distinct styles and point to the absence of a commonly written prose tradition with a balanced vocabulary from which Hindi and Urdu could have split into two styles.

What is more, the "*Bhāṣā Yog'vāśiṣṭh*" refutes claims that Hindus never used a Sanskrit-oriented form of Khaṛī bolī prior to the composition of the *Prem'sāgar*.[13] The other source of evidence which proves that Khaṛī bolī Hindi was used as a prose language more than four decades before the establishment of Fort William College is the Hindi adaption of the Jain *Padmapurāṇa*, the *Bhāṣāpadmapurāṇ*, written by Pandit Daulatram, a resident of Jaipur, in 1766.[14] The author says about himself in the introduction:

yah baṛā āścarya hai ki jo ham sārīkhe alp'buddhi puruṣ bhī un'ke caritrako kahaiṃ haiṃ yadyapi ham sārīkhe caritrako kah'neko samarth nahīṃ tathāpi paraṃparāse mahāmuni jis prakār kah'te āe haiṃ un'ke kahe anusār kuch ik saṃkṣep'tā kar kahaiṃ haiṃ.[15]

(Daulat'rām 1950: 6f.)

The Language of the *Prem'sāgar*

The *Prem'sāgar*, published in 1810, is the first major Hindi prose work of the nineteenth century and the first printed book in Khaṛī bolī Hindi. It was composed by Fort William's Bhākhā Munshi Lalluji Lal (1763–1825) by the order of John Borthwick Gilchrist, the first professor of Hindustani (1800–1804) at Fort William College, a language school established in Kolkata in 1800. In the introduction, the author states that he wrote this work "*yāmanī bhāṣā choṛ dillī āgre kī khaṛī bolī meṃ*". Lalluji Lal simply states here that he used the "Khaṛī bolī of Delhi and Agra, leaving aside its Urdu variety". This statement eventually led to a colossal misunderstanding with far-fetched suppositions that have been uncritically passed on from one generation of scholars to others. I believe that the one crucial source of contestation that led to the assumption of a purist agenda of Lalluji Lal is his use of the term *yāmanī* for Urdu. *Yavan* has certainly been used at times as an ethnophaulism for Muslims. However, the *tadbhav* word *yāmanī* in collocation with *bhāṣā* ('language') was in Hindi a neutral term for Persian or in our case a variety of Khaṛī bolī heavily influenced by that language and written in the Arabic script. In this sense, Bharatendu Harishchandra uses this Hindi synonym for *Fārsī* when he admiringly notes that his great-grandfather was an erudite scholar in *yāvanī vidyā*, i.e., "Persian historiography" (Bhāratendu 2000: 732). Thus, to connect the sole mention of the glossonym *yāmanī* to a Hindi/Hindu nationalist agenda would not be appropriate.[16]

George Abraham Grierson was perhaps the first Orientalist to postulate the creation of Kharī bolī Hindi through the *Prem|sāgar*:

> In 1803, under Gilchrists's tuition, Lallū jī Lāl wrote the Prem Sāgar in the mixed Urdū language of Akbar's camp-followers and of the market where men of all nations congregated, with this peculiarity, that he used only nouns and particles of Indian, instead of those of Arabic or Persian, origin. The result was practically a newly-invented speech; for though the grammar was the same as that of the prototype, the vocabulary was almost entirely changed.
>
> *(Grierson 1889: 107)*

The Indologist Jules Bloch more or less reiterates Grierson's postulate in the introduction of his dissertation *La formation de la langue marathe* in 1914:

> Hindi is the language of literary prose for those Hindus who do not use Urdu. It is modern in origin and owes its creation to English influence in the beginning of the last century. Upto that time, when a Hindu wrote prose and did not use Urdu, he wrote in local speech: Avadhī, Bundelī, Braj Bhākhā, etc. Under the inspiration of Gilchrist, Lalluji Lal, by writing his celebrated Prem Sagar, changed all this. The prose parts of this work were in short in Urdu, with Persian words replaced everywhere by Indo-Aryan words. This experiment was a great success: the new dialect gave a 'lingua franca' to the Hindus.
>
> *(Bloch 1970: 14)*

In a recent work, Vasudha Dalmia takes on this narrative:

> A Gujarati Brahman originally from Agra, Lallujilal was employed by the Fort William College to produce instructional material for teaching Hindavi in the Nagari script. Of Premsagar, one of the first works written with this express intent, Lallujilal is at pains to point out that it has been written in Khari Boli, the 'upright' speech of Delhi and Agra, setting aside the language of the Yavanas, marking thereby the moment in which the deliberate process of extracting a purer Hindi form from the speech of Delhi and Agra, cleansed of its Perso-Arabic elements, begins.
>
> *(Dalmia 2017: 58f.)*

In another recent essay, Rashmi Dube Bhatnagar finds more drastic words:

> Premsagar is at the heart of the disciplining of the other linguistic cartography in the eighteenth century in which Indo-Persian, Perso-Arabic, and Turkic linguistic traces of peoples' histories underwent a secular linguistic purge. Premsagar calls this linguistic purge the abandonment of the Bhāṣā of the Yavanas, or geographically identified outsiders. Secular purges of language are thus part and parcel of the invention narrative around Premsagar and explain the constitutive violence at the birth of the linguistic modern subject.
>
> *(Bhatnagar 2012: 78)*

From the last quotation, we can see how the mere use of the Hindi synonym *yāmanī* for Urdu has fired the imagination of a scholar to construct a whole ideology.

To put the matter straightaway: The language of the *Premˈsāgar* is not a modern invention of an artificial Hindi but rather a continuation of a deep-rooted literary tradition in North West India, oral and textual, that was due to the confluence of different cognate dialects morphologically hybrid but lexically predominantly characterised by *tatsam*, *tadbhav* and *deśī* words, especially when adapting religious works that were originally written in Sanskrit. In the previous chapter, two literary testimonies of eighteenth century Khaṛī bolī Hindi, marked by an admixture of other dialects and a heavily Sanskrit-oriented vocabulary, were presented to corroborate this fact. The *Premˈsāgar* is based on a Braj adaption of the tenth canto of the *Bhāgavatapurāṇa* written by Chaturbhuj Mishra in 1567. So, not surprisingly Lalluji Lal retained a lot of Sanskrit words from the original work in his Khaṛī bolī adaptation. What is the need to replace Sanskrit words of the original text of the sixteenth century if these words are still commonly used and understood by Hindi speakers in the nineteenth century? If we look at the text from this angle, what was replaced was not Perso-Arabic lexical items by Sanskritic ones, but the Braj morphology by a Khaṛī bolī one. The following passage will give an idea of the Hindi Lalluji Lal uses in the *Premˈsāgar*:

> *Śrīśukˈdevˈjī bole ki mahārāj, ek din Nandˈjī ne saṃyam kar ekādaśī vrat kiyā. din to snān, dhyān, bhajan, jap, pūjā meṃ kāṭā aur rātri jāgˈran meṃ bitāī. jab cha ghaṛī rain rahī au dvādaśī bhaī, tab uṭhˈke deh śuddh kar bhor huā jān dhotī, aṁgochā, jhārī le jamunā nhān cale, tinˈke pīche kaī ek gvāl bhī ho liye.*[17]
>
> *(Lāl 1953: 86)*

Apart from its colloquial style, the comprehensibility of the *Premˈsāgar* is such that a reader familiar with basic Hindi literature hardly has to look up a

Sanskrit word in the dictionary. I am not sure if this can be said about the numerous native words that have fallen into oblivion in Modern Standard Hindi as they have become practically extinct over time or were replaced by Sanskritisms or Persian-Arabic words. Take, for example, the *tadbhav* word *begī*, which is frequently used in the *Premˈsāgar*, and is an adverb meaning 'fast, quickly'. This word, which is derived from Sanskrit *vega* ('impetus, speed'), has been totally replaced in today's common parlance by the Arabic word *jaldī* or a corresponding Sanskritism in formal Hindi. In this sense, the text of the *Premˈsāgar* preserves in its lexicon a style in Hindi that often favours *tadbhav* words over *tatsam* words, making the language thereby more vernacular as has always been the common practice in *bhākhā/bhāṣā* literature.

Another interesting example is the Sanskrit word *vilamb* ('delay'; related to Hindi *lambā* 'long'), which is frequently used in the *Premˈsāgar*: *acchā jāo dekh āo, par bilamb mat kījau* (Lāl 1953: 129). Though this *tatsam* word is in today's speech more restricted to formal usage, it was not coined to substitute the Persian synonym *der*, which, by the way, is etymologically related to Sanskrit *dīrgha* 'long'. In fact, *vilamb* was part of everyday speech in the Hindi heartland, as can be seen in the *Vārtā* of the seventeenth century: *tū vegī āiyau bilamb mati kariyau* [...] *itˈne din vilaṃb bhayau* (Gokulˈnāth 2008: 103). Apart from its use in Braj bhāṣā, *bilamb/vilamb* is also used in Tulsidas's adaptation of the Rāmāyaṇa, the *Rāmˈcaritˈmānas* (1574), more than a dozen times, which shows that this word was also common in Avadhī. That *vilamb* was still in use in Khaṛī bolī Hindi 200 years later is corroborated by the fact that John Gilchrist enlists this word as a common Hindvī word ('bilumb') in his dictionary *English and Hindoostanee* (1797). Gilchrist's dictionary, for that matter, serves as a useful yardstick to determine which Sanskrit words in Hindi were inherited and which were to be coined in the course of the 19th century.

With regard to the choice of words the *Premˈsāgar* quite resembles the language of *Rānī Ketˈkī kī kahānī* (1803), written by the polyglot author Insha Allah Khan (1752–1817) at almost the same time Lalluji Lal composed his work. Insha Allah Khan in the introductory statement of his work declares to deliberately leave out all words of foreign origin: *bāhar kī bolī kuch usˈke bīc meṃ na ho* (Khan 1945: 2). Though his story is devoid of Persian-Arabic words, no one would accuse Insha Allah Khan of inventing a new language for the Hindus by cleansing the common speech of Delhi of its foreign elements, as has been the case with Lalluji Lal. On the contrary, in Rai's tract we will find the following juxtaposition of these two contemporary authors: "It was Inshah's declared intention to write an authentic (theth) Hindavi, abjuring both Perso-Arabic and Sanskritic excess. Lalloji Lal, on the other hand, is believed to have 'practically newly-invented' modern Sanskritised Hindi [...]" (Rai 2001: 21). This belief, again, goes back to the wrong assumption Grierson made in 1889 and since then moves on like a perpetuum mobile in the academic evaluation of early Hindi prose.

One reason why most Indian literary historians held the language of *Rānī Ket'kī kī kahānī* in higher esteem is because the Hindi of *Prem'sāgar* bears some morphological influences of Braj bhāṣā. Ramchandra Shukla in his standard work of literary history *Hindī sāhityā kā itihās* (1929) calls Lalluji Lal's language therefore "*braj'raṃjit Khaṛī bolī*", "a Khaṛī bolī influenced by Braj" (Śukla 2002: 289). But this only shows how conventional the language of the *Prem'sāgar* was because such an admixture was a characteristic feature of early Khaṛī bolī Hindi writings. In today's times when there is a strong demand to give local dialects more space in Hindi writings by adapting the standard language to the regional idiom, as we can see in the Hindi *āṁcalik* literature of the past decades, Lalluji Lal's *braj'raṁjit* style would have been more than welcome, as it offers a viable template for rendering regional speech. But in the course of standardising the Hindi language, at the beginning of the twentieth century, any deviation from the norm was generally considered detrimental and qualified as a *aśuddhi* ('impurity').

Bhatnagar's claim that Bharatendu Harishchandra (1850–1885), the literary pioneer of the Hindi renaissance, rejected the model for Hindi prose provided by the *Prem'sāgar*, as it stands for a "Pandit Hindi riddled with Brahminical pedantry", and that it was "prescient for Hariśchandra to recoil from Premsagar's linguistic purges" (Bhatnagar 2012: 91) is totally unaccounted for in any of his statements. In fact, according to Bharatendu's classification of the different styles of Hindi the choice of words in the *Prem'sāgar* would perfectly correspond to the style Bharatendu deems best. In his essay *Hindī bhāṣā* (1883), Bharatendu presents 11 different styles of Hindi, from which, according to him, specimens 2 and 3 "*likh'ne yogya haiṃ*", "are worth to be written" (Bhāratendu 2000: 1051). He describes specimen 2 as a style *jis'meṃ Saṃskṛt ke śabd thoṛe haiṃ*, "which has few Sanskrit words":

> *sab videśī log ghar phir āye aur vyāpāriyoṃ ne naukā lād'nā choṛ diyā pul ṭūṭ gaye bāṃdh khul gaye paṃk se pṛthivī bhar gaī. pahāṛī nadiyoṃ ne ap'ne bal dikhāye vṛkṣ kūl samet toṛ girāe sarp biloṃ se bāhar nik'le mahānadiyoṃ ne māryādā bhaṃg kar dī aur svataṃtratā striyoṃ kī bhāṃtī umaṛ calī.*[18]
>
> *(Bhāratendu 2000: 1050)*

I have counted 14 tatsam words in those two sentences vis-à-vis 1 Persian word (*pul*). Specimen 3, the one Bharatendu calls *śuddh Hindī*, "pure Hindi", contains virtually only *tadbhav* words and not a single word of foreign origin. The language of the *Prem'sāgar* is nothing but a mixture of the two templates Bharatendu considered as ideal Hindi prose.

Bharatendu did, however, have strong reservations about the *Prem'sāgar*, owing to its contents. In a statement to the Hunter Education Commission (1882), he wrote: "I fully agree with Miss Rose Greenfield that the Prem Sagar must not be put into the hands of 'big girls'" (Bhāratendu 2008: 411).

The descriptions of Krishna's *līlā* with the Gopīs evidently did not conform to the prevalent Victorian moral code of that era.

A Conceptual Misunderstanding

Bhatnagar's assertion that the *Prem|sāgar* initiated "*a secular linguistic purge*" (Bhatnagar 2012: 78) results from a conceptual misunderstanding. Owing to the Puranic genre, the vocabulary of *Prem|sāgar* contains many Sanskrit words. It was and is general practice in Hindi adaptions of Puranic literature to abundantly use words of Sanskrit origin. To relate to modern times, no one would blame the Hindi and Urdu author Rahi Masoom Raza (1927–1992), who wrote the Sanskrit-oriented Hindi script for the popular TV serial *Mahābhārat*, which was aired in Doordarshan National from 1988 to 1990, for deliberately cleansing the Hindi language of words from foreign origin to pursue a purist agenda.[19] As already mentioned, nearly all the Sanskrit words Lalluji Lal uses in the *Prem|sāgar* are commonly understood by readers familiar with basic literary Hindi, which is one of the main reasons this work has enjoyed great popularity in the last two centuries.[20] Samuel H. Kellogg notes in the preface of his *Grammar of the Hindi Language* (1876):

> Hindus, from the highest to the lowest, learned and unlearned, greatly admire their style [of the *Prem|sāgar* and *Rām|carit|mānas*]. Crowds, even of the most illiterate rustics, may often be seen listening eagerly to some Brahman intoning the measured rhyming tone of the *Prem Sāgar*.
>
> *(Kellogg 1965: x)*

Another important fact that hardly gets any attention is that Lalluji Lal occasionally does use Persian-Arabic words in the *Prem|sāgar*.[21] The author uses the Arabic word *vidā* ('farewell') innumerable times, not trying to find a Sanskrit-based alternative even once. Replacing that word with an uncommon Sanskritism would have certainly constituted a case of lexical intervention that would have justified the claim of Lalluji Lal's creation of a pure style. But then he also refrains from substituting the Persian conjunct *ki* with the native equivalent *jo*. Other Persian-Arabic loanwords that he could have replaced with Sanskrit synonyms are (page number in brackets): *ekāekī* (32, 86, 181, 264, 373), *gulāb* (207, 267), *der* (73), *band* (9), *bak|rā* (119), *mahīnā* (9, 26, 32, 64, 89, 145, 166, 220, 222, 245), *lāl* (3, 117, 264, 308, 310), *sahī* (389) and *sāmān* (271, 362).[22] We can safely conclude from this fact that purging the Hindi language of all its foreign elements out of a purist agenda was evidently not the intention of Lalluji Lal. One has to also keep in mind that Lalluji Lal translated Braj works into Hindustani (i.e., Urdu) in corporation with other Munshis, too, such as the *Baitāl paccīsī* and *Siṃhāsan paccīsī*. Owing to the secular genre of those works and the target language Urdu, those adaptions contain much less words of Sanskrit origin.[23]

Thus, Lalluji Lal wrote Kharī bolī in two different styles, Hindi and Urdu, as was the common practice in the previous eighteenth century and exactly what Premchand (1880–1936), the pioneer of modern Hindi and Urdu realism, would do, though admittedly to a lesser extent, in the following twentieth century: keeping these two literary styles apart by using a considerable different lexical register in the respective Hindi and Urdu writings. It is only legitimate then to exonerate the *Prem'sāgar* of the allegation of having invented an artificial Sanskritised Hindi.

The Underlying Agenda against the *Prem'sāgar*

With the publication of Shukla's *Hindī sāhitya kā itihās* in 1929, it should have become clear to everyone that Sanskrit-oriented Kharī bolī Hindi was not an invention of a language tutor in Fort William College who deliberately wanted to divide a unified language. Orientalists such as Grierson and Bloch can be given the benefit of the doubt as they didn't have access to those Hindi works preceding 1800. But then their narrative of the invention of an artificial style in a colonial institution came in handy for the propagation of Hindustani, which the Indian National Congress on behest of Mahatma Gandhi declared in 1925 as the future national language of India. The project of a unified language was intrinsically linked to the idea of an undivided India. It influenced the academic discourse on the origins of Hindi and Urdu from the perspective of a pro-Hindustani ideology. Although the Sanskrit-oriented variety of Kharī bolī has deep roots, it posed an obstacle to the masterplan of merging Hindi and Urdu into a common idiom. It was practical then to refer to Grierson and Bloch and project this traditional style as a recent artificial invention. Just get rid of the burden of so-called highbrow Sanskrit and Persian-Arabic words in Hindi and Urdu respectively and the true vernacular will emerge, so the myth. This is the style that Gilchrist had envisioned for Hindi and Urdu, calling it a "*conciliating Hindoostanee*" (Gilchrist 1798: iii). His rendering of *Hindoostanee tales* was written for that purpose as can be seen in the following salient passage from the *tiriyā carittar* genre[24]:

> *vah brāhmaṇ ek vaidyāin kī sūrat pākar kuch jaṛī-būṭī hāth meṁ le darvāze par baiṭhā thā. uske śauhar ne dekhkar pūchā: "tū kaun hai jo hamāre darvāze par baiṭhī hai", javāb diyā ki "hakīmnī", kahā "tumhārā hī kām hai, tum mere marīz ko dekho". tab vah bhītar ākar, bīmār kī nāṛī dekh kahne lagī: "yah kaṭhin dukh hai, jis tartīb se upāy batlāūṁ jo qabūl karo is alīl ko abhī ārām hotā hai." bole, hameṁ manzūr hai". kahā, "maiṁ aur yah rogī ek koṭhrī meṁ raheṁ au us ke dar par ek pardā paṛe, ou is dukhī kā sir parde ke bāhar is ke svāmī kī jāṁgh par rahe, ek ghaṛī meṁ bhalā kar detī hūṁ.*[25]
>
> *(Gilchrist 1798: 127f.)*

The fairly balanced mixture of words of different origin (Sanskrit: *kaṭhin, dukh, upāy, rogī, svāmī*; Persian-Arabic: *sūrat, śauhar, marīz, tartīb, alīl*, etc.) in the passage quoted above shows which style Gilchrist wanted to promote. We can conclude from this that the endeavour of creating a bridge between Hindi and Urdu with a strong focus on the colloquial idiom was a linguistic project initiated by Gilchrist for Hindustani prose. There should, however, be no misgivings whatsoever that apart from all practical considerations that can be availed by a mixed register, the attempt to unify both styles of Kharī bolī under the umbrella of Hindustani was part of Fort William College's linguistic agenda to cater to colonial interests. For the East India Company, it would have been more convenient and effective to rule the people of the North-Western Provinces by using one language instead of taking recourse to two different styles that required much more effort to master. With regard to language, the principle of *unite et impera* was obviously the guiding principle.[26] When Gilchrist calls the abundant use of Persian-Arabic in Urdu and of Sanskrit in Hindi "pedantry",[27] then we have to qualify this disparaging view as part of a colonial mindset that completely ignores indigenous conceptions of aesthetics when it comes to the written form of the language. To adapt the style of writing to the colloquial language has never been the one and only criterion that counts in South Asian literature. Of equal importance is the aura of the text that is created through consciously chosen words different from everyday speech. For expressing more complex matters, Sanskrit and Persian provided the necessary terms. The British officials were never interested in developing Hindi and Urdu into full-fledged languages of literature, administration and modern sciences. All they wanted is to master a colloquial mixed variety of Kharī bolī to command their sepoys and servants.

In this sense, the refusal of the Munshis of Fort William College to provide their colonial masters with such a hybrid prose work can be interpreted as a subversive act of resistance against the British language policy in order to preserve the indigenous literary traditions. As a matter of fact, most contemporary Hindi and Urdu writers ignored colonial interventions to arbitrarily unify these two styles that were still in their nascent stage of literary development. It would have been so much easier for the British officials to learn from a book written in colloquial Hindustani. Instead, they had to study the Sanskrit-oriented *Premˈsāgar* and the Persian-oriented *Bāġ-o bahār* to pass the vernacular examination. Paradoxically, or rather tragically, the native language tutors of Fort William College are generally regarded as collaborators in a colonial project to divide society by using two distinct styles of prose.

Epilogue

The emblematic description of Kharī bolī-based Hindi–Urdu as "one language, two scripts" was never true. It has always been "one language, two styles". I do not see why the co-existence of two different literary styles of one language should be seen as an anomaly. It should rather be regarded as an enrichment that preserves the colourful diversity of Khaṛī bolī in two forms, Hindi and Urdu. A nice example of this co-existence can be seen in the period film *Sikandar* (1941), in which Alexander the Great (Sikandar), played by Prithviraj Kapoor, speaks the Urdu style of Khaṛī bolī, by using Persian-Arabic words such as *mulk*, *tārīkh*, *fauj*, *taslīm* and *yaqīn* and Puru, played by the director Sohrab Modi, speaks the Hindi style by using the corresponding Sanskrit words *deś*, *itihās*, *senā*, *svīkār* and *viśvās*. It is important to mention here that there have always been mutual exchanges between these two styles and under the umbrella of Standard Hindi and Urdu there are again several substyles.

The *Prem|sāgar* provided the necessary literary template for Hindi in the early phase of colonial rule. It is due to Lalluji Lal's efforts in preserving the Sanskrit-oriented style of Khaṛī bolī that the British authorities had to give recognition to the fact that there was not one way, but two ways of doing Hindustani, though Urdu was the sole court language in the North-Western Provinces till 1900. As the *Prem|sāgar* was practically the only Hindi book in the vernacular curriculum throughout the nineteenth and beginning of the twentieth century, thousands and thousands of colonial officers were being made aware of the composite linguistic culture in North India while studying the Hindi language with the help of Lalluji Lal's magnum opus. We should at least appreciate Lalluji Lal's contribution in this regard.

Notes

1 Cf. the register of the historical novel *Divyā* (1945) set in an ancient Buddhist kingdom in Northern India by the progressive Hindi author Yashpal (1903–1978).

2 To be fair towards Pathak, the quoted passage stands as a singular exception in view of the language he used in all of his other letters. In a letter to Mahavirprasad Dvivedi, Pathak writes: *āp to kuch khafā se ho cale! maiṃ muāfī māṁg|tā hūṁ. mitroṃ meṃ vivād uṭh|nā sac|muc anucit hai. maiṃ āp|ke patra kī unnati kī nīyat se mitratā kī rīti par āp|ko do-ek bāteṃ sujhāne kā abhilāṣī thā, āp se virodh khaṛā kar|nā merā abhiprāy na thā* (Pāṭhak 2003: 285). In another letter to Banarsidas Chaturvedi, he writes: *abhī 'viśāl bhārat' nahīṃ nik|lā. śāyad āp|ko bahut sī muśkiloṃ kā mukābilā kar|nā paṛā hai. āraṃbh meṃ aisā hotā hai* ((Pāṭhak 2003: 331). From these two examples, we can see that Shridhar Pathak profusely uses Urdu words such as *khafā*, *muāfī*, *nīyat*, *śāyad*, *muśkil* and *mukābilā*, which he could have easily substituted with Sanskrit synonyms.

3 Orsini is right in the following observation regarding the absence of Khaṛī bolī literary culture between the 13th and the 18th century in North India:

> The later 'discovery' of the production of vernacular poetry in Dakkani and Gujri by Sufis and at Sultans' courts seemed to fill this gap in Urdu's historical narrative by way of a geographical detour, but the question about Urdu's absence from the north Indian literary landscape still remained unanswered. Unlike other Indian vernaculars, which seemed to establish their regional literary presence either before or after the first millennium, Hindi and Urdu seemed to struggle on their own soil.
> *(Orsini 2010: 5)*

For this reason, I could not reproduce northern Khaṛī bolī texts from the 17th century. Though Dakhini is generally acknowledged as Khaṛī bolī, its morphological differences to the standard northern idiom are considerable. An advantage of the very recent literary development of Modern Standard Hindi and Urdu in contrast to several other Indian languages that have preserved historical forms as a concession to their classic literary style is that there are practically no morphological differences between the spoken and the written language.

4 "At that time Śrīācāryajī Mahāprabhū asked: 'Dam'lā, did you listen'? Dāmodar'dās pleaded: 'Mahārāj, I sure did listen to the words of Śrīṭhākurjī but I could not grasp anything. Then Śrīācāryajī Mahāprabhū replied that Śrīṭhākurjī has given me the [following] order: 'Initiate (lit. 'connect with brahma') the living beings whom I [then] will embrace. [By that] all of their faults will vanish. Therefore, you should initiate at all costs" (translation by the author).

5 "[Once] there was a town called Sistan. The ruler of that Sistan was called Intelligence. Spiritual and worldly matters followed his will. Without his order nothing moved. Whoever abided by his command gained both worlds. In society he was well-spoken of [and] honoured by people. Wherever he settled, he was welcomed. Neither did he have to face disasters or earthquakes. When one is content with oneself, the whole world appears benign. one is at peace with the world. Talking bad about someone is [caused by] a false apprehension, [as] all good and evil exits [only] in oneself" (author's translation).

6 The estimated ratio of Persian-Arabic words in the *Sab ras* is 53–57 percent (cf. Oesterheld 2016: 291). I would say that the ratio of *tatsam* and *arddh-tatsam* words in the *Vārtā* has a similiarly high percentage.

7 The fact that Agra, which lies along with Lord Krishna's hometowns Mathura-Vrindavan in the very centre of that dialect region, used to be the Mughal capital from 1506 to 1648 has surely also played an important role in the consolidation of Braj as a literary lingua franca. This might be the reason why Abdul Haq (1870–1961), the Bābā-e Urdū, i.e., the 'Grand Old Man of Urdu', stated that Urdu *Brij bhāśā aur Fārsī ke mel se banī hai*, "originated from a mixture of Braj bhāṣā and Persian" (Shackle and Snell 1990: 121). Although this statement is not correct as Hindi and Urdu are based on *Khaṛī bolī*, the dialect of the Delhi region, the phono-morphological influences of Braj on the modern standard varieties is considerable. If Agra had remained the capital and a flourishing metropolis in the decades to come, Hindi–Urdu might have as well developed into a Braj variety with many Khaṛī bolī elements.

8 For Urdu denoting the city of Delhi, see Rahman (2011: 49f.). In this sense, Bharatendu Harishchandra notes in his essay *Agar'vāloṃ kī utpatti* (1871) that the members of the Agarvāl cast, whose ancestors hail from the region of Delhi, speak "*Khaṛī bolī arthāt· Urdū*", "Khaṛī bolī, that is to say, Urdu" (Bhāratendu 2000: 586).

9 Due to its widespread use, Braj bhāṣā was retained as the standard variety to write poetry in Hindi till the beginning of the 20th century. For Urdu, the only option to replace Persian with a native tongue was Khaṛī bolī. Thus, with regard to poetry Urdu has a longer tradition than Modern Standard Hindi. But even then, Persian was given a much more prominent role in poetry than Urdu throughout the first half of the 19th century, as can be seen from the fact that Ghalib's Persian compositions outnumber his Urdu verses by far.

10 According to Bachchan Singh, the Khaṛī bolī manuscript of *Bhāṣā Yog'vāśiṣṭh* available in the library of the Patiala Darbar is dated 1745, and its language bears more resemblance to the one used in the contemporary *Bhāṣāpadmapurāṇ* (Siṃh 2000: 288). Whatever the differences might be, the vocabulary in both versions is dominantly shaped by words of Sanskrit origin.

11 "[When] a doubt arose in the mind of Agast'jī's disciple Sutīkṣaṇ he went with the intention to remove this [doubt] to the ashram of the sage Agast. He bowed to him accordingly, sat down and pleadingly asked him: 'O Sire! You are the knower of all

essential truths and scriptures, remove a doubt from me. Is the cause of liberation action or knowledge or both of them, explain [this to me]'" (author's translation).

12 "The people of virtue, whose testimony can be trusted, narrate the following to Haidar, the Commander of the Faithful: After the Battle of Nahrawan Hazrat amīr asked who would deliver the news of my victory to Kufa. Ibn Muljam, curse upon him, said: Oh, Commander of the Faithful, if you order, I will go and deliver the good news of victory to the people of Kufa" (author's translation).

13 These findings were first presented in Ramchandra Shukla's work *Hindī sāhitya kā itihās* (1929). Christopher King qualifies Shukla's claim based on "only a handful of examples before 1800" as "tenuous" (King 1994: 25). Although the number of textual sources predating 1800 is quite modest, the existence of a Sanskrit-oriented Khaṛī bolī Hindi tradition in the 18th century cannot be denied. When King quotes Shukla, saying that the literary historian "admits that 'in reality at that time [c.1800] prose works existed in neither Urdu nor Hindi'", he leaves out the context of the previous sentence, that the British had searched in vain for works from which they could learn the language. Because right after this admittedly ambiguous sentence ("*us samay gadya kī pustakeṃ vāstav meṃ na Urdū meṃ thīṃ na Hindī meṃ*"), when torn out of its context, Shukla clearly states: "*jis samay Fort William College kī or se Urdū aur Hindī gadya kī pustakeṃ likh'ne kī vyavasthā huī us'ke pah'le Hindī khaṛī bolī meṃ kaī pustakeṃ likhī jā cukī thīṃ. 'Yog'vāsiṣṭh' aur 'Padmapurāṇ' kā ullekh ho cukā hai*", "at the time the writing of Urdu and Hindi prose works was organised by Fort William College, several Hindi Khaṛī bolī works had already been written before. The '*Yog'vāsiṣṭh*' and '*Padmapurāṇ*' have already been mentioned" (Śukla 2002: 285).

14 Shukla's dating of this work (1761) slightly differs from the one I have taken from the edited book. The editor Hiralal also describes him as a resident of Jaipur, whereas Shukla locates him in Basva (Rajasthan).

15 "It is truly astonishing that even a person of little intelligence like me is narrating his life. Although [men] like me are not capable of narrating [his life], still I am narrating in brief some [aspects] in the way Mahāmuni told [them] according to tradition."

16 It was only in later times around 1900 *yāmanī* as a glossonym got a negative connotation, when partisans of the Braj bhāṣā camp would call Khaṛī bolī Hindi disparagingly "*yāmanī*" (Caturvedī 2017: 20) or "*mlecch'bhāṣā*" (Gulerī 1991: 89).

17 "Śrīśuk'dev'jī said: 'Mahārāj, one day Nand'jī observed the vow of Ekadashi in a disciplined manner. The daytime he spent in taking baths, meditating, singing hymns, muttering mantras, doing puja and stayed awake all night. When it was six *ghaṛī* (time unit of 24 minutes) in the night and Dvadashi dawned he got up, cleaned his body, and noticing the daybreak took his dhoti, towel and pitcher and set off to take a bath in the Yamunā. Several cowherds were also following him'" (author's translation).

18 "All foreigners returned to their homes and the traders stopped loading [their] boats; The bridges broke away and the dams opened; the soil got covered with mud. The mountain rivers displayed their power and uprooted trees along with the banks; snakes crawled out of [their] holes; the great rivers broke [all] boundaries and overflowed like unrestrained women." (author's translation).

19 Here is a specimen out of a dialogue between King Bharat and his Rajguru , wherein the latter tells the king in a heavy Sanskrit-oriented style of Hindi that would still be totally comprehensible to any average viewer:

> *yadi manuṣya apnī ā̃khem̐ band kar legā to use andhakār ke atirikt aur kuch bhī dikhāī nahīm̐ de saktā, mahārāj. is'lie ā̃khem̐ kholie aur dekhie. sūrya ap'ne samay ke anusār uday bhī hotā hai aur ast bhī. candramā vaise hī nikal'tā hai aur vaise hī*

> *ap'ne śītal prakāś kī varṣā kartā hai. prakāś to ātmā hai, mahārāj, aur ātmā ke binā kuch bhī sambhav nahīṁ hai.*
>
> *(accessed January 4, 2021)*

20 Cf. the following observation by Ulrike Stark:

> Arguably, the initial impact of Fort William College publications was limited, the texts being designed for a non-Indian audience and at first hardly read outside the college. Yet it must not be overlooked that works such as Lalluji's *Premsāgar*, Mir Amman's *Bāgh o bahār*, and Maulvi Ikram Ali's Urdu version of *Ikhwān al-safā* (1811) subsequently gained immense popularity among Indian readers and, even if somewhat belatedly, came to figure among the most frequently reprinted works in the nineteenth century.
>
> *(Stark 2007, 41)*

21 Though Kellogg points out that the *Prem'sāgar* is not "free from any Arabic and Persian admixture", he fails to provide a corresponding list of words to prove his assertion, as he did for the *Rām'carit'mānas* (Kellogg 1965: 26).

22 Ramchandra Shukla quotes '*bairakh*', the Turkish word for 'flag', as the only example of a word of foreign origin used in the *Prem'sāgar*. He conjectures that Lalluji Lal did this in ignorance of the word's etymology and that this example is a rare exception: "*par aise śabd do hī cār jagah āe haiṃ*", "such words only appear in two to four places at most" (Śukla 2002: 289). As we have seen, the use of Urdu words in the *Prem'sāgar*, though quite moderate, is not restricted to two to four instances and thus far from being accidental.

23 Shukla's verdict that "*Baitāl paccīsī kī bhāṣā bilkul Urdū hai*", "the language of the *Baitāl paccīsī* is entirely Urdu" (Śukla 2002: 301), is not correct as this Hindustani adaption has retained a fair number of Sanskrit words of the original Braj language such as *nagar, mantrī, tapasyā, cintā, ajñān* and so on.

24 The Roman letters I have phonetically modified with the corresponding diacritics; Gilchrist does not use any.

25 "That Brahmin took the form of a female *vaidya* and sat with some medicinal herbs at [his mistress'] door. Her husband saw him and asked: 'Who are you that you are sitting at my door?'. [The Brahmin in disguise] replied: 'A lady doctor'. [The husband] said: '[So] this is your work, have a look at my sick [wife]'. Then she went inside and checked the pulse of the patient: 'This is a persistent condition. If you agree to the method of the treatment I am going to tell you, this illness will immediately stop.' [The husband] said: 'I consent'. [The lady doctor] said: 'Me and this patient will stay in a room and at its threshold shall be put a curtain. The patient's head should be outside the curtain in her husband's lap. [In this way] I am going to cure her in one *ghaṛī*' (time unit of 24 minutes)."

26 Cf. Stuart McGregor's remarks on Gilchrist's agenda:

> He was uneasy about the fact that both Devanagari and Persian scripts were in use to write Hindustani. To use both scripts for this particular purpose seemed an unnecessary complication to Gilchrist, one to be removed from the study of Hindustani if possible since it would create problems almost impossible to resolve in the future. To Gilchrist's classicist imagination these problems presented themselves as a 'Gordian knot', meriting nothing less than to be decisively 'cut asunder'.
>
> *(McGregor 2001: 30)*

27 In the preface to his English-Hindustani dictionary of 1787, Gilchrist states: "In a country where pedantry is esteemed [as] the touchstone of learning, the learned Moosalman glories in his Arabic and Persian [...]. The Hindoo is not less attached to Sunskrit and Hinduwee" (Cohn 1996: 36).

References

Bhāratendu, Hariścandra. 2000. *Bhāratendu samagra*. 4th ed. Edited by Hemant Śarmā, Pracārak granthāvalī pariyojnā 9. Vārāṇasī: Hindī Pracārak Pablikeśan.

———. 2008. *Bhāratendu Hariścandra granthāvalī. Khaṇḍ 6*. Edited by Omprakāś Siṃh. Dillī: Prakāśan Saṃsthān.

Bhatnagar, Rashmi Dube. "*Premsagar* (1810) and Orientalist Narratives of the 'Invention' of Modern Hindi." *Boundary 2* 39, no. 2 (2012): 75–110.

Bloch, Jules. 1970. *The Formation of the Marāṭhī Language*. Translated by Dev Raj Chanana. Delhi: Motilal Banarsidass.

Caturvedī, Rām Svarūp. 2017. *Hindī sāhitya aur saṃved'nā kā vikās*. 22nd ed. Ilāhābād: Lok'bhāratī Prakāśan.

Cohn, Bernard S. 1996. *Colonialism and its Forms of Knowledge. The British in India*. Princeton: Princeton University Press.

Dalmia, Vasudha. 2017. *Fiction as History. The Novel and the City in Modern North India*. Ranikhet: Permanent Black.

Daulat'rām, Paṇḍit. 1950. *Padmapurāṇ*. Edited by Hīrālāl Siddhānt-Śāstrī. Sastī granth'mālā 8. Dillī: Vīr Sevāmandir.

Dvivedī, Hajārīprasād. 2000. *Hiṃdī sāhitya: Udbhav aur vikās*. Nayī Dillī. Rāj'kamal Prakāśan.

Faẓlī, Faẓl ʿAlī. 1965. *Karbal Kathā*. Edited by Mālik Rām and Muẖtār-ad-Dīn Aḥmad. Paṭna: Idārah-i Taḥqīqāt-i Urdū.

Gilchrist, John Borthwick.1798. *The Oriental Linguist. An Easy and Familiar Introduction to the Popular Language of Hindoostan*. Calcutta: Ferris and Greenway.

Gokul'nāth. 2008. *Caurāsī Vaiṣṇavan kī vārtā*. Edited by Kam'lā Śaṃkar Tripāṭhī, Granth'mālā 3. Lakh'naū: Uttar Pradeś Hindī Saṃsthān.

Grierson, George Abraham. 1889. *The Modern Vernacular Literature of Hindustan*. Calcutta: Asiatic Society.

Gulerī, Candradhar Śarmā. 1991. *Gulerī rac'nāvālī. Khaṇḍ 2*. Edited by Dr. Manoharlāl. Dillī: Kitāb Ghar.

Kellogg, Samuel H. 1965. *A Grammar of the Hindi Language*. 3rd ed. London: Routledge and Kegan Paul.

Khan, Insha Allah. 1945. *Rānī Ket'kī kī kahānī*. 3rd ed. Edited by Śyām'sundar Dās, Nāg'rīpracāriṇī granth'mālā, 34. Vārāṇasī: Nāg'rīpracāriṇī Sabhā, Kāśī.

King, Christopher R. 1994. *One Language, Two Scripts. The Hindi Movement in Nineteenth Century North India*. Bombay: Oxford University Press.

Lāl, Lallūjī. 1953. *Prem'sāgar*. 3rd ed. Edited by Vraj'ratna Dās, Nāg'rīpracāriṇī *granth'-mālā* , 27. Vārāṇasī: Nāg'rīpracāriṇī Sabhā, Kāśī.

McGregor, Stuart. 2001. *The Formation of Modern Hindi as Demonstrated in Early 'Hindi' Dictionaries*. Gonda Lecture 8. Amsterdam: Royal Netherlands Academy of Arts and Sciences.

Oesterheld, Christina. 2016. "Mullā Vajhī's Sab Ras." In *Islam, Sufism and Everyday Politics of Belonging in South Asia*, edited by Deepra Dandekar and Torsten Tschacher, 279–293. Milton: Taylor and Francis.

Orsini, Francesca, ed. 2010. *Before the Divide. Hindi and Urdu Literary Culture*. Hyderabad: Orient Blackswan.

Pāṭhak, Śrīdhar. *Śrīdhar Pāṭhak granthāvalī. Khaṇḍ 3*. Edited by Padmadhar Pāṭhak. 2003. Jodh'pur: Minarvā Pablikeśan.
Rahman, Tariq. 2011. *From Hindi to Urdu. A Social and Political History*. Karachi: Oxford University Press.
Rai, Alok. 2001. *Hindi Nationalism*. Hyderabad: Oriental Longman.
Shackle, Christopher and Snell, Rupert. 1990. *Hindi and Urdu Since 1800. A Common Reader*. Delhi: Heritage Publishers.
Siṃh, Baccan. 2000. *Hindī sāhitya kā dūs'rā itihās*. Dillī: Rādhākṛṣṇa Prakāśan.
Stark, Ulrike. 2007. *An Empire of Books. The Naval Kishore Press and the Diffusion of the Printed Word in Colonial India*. Ranikhet: Permanent Black.
Śukla, Rām'candra. *Hindī sāhitya kā itihās*. 2002. Ilāhābād: Lok'bhārtī Prakāśan.
Vajhī. 1964. *Sab ras*. Edited by Saiyid ʿAbdallāh. Lāhor: Lāhor Akaiḍ.

14

VERNACULARS ACROSS TEXTS

Modern Islam and Modern Literature in Bengal

Neilesh Bose

Introduction

The study of religion, and particularly comparative religion, alongside philosophy, ethics, and other modes of intellection, poses areas for reconsideration within recent paradigms of intellectual history in South Asia. Sanskritist Sheldon Pollock has studied the historical presumptions embedded in the *Sanskrit Knowledge Systems on the Eve of Colonialism*, the international collaborative project which has studied Sanskrit knowledge systems before the nineteenth century (see Pollock 2008: 533–542). As opposed to Pollock's declaration of a rigid break between the premodern and the modern, I argue that comparative religion as practiced by Indian scholars in the late nineteenth century must be seen as a form of vernacular religion and, therefore, Indian intellectual history (see also Kaviraj 2005: 119–142). Comparative religion, as a practical and intellectual focus of Indians in the late nineteenth century, drew from a long tradition of thinking in universal and comparative terms about religion, built out of Indian sources and not only shaped by modern European imperial influences or sources of knowledge.

Even within scholarly studies of Sanskrit intellectual history, approaches to this question of whether an Indian intellectual history exists before Pollock's intervention have qualified and rejected the historical presumptions of epistemic rupture and totalizing intellectual erasure. Historian Michael Dodson, whose study of pandits in Banaras in the nineteenth century demonstrates a multifaceted set of concerns in and of Sanskrit, argues for scholars to write histories of the "knowledgeable," in the nineteenth century. Such scholars adapted to changing circumstances in the nineteenth century without presuming an essential core of Sanskrit form or content (see Dodson 2007, chapters 2

DOI: 10.4324/9781003279921-18

and 3). Another historian of modern religion, Brian Hatcher, argues for a reconsideration of Sanskrit's role in the nineteenth century through a close look at the life and thought of Iswar Chandra Vidyasagar (1820–1891), the Bengali pandit and social reformer (Hatcher 2007). Vidyasagar maintained a serious engagement with Sanskrit traditions and used Sanskrit polemics in order to argue positions relevant to the social world of the nineteenth century regarding widow remarriage (see Hatcher 1996, 2014). In both Dodson and Hatcher's approaches, an intellectual history for India most definitely existed in the nineteenth century, if only the presumptions of a static Sanskrit tradition are abandoned and "problemative normative judgments" about Sanskrit are given up.

A similarly historically rigorous approach would also apply to the project of comparative religion in the late nineteenth century, a point of interest across the world in the nineteenth century, notably among European intellectuals whose reflections remain important to the modern discipline of religious studies as well as the social sciences, such as Max Weber (1864–1920) and Emile Durkheim (1858–1917). In this chapter, I will explore how comparative religion in the late nineteenth century as understood by Indian intellectuals, such as Girish Chandra Sen (1835–1910) and Aghore Nath Gupta (1841–1881), informed a significant portion of Indian intellectual history. Comparative religion in India drew from a range of traditions and was not simply a matter of indoctrination by missionaries, European modern Orientalists, or Theosophists, but, rather, emerged out of layers of engagement with finding solutions to problems facing India at the time. This chapter will first introduce the Brahmo Samaj, the site of my investigation of the notion of comparative religion as it developed primarily in the 1880s. It will then discuss the ways that Islam and Buddhism are featured in this project, and end with a reflection on why the comparative religion of the Brahmo Samaj deserves consideration as a significant context for the development of vernacular languages of India, with specific reference to the history of Bengali in the nineteenth century. It bears in mind the given twentieth-century legacies, including the work of the poet Kazi Nazrul Islam as an exemplar of the vernacular tradition.

Within recent intellectual histories of nineteenth- and twentieth-century India, a common thread has emerged, notably the realization that various subfields of intellection (science, race, linguistics) become comprehensible only alongside various other subfields, so the study of linguistics was impossible without the various developments in the study of race, and the study of science was likewise animated by a taxonomic impulse that emanated out of various cognates. Finding a true or isolable variant of race, language, and scientific knowledge became a key endeavor throughout the nineteenth century. Finding a true, and for religion a universal, religion animated the work of Indian scholars of religion from the 1800s to the 1950s before and outside of any direct European encounter. Projit Mukharji's recent study of Ayurveda and "braided histories" explores how the forms of knowledge brewing in the nineteenth century, such as science, alongside race, and language, cannot easily be separated from one another within India or between India and sources and forces elsewhere.[1] In my view, these methodological directions link to a conception of religion, like the study of linguistics in a recent work by Majeed, as a "project with many different strands and narratives, some of which were in tension with each other" (Majeed 2018: 8). Rather than point to an indigenous and allegedly pure form, the term "vernacular" here refers to a comparative project that takes Indian sources seriously within a mission to critically examine religion anew.

The Brahmo Samaj

Discussions of comparative religion in modern India began in earnest with the formation of the Brahmo Samaj, the reformist organization that emerged in Calcutta in the 1820s. Though this organization boasts a detailed social and cultural history regarding social activism (such as advocacy for widow remarriage and the abolition of *satī*) as well as creating new spaces for religious discussion and worship, linked to the history of Company-era Calcutta,[2] an intellectual emphasis on universal and comparative religion began in fact with Rammohan Roy (1772–1833), the turn of the century polymath and scholar. A focus on universal and comparative religion began with his emergence as a philosopher of religion in the 1800s, i.e., in the two decades before the creation of the Samaj itself. Roy grew up in post–Plassey Company Bengal of the 1780s and 1790s, studying law and inheriting his father's estate in 1796, which enabled him to enter into both real estate and money-lending, signature occupations of many rising elite groups in Company India, as well as work in service of the East India Company.[3] Proficient in Persian and with working skills in Arabic and Sanskrit, as well as the newly "vernacularized" Bengali, Roy left the comfortable confines of colonial Calcutta and traveled throughout the Himalayas as well as the northeast, reaching areas near Bhutan and Tibet.[4] From the opening of the nineteenth century, he began to write and translate a long range of works about Indian religion.

In line with the broader global focus on monotheism and true religion in the late eighteenth and early nineteenth centuries, in 1803 or 1804, the discussion on universalism in Indian religion opens with the publication of *Tuḥfat al-Muwaḥḥidīn*, a small 14-page book written in Persian, with an Arabic preface, translated usually as "A Present to the Believers in One God," and frequently glossed as a "A Gift to the Monotheists." Its early incarnation circulated in the Persianate and quickly, in the vernacular Bengali world, in colonial Calcutta, and, by the late nineteenth century, in English to Anglophone readers in North America and Great Britain, where Roy spent the last two years of his life, hosted and appreciated by a range of Unitarians and others, from 1831 to

1833, where he died, buried now in Arnos Vale in Bristol, in a chhatri (*chat'rī*), a traditional Indian cenotaph.

After an introduction (written in Arabic) in which he explains how he has traveled in the "remotest parts of the world" and concludes that a broad swath of people agree on the existence of One being as the source of all existence, his opening places habits trained by socialization aside in search for a greater, transcendent truth, citing that "it is not the numbers of people behind or against truth that make it true; as one constant element is a belief in one Almighty God, the 'fundamental principle of every religion'" (Roy 1906: 955). He tackles a topic of contemporary deist interest, that of miracles and birth without parents (and he rejects the possibility of either) and also the inherent denial of history when resistance to conversion was raised (by defensive Hindus) as he recounted many episodes of conversion and change in the Indian religious landscape.

What is the history of thought that informed the making of this remarkable text? Like in the European case, when comparative religion entered the vocabulary in the seventeenth century through an engagement with then-dominant Christian understandings of religious diversity,[5] the broader world of Muslim India, as well as the particular context of Mughal India in the 1660s, provides a starting point for Roy. The structure of the *Tuḥfat* bears a close resemblance to the late sixteenth-century *Ā'īn-i-akbarī*, especially through a reading of its "The Learning of the Hindus" (Abu'l Fazl 1877: 210–20). Roy's framework for understanding each religion as he sees it is akin to each branch of learning covered in the *Ā'īn-i-akbarī*, as the latter reviews many different systems of Indian philosophy as well as Jaina and Buddhist traditions. Roy also reviews the religions of India but assesses religions by determining a relationship to a Supreme Being, as this is one marker of true religion for Roy. Roy's approach also appears to draw on the *Dabistān-i-Maẕāhib* (The School of Manners), a Persian text written by Kaykhusraw Isfandiyar in the 1640s CE, a member of the Ādhār Kayvān (d. 1027/1618) sect, a breakaway Parsi subgroup established in India by the rise of the Mughal Empire.[6] In 12 chapters, this text offers a description of a different tradition or set of traditions in each chapter, including Parsis, Hindus (which included Buddhists and Indic philosophical traditions), Muslims of various kinds, and others. Notable is the inclusion of a chapter on "Ilahiyya," or followers of the Emperor Akbar, as well as a running theme of assessing religions from the perspective of a Supreme Being as the common thread running through religions, but with the diversity of India as the framework through which such a conclusion could be determined. In the *Tuḥfat*, Roy opens with a discussion of the "One Being Who is the source of all that exists and its governor, and disagreeing in giving peculiar attributes to that Being and in holding different creeds consisting of the doctrines of religion and precepts of haram (forbidden) and halal (lawful)." Turning to one being is, for Roy, a natural tendency and common to "all individuals of mankind equally" (Roy 1906: 944). Finally, another probable context would have been the work of Baladev Vidyabhusana (1700–1793), who worked with the demands of Jaisingh II, king of Jaipur in the 1700s–1740s. Baladev created, as scholars of Vaishnava thought and practice such as Okita (2014) have established, a normative ideal with reference to the *Brahmasūtras* – a key starting point for defining true religion in the eighteenth century, which appeared later in Rammohan's thought in his own commentaries on particular Upaniṣads as well as his translations.

Zoroastrian-centric, Mughal-inflected, notionally Christian, and Gaudiya Vaishnava parameters for universalisms and comparisons comprise precedents for the *Tuḥfat*, which serves as the origin point of debate and discussion about the meanings and ends of comparative religion in modern India. Roy's primary goal throughout much of this textual work on "uncovering" the primary sources of Indian religion led him to conclude that various rituals, ceremonial practices, and external manifestations of religion were in fact not derived from any textual source, but formed as social distortions of religion's initial messages, hidden as they were in languages (like Sanskrit, termed by him a "dark curtain"). His goal was to clarify that, indeed, monotheism, as well as freedom from any ritual, lay at the source of Indian religion.

Roy also began to systematically study Upaniṣads, or theological critiques written after the Vedas in the post-500 CE period. He translated several Upaniṣads into Bengali over the course of the 1810s. In particular, he focused on five texts – the Kena, Īśa, Kaṭha, Muṇḍaka, and Māṇḍūkya-Upaniṣad. In the 1810s, these selections demonstrated a way to define religion not out of ritual but out of an investment in a belief in a Supreme Being addressed the particular audience of Christians entering Calcutta at this hinge moment in global history. From the 1790s, Christian missionaries had been pressuring the Company to allow missionaries into Company territory, which was formally forbidden according to the Company's charter until 1813. Whereas Christians themselves were certainly not new to India, given the long history of the Portuguese Empire in India from the late fifteenth century, and its "empire of Apostles," as well as premodern Christian groups scattered throughout southern India, this variant of Christians in the world of abolitionist and imperially situated Britain is a product of the political economy of the post-Plassey and, crucially, post-1813 landscape.

His last substantive work was *The Universal Religion: Religious Instructions Founded on Sacred Authorities* in 1829. Framed as a set of questions and answers between a teacher and student, this includes 12 questions with answers, in English, and then in Sanskrit, and later in Bengali. For questions about the manner, regulations, and spaces of worship, the answers offer the mode of reason as the approach to understanding the sacred writings, which he uses in the general, not specific, and which is the same answer offered in the *Tuḥfat*. In the Bengali version, each page is adorned with the word for truth, or *satya*, whereas in English it is universal religion being the analogue of truth. This universal religion, which is eagerly promoted by his friends the Unitarians of Calcutta, animates the work of the Brahmo Samaj (*brāhma samāj*), a reformist organization begun in 1828.

In 1828, a Trust Deed introduced a set of rules for the Samaj's members. By the 1840s, the organization began their journal *Tattvabodhinī Patrikā* (1843–1883) and through a process initiated by Debendranath Tagore, like Rammohan a layman in Sanskrit, began to initiate vows. Through this process, a broad definition of religion out of ancient Indic sources, as outlined in the book *Brāhma Dharma*, led to the creation of a religion of the householder.[7] Such a religion was born through readings of the same Upaniṣads – the Kena, Īśa, Kaṭha, Muṇḍaka, and Māṇḍūkya – emphasized by Roy.

Keshab Chunder Sen and Comparative Religion

About a decade after the appearance of *Brāhma dharma* during the 1857–1858 mutiny/rebellion, a young Keshab Chunder Sen (1838–1884) stayed with Debendranath Tagore in Calcutta and began to learn about, join, and eventually preach for the Brahmo Samaj. For a variety of reasons, he split from Debendranath in the 1860s, started the new Brahmo Samaj of India, began to publish books of theistic texts from across the world, and in 1869 created the *Brāhma mandir*, built in a new style aiming to synthesize and mix the religions of India into one new religion. Also, in Calcutta he started the Bharat Ashram (*bhārat āśram*), in 1872, an experimental living community where Brahmo members would live, learn, and have access to the world's traditions. Underneath this new dispensation, under the leadership of Keshab, beyond various splits and schisms, there emerged a project of studying the various religions of the world from 1879, with missionaries ordained to study Christianity, Islam, Buddhism, Bhakti, Vaishnavism, and initially many other traditions including Sikhism, but for various reasons this did not pan out. The New Dispensation had its apostles, those who would spread out into India, and were seen as science that found, explained, and, most importantly, harmonized all the religions of the world.

The religion of Islam was part and parcel of the various investigations of the Brahmo Samaj, and consequently, this iteration of vernacular religion. By most historical accounts, Islam entered Bengal via the conquests of the Turkic Khilji tribesman Muhammad Bakhtiyar (1198–1206) and his cavalry, who raided parts of eastern India, beginning with attacks on Buddhist monasteries in Bihar in the late sixth/twelfth century and conquered Nabadwip, a center of ancient learning, and Gaur (Gauṛ), the erstwhile capital of the Sena dynasty that had ruled most of Bengal since the late fifth/eleventh century. There is suggestive evidence that Islam existed in Bengal before the rise of Khilji, as material remains and folk traditions point to the existence of a mosque built in

Lalmonirhat in northern Rangpur in the 8th century, as well as Arab presence in Arakan and Chittagong between the 8th and 13th centuries.

Bengal remained nominally under the rule of the Delhi Sultanate until 1342, when Sultan Ilyas Shah (r. 740–59/1339–58) established an independent Bengal sultanate. From the fourteenth century to the late sixteenth century, Bengal was transformed into an independent political entity and developed localized literature, architecture, and religious practice and local memorialization of saints arriving from various parts of the Muslim world, as the structures in Pandua show. Tied to this process of Islamization was the growth of literature in Bengali intended as instruction for readers about proper forms of religious practice. Such works as *nasīhat-nāmā*s (*naṣīhat-nāma*s, books of advice) were composed from the tenth/sixteenth century to the thirteenth/nineteenth and used Arabic terms such as *nabī* (prophet) and *kalima* (word of God), as well as terms such as *puṇya* (merit) from Sanskrit. Literature that preached Islam within Bengali linguistic, literary, and philosophical registers began to emerge in the late tenth/sixteenth century.

During the period of Company (1764–1858) and imperial rule (1858–1947), Bengal was home to a series of reformist movements in line with the modern forms of religiosity and politics ushered in by that rule. Men such as Haji Shariatullah (d. 1840), from Faridpur in eastern Bengal, studied in Mecca and al-Azhar (in Cairo) between 1798 and 1818 and began to critique allegedly Hindu practices such as praying and worshipping at *dargāh*s and observing Hindu customs such as Dīpāvalī (the festival of lights) as "accretions" antithetical to Islam. He began a movement called Faraizi (*farāʾiḍī*, from *farāʾiḍ*, obligations to Islam). Shariatullah's son, nicknamed Dudu Miyan (d. 1862), continued this movement in the eastern countryside in the 1830s, transforming it into an explicitly political peasant movement, aimed at exposing and curtailing abuses of Muslim riots against land tenants as well as at establishing a system of justice alternative to British courts.

In the early twentieth century, as a small but increasingly visible Muslim middle class developed in Bengal, Muslims began to take new jobs available in the public sphere, in business, universities, and the government. Muslims also began to produce new journals and newspapers in Bengali, suggesting proper Muslim practices, criticizing Christian missionary practices, and creating a space for discussion of the Muslim community in the popular press. It is just before this stage after several centuries of Muslim presence in Bengal that a figure like Girish Chandra Sen enters the history of Islam in Bengal.

The missionary deputed to study Islam was Girish Chandra Sen (1835–1910), born a Hindu, but converted to this new movement of the Brahmo Samaj in the early 1870s and became a missionary for it. He left a past life filled with caste-based ritual and obligation, confronted a great amount of resistance from the family and life he left, and spent much of the 1870s in Lucknow, learning Persian, Arabic, and immersing himself mostly in studies of *tafsīr*.

Whereas Rammohan Roy a century earlier had come from the rising riches of Company Calcutta, Sen grew up in agrarian east Bengal, and also lived where "vernacular" Bengali was being standardized over the course of the nineteenth century into a language with a grammar and primary teaching methods. This new "vernacular" was cemented into existence primarily through Hindu elite collusion, that of pandits and other highly placed Hindu Bengalis who interpreted Bengali as a "Hindu" language with Company officials from the 1790s onward.

In the nineteenth century, though, a rising and increasingly literate Muslim small peasant, and emergent middle class, began to engage with their religion not in Arabic and Persian, but in this "vernacular," a language which in the newly standardized form held little about Islam (though much in the *battala* [*baṭ'talā*] literature certainly did, such as tales like *Ḥātim Ṭā'ī* and *Yūsuf-Zuleykhā*). Before Girish Chandra Sen embarked on a five-year immersion into the Qur'an, he translated from Persian into Bengali Rammohan Roy's *Tuḥfat* in 1878, published in Keshub Chandra Sen's *Dharmatattva* journal. In the late 1870s and the early 1880s, he studied with a maulvi in Lucknow, who taught him Arabic grammar, manners of reading the Qur'an, and selections from Hafiz. Sen translated the Qur'an, for the first time in its entirety, into vernacular standard Bengali accessible by everyday people literate in Bengali. Though bits and pieces had been accessible in Bengali in scattered places, by 1886 a thousand copies of Sen's full translation were available, mostly read by Muslim Bengalis and Brahmos like Sen. It was published in four editions, in 1892, 1908, and 1936. The fourth edition garnered lavish praise from the Muslim League leader and social activist Muhammed Akram Khan, who wrote its preface. What is new about Sen is not the rendering of the Qur'an itself, but the sort of language it was written in – vernacular Bengali – as earlier versions were available in *dobhāṣī* forms. Furthermore, the earlier version of Bengali Quranic literature did not include the whole text, but selected portions, as in the Ampara edition produced by Amiruddin Bosunia in the 1860s.

Sen explains pertinent information about Islam, catering to a non-Muslim readership. He conducts a line-by-line translation in an idiomatic fashion, often combining lines and rendering the meaning as opposed to only a literal translation of Arabic. As his preface lists a set of obligations Muslims in South Asia in particular would be aware of, such as facing west while praying and ritual recitations common among those around him in both Bengal and Lucknow, he demonstrated a sensibility around the living experience of Islam during his time. He used three primary sources for his commentary: *Tafsīr ḥusaynī*, *Tafsīr fā'ida*, and *Tafsīr jalālayn*. For the *Tafsīr ḥusaynī*, one of the most widely read works in India, Sen used the Urdu commentary, by Shah Abdul Aziz (d. 1823), a son of the heralded Shah Waliullah. He never uses the term "Allah," but terms like *īśvar*, *parameśvar*, and *adhipati*, and aims to be both universalist and true to the original.

He also includes a translation of the first *sūra*, *al-Fātihah*, using terms from Bengali of the nineteenth century. This move likely was made for the Brahmo Samaj to be receptive to the ideas presented, and not alienate primarily caste Hindu audiences from accessing ideas about God, monotheism, and ethics from the Qur'an. This maneuver in Bengal has been commented on by scholars of Islam in Bengal (Sufia Uddin 2006; Stewart 2001; Irani 2010), but this moment of Sen's translation marks an opening for those interested in Islam in a wholly new context, as concepts from the Bengali linguistic environment for Muslim and Hindu readers alike. Bengali Muslim critics in contemporary Bangladesh have consistently highlighted particular *sūra*s where these terms are deployed, such as *al-Fātiha, al-Baqara*, and *an-Nisāʿ*, in all of which terms such as *īśvar*, and significantly no Arabic, are used. Girish Chandra Sen's work comprises here an example of this regional tradition extending to non-Muslims writing about Muslims in Bengali (Hannan [ed.] 2014).

A prolific translator, Sen wrote 44 books in Bengali about various subjects related to religion, the nature of God (including *Īśvar ki īśvar*? – a dialogue detailing the long history of the Brahmo Samaj), biographies of the Prophet, key landmarks in Muslim history, like Karbala, and biographies of Ramakrishna. His work *Tāpas-mālā* contains biographies of Muslim saints, translated from the Persian original *Tazkīrat al-Awliyāʿ*. In the 1880s through the 1900s, he also wrote a great deal about the Brahmo Samaj, the *Naba bidhān*, or new dispensation, and the nature of religion and ethics. His last book was, fittingly, titled *Natural Religion*, which compels attention to Rammohan Roy's 1829 *Universal Religion*, Rammohan's last major contribution.

Sen's efforts emerged after nearly a century of reformist activity among the Muslims in India. A good portion of reformist activity also predates formal European imperial presence in India, such as the work of Shah Waliullah (1703–62), his son Shah Abdul Aziz (1746–1824), as well as post-1858 institutions such as the Deoband madrasa, begun in 1867, and social movements like the Tayuni movement led by Karamat Ali of Jaunpur in the 1860s and early 1870s, among many others.[8] Each strand of Muslim reformism in modern India put a new emphasis on personal action and will, self-consciousness and self-examination, and rationalization of religious belief and practice. What remains of enduring importance for the intellectual history of India is the fact that Sen conducted his labors neither on behalf of a Muslim political interest that began to develop in post-1858 India nor as an individual Muslim, but rather in the service of the Brahmo Samaj, which was exploring the various religions of India in their totalities, primary sources and expressions, and literal manifestations. His translation then comprises a chapter on the intellectual history of religion in India, both at the level of how creating a synthesis of different religions extant in India to produce a reformed new religion, as per the dictates of the Brahmo Samaj, forms a tradition in the religious history of India. Early modern histories of *bhakti*, the development of a stand-alone Sikh tradition, comprise important precursors to this Brahmo development. Such precursors are to be seen both in the form and manner in which major Brahmo activists conducted their work, as Rammohan Roy, the founder of the organization, as well as Keshub Chandra Sen, the pioneer behind comparative religion, engaged in comparable embodied and intellectual labor. They traveled both far and wide within the bounds of the India of their time, to points as varied as Tibet and Bhutan, north India, and areas outside of urban India, and also pondered the nature of religion in philosophical terms. In both cases, the presence of precursor efforts, whether by Guru Nanak, or even Siddhartha Gautama, or other such luminaries, bears heavily on their practices.

The focus on Islam by Sen is not an outlier to broader histories of religious change in Bengal, as the longer histories of religion demonstrate changes that emerged as responses to various forces, including the creation of the *Maṅgal'kābya* tradition, *kāvya* texts that focused on gods and goddesses not mentioned in the Purāṇas. These texts included iterations of local deities, such as Manasa, into a synthetic form of religion that integrated local gods and goddesses into narratives and reference points familiar to, but distinctive from, classical Sanskrit traditions. The emergence of the Chaitanya variant of Vaishnava thought and practice also arose in response to the enduring problems of caste-based restrictions. Finally, Islam in particular regions of eastern and southern Bengal had arisen due to a variety of social and ecological factors, including the spread of ideologies of agriculture.[9] Sen belongs then in a long line of engagement with sources, in this case, from Islam, within a broader mission to remake religion in India. In each and every case, the language of Bengali was enriched by these developments in religious life.

If we compare him to his eighteenth-century predecessor Ali Raja as studied by Tony K. Stewart (2001), we find that the reformist impulse is not only a reflection of Protestant literalism or religious communalism but, rather, also a continuation of the trends set in motion in premodern times. In *Witness to Marvels*, Stewart expands on his approach to Bengali religious life by outlining a detailed framework in which he interprets a range of texts nominally directed at Muslim audiences, but built out of the diverse Bengali set of references and textual precedents available to Muslims from the sixteenth century onward.[10] Stewart excavates the ranges of reading vis-à-vis logical or pragmatic suppositions (references from either the literal environment or the preceding textual landscape) as well as overt or implicit intertextuality. Extending the insights of Stewart's work on the early modern, one may interpret Sen via the *imaginaire* of nineteenth-century Bengal. An important element of this moment is not reform via caricature of traditions and political identity, but rather an investment in the vernacular traditions of Bengal. Rather than inputting Muslim reference points into a narrative landscape filled with Hindu references, he sought to make the text accessible to Brahmos first and foremost, but to

Hindus who would have had little to no experience with terms such as *paiġambar* or *rasūl* (terms for Prophet) in Bengali texts.

Sen's word choices demonstrate the sort of vernacular tradition known to Bengali audiences since the rise of Islam itself. He uses the term *adhipati* for sovereign (*al-Fātiha*), *Biśva-pālak* for Lord of the Universe (*al-Fātiha*), and *pratipālak* for Lord in most other *sūra*s. For God, he uses the term *parameśvar* throughout. Some phrases indicate an implicit familiarity with the pre-existing Sanskritic Indic culture, such as the transition into light from darkness, a common theme in Upaniṣads, emphasized since Rammohan Roy. Sen's translation appears in the same decade as the heralded Syed Ahmed Khan's 1880 translation. Notably Sen's is done from within a Bengali tradition, and not at all highlighting science, Christianity, or Muslim defensiveness, in the manner of Khan or other high-profile Muslims of the era.

In his preface, he mentions how translation into Bengali is difficult and some words will be complicated. He relies on *Tafsīr ḥusaynī* and Shah Abdul Kader's *Tafsīr fā'ida*, as well as *Tafsīr jalālayn*, like many of the English translations that came out later, including the oft-cited version by Dawood. Other translations of this era in other languages are usually studied by scholars of Islam in India, such as that by Waliullah, as well as Obeidullah Sindhi, and Sayyid Ahmad Khan. The emphasis in those translations focuses on a defence from missionaries as well as rationality and science.

Unlike Sindhi and Khan, who translated into Urdu, Sen's is the only translation of his time (though many follow just after him) in Bengali. He includes a lengthy, nearly a page-long note in his translation of *Sūra Fātiha* about his usage of language, as well as cites *Tafsīr fā'ida*. He did not see himself as Hindu and did not see himself as Muslim, but felt it was imperative to make the Qur'an accessible to non-Muslims. Terms like *īśvar, parameśvar*, and *adhipati* were used in his translation, but as Muhammed Hannan in a recent study has shown, these words have been excised from recent editions, especially those from the Islamic Foundation of Bangladesh in 2004. He aimed at enabling the recognition of what had already been in Bengal, but had been invisible to Bengali Hindus primarily, even though it had been on the minds of Brahmos since at least Debendranath Tagore, if not Rammohan himself.

In terms of Sen's impact on Islam in Bengal, after him, a range of translations emerged, mostly by Muslims, but some by Hindus and Brahmos. Translations did exist, but of bits and pieces and in *pūthi* style, by Amiruddin, Ghulam Akbar Ali, and Khondkar Mir Waleed Ali. G. C. Sen comes in the 1870s, a disciple of K. C. Sen, with the goal of finding the links between all religions. Before Sen, most works in Bengali regarding the Qur'an were translations of particular *sūra*s or poetry inspired by particular *sūra*s. The first is Shah Mohamed Shagir, who writes on *sūra Yūsuf*. Particular *sūra*s were of interest to common people before the nineteenth century, such as *sūra Fātiha*, and *sūra Yāsin*.

When we get to the colonial period, we find that according to the last count, 67 translations were produced, but mostly of bits and pieces. In 1808, Amiruddin Bosunia offered a variant of the Qur'an in Bengali, but in *pūthi* style. Sen, with his vernacular Bengali words, comes in 1881, followed by Naimuddin. A prominent religious leader, Naimuddin signals how it is because of Sen's work that then later translations occur, whereas before that the *ʿālim* looked at Arabic, Farsi, and Urdu. At that time, Farsi and Urdu were prevalent among elites of Hindu and Muslim classes. From the 1890s to the 1940s, mostly Muslims offered translations following Naimuddin, but there were others, including Christians, such as Philip Biswas and one Reverend Goldsack. Also, Hindus such as Sri Kiran Gopal Singh and Brahmos such as Dwidas Datta, following in Girish Chandra Sen's footsteps, translated the Qur'an in 1926. Whereas very few Hindus were interested in studying or learning about Islam in this time period, Brahmos had always held a strong attachment to monotheism and so this is one reason possibly why Girish Sen and Dwidas Datta devoted their energies to it.

Unlike the translations and creative products from earlier times, the nineteenth-century Bengali world featured a drive toward standardization and inclusion into the Bengali public sphere, though the form of translation here appears to fall in between a literal and dynamic translation (in the fourfold schema laid out by Stewart). Though the language does not contain the levels of depth and generic complexity, say of parody and satire, that is seen in earlier periods, the efforts by Sen must be placed in a longer context of Islam's presence in Bengal, one not oriented toward a political interest or public Muslim identity. This approach to religion may be seen as the vernacular understanding of religion from within Bengali starting points.

Aghore Nath Gupta

Like his compatriot Girish Chandra Sen, Aghore Nath Gupta also hailed from a region outside of the Calcutta metropole – Shantipur, in Nadia above Calcutta, a center of older Sanskrit education under Krishna Chandra. Aghore Nath, who also grew up in a caste Hindu home, lost his father at a young age and found the Brahmo Samaj in Calcutta, when he was studying in the 1850s at Hindu College. Gupta met Keshub in the late 1850s, and after meeting him became a Brahmo. From 1866 and till the creation of both the New Brahmo Samaj for India, he joined the movement as a worker and preached in Dhaka, Rangpur, Mymensingh, and Bogra, all regions in eastern Bengal. From the 1870s, he joined the Bharat Ashram in Calcutta and mingled with a variety of figures in addition to Keshub, such as Kedarnath Datta, the noted Vaishnava theologian, Bijoy Krishna Goswami, a key reader of the *Caitanya caritāmṛta*, as well as Girish Chandra Sen and Sibnath Sastri.

He was deputed to study Buddhism in 1879 and spent most of that year and 1880 studying Pali, English, and Sanskrit, to write one major masterwork,

Śākyamuni carit o nirbāṇ'tattva, a Bengali book that emerged in print in three volumes, in 1904 and 1905. It is a detailed study of the life of Siddharta Gautama in vernacular Bengali, paralleling, in ways, the project of translating the Qur'an by Sen, as both emerge in the decade of the 1880s as elements of the comparative religion wing of the Brahmo Samaj.

His interest in Buddhism fits into a wider revival of thought and practice in India, and in particular in Bengal, in the late nineteenth century. However, he is a unique figure in this history. Four broad forces converged in the late nineteenth century in Bengal and eastern India at this time. One is the work of Chakmas, including Queen Kalindi, who invites the Venerable Saramedha Mahasthavira to Rajanagar to revive Buddhism in the Chakma country in 1857, which leads to both more followers and a reformist Buddhism purge of heterodox elements. Another is the institutional basis for the study of Buddhism, which occurs both in the Brahmo Samaj and, in 1880, in the creation of Keshab Chunder Sen, the Śākya Samāgam, an annual program for religious discussions, after his visit to Bodh Gaya, to focus on Buddhist texts and sources. Within this broad ambit would be the intellectual work of Rajendralal Mitra, and his work *Sanskrit Buddhist Literature of Nepal*, the basis of much of Rabindranath Tagore's plays and stories about Buddhism, as well as Haraprasad Sastri, and his *Discovery of Living Buddhism in Bengal*, which emerges in 1897. Mitra and Sastri were part of the Buddhist Text Society based in Kolkata, established in 1893. After the Asiatic Society of Calcutta had been in existence for over a century, this society held the goal of "making researches into the religious and social literature of the ancient Indian Buddhists found in original Sanskrit works, as also in Pali, Tibetan, Burmese, Siamese, Chinese, Corean, and Japanese literature." The journal aimed to "furnish materials for a history of Indo-Aryan thoughts on Buddhism, as also, of a history and geography of ancient India and all Buddhist countries."[11] In addition to a focus on Buddhism amongst the intelligentsia of Calcutta society – its sources, texts, and histories – an institutional life of organizations for Buddhists began to emerge in Bengal at this time. In 1891, the Mahabodhi society, aimed at reviving Buddhism in India, was founded in Calcutta. In 1892, the Bauddha Dharmankar Sabha, by Ven. Kripasankar Mahasthabir, was founded for the revival and reform of Bengali Buddhism began also in Calcutta.

What marks out Aghore Nath Gupta is that, unlike others, he was not an urban intellectual supported by a university or learned society. His activities are interspersed with his social work and engagement with people in various parts of India in the *mufassil*, and aimed at contributing to the Brahmo religion, not necessarily for the sake of the science of comparative religion (which for Max Müller, of course, relied on the telos of Christianity) but in the service of remaking religion itself. Whereas Girish Chandra Sen worked with a Muslim tutor in Lucknow, Aghore Nath, from available evidence, did not have contact with Buddhist monks, but worked with Rajendralal Mitra and others in

Pali and Sanskrit. Unlike Dharmapala, as Steven Kemper in his recent detailed study of his life and work shows,[12] Aghore Nath's Brahmo message was not transformed into nationalism.

Aghore Nath retains the Brahmo Samaj comparative religion approach by including both religions of revelation and practices observed in India, with the most important practice of *bhakti*, developed by Keshub Chandra Sen, Sitanath Tattvabhusan, and Protap Mazoomdar, in the field of eligible sources for remaking religion in India. This field of religion – not the only one in late nineteenth-century India, to be sure – is not simply redolent of the Protestant impositions on the world but the creation of a new synthetic religion that positively engaged with, and integrated aspects of, religions such as Islam and Buddhism, through an appreciation of the disciplinary process that both religions allowed for as well as the deep reservoir of inspiration that the stories of the Prophet Muhammad and Siddhartha Gautama provided Indians. The history of Buddhism in modern South Asian contexts usually fixates on figures such as Dharmapala in the late nineteenth-century or early twentieth-century figures such as Rahul Sankrityayan and B. R. Ambedkar. Gupta's importance lies precisely in his investment in Buddhism for the vernacular religious world of Bengal, not a development of Buddhist revival or politics.

Language Politics and the Bengali "Vernacular"

The long history of the Bengali language and its literary and social histories have been documented and analyzed by numerous scholars, from various vantage points in linguistics, social history, and literary criticism.[13] Common to all literary histories is a focus on the nineteenth century as a site of enduring contestation. Termed by Sudipta Kaviraj as the "second history of Bengali literature" (the first history featuring works from the tenth-century *caryāpadas* to the *maṅgal'kābyas*), most colonial histories have tended to focus on the rise of the *bhadralok*, Sanskritization, and standardization. Equally important to this history is a focus on cleansing from past literary works any traces of obscenity or vulgarity.

What remains understudied is the role of Islam and Muslim reference points and inspirations within the making of vernacular sources of religion and language in Bengal. Religion has long been seen as a site of active change within Bengali, from the perspective of dissident traditions, beginning with the tenth-century Buddhist religious songs, the *caryāpadas* (the first examples of Bengali literature), and the *maṅgal'kāvyas*, as both belong to a way of "doing religion, a way of inviting people who are usually excluded from a high religious experience into its center" (Kaviraj 2003: 519). In the world of premodern Islam, a consciousness of Islam certainly has been noted in various appreciations of literary and religious life, from the ways that Mukundaram Chakravarti's *Caṇḍīmaṅgal* demonstrates an awareness of Islamic locutions to the imprint of

Islam in medieval Bengali more broadly. However, the colonial period, usually noted for Sanskritization and standardization, stands apart from studies of Islam's presence in Bengali literary pursuits. What remains is a full study of translations of the Qur'an, from Amiruddin Bosunia in the early nineteenth century through Dwijas Datta and Nazrul Islam in the early twentieth century, adding to the storehouse of content expressed in Bengali. Though retaining aspects of Sanskritization, Sen's Qur'an shows a deep awareness of Persian and Arabic, following in a new sort of dissident tradition, but keeping in line with how Bengali has been a vehicle for new religious ideas, disturbing orthodoxies, ever since its inception with Buddhist religious songs in the tenth century.

One figure who also translated the Qur'an into Bengali is Nazrul Islam. As a prominent litterateur and activist, Kazi Nazrul Islam, born in 1899 and reared in various parts of rural Bengal, only to come to Calcutta as an adult, has been studied through frameworks of literary criticism and cultural history, with a focus mostly on his youth, his marriage, and activities and writings during and just after World War I. Building upon these foundations but sticking to the historical framework of the interwar period, Nazrul's creative expression during the interwar years from the early 1920s through 1939, built upon the vernacular traditions highlighted by Sen.

During this time, Nazrul produced an explosion of lyrics, original compositions of music for stage and screen, prose criticism (including his 1933 essay "Modern World Literature"), in addition to his well-known poetry. From the late 1920s through the end of the 1930s, he transitioned into cinema, working as a song and music writer and director, as well as working for Calcutta radio. His work retained localized Hindu and Muslim themes (primarily his devotional songs) as well as a broader internationalist vision that began to develop from the early 1920s and appeared throughout most of his work. I suggest his ethos drew from the Brahmo Samaj's long legacy in Bengali literary and activist spaces, even though he was attacked and condemned by some Brahmos in the 1920s.

During the war years in Karachi, Nazrul developed a political and aesthetic investment in Islam as a source of inspiration and, as the Ottoman Empire fell, a feeling for the Muslim world under attack. The war put him in contact with Muslims from other regions and broadened his sense of Muslim identity and culture. He also nurtured his passion for Bengali literature as he read literary journals from Kolkata, such as *Saogāt* and the *Baṅgīya musal'mān sāhitya patrikā*. Nazrul returned from Karachi in early 1920. Ahmad had been corresponding with him through letters and had noticed his prodigious talent. They finally met in person in April 1920, soon after Nazrul landed in Kolkata. By this time, his name was reaching literary circles and his novel *Bandhan'hārā* (Free from Bondage) was being serially published in *Mos'lem bhārat*, a journal also housed at 32 College Street in Kolkata. It served as another venue for the development of Bengali Muslim radicals and progressives and started just as Nazrul was returning from the war. The office at the famed 32 College Street was a long-standing center of intellectual and political addas. During this formative period in Nazrul' s life, he came into close contact with great personalities of Bengali letters, such as Kazi Abdul Wadud, Muhammed Shahidullah, Saratchandra Chattopadhyay, and Satyendranath Datta.

The years between 1920 and 1922 saw Nazrul develop his talents and reputation as a poet, journalist, and an anti-colonial critic. In summer 1920, after meetings with Muzaffar Ahmad, M. Wajed Ali, the noted journalist, editor, and social critic, Moinuddin Hussein, a prominent supporter of journalism and literature, and the rising politician Fazlul Huq, the group decided to publish a daily journal in Bengali, suffused with progressive ideas and anti-colonial writings. The 1920s was a decade of both fierce political agitation and organization on Nazrul's part but also the era of his most explosive poetry, including *Dhum'ketu*, which landed him in jail for nearly all of 1923. To emphasize Nazrul as an Indian thinker, he was a reader of Dara Shukoh, as Rammohan Roy was about 120 years before him, and not only noticed but also thought expansively about the various religious traditions of India. The 1920s saw a range of poems published by Nazrul that showcased an integration of various images and devices from Hindu and Muslim – broadly an Indic imagination, within a poetic framework. These include the 1920 *Korbānī*, a term popularly associated with Muslims, but that portrayed the *satyāgraha* of the time as a harbinger of both *pralaya* and *qiyāmat*, Hindu and Muslim end-times, respectively. In both *Bidrohī* of 1921 and *Ānandamaẏī āgamane* of 1922, apocalyptic imagery is used. In particular, in the latter poem, Durga is invoked as the spirit of war in the fight against the British Empire. These were excursions into various sensibilities, inclusive of images and gods and goddesses as well as philosophy from Hindu and Muslim sources, conjoined to the causes of workers and peasants.

The line between religion and creative expression is never possible to fully draw. We know that Nazrul accessed both Rammahon's works in Bengali but significantly through the labors of Sen, who both wrote an early biography of Rammohan in Bengali and translated the Qur'an into vernacular Bengali. Sen and Roy, two figures born into caste Hindu families but shunned at some level by those networks, were keen readers of Persian as well, such as the seventeenth-century Persian comparative religious treatise, the *Dabistān* and Dara Shikoh's *Majmaʿ al-baḥrayn*. The enduring ethos was a view of religion as a source of wisdom, which drew from multiple genres of expression. Nazrul could be said to be carrying on that tradition not as a science (one of Keshub Chandra Sen's goals) but as an art form, conveyed through multiple genres. Nazrul, as we know, found Persian through training with a maulvi during his time in Karachi. He studied not from within a tradition that would have shaped elite Indian Muslim men in formal systems but rather he devoured the classics through specific study. This would place him in a Brahmo tradition, as we see in his repeated emphasis on one without second, or *ekam evādvitīyam*, translated loosely as one god, promoted by Brahmos since at least 1828. In 1941, Nazrul mentioned in his article "Āmār līg kaṃgres" (My League and Congress), written as a response to Muslim communalists who attacked him, that he saw Allah alone as the king of kings of this world, and the human was the *khalīfa* of Allah, or his representative, his viceroy. In line with his broader practices, he described Allah as one without second, or *ekam evādvitīyam*, and that he has a religion, that of humanity, *mānab'dharma*.

From 1928 to 1932, he worked for His Master's Voice as a lyricist and composer. Here, he focused on music that drew upon the Brahmo tradition of seeing and engaging with devotional content from Islam, such as songs about Namaz, Roza, Hajj, and some issues about Islam in a broader context were dealt with in his poetry and prose in the early 1920s. Also, he composed songs drawing on Hindu precedents, including devotional songs to Kali; his poems from the 1920s period repeatedly feature references to the Ramayana and other aspects of Hinduism. He published 10 volumes of songs, which included a total of over 800 songs, the majority based on classical ragas, about 100 on *kīrtaṇ*, and 30 on patriotic themes. He built upon his vast imagination and connections to various parts of the world seen from back in the World War I and the immediate postwar era but always from a base in the geography of Bengal and the city of Kolkata. There we now find the Nakhoda Mosque, built in 1926, which inspired a generation of Bengali Muslim intellectuals in the interwar India to write about aspects of the Islamic world from Egypt to Turkey to Iran, just like Nazrul.

Although parts of the city figured as a prominent site from which ships transported laborers of all types from the Bay of Bengal in the late nineteenth century, Nazrul imagined the world from the perspective of Calcutta. Active just before and after the Great War, Nazrul trained for service in the Great War, but never went west of the Khyber Pass. He wrote about the world of Islam outside of the local in his poems *Śāt·-il·-ārab* and *Kāmāl pāśā* as well as in the scenic play *Khāled* (Is'lām 1993: 34–35, 435–41, 18–27). In these Bengali compositions, he recounts the sacrifices of Muslims and the physical geography of a world known through the trans-regional life force of Islam in South Asia, where the Arabian dates were consumed on Eid, but enjoyed among those who eat rice, dal, and riverine fish. In *Śāt·-il·-ārab*, he mentions the bones of "Arab, Egyptian, Turk, Greek, and Bedouin" and the "crimson flame-like roses of Basra"; to him "radiant emblems of war and glory [...] they flourish on soil where heads have tumbled, forever glorious, forever holy" (Is'lām 1993: 34–35). In 1934, he published an essay about two conceptions of world literature, one about looking to heaven, citing Shelley and Skylark, and another about people, the earth, and the brutish nature of reality, citing literatures of revolution. There was always a world outside but grounded in the local soils of Bengal.

Nazrul's heralded collection *Sāmyabādī* (Is|lām 1993: 231–45) showcases how he sings of equality, literally, but also of God. That landmark publication included 11 poems, starting with *Sāmyabādī*, and ending with *Sāmya*. In the second position, there is a poem about god, or *īśvar* (again a term used by Sen in his 1881 Qur'an translation for God), and the last three poems are adorned with the line *gāi sāmyer gān*, or *sāmyer gān gāi*, "let us sing the song of equality" (Is|lām 1993: 232, 241–45). The sentiment at the end of the poem *Samyabadi*, after a list of the various traditions and their truths, comes back to one recurring theme, emphasized by Brahmos since Rammohan Roy and reiterated by many ever since, as he ends by stating that *mithyā śuni ni bhāile hṛdaẏer ceẏe kono baṛa mandir kābā nāi*, or that "what I've heard my friend is no lie, that there is no Kaaba and no temple bigger than the heart," another way of seeing the vernacular of both religion and literature in a Bengali register.

Conclusion

Without a specific history of nineteenth-century developments, there is no way to assess how the changes of that century draw from either continuous intellectual currents or from alterations whose ultimate origins lie in the West, whether via formal missionaries or Orientalists. In *Empires of Religion*, David Chidester shows how in another context African interlocutors were able to use the rising tides of race and science to pursue their own agendas and endeavors (Chidester 2014). Indians like Gupta and Sen, in service of a bigger project to reform religion, both not only derived parts of their apparatus from pre-1800 knowledge systems but also were deeply invested in the worlds in which they were living, following the work of Brian Hatcher and Michael on Sanskrit in the nineteenth century. For the Brahmo Samaj, religion as a discrete object, replete with the possibility to include a synthesis of the texts and practices of the world, by the 1880s and 1890s explicitly including Islam and Buddhism as I have shown; and as the scholarship of Abhishek Ghosh (2019) demonstrates, the world of *bhakti*, or devotion, was also included in the expanding project of comparative religion.

To think of religion in these terms compels an engagement with the history of religions subfield of religious studies. Hans Kippenberg (2002) argued that thinkers from Müller to Tylor and Frazer from the 1850s to the 1930s, in short the time of the flowering of the Brahmo Samaj, restored to "modern society its other, officially ignored half, the power of life that does not serve progress." While full-scale scientific approaches demanded a rejection of religion, historians of comparative religion focused on what was superseded by modernization and conceived of it as remaining valid in the present world, including social obligations and social bonds. If we substitute "nationalism" in an intellectual history of comparative religion in the Indian nineteenth century for what Kippenberg claims for "modernization," we will find some common ground in the exploration of options for a variety of purposes. Though formal nationalism emerges in the era of the comparative religion project I have sketched out, the work of Sen and Gupta proceeded according to a mission and guideline that is not easily captured in terms of nationalism or modernity. Rather, Islam and Buddhism are part and parcel of the reformation of religion in India, part of a longer history of thinking about universal and comparative religion.

The investment in religion shown by the Brahmo Samaj reveals the importance of the vernacular sphere of "religion-making" (Pal-Mandair and Dressler 2011). Making and remaking religion for Bengali Brahmo Samaj members were both a feature of religious life manifested through the creation of translations and a textual record of a new religion built out of various sources in Bengal's past and present. Religion was one vehicle through which the vernacular expanded and flourished in the nineteenth century.

This "vernacular," a concentrated effort to remake religion out of various sources and express this religion in the language of Bengali, did not simply mean anything and everything that was not imposed on Bengalis by Western social actors such as missionaries or Orientalists. Rather, the form of religion-making, one that sought to integrate the various forms of religion in Bengal into a new universal religion, is vernacular for this context. Experiments with religions like Islam, as Sen explored in his translation of the Qur'an, were not meant to displace or erase forms of Islam that had existed in India for centuries, but to recognize them, and place them into a form that late nineteenth-century *bhadralok* could not fully comprehend in their own language before his efforts. Kazi Nazrul Islam, whose interplay between Hindu and Muslim references in his poetry, finds a nineteenth-century precedent in this translation of the Qur'an, given his 1933 translation of the Qur'an into Bengali, which included both Arabic and Bengali unlike Sen's. Sen's translation in Bengali has been thus far ignored in scholarship on South Asian Islam, such that the most recent analysis of Qur'anic commentaries in 2020 lists the languages of Urdu and Persian and explores individual works by Syed Ahmed Khan and Maulana Azad, but ignores Bengali and Sen completely (Tareen 2020). This points to one of the many reasons why Sen's pioneering translation is so important. Muslims had been engaging with *tafsīr* in Bengali for some time. Muslims engaged in their own ways with Islam in Bengal ever since the seventeenth century at least, but from the 1880s,it would be impossible for a vernacular-educated Bengali *bhadralok* to ignore the manifold presence of Islam in Bengal. For Gupta's work on Buddhism, the *bhadralok* were also similarly involved. Both point to the existence of vernacular religion in modern India. Such a vernacular forms not a "local" or "little" counterpart to "great" traditions but rather a method to encounter the vast diversity of religion from within parameters set by Indic precedents, such that changes in language and religion are inseparable from one another.

Notes

1 See Projit Mukharji (2016: 30). The term "braided histories" has been deployed by scholars from various fields attempting to grasp intellectual and cultural histories without presuming ahistorical essences. Mukharji draws on Sanskritist Sheldon Pollock, art historian Finbarr Barry Flood, and, most explicitly, art historian Monica Juneja, who introduces the notion of "transculture," which highlights "braided histories" most clearly. See Juneja (2012: 418).

2 See Kopf (1979) for an overview of its intellectual and cultural history. For a historical account from a key member of the organization, see Sibnath Sastri (1911).

3 For the most recent and up-to-date biography, see Amiya P. Sen (2012), esp. Chapter 2.

4 Rabindranath Tagore termed Rammohan Roy a "Bhārat'pathik," or India-traveler.

5 See Will Sweetman (2003, chapter 3) for a discussion of how authors such as Brerewood, Baxter, Ross, and Purchas grappled with the plurality of religions in India and laid the foundation for later eighteenth-century writers such as Ziegenbalg, and finally, Holwell, to change their earlier fourfold schema of Christian, Muslim, Jew, and Heathen to include new conceptions of Hinduism.

6 For details on authorship and manners of reading the text, see Aditya Behl (2011), as well as Azfar Moin, "Dabistan-madahib" in *Encyclopedia of Islam* (Vol. 3): 72–73.

7 See my forthcoming *Religion before Gandhi: Meanings and Ends of Religion in Nineteenth Century India*.

8 See Osella and Osella (eds.) (2013); Robinson (2008); Jalal (2000).

9 For discussions of West Bengal and the history of *Maṅgal'kābyas*, see Sircar (2016). Regarding the rise of Islam in Bengal, see Eaton (1993).

10 See Stewart (2001), especially chapter 4, "Mapping the Imaginaire: The Conditions of Possibility," 110–154.

11 Cf. the blurb titled "Buddhist Text and Anthropological Society" in the inaugural edition, August 1893, of the *Journal of the Buddhist Text Society of India*, n.p.

12 Steven Kemper, *Rescued from the Nation: Anagarika Dharmapala and the Buddhist World*. Chicago: University of Chicago Press, 2015.

13 See S. K. Chatterji (1970–72); Sukumār Sen (1965); Haraprasād Śāstrī (1956); Sudipta Kaviraj (2003); and Anindita Ghosh (2006).

Bibliography

Abu'l Fazl, Sheikh. 1877. *Ain-i-Akbari*, vol. 2. Ed. H. Blochmann. Calcutta: Asiatic Society of Bengal.

Chatterji, S.K. 1970–72. *The Origin and Development of the Bengali Language*. 3 vols. London: Allen and Unwin.

Behl, Aditya. 2011. "Pages from the Book of Religions: Encountering difference in Mughal India." In Sheldon Pollock (ed.): *Forms of Knowledge in Early Modern Asia. Explorations in the intellectual history of India and Tibet, 1500–1800*. Durham: Duke University Press, 210–239.

Chidester, David. 2014. *Empires of Religion: Imperialism and Comparative Religion*. Chicago: University of Chicago Press.

Dodson, Michael. 2007. *Orientalism, Empire, and National Culture India, 1770–1880*. Basingstoke: Palgrave Macmillan.

Eaton, Richard. *The Rise of Islam and the Bengal Frontier, 1204–1760*. Berkeley, CA: University of California Press, 1993.

Ghosh, Abhishek. 2019. "Innate Intuition: An Intellectual History of Sahaja-jnana and Sahaja-samadhi in Brahmaism and Modern Vaishnavism." *Religions* 10(6): 384.
Ghosh, Anindita. 2006. *Power in Print: Popular Publishing and the Politics of Language and Culture in a Colonial Society*. Delhi: Oxford University Press.
Gupta, Aghor Nāth. 1957. *Śākyamuni carit o nirbāṇ'tattva* (The Life of Buddha and the Truth of Nirvana). Kalikātā: Nababidhān.
Hannan, Muhammed Abdul (ed.). 2014. *Bengali Translation of The Holy Quran by Girish Chandra Sen*. Dhaka: Bishwashahittya Bhaban.
Hatcher, Brian. 2007. "Sanskrit and the Morning after: The Metaphorics and Theory of Intellectual Change." *Indian Economic and Social History Review* 44(3): 333–361.
———. 1996. *Idioms of Improvement: Vidyasagar and Cultural Encounter in Bengal*. New Delhi: Oxford University Press.
———. 2014. *Vidyasagar: The Life and After-life of an Eminent Indian*. New Delhi: Routledge.
Irani, Ayesha. 2010. "Mystical Love, Prophetic Compassion, and Ethics: An Ascension Narrative in the Medieval Bengali Nabīvaṃśa of Saiyad Sultān." In *The Prophet's Ascension: Cross-Cultural Encounters with the Islamic Mi'rāj Tales*, edited by Christiane Gruber and Frederick Colby, 225–251. Bloomington: Indiana University Press.
Is'lām, Kājī Naj'rul. 1993. *Naj'rul-racanābalī*, Vol. 1. Ḍhākā: Bāṃlā Ekāḍemī.
Jalal, Ayesha. 2000. *Self and Sovereignty: Individual and Community in South Asian Islam since 1850*. New York: Routledge.
Journal of the Buddhist Text Society of India. Ed. Śarat Chandra Dás. Vol. 1, 1893. Calcutta: Baptist Mission Press.
Juneja, Monica. 2012. "Objects, Frames, Practices: A Post Script on Agency and Braided Histories of Art." *Medieval History Journal* 15(2): 418.
Kaviraj, Sudipta. 2005. "The Sudden Death of Sanskrit Knowledge." *Journal of Indian Philosophy* 33(1): 119–142.
———. 2003. "The Two Histories of Literary Culture in Bengal." In *Literary Cultures in History: Reconstructions from South Asia*, edited by Sheldon Pollock, 503–566. Berkeley, CA: University of California Press.
Kemper, Steven. 2015. *Rescued from the Nation: Anagarika Dharmapala and the Buddhist World*. Chicago: University of Chicago Press.
Kippenberg, Hans. 2002. *Discovering Religious History in the Modern Age*. Princeton, NJ: Princeton University Press.
Kopf, David. 1979. *The Brahma Samaj and the Making of the Modern Indian Mind*. Princeton, NJ: Princeton University Press.
Majeed, Javed. 2018. *Nation and Region in Grierson's Linguistic Survey of India*. Delhi: Routledge.
Metcalf, Barbara. 1982. *Islamic Revival in British India: Deoband, 1860–1900*. Princeton, NJ: Princeton University Press.
Mukharji, Projit. 2016. *Doctoring Traditions: Ayurveda, Small Technologies, and Braided Sciences*. Chicago: University of Chicago Press.
Okita, Kiyokazu. 2014. *Hindu Theology in Early Modern South Asia*. New York: Oxford University Press.
Osella, Filippo and Caroline Osella (eds). 2013. *Islamic Reform in South Asia*. Delhi: Cambridge University Press.

Pollock, Sheldon. 2008. "Is There an Indian Intellectual History? Introduction to "Theory and Method in Indian Intellectual History"" *Journal of Indian Philosophy* 36: 533–542.

Robinson, Francis. 2008. "Islamic Reform and Modernities in South Asia." *Modern Asian Studies* 42(2/3): 259–281.

Roy, Raja Rammohun. 1906. "A Present to the Believers in One God: Being a Translation of Tuhfatul Muwahhiddin by Raja Rammohun Roy." In Jogendra Chunder Ghose (ed.). *The English Works of Raja Rammohun Roy*. Allahabad: Indian Press.

Śāstrī, Haraprasād. 1956. *Haraprasād Śāstrī racanābalī*, 2 vols. Kalikātā: Eastern Trading Company.

Sastri, Sibnath. 1911. *History of the Brahma Samaj*, Vol. 1. Calcutta: R. Chatterji.

Sen, Amiya. 2012. *Rammohan Roy: A Critical Biography*. Delhi: Penguin.

Sen, Sukumār. 1965. *Bāṃlār sāhitya-itihās*. Dillī: Sahitya Akademi.

Sircar, Jawhar. 2016. "The Construction of the Hindu Identity in Medieval Western Bengal: The Role of Popular Cults," Unpublished paper.

Stewart, Tony K. 2001. "In Search of Equivalence: Conceiving Hindu-Muslim Encounter through Translation Theory" *History of Religions* 40(3): 260–287.

Sweetman, Will. 2003. *Mapping Hinduism: "Hinduism" and the study of Indian Religions, 1600–1776*. Halle: Franckesche Stiftungen.

Ṭhākur, Debendranāth. 1848. *Brāhma dharma*. Kalikātā: Brāhma Samāj.

Tareen, SherAli. 2020. "South Asian Qur'an Commentaries and Translations: A Preliminary Intellectual History." *ReOrient* 5(2): 233–256.

———. 2019. *Witness to Marvels: Sufism and Literary Imagination*. Berkeley, CA: University of California Press, 2019.

Uddin, Sufia. 2006. *Constructing Bangladesh: Religion, Ethnicity, and Language in an Islamic Nation*. Chapel Hill, NC: University of North Carolina Press.

Yelle, Robert. 2018. *Sovereignty and the Sacred: Secularism and the Political Economy of Religion*. Chicago: University of Chicago Press.

15

READING CASTE IN VERNACULAR JOURNALS

Meenakshi Yadav

> *Large native publishing-houses have risen in Luck'nau, Banaras, and Patna from which have issued floods of printed works, old and new, good, bad, and indifferent. At the same time, a mushroom growth of smaller establishments has sprung up all over Hindustan, and there is now scarcely a town of importance which does not possess its printing-press or two. Every scribbler can now see his writings in type or lithographed for a few rupees, and too often, he avails himself of the power and the opportunity.*[1]

In his seminal work *The Modern Vernacular Literature of Hindustan* (1889), George Abraham Grierson is hinting at not just the expanding potential of print capital but also how it challenged the existing knowledge hierarchy. His complaint about inflated access to print signals that people gained access to knowledge that had been meant for a few elites, and also asserted the power to create new forms of knowledge. Therefore, printing technology not only commercialized but also democratized the existing knowledge systems by providing open access to diverse knowledge(s) and cultural spaces.[2] Exposure to the "traditional" knowledge also urged some to question and challenge them. The cultural space was constituted by those who were striving to sustain the status quo and those who were supporting and constituting the new ideological frameworks.

The modern means of communication – print technology, railways, and postal services – not only enhanced the mobility of information, discourses and people but also initiated a totalizing phenomenon that stimulated people to coagulate as *jātīya saṅgaṭhan* (caste associations). In the late nineteenth century, India witnessed an unprecedented increase in community consciousness (*jātīya cet'nā*). Several social movements gained momentum in the name of

DOI: 10.4324/9781003279921-19

communities like *Bhāratīya jāti, Hindū jāti, Ārya jāti, Rāj'pūt jāti, Mus'lim jāti, Brāhmaṇ jāti, Kṣatriya jāti, Kāyastha jāti*, and so on.

The native social structures did not just adopt the modern technology of print but vernacularized it to reaffirm the traditional ideological frameworks and to selectively appropriate the modern thinking: the awareness regarding education was one such example. The relationship between the indigenous and colonial knowledge systems was one of mutual exchange. On the one hand, the colonial government took into account traditional ideologies of social organisation such as *varṇa* to inform their policies; on the other, the caste communities appropriated the modern means of information diffusion to assert their identities and asserted themselves as pan-Indian communities by establishing *sabhā*s and publishing periodicals. These periodicals were published in vernaculars which propelled the natives to increase literacy in these languages. The use of language in these Hindi periodicals was not uniformly Sanskritized but hybrid. While the influence of colonial modernity was making inroads into the sinews of Indian society, institutions like caste boosted their older communication networks by appropriating the technology of print and new ways of organization (of people and information). In this way, they refashioned themselves as what they perceived to be modern, but rigid social categories.[3] Nonetheless, the underlying motive was also to represent the interests of (caste community) people at large. Rudolf (1965) also observes this somewhat democratic thrust in the caste associations.

In fact, caste journals were borne out of the alliance between the older communication networks and the modern technologies in shaping and freezing identities along caste lines.[4] The traditional pattern of dissemination of word from mouth to mouth assured a conducive environment for the print market; the printed word was held as a reference to attest the reliability of the spoken word. Caste associations were modernized forms of the *kunba* (clan) meetings under a tree or at the *caurāhā* (the intersection point of four roads), and serious councils known as panchayats (caste community meetings).

This chapter unravels the interconnection between the emergence of journals and their patron caste associations to delve deeper into their functioning mechanism. The reason to choose *Rāj'pūt*[5] *and Ahīr Gazette*[6] lies with the historical fact that the maximum number of lower castes sought assimilation to the Kshatriyas rather than any other *varṇa*. History bears many examples where lower castes appropriated Kshatriya identity; e.g., Kayasthas, Kurmis, Jats, Gujars, and Ahirs claimed to be Kshatriyas in nineteenth-century India. Obviously, such assertions received a backlash from the Kshatriyas. The magazines, pamphlets, and agendas in caste councils were devoted to counter this intrusion of 'other' castes into Kshatriya ranks. *Rāj'pūt* was one of the many Hindi periodicals that sprung up in the late nineteenth century.[7] In fact, the caste journals were engaged in a print dialogue, which was reflected in the content of the journals. Considerably, such discursive engagements happened in the day-to-day language rather than Sanskritized Hindi; the underlying idea was to sustain communication. This chapter throws light on the issues that found their way to the pages of the caste journals with specific reference to these two journals, while looking at other journals as well. Caste journalism in the vernacular was a thriving popular discursive space which took cognizance of all events – regional, national, and global – to gauge their impact on the caste community. The chapter also undertakes a comparative analysis of various journals to analyse the ideological variance on prominent issues of the contemporary society. It looks into the phenomenon of vernacularization of print media with a focus on how language came across both as a strategical tool and as a means of information diffusion.

Advertisement and Notice Sections

The first page of all journals begins with the name of the patronizing body. The caste journals were the mouthpieces of distinct caste associations. *Rāj|pūt* proclaimed itself a "*kṣatriya varṇ sambandhit pākṣik patra*" ('A bi-weekly related to the Kshatriya *varṇa*'), and was patronized by the Rajput Mahasabha. *Jain Gazette* was started as the weekly mouthpiece of the Jain Mahasabha. *Ahir Gazette* and other journals followed the same tradition of specifying their institutional affiliation. The journals were meant to advertise the activities of their respective *mahāsabhā*s. The diffusion of the printing word through journals accorded credibility to the oral discourse of the *sammelan* (conventions) and prevented the adulteration of the message. As the official organ of a specific caste body, the journal was meant to popularize the association and mobilize the caste people to join the *sabhā*. Akhil Bhartiya Brahman Samaj also proposed to "first, appoint *upadeśak*s [advisors] who would propagate the activities of the *sammelan*, and second, to start a weekly paper to popularize the decisions of the *sammelan*".[8] *Ahīr Gazette*, an Urdu journal, was also started in 1901 to create caste consciousness among Yadavs.

The first and second pages of *Rāj|pūt* enumerated the rules pertaining to the dates of publication, the price, modalities of subscription with attractive offers to increase the sale, and the advertisement policy. The advertisements in these journals were scattered throughout the pages. A close reading of the advertisement section in the journals reveals their exclusivist politics. The *jātīya* identity determined the availability of job opportunities, as practised by the patrons of the journals. For example, *Gaur hit|kārī* advertised a job opening for someone who knew Hindi, on the condition that the candidate was from the Gaur caste or Brahman *varṇa*.[9] *Rāj|pūt*'s rules reflected similar exclusive tendencies; it declared a free advertisement policy for caste members, whereas 'others' had to pay to publish. The caste-specific journals had limited commercial prospects as their prime readership belonged to their respective communities only. Therefore, journals urged the community members to subscribe and popularize the journal in the name of *svajāti*.[10] The advertisement section was also utilized to publicize the meetings organized by other affiliated *sabhā*s; on 15 May 1901, *Rāj'pūt* published an open invitation to a meeting held by the Kshatriya Hitkarini Sabha (p. 17). The advertisement also revealed the agenda, which was to overcome all the animosities among the caste members and unite as Rajput brethren. Understandably, the unity was called for to counter the intervention by the lower castes in the Rajput community, as *Rāj'pūt*'s news section reported the *sabhā*'s constant surveillance of the activities organized by other castes like Kayasthas and Kurmis.

Language and Literature

The literature review section in *Rāj'pūt* critically reviewed the Hindi journals and texts. Some of the reviewed texts were *Hindī Lecture, Śrīgopāl patrikā, Bhārat hitopadeśak patra, Jain patrikā, Vaiśya Agravāl itihās, Mukti mārg prakāś, Sundarī sudhār*, and *Vyavahār patra darpaṇ*. The catalogue of the texts selected for the review section is conspicuous by the absence of negative editorial remarks and the selection of only-Hindi texts; the journals associated with other caste communities, arguably all upper caste, were praised, and the support for Hindi and Nagari was evident. *Vyavahār patra darpaṇ*, for instance, was published by the Nagari Pracharini Sabha to propagate Hindi in Nagari script as the language of the public sphere. The periodical was meant to guide Hindi speakers in technical terms used in courts and administration. Obviously, it was a part of the larger Hindi movement that started in the late nineteenth century to demarcate the contours of the Hindi public sphere by educating the masses about discursive vocabulary and, thus, preparing the ground to supplant Urdu in official and administrative discourses. High castes like Rajput and Gaur supported the claim of Hindi and assisted it in an implicit manner. Furthermore, the wealthy caste members funded the movement, as the news section of *Rāj'pūt* reveals: on 15 October 1901, the editor eulogized Raja Saheb Bahadur for donating 500 rupees to the Nagari Pracharini Sabha (p. 23). The news section also brought to light the project undertaken by the Nagari Pracharini Sabha to compile the grammar of Hindi.

On October 15, 1901, *Rāj'pūt* published an advertisement for the Rajput Anglo-Oriental Press to seek a worker who was proficient in both English and Hindi. The point to ponder upon is that an upper-caste-specific printing press was publishing bilingually in Hindi and English. For a caste which did not boast of its literacy, the Rajputs' diving into the print market invites many questions – whether there was scope for Hindi journals that catered to targeted caste sensibilities and how branding Urdu as the alien language was to reconcile with the acceptance of English in cultural discourse. In fact, *Kanyā-kubja hit'kārī*, a Brahman journal, proclaimed English to be the *rāj-bhāṣā* and Hindi the *mātṛ-bhāṣā*.[11] The contradiction alerted one to take the propaganda of essential categories like honour, *ārya jāti*, and *ārya bhāṣā* on the face value, since the ambivalence was rooted in the contemporary sociopolitical contexts. Allegiance to Hindi and Nagari was derived from loyalty towards religious and cultural kinship, whereas prospective economic interests translated into acceptance of English.

The relative appropriation of Sanskritized Hindi by the caste-specific periodicals in proportion to their *varṇa* status is striking. To begin with Brahman journals (*Brāhmaṇ sarvasva* and *Gaur hit'kārī*), the endeavour to embrace Sanskrit-laden vocabulary rendered the articles incomprehensible for the masses.[12] *Rajput*, by contrast, nominally supported the Hindi movement, which was evident from the advertisements and editorials, but it is observed that the language of the journal was largely Hindustani, infused with regional linguistic variations. The cover page of the journal exhibits the co-existence of Hindi and Urdu; the incorporation of a Sanskrit *śloka* reflected the editor's allegiance to the cause of cohesion of Hindu *jati* that coincided with the nationalist discursive formation of a community (*ārya jāti* and *bhāratīya jāti*). On the other hand, the rules under the title "*Rāj'pūt ke niyam*" were listed in Hindustani; see an excerpt from *Rajput* on 15 May 1901: "*kṣatriyavarṇ up'yogi vijñāpan muft chāpā kareṃge parantu anya vijñāpanoṃ kī chapāī evaṃ bāṭāī kī śarah patra dvārā manager Rāj'pūt se daryāft kar'ne se ho sakti hai*".[13] The title page, unlike the aforementioned journals patronized by Brahman associations, manifested stylistic mixture. Furthermore, the content in the inner pages of the journal also exhibited an inclination towards a hybrid language; words were drawn generously from Urdu vocabulary in articles. The vocal support for Hindi and Nagari did not prevent the editor and other contributors to the magazine from employing Hindustani. Chhotu Ram – leader of a backward-caste community, the Jat – started the Urdu weekly *Jāṭ Gazette* in 1916, and remained its editor till 1924. Possibly, Hindustani was the most known language and the owners of the backward-caste vernacular journals, who were already struggling to sustain the print due to lack of literacy, found it convenient to retain the language of communication rather than appropriating Sanskritized Hindi. The same logic rationalizes the appropriation of Urdu by Ahirs (a backward caste, also known as Yadavs); their neutral stance on Hindi was evident from their publishing pattern. *Ahīr Gazette* started as an Urdu journal in 1901 and shifted to Hindi only in 1910. An ethnographic monograph was written in Urdu entitled *Yādav Abhīr kul'dīpikā* in the late nineteenth century; another journal, *Yādav* (1925), was started from Allahabad in Hindi. My aim is to underscore the fissures within different cross-sections of society regarding the Hindi movement; as the foregoing examples indicate, not all upper castes supported the nationalist movement, and Hindi and nationalist movements overlapped to a large extent but did not coincide absolutely. *Rāj'pūt*'s silence about, and occasional eulogization of, the colonial government implies otherwise.[14] The explicit support for Hindi and Nagari could not translate into concrete support in the formulation of a Hindi public sphere. The vocal support for Sanskritized Hindi as the pure (owing to its traditional association with Hinduism), and *matṛbhāṣā* (mother tongue) did not necessarily result in its wholesome adoption. The marginalized castes like Ahirs, in contrast, did not share the aversion to Urdu (yet), which possibly contributed to the flourishing of the Urdu public sphere until the early twentieth century.[15] Undoubtedly, however, the influence of the Arya Samaj on the Ahir movement in the 1890s eventually increased Ahirs' interest in Hindi.

Construction of Histories

Rāj̍pūt published a series on history entitled "Vīr̍caritāvalī" from 15 October 1900. The journal was not unique in retracing the past, as many journals were redeeming the history to entertain, introspect, and insinuate caste consciousness (*jātīya cet̍nā*). The histories in Sanskritized Hindi were to be treated as the treatise on Kshatriyahood. Using an apt language became all the more important not just to make the past more believable but also to bring forth a sense of reverence towards the past. The glorification of the martial stereotypes became more compelling when textualized in Sanskritized Hindi. The stark contrast between the language used in advertisements and these histories underscores this strategy of mobilization using language as the tool. The nationalist, religious, and caste mobilizations relied on the historical discourse to achieve the cohesion of a selective mass with a particular belief system. (Re)Writing history is not an innocent enterprise as it is always motivated by a predefined objective and refined by the ideological framework of the writer/historian. Following this line of argument, one needs to delve deeper into the implicit politics in identifying India (*bhārat̍varṣ*) with *Āryavarta* in an upper-caste journal like *Rāj̍pūt*.[16]

The only way to understand the formation of caste associations and their respective movements is by juxtaposing the upper-caste *sabhā*s with those of the marginalized sections. The former fought to retain the *varṇa* hegemony, to forward their communities' claim for better education and job opportunities, and to bring reforms. The Kayasthas' association and Rajput *sabhā*s, for instance, created awareness for education and jobs through their journals. In contrast, the deprived sections interrogated the traditional power frameworks, usually targeted against some 'reference groups', and devoted themselves to alleviating their 'relative deprivation'.[17] Where the former sought to improve their existing socio-economic standing, the latter were campaigning for basic amenities like education, social respectability, and job opportunities. Their organized protests faced backlashes from the reference caste groups; the mass movement organized by the Gopajatiya Sabha in 1911 to protest against the monopoly of *dvija* castes in religious discourses like the donning of sacred threads, and the forced and unpaid labour by the lower castes, culminated in a violent clash between the local landlords and protesters (Rao 1987: 213).

The history series in *Rājpūt* presupposed Muslims as the reference 'other', and the narratives underscored the cultural and religious distinctions as binaries. There was a glorification of Rajputs at the expense of the Muslim 'other'. The print histories selectively retrieved the symbols from the past and refined them to present as the ideal. The nationalist discourse posited an ideal endowed with masculine strength and *dharma*. The heroic portrayal of Ranaji in the Rajputs' history fitted into this nationalist imagination of the hero, as did the assumption of the alien invader as the common enemy. The upper castes' journals regarded the mythical figure of Ram, the Aryan ruler, as the epitome of an ideal man. However, that does not necessarily imply absolute complicity between the nationalist and Rajputs' imaginations of the hero, as the nationalist discourse also unearthed the figures of Rajputs like Birbal, Todarmal, and Mansingh – all of them enjoyed prominent positions in the Mughal period – to caution against those who had sold their honour (*izzat*) for material gains (Orsini 2002: 211).

The decennial census of 1901 came across as a historical moment of introspection for the indigenous populace. The categorical compilation of natives' information also provided an opportunity for Indians to interrogate about themselves. The abstract construction of certain castes or caste-cluster, as elucidated by Iravati Karve (1959), mobilized the castes to fashion themselves in the official framework to gain a maximum out of the legal negotiations that were already in place. Around 1911, various regional associations sent petitions to the Census Commissioners to recognize Golla, Gollavvar, Gavli, and Ahir as Yadavs to appear as a community with numerical strength, and thus deserving a representation in the legislative council and a greater proportion in the job opportunities (Karve 1959: 226).

The backward castes did not lag behind in fabricating their own set of historical narratives. The mythical figure of Krishna was employed as a unifying symbol to refashion the Ahirs as a caste cluster, overcoming all distinctions (Jaffrelot 2000: 763). The myth of Krishna as the ruler and warrior ascribed credibility to the Yadavs' claim to Kshatriyahood. From finding an ancestor in the mythical figure of Krishna to employing him as the unifying factor, the thrust was to incorporate the maximum number of (sub)castes. The numerical superiority of any caste association empowered their position in the eyes of the colonial authorities. To the colonial outsider, numerical strength and common traits (physiological and economic) were important determinants of a community.

Modernity and Caste Associations

The caste members were mobilized by the indigenous elites of the specific caste groups.[18] Vasudha Dalmia (1997: 4) opines that caste associations "were organized according to British models, had presidents, executive boards and secretaries and often functioned in strict accordance with British parliamentary procedure". In the notice section of the journals, readers were informed about the meetings that had taken place recently with detailed minutes to acquaint the readers of any resolution that the association members had taken for the entire caste community. The information consisted of the names of the president and other eminent caste members and the strength of the people who attended the meetings. Not only this, the caste associations refashioned the older institution of the panchayat in modern robes. The caste associations came across as organizations with various branches/organizations devoted to distinct objectives, and the journals functioned as their point of convergence. For instance, All India Yadav Mahasabha (1923) was coordinating with Ahir Yadav Kshatriya Mahasabhā (1908), Yadav Sangam (1905), Bangiya Yadav Mahasabha (1922), and Hyderabad Rashtra Yadav Mahajan Sangam (1922) in early twentieth century. Likewise, the Madyastha Sabha (mediatory association) was an organ of the Rajput Mahasabha, dedicated to resolving the property issues, civil cases, and criminal cases among caste members.

The last page of the journals was reserved to thank the new members and those who brought the new subscribers. From listing the names of the new subscribers to providing the statistical data of members of the Rajput *sabhā* and other caste associations, *Rājpūt* adopted the modern "information system"[19] to revolutionize the older ways of organizing knowledge. First among the non-*dvija* castes to start an association, the Kayasthas prepared an All India Directory of Chandraguptavanshi Kayasthas as early as 1887 in order to unite them. By popularizing the *sabhā*s and advertising their meetings, the journals managed to connect the *sabhā*s with the masses. Obviously, the patrons of caste-journals knew that the masses consisted of caste-community members only. The organizational structure expanded the scope of existing panchayats, and railways and postal services ensured that people from distant places participated in the annual conferences. Rudolph and Rudolph (2012: 372) argue that caste associations became partly ascriptive, partly voluntary with time, as membership in caste associations was not ascriptive and people had to "join" these associations. In fact, the associations selected leadership on the basis of their qualifications as intellectual, political, and administrative elites (Rao 1987). A duality characterized the encounter between modern knowledge and castes (as native knowledge communities); on the one hand, the modern techniques aided the 'rearmament of conservatism' (Bayly 1999a: 338), and on the other, the associations ensured negotiation with the political authorities and thus emerged as an egalitarian alternative. Thus, any reading of caste associations as 'democratic incarnation of caste in India' (Rudolph 1965: 982) seems problematic, considering this ambivalence as intrinsic to all debates on caste associations. For instance, traditional customs of marriage and commensality, which were orally transmitted through generations and therefore open to reinterpretation with the changing times, now acquired rigidity when journals published them. Caste journals, indeed, were meant to improve the existing status of their respective communities, and thus adhered to an agenda in which the larger society's interests were not always embedded.

The spatial displacement in the wake of industrialization rendered people psychologically dismembered, too. In a society where caste determined one's religious, cultural, and occupational practices, dislocation fractured the sense of coherent existence. In the wake of 'secular mobility' (Khare 1970: 209), traditional social identity was no longer assumed spontaneously. Printed journals in the known language in such contexts became a nostalgic reminder of their community kinship. Caste associations firstly gave them a semblance of identity, and attempts were made to reinstate the traditional practices; secondly, caste associations emerged as a counterforce (Jaffrelot 2003: 185–187) against the growing impact of Kayasthas, Baniyas, and other Brahmans of North India. Therefore, printed journals played a crucial role in intensifying the mobilizations of caste associations.

Viewing caste as the defining factor in understanding Indian people, the colonial authorities adopted the census as a central pillar of their administration (Carroll 1978). In the process, they tended to (re)define, interpret, and categorize Indians. Consequently, the enterprise evoked the predictable response from the natives who in turn strived to (re)define and assert themselves. The data collection enterprise was significant not only for the authorities but also for the natives since for the first time the statistical data pertinent to indigenous identities was available in natives' terms and, thus, open to analysis.[20]

The government intended to collect census data for administrative purposes, but problems arose when caste became the nucleus for issuing political and economic policies, granting patronage and job opportunities.[21] Such policies welcomed an era of petitions and memorials. Requests to reconsider the rank of some castes, to terminate the social precedence framework altogether, and to protest against the categorization of some castes with others deemed higher than them (such petitions were filed by the upper castes) were commonplace.

On 15 May 1901, an article entitled "*Hindū jātiyōṃ ke vibhāg*" (p. 19) pondered upon the classification and categorization of Indian population in accordance with the *varṇa* system. The article carried information including the categories used in the census. It also provided information on the communication nexus between the indigenous communities and the colonial government. The writer clarified that the superintendent had specifically asked the Mahāsabhā to send a report on Kurmis', Kayasthas', and Khatris' claim on Kshatriyahood. The editor registered his apprehensions on account of *Rāj'pūt* honour, which was doomed to tarnish in case the foregoing castes would be recognized as Rajputs. The editorial also emphasized that the three castes had the maximum number of members in the colonial administration who would vouch on behalf of their caste communities to upgrade their *varṇa* status; the apprehensions were not without any reason as the Kayasthas and Kurmis actually approached the government afterwards with petitions and memorials to register their disagreement over the assigned status of *Sudras* in official records (Carroll 1978: 242). The role of administrative and intellectual elites in such official negotiations became of paramount importance. Munshi Kali Prasad wrote *Kayastha Ethnology* to strengthen their claim to Kshatriyahood, and started a periodical *Kāyastha samācār* in the late nineteenth century (Jaffrelot 2003: 186). Its editorials were marked with rhetoric to exhort the readers to organize themselves against such intrusions.

The journals came across as the discursive space where mutual exchange of information and perspectives took place. It is pertinent to explore how the caste journals maintained their own networks to acquaint themselves with the salient news of contemporary times. The other noticeable aspect is how the news about political, social, and cultural importance was received by the editors and then reproduced for the readers.[22] As expected, the upper-caste journals registered their inhibition against the infiltration of traditional lower castes into the upper castes through editorials, while the lower castes urged fellow community members to support the protest movements against Brahmanical social structure in their journals. M. S. Srinivas maintains in "Caste in Modern India" that census provided the opportunity for social mobility, as the lower castes appropriated "new and high-sounding Sanskrit names" (Srinivas 1957: 531). The census project enabled a reshuffling of the traditional caste structure. In some cases, the census became an agency for Hinduization; some tribal communities, as Srinivas observes, such as the Bhils of Western India, Gonds and Oraons of Central India, and Pahadis of the Himalayas claimed to be upper castes in census surveys, and came into the Hindu fold (Srinivas 1957: 531). In another paper (1972), he explains the lower castes' claim to higher social rank through the lens of Sanskritization.[23]

Nevertheless, the emphasis on the logic of Sanskritization to discern every caste-related sociocultural movement seems problematic, for some historical movements break the monotony of singular mainstream narrative. When Ahirs adopted the *janeū* ceremony (donning of sacred thread) in the Gopa-jātīya Sabhā held in 1911, it was a univocal symbolic act of protest deprived of its multivocal significance for *dvija* castes (Rao 1987: 213); Rao refers to this protest as egalitarianism (p. 236). Jaffrelot in *India's Silent Revolution* (2003) discerns the establishment of Goraksha Sabha (*gorakṣā sabhā*, Cow Protection Association) by Ahirs as an instance of Sanskritization. Nevertheless, the alternative perspective perceived the act as an assertion of identity by a caste which had been associated with the cow traditionally; their community God, Krishna, was also a cow herder, which justified their preoccupation with cow protection as a feature of self-assertion rather than Sanskritization. One needs to be wary of romanticizing the token acts as 'egalitarianism' for Sanskritization was a historical reality, and like with many lower castes, the Ahirs' claim to Kshatriya status was preceded and followed by emulation of the cultural and ritual practices of *dvija* castes. However, interpreting all anti-caste discourses from the lens of Sanskritization amounts to negating the protesting voices of the subalterns. A reading of the anti-caste movements is not possible without taking into account both perspectives, which do not necessarily exclude one another, but often run parallel to each other.

Education and Caste Journals

The significance of education was recognized by almost all caste communities. Thus, all caste associations promoted the establishment of schools and colleges, and urged their members to financially aid such projects.[24] To borrow Gramsci's (1971) idea of hegemony, the caste communities strove to instil a specific ideological set of values into the minds of the members that would ensure the propagation of the communities' interests, and arm the existing knowledge communities with the modern knowledge systems to sustain them in the wave of industrialization and colonization.[25] The new sociopolitical contexts demanded a new set of skills, and all communities recognized the need of the hour and restructured the traditional structures. English, as the modern language, was accepted across all caste communities. Interestingly, the journals that were supporting the cause of Hindi movement also promoted English as the language of power and possibilities; the upper castes acknowledged the relevance of English to acquire government jobs which would ensure their social standing. Likewise, the depressed castes, also favoured English education to improve their social standing and destabilize the hierarchical social structure.

The editorials and readers' letters reflected on the lack of education in Kshatriyas. Their disappointment derived from the degrading occupational status of Kshatriyas – from zamindars they had been reduced to farmers.[26] Their minuscule presence in the government jobs set them backward sin comparison to other castes. Therefore, investment in English education was a well-defined move to reinstate the older social framework, while striving forwards to have a stake in the new world order in the wake of colonial government. Khare identifies the lack of enthusiasm for education as the chief concern among Kanya-kubja Brahmans in the face of "the growing fact of inter caste competition for the same secular ends" (Khare 1970: 44). The Vaishya Mahasabha (*vaiśya mahāsabhā*) came to the fore in 1907, and started *Vaiśa patrikā*, and *Vasavī* to create awareness about education (Reddy 1998: 648). M. S. A. Rao in *Backward Classes Movement* maintains that Yadavs were conscious of English education and established their own schools at the beginning of the twentieth century (Rao 1987: 226). *Ahīr Gazette*, started in 1910 from Etawah (in present Uttar Pradesh), was devoted to enlighten Ahirs about the importance of English education.

Education, for upper castes, was not a means to social mobility owing to the fact that they already were at the top of the social hierarchy; arguably, it had something to do with economic prosperity. However, for lower castes, English education was strategic to social revival; it provided them with an entry point into mainstream social processes. It opened a world of opportunities in the colonial government. The journals emerged as the printed mouthpieces of the respective caste associations, but literacy was prerequisite for their efficient functioning. There was a direct relationship between Hindi journalism patronized by caste *sabhās* and collective mobilizations. Possibly, that was why the caste associations chose journals as the means to reshape the contours of their respective knowledge communities. The education sector was instrumental not only as an ideological vehicle but also for the formation of the group of administrative and intellectual elites who are a prerequisite for any social movement.

In tandem with *Manusmṛti*'s idea of the *varṇa* system, *Rāj'pūt* charted the possible educational curriculum for its caste members. Alluding to Manu for accrediting specific vocations for each caste, the editor believed that as Brahmans derive their supremacy from knowledge, and Vaishyas from wealth, Rajputs ought to acknowledge the importance of physical strength to retain the traditional social standing.[27] The articles in *Rāj'pūt* recurrently stressed on the importance of exercise.[28] The journal emphasized on an education system that would fetch them jobs, while focusing on physical strength. Other caste associations also insisted on maintaining a balance between their traditional knowledge systems and modern knowledge. Reddy (1998) also observed how Vaishya Mahasabha, in its annual conference in 1911, encouraged youths to travel overseas to learn new technical skills. Chhotu Ram, the editor of *Jāṭ Gazette*, proclaimed that the Anglo-Sanskrit Jat High School in Rohtak was opened in 1913 to train students for jobs in the army.

Conclusion

The colonial policies and projects functioned as a 'catalyst' (Bayly 1999b: 345) that spurred the formation of caste associations. Indian society was caste-ridden and readily adopted the modern means of information diffusion to preserve their identities. Ironically, the modern systems of knowledge intensified rather than dissolving the caste distinctions in the society. Nevertheless, the colonial practices including decennial census, surveys, and preparing ethnographic monographs narrowed down the focus of natives to the issue of caste. The caste associations in late nineteenth and early twentieth century India were manifestations of negotiation between tradition and modernity (Khare 1970: 161). Modernity also created a chasm between textual and oral discourses. The history of the Hindi language is one example where the textual was privileged over oral literature. A study of caste journals seems to alleviate such gaps in historiography. From announcing the important community and national events to urging the readers to spread the word by mouth,[29] the caste journals managed to bridge the gap between the older and modern communication networks. In fact, the journals invited the readers to share news regarding other castes, thus ascribing a sense of power to the latter; consequently, caste journals emerged as a shared discursive space. Of course, language politics played a prominent role in (a) choosing the vernacular as the means of ideological insinuation, (b) supporting (or not supporting) the Hindi movement, (c) using a hybrid language for selected sections in caste journals, and (d) introducing English as the aspirational language of opportunities. Caste associations functioned as pressure groups that represent their respective communities, and thus endeavoured to represent their interests in social, political, and cultural discourses. The colonial government acknowledged the role of caste associations. Their journals became the manufacturing units where histories, ethnographic studies, and respective curriculum frameworks were constructed, and served the purpose of ideological insinuation and perpetuation. An analysis of caste journals underscores the impact of language, modernity, education, and colonial policies and administration on upper-caste and lower-caste subcultures.

Acknowledgement

I thank Prof. Nishat Zaidi and Prof. Hans Harder for giving me the opportunity to be a part of this esteemed project. I also thank Dr. Saroj K. Mahananda for his guidance throughout.

Notes

1 Grierson, G.A., *The Modern Vernacular Literature of Hindustan* (1889), p. 145.
2 Stark (2008: 19) dwells on how Munshi Nawal Kishore, a Hindu publisher, provided the printed Quran for a minuscule price of Rs. 1 and 8 annas for the common man irrespective of his/her religion.
3 Chakrabarty (1995: 375) articulates that the British set into motion the process to restructure the Indian society into a "modern state" by introducing railways, print, census, and so on.
4 See Cohn (1990).
5 *Rāj'pūt* was started in 1899 from Agra as the official journal of Rajput Mahasabha. Rajput is the most prominent Kshatriya caste.
6 Ahir (*Ahīr*) is a socially backward-caste community popularly known as Yadavs; Rao Daleep Singh was the editor of *Ahīr Gazette* which was started to mobilize the anti-caste movement and uplift the Yadav community. See Rao (1987) to read more on anti-caste social movements.
7 There were many other caste journals like *Ārya mahilā* (1917 from Banaras), *Brāhmaṇ* (1883 from Kanpur), *Caturvedī candrikā* (1891 from Calcutta), *Caturvedī patrikā* (1895 from Agra), *Pāñcāl paṇḍit* (1900 from Jallandhar), *Jāṭ samācār* (1890), etc.
8 'Sampādakīya vicār': Akhil Bharatiya Brahman Mahasammelan, *Brāhmaṇ sarvasva*, September 1928; p. 324.
9 "Āvaśyak'tā", *Gaur hit'kārī*, October 1919, p. 26.

10 For reference, see *Rāj'pūt*, 15 July 1901, p. 26.
11 "Hindī sāhitya kā mahatva", *Śrī kanyā-kubja hit'kārī*, 10 January 1923, p. 14.
12 *Gaur hit'kārī* was patronized by Narayan Samiti from Mainpuri; *Brāhmaṇ sarvasa* was associated with *sanātana dharma* and printed from Etawah. Both journals were publishing in the beginning of the twentieth century.
13 *Rāj'pūt*, 15 May 1901, p. 1.
14 The editor crowned Kshatriyas with adjectives like *param bhakt* of government in *Rajput*; 15 May 1901, p. 17.
15 See Jaffrelot, *India's Silent Revolution* (2003), p. 194; and MSA Rao, *Social Movements and Social Transformation* (1987), p. 214.
16 Ibid., "Vīr'caritāvalī ", 30 September 1901, p. 21.
17 The social movements by the lower castes were usually targeted against the immediate opposition group that served as the reference group. The relative deprivation of the lower castes was estimated vis-à-vis the reference caste. See Rao (1987) for a detailed explanation.
18 The elites can be referred as political elites; see M. S. A. Rao (1987).
19 Bayly (1999a) reflects on the idea of "information system" in *Empire and Information*.
20 An official circular was published in Pioneer on 29 April 1901, "to constitute district committees to issue decisions on the social standing and precedence of castes in their respective districts; there were specific instructions to enumerate names of representatives of 'any caste *sabhā*s' that might be found in the district"; quoted in Carroll (1978: 241). Apparently, the announcement mobilized different caste communities to assimilate as *sabhā*s.
21 Caste was the centre of administration even in pre-colonial times. C. A. Bayly (1999b: 169) also asserts that caste was presumed to be the natural scheme of the Indian society, and history has examples like Peshwa rulers, who organized data collection on the lines of caste.
22 *Rajput*, "Vividh samācār ", p. 22. *Rāj'pūt* published about the second Khatri conference, and specifically referred to the number of participants.
23 M. N. Srinivas in Social Change in Modern India (1972: 6) defines Sanskritization as the process by which a 'low' Hindu caste, or tribal or other group, changes its customs, ritual, ideology, and way of life in the direction of a high and frequently 'twice born' caste.
24 Both Rajputs and Ahirs published recurrently on the importance of education in their caste journals. See *Rāj'pūt*, 31 October 1901, p. 19 and Rao (1987), p. 187 for reference.
25 *Rāj'pūt*, 31 July, 1901, p. 12. The article underlines the educational endeavours by Kayasthas and Muslims, which culminated into Kayastha Pathshala and Aligarh College, respectively. Such writings underscore the conceptualizations of self-identity which were asserted in contrast to the *other*. The increasing sense of competition propelled the caste communities to enhance the education status of their caste members.
26 *Rāj'pūt*, 31 August 1901, p. 19–21.
27 *Rāj'pūt*, 15 June 1901, p. 2.
28 *Rāj'pūt*, 15 July 1901, p. 21. In an article titled "Vyāyām", the writer religiously quoted from *Manusmṛti* to emphasize the importance of physical exercise.
29 *Jain Gazette* requested its subscribers to read the journal aloud: "kṛpā kar is patr ko ādyopānt paṛh'kar sarv bhāiyoṃ ko sunāiye"; it was presumed that many caste members were not literate enough to read the paper so the printed content was read out by the schoolmaster or any literate person as part of *jātīya sevā*, 'caste service'. *Jain Gazette*, 16 October 1899, p. 1.

References

Official Publications

Census of India. 1901. *North Western Provinces and Oudh*. Allahabad: Government Press.

Periodicals

Brāhmaṇ sarvasva, April 1920.
Gaur hit"kārī, Oct. 1919.
Jain Gazette, 1899–1927.
Rāj"pūt, Jan.–Dec. 1901.

Other Publications

Bayly, C. A. 1999a. *Empire and Information*. Cambridge: Cambridge University Press.
Bayly, S. 1999b. *Caste, Politics and Society in India from the Eighteenth Century to the Modern Age*. Cambridge: Cambridge University Press.
Carroll, Lucy. "Colonial Perceptions of Indian Society and the Emergence of Caste(s) Associations." *The Journal of Asian Studies*, vol. 37, no. 2, 1978, 233–250.
Chakrabarty, Dipesh. "Modernity and Ethnicity in India: A History for the Present." *Economic and Political Weekly*, vol. 30, no. 52, 1995, 3373–3380.
Christophe Jaffrelot. 2003. *India's Silent Revolution: The Rise of the Lower Castes in North India*. London: C. Hurst & Co. Publishers.
Cohn, B. S. 1996. *Colonialism and Its Forms of Knowledge: British in India*. New Jersey: Princeton University Press.
Cohn, B. S. 1990. "The Census, Social Structure and Objectification in South Asia." In *idem*: *An Anthropologist among the Historians and Other Essays*. Delhi: Oxford University Press.
Dalmia, Vasudha. 1997. *The Nationalization of Hindu Traditions: Bharatendu Harischandra and Nineteenth Century Banaras* . Delhi: Oxford University Press.
Gramsci, Antonio. 1971. "Hegemony (Civil Society) and Separation of Powers." In *Selections from the Prison Notebooks of Antonio Gramsci*. Ed. and trans. Quintin Hoare and Geoffrey Nowell Smith. New York: International Publishers.
Grierson, G.A. 1889. *The Modern Vernacular Literature of Hindustan*. Calcutta: Asiatic Society of Bengal.
Jaffrelot, Christophe. 2000. "Sanskritization vs. Ethnicization in India: Changing Identities and Caste Politics before Mandal." *Asian Survey*, vol. 40, no. 5, 756–766.
Karve, Irawati. 1959. "What is Caste? Caste Society and Vedantic Thought". *The Economic Weekly Annual*, January 1959, 149–163.
Khare, R.S. 1970. *The Changing Brahmans: Associations and Elites among the Kanyakubjas of North India*. Chicago and London: The University of Chicago Press.
Orsini, Francesca. 2002. *The Hindi Public Sphere, 1920–1940: Language and Literature in the Age of Nationalism*. India: Oxford University Press.
Rao, M.S.A. 1987. *Social Movements and Social Transformation: A Study of Two Backward Classes Movements in India*. Delhi: Manohar Publications.

Reddy, G. S. 1998. "Caste Mobility in Andhra: A Study of Vaisya Mahasabha 1907–1930." *Proceedings of the Indian History Congress*, vol. 59, 647–653.

Rudolph, Lloyd I. 1965. "The Modernity of Tradition: The Democratic Incarnation of Caste in India." *The American Political Science Review*, vol. 59, no. 4, 1965, 975–989.

Rudolph, Susanne Hoeber, and Lloyd Rudolph. 2012. "Caste Associations to Identity Politics: From Self-help and Democratic Representation to Goonda Raj and Beyond". *Pacific Affairs*, vol. 85, no. 2, 1965, 371–375.

Srinivas, M. N. 1957. "Caste in Modern India." *The Journal of Asian Studies*, vol. 16, no. 4, 1957, 529–548.

Srinivas, M.N. 1972. *Social Change in Modern India*. Hyderabad: Orient Longman.

Stark, Ulrike. 2008. *An Empire of Books: The Naval Kishore Press and the Diffusion of the Printed Word in Colonial India*. Ranikhet: Permanent Black.

16

A SOUTH ASIAN VERNACULAR PUBLIC OVERSEAS

Tamil in the Straits Settlements, c. 1870–1942

Torsten Tschacher

Introduction

The idea of a 'South Asian vernacular' during the colonial period conjures up the idea of a relatively simple language hierarchy, with English as the dominant idiom of colonial power, a few privileged South Asian vernaculars recognized by the colonial government, and a large number of languages that did not receive any public support. But how did this language-hierarchy look from the perspective of South Asians settled overseas, as traders or laborers in another colony? How were South Asian publics constituted in conditions that were different from those at home? In how far were patterns reproduced or changed? And what language ideologies were formulated in the diaspora, in comparison to developments in South Asia? One interesting case to consider these questions is the development of Tamil print and publishing in the Straits Settlements (Singapore, Penang, and Melaka) between the late nineteenth century and the Japanese occupation in 1942. From the 1870s onward, Tamil newspapers and books began to be published locally, mostly by Muslim printers. Until World War I, Tamil publishing in the Straits Settlements largely followed local patterns that were determined by the complex interconnections between various Asian communities settled in the Straits Settlements. After the war, the situation changed, and with the impact of both Indian and Dravidian nationalism, the local Tamil public sphere became more 'diasporic' in the sense that it became more dependent on discourses produced in India.

In this chapter, I aim to provide a history of the development of a Tamil print industry and the creation of Tamil-language publics in the colonial Straits Settlements before the Japanese invasion in 1942 and to analyze the specificities of this environment in terms of the position of Tamil in the local

DOI: 10.4324/9781003279921-20

language order and the language ideologies emerging from this order. In the first section, I will survey the early history of Tamil public in the Straits Settlements prior to the development of a local Tamil print industry. This is followed by a survey of Tamil publishing between 1887 and 1941, to sketch the publications of this industry, especially newspapers, and to elucidate some important general trends. The third section will then address the strangely delayed formulation of a common Tamil linguistic identity in the Straits Settlements, and the conditions that aided that delay. Finally, I will briefly outline the interconnected questions of the relationship between English and the political currency of Tamil in the Straits Settlements, in order to provide some explanations for the peculiar development of the Straits Tamil public sphere.

Toward Print: The Early History of Tamil-Language Publics in the Straits Settlements

The beginnings of contemporary Tamil-language publics around the Malacca Strait are deeply entwined with the extension of European colonial control. While there is evidence that individual Tamil texts and manuscripts circulated in the region before and beyond the control of European colonial powers – Portuguese, Dutch, and British – these remained within the realm of individual practice and did not, apparently, impact the public order. There is good evidence of the public use of Tamil-language documents in Malacca already during the period of Portuguese (1511–1641) and Dutch (1641–1825) rule over the town (Gallop 2006, 55; Stephen 2019: 167).[1] These patterns – the individual circulation of Tamil-language texts and literature and the utilization of Tamil legal documents in communication with the authorities – are similarly found in the early British outposts, in Penang after 1786 and in Singapore after 1819. The circulation of Tamil texts in Penang is clearly attested by the Scottish Orientalist John Leyden (1775–1811), who visited the island late in 1805. However, this observation came with an important caveat: the Tamil literature encountered by Leyden in Penang were predominantly Muslim texts, often written in Arabic script, a result of the overwhelmingly Muslim composition of the island's South Indian inhabitants (Brown 1955: 447; [Leyden] 1810: 120).[2] The importance of Tamil among local merchant communities is also confirmed by the famous Malay writer Munshi Abdullah b. Abdul Kadir (1796–1854), himself of South Indian ancestry, who described in his autobiography how, as a child, "my father sent me to a teacher to learn Tamil, an Indian language, and its letters, because it had been the custom from the time of our forefathers in Malacca for all the children of good and well-to-do families to learn it" (Abdullah 1970: 45, translation slightly modified).[3]

Neither the literary uses of Tamil described by Leyden nor the mercantile uses enumerated by Munshi Abdullah really translated into the creation of any kind of Tamil 'public' in the modern sense. But in an important manner, they were forerunners of such a public. The recognition bestowed on Tamil documents as valid legal instruments by the colonial order enabled more political usage of the language. Petitions could be directed to the government directly in Tamil, though the translation process that inevitably ensued often delayed these petitions or even rendered them obsolete. The earliest surviving Tamil-language petition from Singapore, though dated 2 December 1822, was obviously added to the respective file of 1822 only after the month of December had ended, when the issue it pertained to had already been overtaken by other events (SSR L6, No. 91, 2 December 1822). Therefore, while having some legal authority, Tamil was not a particularly useful language in the public domain, where English and Malay were of prime importance. Until the 1860s, processions and the public celebration of festivals and rituals remained the primary means for publicly engaging and contesting the colonial state and elite European society. Chief among these public displays of power were the annual Muharram processions, which increasingly came under the control of the so-called White Flag and Red Flag societies. While the British state came to perceive these societies as trans-regional criminal gangs composed of South Indian Muslims and Hindus, Malays, and Arabs, in reality, they were primarily local pressure groups contending with each other in contesting control over the Indian and Malay population in individual neighborhoods and towns, with only loose connections to similarly named groups elsewhere (Musa 2006; Pieris 2009: 165–87; Tschacher 2022).

A series of disturbances and riots in the mid-1860s finally led to the suppression of the White and Red Flag societies and effectively brought Muharram processions to an end in the Straits Settlements. This fundamentally transformed the political landscape of the Straits Settlements as far as South Indians were concerned, especially since the Straits Settlements, which had traditionally been governed as a part of British India, became a crown colony in 1867, transforming the government of the Straits Settlements from a merely regional authority into an independent institution with its own constitution and legislative council. It was in this context that the first Tamil book printed in the Straits Settlements, an anthology of Muslim devotional poetry entitled *Muṉājāttuttiraṭṭu*, was published by the government printer in Singapore in 1872. Within a year from this publication, Denodaya Press, the first privately owned Tamil printing press in the Straits Settlements, was formed in Singapore as a joint venture between 'Singapore' K. Makhdum Sahib, a local printer, and a poet by the name of Mohamed Abdulkadir Pulavar, though the latter withdrew from the partnership on 29 December 1875 ("Notice," *The Straits Observer*, 29 February 1876). Both had been directly involved in the publication of *Muṉājāttuttiraṭṭu* in the year before, 'Nagore' M. Mohamed Abdulkadir Pulavar as the author and Makhdum Sahib as the largest subscriber (Mukammatu Aptulkātiṟuppulavar 1872). The formation of Denodaya Press came at a time that also saw the expansion of privately owned Malay printing presses, and, indeed, the main presses printing Tamil before 1900 were multilingual enterprises. In Singapore, where the evidence is clearer than in Penang, much of Tamil printing in this early period was published by just two presses, Makhdum Sahib's Denodaya Press and Muhammad Said's Matbaʿ Saʿīdī (later Jawi Peranakan Press), which were also among the most important Malay presses of the late nineteenth century. The owners of both presses had a similarly 'creolized' background in the so-called Jawi Peranakan or Peranakan Kling community, i.e., locally born South Indian Muslims, often with Malay mothers (Fujimoto 1988; Khoo 2014: 121–34; Proudfoot 1993; Roff 1967: 48–55; van der Putten 2009: 92–95). While both presses published Tamil literature (mostly Muslim religious tracts and devotional poetry), they are more important for their early attempts at publishing Tamil weekly newspapers. Prior to 1887, Denodaya Press started two attempts at running Tamil-language periodicals, *Ciṅkaivarttamāṉi* ('The Singapore Newspaper,' 1875) and *Ñāṉacūriyaṉ* ('Sun of Knowledge,' 1882), while Muhammad Said's press published *Taṅkai Ciṉēkaṉ* ('Friend of *Taṅkai*,' 1879).[4] In Penang as well, the first Tamil newspaper, *Vittiyāvicāriṇi* ('The Scientific Enquirer,') was started in 1883 by Ghulam Kadir Navalar, himself a prolific Tamil poet and later involved with the so-called Madurai Tamil Sangam, a prominent literary and scholarly society founded in 1901 (Amrith 2013: 165–8; Birch 1879; Tschacher 2011: 69–72; regarding the Madurai Tamil Sangam, cf. Ebeling 2010: 126–7). However pioneering, these enterprises met with relatively little success: all of these newspapers seem to have folded up within a year, in contrast, for example, to Muhammad Said's Malay weekly *Jawi Peranakan*, which ran uninterrupted from 1876 until 1895, seven years after the founder's death. Consequently, little evidence survives of these newspapers, apart from references by contemporaries, so that we can only speculate about their content (cf. Birch 1879).[5] This situation only changes with legal transformations in 1886 that reflected the recent growth of a local, non-English print industry.

Tamil Publishing in the Straits Settlements: A General Overview

On 18 November 1886, the Legislative Council of the Straits Settlements passed the *Book Registration Ordinance* (Ordinance XV of 1886), the first, and for a long time only, piece of legislation in the Straits Settlements aimed at the local print industry. The Ordinance primarily regulated the submission of three copies of every book, newspaper, and similar printed material to the government for preservation (§3–4), their registration in a catalog (§5), and the regular publication of this catalog by government (§6) (Garrard 1898, vol. 2, 967–9). In contrast to laws controlling the press in British India that had been passed in the preceding two decades, this ordinance provided little powers for policing publications. In this period, the Straits Settlements' government saw the biggest threat to its authority as emanating from so-called secret societies.

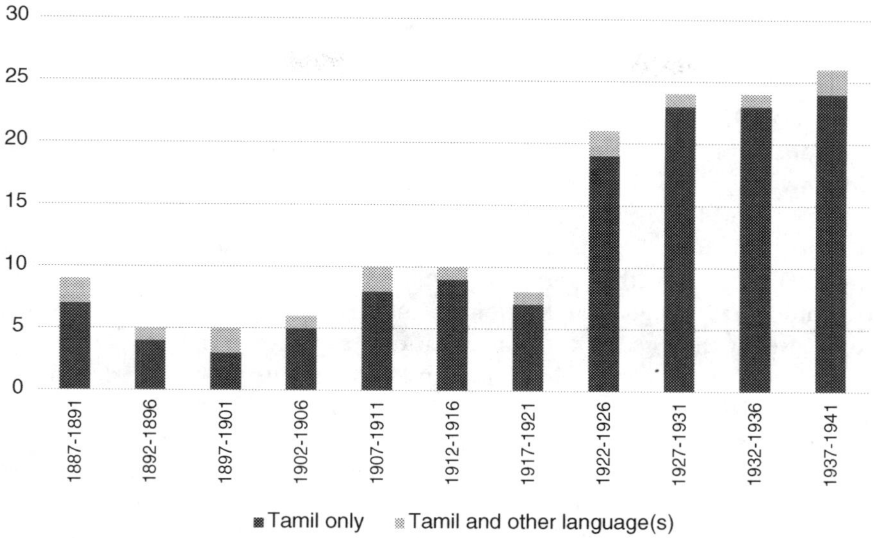

FIGURE 16.1 Number of Tamil publications in the Straits Settlements per five-year period, 1887–1942

Source: MoB.

Consequently, the ordinance was solely focused on the aim of preserving copies for public record (SSSHLC 1886, B143).[6] Both the policy of keeping a deposit of local publications in Britain and the Straits Settlements, and the quarterly publication of memoranda listing the publications registered, enable us to gain a much better understanding of Straits Settlements' publishing in general, and Tamil publishing in particular, than is possible for the period before 1887.

The information contained in the *Memoranda of Books* allows us to sketch the development of Tamil publishing in the Straits Settlements. Figure 16.1 shows the number of Tamil publications registered in a 5-year period in the 55 years between the coming into effect of the *Book Registration Ordinance* on 1 January 1887 and the Japanese occupation of Singapore on 15 February 1942. In total, 148 Tamil publications were registered in this period, with 132 being exclusively in Tamil, and 16 where Tamil formed part of a multilingual publication. In the language order of the Straits Settlements, this was a far cry from the two main languages, English (1,354 exclusively English publications) and Malay (1,071), but part of a second tier consisting, besides Tamil, of Chinese (192) and Arabic (56). Publications in other Indian languages were negligible, with a total of five Malayalam publications and one publication each in Gujarati, Hindi, and Urdu registered during the whole period. Singapore remained the primary center of publishing in all languages, though in Tamil the distribution was a bit more equal: 82 out of 148 publications (55%) were registered in Singapore, the other in Penang; no Tamil publication was registered at Malacca. After an initial boost of Tamil publishing in the wake of the *Ordinance* in 1887, the next 15 years saw a relative slump in publications, with less than one publication registered per year. After 1906, publishing slowly picked up, only to be stalled again with the paper shortages in the wake of the outbreak of World War I. From 1922 onward, Tamil publishing picked up again, with more than double the number of publications registered than in prewar times. Throughout this period, though monolingual publishing kept on expanding, multilingual publications including Tamil remained steadily at the same level, with only one to two publications per five-year interval.

In terms of the types of publications, throughout the period, devotional poetry (with Hindu publications overtaking the number of Muslim ones in the second decade of the twentieth century) and practical publications, such as school books and calendars, dominated the market. Literary works were largely conventional, though some of the poetry, while in traditional genres, turned to unusual subjects, such as a collection of songs about the horse races at the Singapore racecourse published in 1893 (Iraṅkacāmi Tācaṉ 1893; cf. Tiṇṇappaṉ and Civakumāraṉ 2002; Kanagalatha 2019). Prior to World War I, a number of prose narratives adopted from *hikāyat*-literature in Urdu and Malay was published as well, but the first book registered as a novel is found only in 1926 (No. 25, 31 December 1926).[7] Perhaps the most interesting element in Tamil publishing during this period are the periodicals. No less than 51 of the registered 148 Tamil publications were registered as periodicals, with 4 periodicals registered in 1914 and 7 in 1939 marking the high points. These periodicals included journals published by associations and church magazines, but a good number were weekly, and later daily, newspapers. The high numbers registered of course point toward a significant problem with these periodicals: most of them folded up within a few months of their registration. However, the frequency with which printers attempted to find periodicals, despite the apparent odds, is noteworthy. The first somewhat 'successful' Tamil newspaper was the weekly *Ciṅkainēcaṉ* ('The Singapore Friend,') published between 27 June 1887 and 23 June 1890 by 'Singapore' K. Makhdum Sahib at the Denodaya Press. The first functioning daily, the *Piṉāṅkuñāṉācāriyaṉ* ('The Penang Teacher of Knowledge,') had started as a weekly in April 1912 but turned into a daily in July of the same year. A dispute over the press caused this paper to cease publication in November 1913, but it was succeeded by another daily from basically the same press by the name of *Jaṉōpakāri* ('Benefactor of the People') between February and December 1914. Ultimately, however, a Tamil press was to establish itself permanently only in the 1930s. *Tamiḻ Muracu* ('The Tamil Kettle-drum,') first founded in Singapore as a weekly in 1935 and then transformed into a triweekly, became a daily from 1 December 1937 onward. Its main rival, *Tamiḻ Nēcaṉ* ('The Tamil Friend,') published since 1924 from

Kuala Lumpur (outside the Straits Settlements), had already turned into a daily a few months earlier. Both newspapers came to define the Tamil press in Southeast Asia for decades to come – *Tamiḻ Muracu* is still in print, and *Tamiḻ Nēcaṉ* closed down on 31 January 2019 (cf. Karthigesu 1989; Samy 2000; Sathisan 2019). It is from these attempts at the printing of periodicals that the interplay of Tamil publics, politics, and language ideologies emerges most clearly.

Money Matters, or Language without Community

Two assumptions dominate the scholarly understanding of the development of a Tamil press in the Straits Settlements: one is that Tamil publishing gave voice to the concerns of an already-pre-existent community of 'Tamilians,' or at least encouraged its readers to identify primarily through language. The other common idea is that the early Tamil press was predominantly a phenomenon turned toward India, an expression of diasporic nostalgia, with little interest in the local (cf. e.g. Fakhri 2008: 72–73; Kanagalatha 2019: 177–8; Rai 2014: 140–1 (with some qualifications); Sathisan 2019: 130; Trocki 2006: 68). The notion that South Indians migrated to Singapore with an already-established unifying linguistic identity in place is increasingly subjected to criticism (Kanagalatha 2019: 177–78; Mani 2019; Tschacher 2018b: 23–30), but the question remains: In how far did the development of a Tamil press contribute to the formation of a common Tamil identity in the Straits Settlements, and in how far can we speak about the products of the press formulating a common 'language ideology'?[8]

At the first glance, the early newspapers may indeed appear as logical catalysts for the formulation of a common language identity and a championing of Tamil as the 'mother-tongue' of a unified, diasporic community. Early printers were, unsurprisingly, conscious that their efforts to print Tamil newspapers and books were made meaningful primarily because of the language: what they did enabled Tamil, and by extension those who used the language, to perform a specific role in contemporary society. Print supposedly helped the largely mercantile readership in the development (*apivirutti*) of education (*kalvi*), knowledge (*aṟivu*), wealth (*poruḷ*), the 'common good' (*potu naṉmai*), and generally, the 'reform' (*cīrtiruttam*, literally the 'turning to a good condition') of the individual, with English forming the model for the transformation of the Tamil language (cf. e.g. "Em pattirikai," *Ulakanēcaṉ*, 28 March 1887; "Ippattirikaiyiṉ nōkkam," *Ciṅkainēcaṉ*, 27 June 1887; "Pattirikai," *Ciṅkainēcaṉ*, 24 June 1889; "Varttamāṉap pattirikaiyaiṉ pirayōjaṉam," *Piṉāṅkuñāṉācāriyaṉ*, 12 April 1912). Consequently, it is not surprising to find the concomitant claim that publishing a newspaper was "in advancement of Tamil" (*tirāviṭa virttikkāka*) in local society. In the invocation of a specifically English model of individual development, the Tamil press in the Straits was hardly different from dozens of similar cases all over the British Empire. If the focus on the advancement of the individual through the advancement of language seems like an ideal ground for the formulation of a common linguistic identity, another, perhaps a bit more surprising, aspect of the early Straits Settlements' Tamil press was its transregional reach. Far from being consumed only by a tiny reading public in the colony itself, these newspapers were read in an astonishingly large area. *Ciṅkainēcaṉ*, the best documented case, had readers and subscribers not only in Singapore and Penang but also in various localities in (Dutch) Sumatra and (French) Indochina, in Bangkok and Colombo, and, least surprisingly, in British India, while it simultaneously quoted articles from Tamil newspapers published in Colombo, Madras, and Penang. What, one might wonder, could hold these different life-worlds together other than the common experience of speaking Tamil?

Despite the apparently optimal conditions for the development of a common identity based on the Tamil language, there is next to no evidence of such a development prior to the 1920s and 1930s. While publishers invoked the Tamil language, they made no efforts to address their products to a community of 'Tamilians.' When *Ciṅkainēcaṉ* outlined the aims and purposes of the newspaper in its first issue, it identified its audience simply as the "members of many communities speaking the Tamil language in Singapore".[9] Part of the problem lay in labeling that linguistic community itself. The term *tamiḻār*, 'Tamilians,' did not refer to all speakers of the Tamil language, but to a particular section of the caste spectrum: the upper non-Brahmin castes and, in particular, the Vellalars.[10] However, the most important factor is connected to an aspect of early Tamil printing in the Straits Settlements that set it apart from developments elsewhere where Tamil was used: the identity of its early print capitalists. In contrast to India, early Tamil printing in the Straits Settlements was largely the preserve of Muslims. So important was the role of Muslims in Tamil print that one of the few surviving examples of a nineteenth-century Straits Tamil newspaper not published by Muslims still felt the need to point out that Muslims "have taken countless efforts to create and promote Tamil books".[11] Tellingly, this newspaper, pointedly entitled *Intu Nēcaṉ* ('The Hindu Friend,') did not attempt to formulate a common Tamil identity either, but rather highlighted the fact that Tamil, like Sanskrit, had been promulgated by Śiva himself ("Tamiḻ," *Intu Nēcaṉ*, 16 April 1888). Around the same period, Muslims in Ceylon were engaged in a struggle to be recognized as a community separate from Hindu and Christian Tamils, while seeing no contradiction in formulating specifically Muslim claims to the Tamil language (cf. "Tamiḻpāṣai," *Muslim Nēcaṉ*, 5 Paṅkuṉi 1883).[12]

While the Muslim dominance of early Tamil printing in the Straits Settlements may appear unusual, it was in fact rather unsurprising. To begin with, Muslims had long formed the majority of Tamil speakers in the urban centers of British Malaya, a situation that only began to change in the late nineteenth century (cf. Tschacher 2019: 217). Furthermore, as a community engaging primarily in trade and shopkeeping, Muslims had one of the highest literacy rates among Tamil speakers; for example, in Tanjore district, one of the prime regions of migration to the Straits, 22.5% of Muslim men were literate in Tamil in 1901, while the India-wide male literacy rate stood at 9.8% (figures calculated on the basis of Francis table VIII; Risley and Gait 1903, table VIII, part 1). But the prime advantage of Muslims in operating printing presses in colonial Singapore had nothing to do with Tamil. Rather, it was their role as multilingual entrepreneurs straddling the boundaries of South Indians and Malays that they turned to their advantage. Already in the seventeenth century, English traders in Southeast Asia had begrudged Tamil Muslims their linguistic skills (e.g. Bowrey 1905: 258), and in the multilingual environment of the Straits Settlements, these were of great advantage to a printer. As already mentioned, many of these early printers were actually born in the Straits Settlements and in all likelihood had Malay mothers, giving them close family connections with the local Malays. The Malay printing business was important precisely because, during much of the pre–World War I period, Tamil publishing seems to have been a somewhat uneconomical business. This was not so much due to the lack of readers, but due to the myriad ways in which readers distributed throughout South and Southeast Asia could default on payments. The history of *Ciṅkainēcaṉ* is very much the history of a publisher in constant battle with his subscribers: "Having published a whole column in the last two issues and pleaded to show us a little justice and send the outstanding balance, is it fair for you to pretend that you just do not hear" ("Aṟivippu," *Ciṅkainēcaṉ*, 26 May 1890)? He made enough money with his printing business, Makhdum Sahib claimed, that he was content to publish the newspaper, as long as he recovered the money he had invested in it (cf. "Pattirikai," *Ciṅkainēcaṉ*, 24 June 1889; "Kaiyoppak kaṉavāṉkaḷukkuc calām," *Ciṅkainēcaṉ*, 1 July 1889). When *Ciṅkainēcaṉ* was discontinued in June 1890 precisely because of the defaulting subscribers, Makhdum Sahib still continued his Malay printing works. Denodaya press survived until about 1915, though largely seems to have ceased publishing Tamil by 1893.

To a certain degree, it may thus be fair to say that Tamil piggybacked on the much larger Malay printing industry in the Straits Settlements. However, this alone would not explain the pronounced absence of any sense of a unified linguistic community. The point may rather be that the very creation of such a community may have endangered business, for the individuals who invested in a Tamil press had no intention to artificially narrow their markets by invoking a single language community, even more so as this might empower others who might have a better claim at representing that linguistic community than the multilingual entrepreneurs straddling the boundaries between languages. As long as there was no single community laying claim to the Tamil language, tailor-made products could be sold to different groups, while it was at the same time unlikely that, for example, Hindu readers of *Ciṅkainēcaṉ* would have taken much umbrage at Makhdum Sahib's statement that he was publishing a newspaper "for Muslims" ("Kaiyoppak kaṉavāṉkaḷukku," *Ciṅkainēcaṉ*, 14 April 1890).

The interwar period saw a massive transformation in the way Tamil language publishing was situated within the wider politics of the Straits Settlements and the British Empire. The primary transformation was a shift from the selective invocation of different visions of the Tamil language, and the relationship formulated between the language and its diverse users. In practice, this involved a wholesale importation of discourses raging in India at that time, no matter what their relevance for the local context in the Straits Settlements. The fallout of this importation was an increased competition between particular groups struggling for control over the 'proper' use of Tamil. The question was, in principle, one of caste. On the one side were those who argued that Tamil had suffered at the hands of a Brahmin elite that had unduly Sanskritized and debased Tamil. The other side argued that both Sanskrit and Tamil, Brahmin and non-Brahmin, were legitimate parts of the wider Tamil whole that, however, still required reform on the model of European languages and some of the more developed Indian languages (Bengali and Marathi being the main examples of the latter). This latter position seems to have had the greater currency in British Malaya in the 1920s, represented by newspapers such as *Tamiḻ Nēcaṉ* in Kuala Lumpur and *Potujaṉa mittiraṉ* ('The Common Peoples' Friend') in Singapore (cf. "Tamiḻp pāṣai," *Potujaṉa mittiraṉ*, 05 April 1924; "The Fundamental Difference," *Potujaṉa mittiraṉ*, 20 August 1924), while 'Periyar' E. V. Ramamsamy's visit to Malaya in 1929–1930 and the activities of the publisher G. Sarangapany in Singapore tilted the balance toward the former in the 1930s (Sathisan 2019). There is no need to repeat here the history of the development of the non-Brahmin movement and its vision of the Tamil language. The only matter to point out is that, although these developments greatly transformed the capacity of actors to engage Tamil publics in the Straits Settlements, as I will discuss in the next section, the role of the Tamil language in the formulation of Tamil identities still remained ambiguous.

A good deal of the ambiguity was provided precisely by the divergent visions of who could legitimately lay claim to Tamil, and in what form. And while there were some, generally Śaiva members of the dominant castes, who were able to make those claims with greater authority than others, they still had to contend with the fact that no clear identification between language and community existed, at least not as yet. This required a good deal of willingness for compromise, to convince groups that were not used to identify as 'Tamils' that they indeed were 'Tamils.' When the president of the Tamils Reform Association, perhaps the most important organization in British Malaya to support the Dravidianist ideology and the Self-Respect Movement, was asked – significantly, by a Muslim – at a meeting in 1933 to specify as to whom the label 'Tamil' applied, he answered: "Generally, all who are born in Tamil Nadu, be they Hindu, Muslim, Christian, or Buddhist, are Tamils" ("Tamiḻar makā jaṉak kūṭṭattiṉ alaṅkōlam", *Navanītam*, 3 April 1933). The same notion was frequently repeated in Dravidianist circles right up until the Japanese invasion (cf. e.g. "Tamiḻ nāṭṭavar tamiḻarē," *Tamiḻ Muracu*, 8 October 1936; "Tamiḻar eṉṟāl tamiḻ nāṭṭiṉar," *Tamiḻ Muracu*, 05 February 1941). Yet this definition through territory rather than language, however inclusive, did not really clarify matters. Firstly, it raised the question of what this meant for those who were born in 'Tamil Nadu,' but spoke different languages. This could still be addressed in a relatively straightforward manner: anyone born in Tamil Nadu was supposed to be bound "by the inseparable ties of birth that are country and language", i.e., everyone born of 'Mother Tamil' was supposed to be a 'Tamil' and therefore had a duty to honor the Tamil language, even if speaking a different language at home ("Tamiḻ nāṭṭavar tamiḻarē," *Tamiḻ Muracu*, 8 October 1936). Yet in the context of the Straits Settlements, this was hardly a satisfying definition. What if one was born in Penang or Singapore? It is not surprising that those who were most difficult to convince that they were 'Tamil,' were precisely the members of that community that had pioneered Tamil publishing in the Straits Settlements, and who were the most likely to be 'locally born' (Malay: *peranakan*): Tamil-speaking Muslims. As late as February 1941, G. Sarangapany, the editor of *Tamiḻ Muracu*, lamented that "it is the common opinion of Tamil Muslims that the name 'Tamils' does not denote themselves" ("Tamiḻar eṉṟāl tamiḻ nāṭṭiṉar," *Tamiḻ Muracu*, 5 February 1941). Sarangapany's remark was a candid admission that a straightforward linguistic identity was difficult to achieve, precisely because the Tamil publishing industry in the Straits was shaped by political conflicts, ideologies, and exigencies in which language was often only a secondary consideration.

The Triumph of Nationalism(s): Erasing a Multilanguage Order

As I have mentioned before, a common assumption about the Tamil press is that it was primarily a diasporic, India-oriented enterprise. This assumption is in fact hardly based on evidence, but rather a common idea about the 'vernacular press' in the Straits Settlements as a whole: Indians, it is assumed, were primarily interested in events and ideologies of India, Chinese in what was happening in China, and Malays supposedly were primarily concerned with events in the Muslim World (Harper 1997; Trocki 2006: 68–69). However, a simple glance at the early vernacular newspapers in the Straits Settlements quickly dispels this idea. At least the Tamil newspapers were primarily concerned not with India, but with life in the Straits Settlements, spiced-up with some international reporting. Even in the latter case, given the religious background of most early Tamil publishers, the Muslim World was far more center-stage than India, and Tamil newspapers in this regard even outdid the Malay ones, as can be seen from a comparison of the reporting regarding the

Mahdi-rebellion in Sudan in *Ciṅkainēcaṉ* and *Jawi Peranakan* between 1887 and 1890 (cf. Tschacher 2011). How are we to understand this state of affairs?

Central to an understanding of the discourses and ideologies found in the 'vernacular' press is indeed the colonial language order, in particular, the role of English. Prior to the development of a press in Asian languages, 'the public' in the Straits Settlements had been unambiguously European and English-speaking; moreover, given that Georgetown (Penang) and Singapore, in their modern incarnations, were British-founded entrepots, British public opinion believed that Asian populations from India, Java, or China had no claim as 'natives,' but were, strictly speaking, migrants (cf. e.g. *Singapore Free Press and Mercantile Adviser*, 5 May 1836, 2). The only way in which the Asian population could try to contest this state of affairs was by directly petitioning the government and alleging that the Europeans unfairly excluded them from the definition of 'the public.'[13] The development of 'vernacular' newspapers threatened this balance, especially if the government might be inclined to listen to what was written in these papers. Consequently, the English-language press was quick to dismiss the utility of such a press:

> A "vernacular" newspaper in the Straits must of course mean a newspaper published in Malay [as other Asian languages were not considered 'native' to Singapore; T.T.], a newspaper which is therefore unreadable alike by the Europeans and the Chinese, and in fact cannot be understood by one voter out of a hundred–for while many can speak Malay the reading of it is barred by the fact that it is written in the Arabic character. Yet it is actually proposed that in an English colony, where English is the official language, and the language read not only by Englishmen, but by all the educated Chinese, an important public announcement may be made in half-a-dozen Malay journals, if there were such [...].
>
> *("The Municipal Amending Ordinance," The Straits Times, 11 November 1889)*

The danger that "gharry-drivers, bullock-cart Klings [South Indians; T.T.], and other unsuitable persons" might take part in public life in an "English colony" was, apparently, keenly felt ("The Municipal Amending Ordinance," *The Straits Times*, 11 November 1889). At the same time, the fear was unjustified: the barriers against the development of a unified but truly multilingual public sphere were simply too high. The result of this was, however, that the only way in which the 'vernacular' press, certainly the Tamil one, mattered to the government and the English public was when it was deemed to spread dangerous ideologies. These dangers, it was assumed, would arise not from inside the Straits Settlements, but would be carried into the colony from the Asian populations' 'home countries.' For most of the period preceding World War I, Tamil and the other 'vernaculars' of the Straits Settlements were not considered dangerous at all. Rather, government officials, and modern historians in their wake, emphasized the declarations of loyalty to the British Empire in these papers and their ostensive focus on reforming their 'own' people, and consequently declared them uninteresting (cf. Turnbull 2009: 130–2). The assumption that the Tamil press was unpolitical was, however, fundamentally mistaken, a mis-assessment made on the basis of the idea that any danger emanating from this press would automatically be connected to the development of nationalist ideologies in India. Yet unbeknownst to the British, the Muslim-run Tamil papers actually espoused a rather different cause – pan-Islamic sentiments attached to the Ottoman Empire.

These politics are visible already in the earliest newspapers. While many observers noted the English-language tribute to Queen Victoria published on the frontpage of *Ciṅkainēcaṉ*'s first edition, the blessings requested for the Ottoman Sultan Abdülhamid II (reigned 1876–1909), who ruled in Istanbul, "that is the capital of our Muslims", on the same page have been overlooked ("Taulat Utumāṉiyā," *Ciṅkainēcaṉ*, 27 June 1887). Tamil newspapers like *Ciṅkainēcaṉ* engaged in a subtle discourse that praised the British government locally and at home for its achievements, but criticized it through the coverage of international events. The disadvantages faced by the Tamil press in this context were tackled by drawing a good amount of information from other Tamil as well as Arabic newspapers, as well as a tactic of subversive translation, in which articles were shoplifted from the local English press without crediting the original, and subtly changing the tone, so that what had been an account of 'Muhammadan fanaticism' in the English version became a celebration of Muslim anticolonial resistance in Tamil (cf. e.g. Tschacher 2011: 77, 81). The popularity of all things Ottoman was not lost on non-Muslim Tamil speakers. When in 1912 a certain P. C. Doray made another ill-fated attempt at establishing a Tamil daily in Singapore, he listed among the benefits of his newspaper that it would provide Tamil news on the ongoing Turco-Italian war over Libya, for, currently, Muslims were pestering English speakers for news regarding the war like a "dog that let the squirrel escape" (*Ciṅkai Mittiraṉ*, 21 September 1912: 2). Doray was true to his word, and the fact that the news about the Turco-Italian war soon overtook news about M. K. Gandhi's activities in South Africa demonstrates both the popularity of alternative identifications among Tamil speakers in the Straits Settlements, as well as the readiness of editors to pander to all possible audiences, rather than unifying the discourses on language and political belonging.

This situation changed abruptly with the Ottoman Empire's entry into World War I on the side of the Central Powers on 29 October 1914. These developments clearly surprised many Tamil Muslims in the Straits Settlements – the newspaper *Ciṅkai Vijayakētaṉaṉ* ('Singapore Standard') even sported a masthead with the Ottoman flag and the Union Jack tied together under a crescent moon, obviously in anticipation of a British-Ottoman alliance. It also became clear that the English public was not completely in the dark about the pro-Ottoman sympathies harbored by many Tamil Muslims. Shortly after the Ottoman entry into the war, an English newspaper in Penang spread the rumor that the editor and printer of the *Janōpakāri* had been arrested in connection to a pro-Ottoman article published by the Tamil daily, a claim that was quickly picked up by other English newspapers. The editor denied the allegations, but the fact that the paper had already been denounced as a "Pan-Islamic Organ" earlier in the year, the loss of an unconnected lawsuit, and the general paper shortage led to the demise of this and other Tamil newspapers soon thereafter ("Pan-Islamic Organ," *The Straits Times*, 24 February 1914; "Janopakari Daily News," *Pinang Gazette*, 17 November 1914; "Local and General," *Malaya Tribune*, 20 November 1914; "Claim for Damages," *Malaya Tribune*, 21 November 1914; "Malāya Viḷakkam Pattirātiparavarkaḷukku ," *Janōpakāri*, 27 November 1914).

With the effective disappearance of Pan-Islamism from the political scene after World War I, the scene was set for a restructuring of the 'vernacular' press. With other 'internationalist' movements, especially Communism, banned by newly passed anti-sedition laws, the main field of political engagement for Asian-language newspapers became nationalism. The first effect of this was that 'marginal' link-communities like the Jawi Peranakan and Tamil Muslims, which had hitherto benefited from their capacity of serving various print markets, were pushed out of business in favor of those in a better position to lay claims to representing the 'Malay,' 'Indian,' or 'Tamilian common man.' Malay nationalists actively campaigned against the influence of Arab and Indian Muslims in Malay affairs, but also, on the Indian side, Tamil-speaking Muslims were hardly capable to represent 'Tamilians,' far less 'Indians' as a whole (cf. Kahn 2006: 109–14). The dividing line between English-speaking and 'vernacular' publics similarly shifted: while before the war 'English-speaking' had meant British, the Tamil press now had to contend with a new class of English speakers: an elite of ethnically diverse (predominantly North Indian, Gujarati, and Tamil Brahmin) pro-Congress Indian nationalists, who claimed to represent all Indians, from elite Punjabi administrators and Gujarati merchants to Tamil laborers. Though expressing themselves in English, the language favored by these elites was, ultimately, Hindi – at least symbolically as the national language of India, not as the language of choice for Indians in the Straits Settlements (Chua 2012; Rai 2014: 177–87). Dravidianism was, in this context, the logical solution for the Tamil press to stake a claim at relevance. Ultimately, in the Straits Settlements, it was not Tamil publishing that produced a Tamil identity and nationalism, but rather, the political dominance of English-speaking Indians supporting the Congress opened a field in which a Tamil public could lay claim to a particular identity and be heard.

Conclusion

The development of a Tamil public in the Straits Settlements provides some illuminating contrast to the parallel developments in India (cf. Venkatachalapathy 2012). The relatively small number of individuals literate in Tamil as well as the general social composition of Tamil speakers in the Straits Settlements encouraged business models where printers and publishers were able to tap into several vernacular print markets simultaneously, especially the Malay market. This gave an advantage to a social group that had only a relatively small presence in the Tamil publishing industry in India, but was simultaneously literate and well-connected in local Malay society, namely Muslims. Profitability lay not in unifying linguistic communities, but in maintaining diversified readerships only loosely connected by their use of the Tamil language. This situation delayed the formulation of Tamil language-nationalism until the 1920s in the Straits Settlements, and furthermore, provided challenges right up to the time of the Japanese invasion in 1942 for those aiming to unify Tamil speech communities. The multilingual order of the pre–World War I period was actually strengthened by the hegemonic position of English in the language order, because English kept vernacular publications out of local politics unless they aligned with diasporic interests and political ideologies seen as threatening to the British order. This encouraged transformations after World War I in favor of anti-colonial nationalist ideologies, less in their attractiveness to local Indian populations, but in the fact that only through these 'diasporic' publics could Tamil-language publications hope to be noticed and taken seriously in the wider public sphere of the Straits Settlements.

In comparison to the situation in India, in the Straits Settlements Indian languages faced different kinds of difficulties. First and foremost, in the language ideology of European settlers, Indian languages were not 'vernacular,' but 'foreign Asian languages.' While this ideology was not adopted wholesale by the local colonial government, it nevertheless produced both disadvantages and benefits. The disadvantage was that Tamil could not count in any way on state support, and as few schools utilized the language, Tamil publishers in the Straits Settlements could not count on the income provided by the publication of schoolbooks, as they did in India. The only way to keep Tamil publishing viable was, for a long time, to allow it to piggyback on Malay publishing, Malay being the only language accepted as truly 'vernacular' in the local context. The advantage of this situation, however, lay in the relative freedom from censorship in the years prior to World War I. Even after the war, when stricter patterns of censorship were put into place, Tamil nevertheless was hardly subjected to much control, as the British were more concerned about their mostly Punjabi police and military units stationed in the Straits Settlements. 'Vernacular' in the Straits Settlements' context, therefore, does not simply describe only a hierarchical relationship between English and local Asian languages, but among Asian languages as well, mediated through colonial ideologies of 'native' and 'foreigner.'

Notes

1 An earlier phase of public Tamil-language use in the region between the eleventh to thirteenth centuries is marked by a number of inscriptions, usually set up by trade

guilds, in the wake of the Chola conquest of Kedah, but there is no apparent continuity between these inscriptions and Tamil-language use in the colonial context (cf. most recently Subburayalu 2019).

2 Leyden's notes exist only in manuscript form: British Library Add MS 26562/2, folio 94v-101v (cf. Tschacher 2018a: 16–18).

3 All translations in the chapter are my own unless specified otherwise.

4 The precise title of this newspaper is unclear in form and meaning. The title adopted here comes from E. W. Birch (1879, 51), who uses the spelling *Thangai Snahen*; the synonymous *Taṅkainēcan̲* is found in several articles published in a Tamil newspaper about a decade later (cf. e.g. "Kaṭitam," *Ciṅkainēcan̲*, 2 July 1888; "Kur̲r̲amillātavan̲ yāvan̲?," *Ciṅkainēcan̲*, 9 June 1890; "Namatupattirikai," *Ciṅkainēcan̲*, 16 June 1890). The meaning of the element *taṅkai* is unclear; literally, the word means 'younger sister', but it is more likely in this case to be a shortened placename.

5 A single issue of *Ñān̲acūriyan̲* dating to December 1882 survives at the National Library, Singapore.

6 Straits Settlements, *Short-hand Reports of the Proceedings of the Legislative Council: 1886*, B143.

7 Another novel was published in Penang in 1918, but, significantly, it is not found in the catalog of registered books (Venugopal 1999: 201; cf. also Bala Baskaran 2006).

8 The classical formulation of the role of print capitalism for linguistic homogenization and the development of language nationalisms remains then the work of Benedict Anderson (1991, chapter 5).

9 *ciṅkappūrilē tamiḻp pāṣaipēcum palacātiyār* [...] ("Ippattirikaiyin̲ nōkkam," *Ciṅkainēcan̲*, 27 June 1887).

10 Already the first Tamil petition from Singapore distinguishes Muslim and Vellalar traders in Singapore as *tamiḻar yiculāmān̲avar varttakar* (SSR L6, No. 91, 02 December 1822).

11 [...] *tamiṣnūlkaḷ* [*sic*] *uṇṭākki virutticeyvatil atika muyar̲ciyuṭaiyavarkaḷ* ("Mukammatiyar," *Intu Nēcan̲*, 20 February 1888).

12 *Muslim Nēcan̲*'s publisher, M. C. Siddi Lebbe, was a key figure in the development of a separate 'Muslim' or 'Moorish' identity in Ceylon (cf. McKinley and Xavier 2018; Samaraweera 1979: 258-60).

13 For one surprisingly successful example, cf. "Public Meeting," *Singapore Free Press and Mercantile Adviser*, 05 March 1857: 3-4; *Straits Settlements Records* W24 No. 125, 2 March 1857.

Bibliography

Archival Materials

MoB – *Memoranda of Books registered in the "Catalogue of Books Printed in the Straits Settlements" under the Provisions of Ordinance XV of 1886*, British Library n.d.

SSSHRLC – *Straits Settlements, Short-hand Reports of the Proceedings of the Legislative Council*, British Library n.d.

SSR – *Straits Settlements Records*, National Archives of Singapore n.d.

Other Publications

Abdullah, bin Abdul Kadir. 1970. *The Hikayat Abdullah*, tr. A. H. Hill. Kuala Lumpur: Oxford University Press.

Anderson, Benedict. 1991. *Imagined Communities: Reflections on the Origin and Spread of Nationalism*, 2nd ed. London: Verso.
Amrith, Sunil S. 2013. *Crossing the Bay of Bengal: The Furies of Nature and the Fortunes of Migrants*. Cambridge, MA: Harvard University Press.
Bala, Baskaran. 2006. *The Malaysian Tamil Short Stories 1930–1980: A Critical Study*. Singapore: Bala Baskaran.
Birch, E. W. 1879. "The Vernacular Press in the Straits." *Journal of the Straits Branch of the Royal Asiatic Society* 4: 51.
Bowrey, Thomas. 1905. *A Geographical Account of the Countries Round the Bay of Bengal, 1669 to 1679*. Cambridge: Hakluyt Society.
Brown, I. M. 1955. "John Leyden (1775–1811): His Life and Works." PhD diss., University of Edinburgh.
Chua, Ai Lin. 2012. "Nation, Race, and Language: Discussing Transnational Identities in Colonial Singapore, circa 1930." *Modern Asian Studies* 46, no. 2: 283–302.
Ebeling, Sascha. 2010. *Colonizing the Realm of Words: The Transformation of Tamil Literature in Nineteenth-century South India*. Albany: SUNY Press.
Fakhri, S. M. Abdul Khader. 2008. *Dravidian Sahibs and Brahmin Maulanas: The Politics of the Muslims of Tamil Nadu, 1930–1967*. Delhi: Manohar.
Francis, Walter. 1902. *Census of India, 1901: Volume XV-A: Madras: Part II: Imperial Tables*. Madras: Superintendent, Government Press.
Fujimoto, Helen.1988. *The South Indian Muslim Community and the Evolution of the Jawi Peranakan in Penang up to 1948*. Tokyo: ILCAA, Tokyo Gaikokugo Daigaku.
Garrard, Charles Goodricke, ed. 1898. *The Acts and Ordinances of the Legislative Council of the Straits Settlements, from the 1st April 1867 to the 7th March 1892*, 2 vols. London: Eyre and Spottiswoode.
Gallop, Annabel The. 2006. "Malay Documents in the Malacca Records in the British Library." *Itenerario* 30, no. 2: 54–77.
Harper, Timothy N. 1997. "Globalism and the Pursuit of Authenticity: The Making of a Diasporic Public Sphere in Singapore." *Sojourn: Journal of Social Issues in Southeast Asia* 12, no. 2: 261–292.
Kahn, Joel S. 2006. *Other Malays: Nationalism and Cosmopolitanism in the Modern Malay World*. Singapore: Singapore University Press.
Kanagalatha, K. "Literature Liberated from Landscape." In *Sojourners to Settlers: Tamils in Southeast Asia and Singapore*, 2 vols., ed. Arun Mahizhnan and Nalina Gopal. Singapore: Indian Heritage Centre, 171–184.
Karthigesu, Ranggasamy. 1989. "The Role of Tamil Newspapers in Ethnic Cultural Continuity in Contemporary Malaysia." *Sojourn: Social Issues in Southeast Asia* 4, no. 2: 190–204.
Khoo Salma Nasution. 2014. *The Chulia in Penang: Patronage and Place-making around the Kapitan Kling Mosque 1786–1957*. Penang: Areca Books.
Leyden, John. 1810. "Characters and Localities of Languages Spoken in India." *The Monthly Repertory of English Literature* 10, no. 37: 115–120.
Mani, A. 2019. "Arrival and Settlement: Becoming a Community." In *Sojourners to Settlers: Tamils in Southeast Asia and Singapore*, 2 vols., ed. Arun Mahizhnan and Nalina Gopal. Singapore: Indian Heritage Centre, 45–64.
McKinley, Alexander and Merin Shobhana Xavier. 2018. "The Mysteries of the Universe: The Tamil Muslim Intellectualism of M.C. Siddi Lebbe." *South Asia: Journal of South Asian Studies* 41, no. 1: 51–68.

Mukammatu Aptulkātiṟuppulavar, Mu, Nā. 1872. *Muṉājāttuttiraṭṭu*. Singapore: J. Paton, Government Printer.

Musa, Mahani. 2006. *Malay Secret Societies in the Northern Malay States, 1821–1940s*. Kuala Lumpur: Malaysian Branch of the Royal Asiatic Society.

Iraṅkacāmi Tācaṉ, Nā. Va. 1893. *Ativiṉōtak kutiraip pantaya lāvaṇi*. Singapore: Denodaya Press.

Pieris, Anoma. 2009. *Hidden Hands and Divided Landscapes: A Penal History of Singapore's Plural Society*. Honolulu: University of Hawai'i Press.

Proudfoot, Ian. 1993. *Early Malay Printed Books: A Provisional Account of Materials Published in the Singapore-Malaysia Area up to 1920, Noting Holdings in Major Public Collections*. Kuala Lumpur: University of Malaya.

Rai, Rajesh.2014. *Indians in Singapore 1819–1945: Diaspora in the Colonial Port City*. Delhi: Oxford University Press.

Risley, Herbert Hope and Edward Albert Gait. 1903. *Census of India, 1901: Volume I-A: India: Part II.—Tables*. Calcutta: Office of the Superintendent of Government Printing, India.

Roff, William R. 1967. *The Origins of Malay Nationalism*. New Haven: Yale University Press.

Samy, A. Ma. 2000. *History of Tamil Journals (19th Century)*. Chennai: Navamani Pathipppakam.

Sathisan, Dinesh. 2019. "Power of Print: Agent of Reform." In *Sojourners to Settlers: Tamils in Southeast Asia and Singapore*, 2 vols., ed. Arun Mahizhnan and Nalina Gopal. Singapore: Indian Heritage Centre, 127–140.

Stephen, Jayaseela. 2019. "Multiple Facets of Merchant Interactions with the Straits." In *Sojourners to Settlers: Tamils in Southeast Asia and Singapore*, 2 vols., ed. Arun Mahizhnan and Nalina Gopal. Singapore: Indian Heritage Centre, vol. 1, 158–172.

Subburayalu, Y. 2019. "Tamil Inscriptions in Southeast Asia: Cultural Implications." In *Sojourners to Settlers: Tamils in Southeast Asia and Singapore*, 2 vols., ed. Arun Mahizhnan and Nalina Gopal. Singapore: Indian Heritage Centre, vol. 1, 83–96.

Samaraweera, Vijaya. 1979. "The Muslim Revivalist Movement, 1880–1915." In *Collective Identities Nationalism and Protest in Modern Sri Lanka*, ed. Michael Roberts. Colombo: Marga Institute, 243–276.

Tiṇṇappaṉ, Cupa and Ē. Ār. Ē. Civakumāraṉ. 2002. *Ciṅkappūrt tamiḻ ilakkiya varalāṟu: Oru kaṇṇōṭṭam*. Singapore: The Centre for the Arts, National University of Singapore.

Trocki, Carl A. 2006. *Singapore: Wealth, Power, and the Culture of Control*. London: Routledge.

Tschacher, Torsten. 2022. "The Idea of Religion and the Criminalization of Muharram in the Straits Settlements, 1830–1870." In *Non-Shia Practices of Muḥarram in South Asia and the Diaspora: Beyond Mourning*, ed. Pushkar Sohoni and Torsten Tschacher. London: Routledge, 53–70.

Tschacher, Torsten. 2019. "Between Mosque and Market: Tamil Muslims in Singapore." In *Sojourners to Settlers: Tamils in Southeast Asia and Singapore*, 2 vols., ed. Arun Mahizhnan and Nalina Gopal. Singapore: Indian Heritage Centre, vol. 2, 217.

Tschacher, Torsten. 2018a. "From Script to Language: The Three Identities of 'Arabic-Tamil'." *South Asian History and Culture* 9, no. 1: 16–37.

Tschacher, Torsten. 2018b. *Race, Religion, and the 'Indian Muslim' Predicament in Singapore*. London: Routledge.

Tschacher, Torsten. 2011. "'Walls of Illusion': Information Generation in Colonial Singapore and the Reporting of the Mahdi-Rebellion in Sudan, 1887–1890." In

Singapore in Global History, ed. Derek Heng and Syed Muhd Khairudin Aljunied. Amsterdam: Amsterdam University Press, 67–88.

Turnbull, Constance Mary. 2009. *A History of Modern Singapore 1819–2005*. Singapore: NUS Press.

van der Putten, Jan. 2009. "Wayang Parsi, Bangsawan and Printing: Commercial Cultural Exchange between South Asia and the Malay World." In Islamic Connections: Muslim Societies in South and Southeast Asia, ed. R. Michael Feener and Terenjit Sevea. Singapore: Institute of Southeast Asian Studies, 92–95.

Venkatachalapathy, A. R. 2012. *The Province of the Book: Scholars, Scribes, and Scribblers in Colonial Tamilnadu*. Ranikhet: Permanent Black.

Venugopal, Sababathy. 1999. *Malaysian Tamil Novels before Independence*. Kuala Lumpur: University of Malaya Press.

INDEX

Pages in *italics* refer to figures and pages followed by "n" refer to notes.

Abbās, Ġulām 46
Abdul Kadir, Munshi Abdullah b. 312
Abdullah, Munshi 312
academic social theory 150
Advaita Vedanta 170, 172
Advani, Rukun 84
Agnihotri, R. K. 26
Ahir Gazette 296–297, 299, 305, 307n6
Ahir movement 300
Ahir Yadav Kshatriya Mahasabha 302
Ahmad, Aijaz 77, 86
Ahmad, Muzaffar 288
A House Divided 255, 257
Akhil Bhartiya Brahman Samaj 297
Alexander, R. 29
Ali, Ameer 36, 47
Aligarh Movement 45, 54n1, 238–239
Aligarh Muslim University 127
Ali, Ghulam Akbar 283
Ali, Karamat 281
Ali Khan, Zafar 11, 240
Ali, Khondkar Mir Waleed 283
Ali, Mohammed 11, 248–250; colonial perspective on vernacular emotions 241; *Comrade* 238–239; display of emotions 244; future of Islam 245–247; *Hamdard* 239–240; ideology of language 240; Kanpur 247–249; languages and emotions 241; translator 241; Urdu newspapers 242; voice of the Muslim community 242–243
Ali, M. Wajed 288
Ali, Shaukat 246
Alliances françaises 83
All India Yadav Mahasabha 302
All Parties Conference of 1928 118, 123, 125
Althusser, Louis 3
Ambedkar, B. R. 65, 71, 121, 125–126, 131–132, 286
Anglo-Oriental Press 298
Anglophone orientation 81
Anglophonia 5
Anjuman-i Taraqqī-i Urdū 35
Ansari 246
anti-caste matriarchy 58
applied science 200–201
Apte, V. S. 168–169
"Aryan" invasion 60–61
Askari, Muhammad Hasan 47–49, 53
āstika 165–170, 173
Augustine, Saint 175–176
Aurobindo, Sri 174
autobiography 180, 188, 190, 195n9, 312
Azad, Abul Kalam 11
Azad, Maulana 291
Aziz, Shah Abdul 280–281

Backward Classes Movement 305
Bagchi, B. 28
Bagchi, Jasodhara 77–78
Bagul, Baburao 187
Bakhtiyar, Muhammad 278
Bakunin 170–171
Bandukush 212
Bandyopadhyaya, Shyama Kanta 171
Banerjee, Sumanto 184
Bangiya Yadav Mahasabha 302
barbarisation 219
Bardhan, Adrish 205
Basalla, G 200
Bedroom 193
Before the Divide 255
Bell, Bill 78
Benares Hindu University 127
Bengali 142; inhabitance in the social world 146–149; locutions 143–144; natural world 145–146; notion in English and 143; periodicals 204, 206; purpose of writing in 150; script 150; social theory in 144–145
Bengali vernacular: Kazi Nazrul Islam 287–290; role of Islam and Muslim 286–287; second history of Bengali literature 286; translations of the Qur'an 287
Bengal Partition of 1905 119–120
Bhabha, Homi K. 78–80, 85
bhadralok 184, 186–187, 213n10, 213n12, 286, 291
Bhadralok morality 184
Bhagat Singh's essay 170–171
Bhāgavatapurāṇa 261
Bhagawat, Chaitanya 186
Bharat Ashram 278
bhāṣā literatures 8, 75–88
bhasha worlds 91
Bhatnagar, Rashmi Dube 261
Bhattacharya, Baidik 208
Bhavans, Max Müller 83
Bhosale, Rajaram 58
Bhosale, Tarabai 58
Biswas, Philip 284
Bombay University Reform Committee 129
Book Registration Ordinance 314–315
Bopp, Francisco 169
Bose, Jagdish Chandra 203
Bose, Neilesh 11–12, 273–291
Bosunia, Amiruddin 283–284, 287
Brahmanical Peshwa period 60–61; caste patriarchy 62; *dharma* 64; gender oppression 62
brahminical class-based heteropatriachies 187
Brahmo Samaj: comparative religion 277; Indian religious landscape 276; monotheism 275; social activism 275; Supreme Being 276–277; true religion 275–276; Trust Deed 278; Upaniṣads 277
Braj Hindi 257
Brecht, Bertolt 80
Brennan, Timothy 76
British Council 21
British language policy 266
British-Ottoman alliance 323
Buddhism 61, 65, 167–168, 171, 173, 274, 278, 284–286, 290–291
Business English Lingua Franca (BELF) 17
Butalia, Urvashi 84

caste–gender nexus 62
Caste in Modern India 304
casteist elitism 59
caste journalism 297
Caṭṭopādhyāẏ, Baṅkim[l]candra 154
Cavallo, Guglielmo 183
Central and Provincial Legislatures 124
Chakrabarty, Nilanjana 198
Chakravarti, Mukundaram 286
Chakravorty, Swapan K. 82
Chandrabati 180
Chartier, Roger 183
Cārvāka 167
Chatterjee, P. 82, 90
Chattopadhyay, B. 154, 165, 205
Chattopadhyay, Dhrupadi 10, 180–194
Chattopadhyay, Saratchandra 288
Chaudhuri, Rosinka 78
Chaudhuri, Supriya 82
Chowdhuri, Upendrakishore Roy 206
Christianity 92, 98–100, 103, 110, 165, 167, 171, 175–176, 278, 283
Christian theology 171
Christopher, Isherwood 174
Chughtai, Ismat 80
Ciṅkainēcaṉ 316–320, 322–323, 326n4, 326n9
Ciṅkaivarttamāṉi 314
cognitive capitalism 22
cognitive estrangement 156, 224

Colley, Linda 122
colonial Bengal: circulation' of scientific epistemologies 203; cultural, social and political life 201; early science fiction narratives 199; institutionalization of Western science 202; magazine cultures 202; modernizing scientific-technological icons 201; print language and literature 198; rise of popular consciousness 204–206; vernacular science and Western science 199–200
colonial education system 145, 183
colonial governmentality 202
colonial hegemony 78–79
colonialism 122, 141–142, 145
colonial palimpsest 60
colonial state 123, 200–202, 208, 313
colonial victimhood 75, 80, 86–87
Common Sense 24, 146, 171–172
comparative religion: Aghore Nath Gupta 284–286; Brahmo Samaj 275–278; intellectual histories 274; and Keshab Chunder Sen *see* Keshab Chunder Sen, comparative religion; in late nineteenth century 273–274; modernization 290; vernacular 275, 291; world of *bhakti* 290
Cons, J. G. 208
corpus planning 3, 7, 218
cosmopolitan identity of Hindi 218, 227
cosmopolitan languages 68, 141, 156, 160, 226, 237–238, 250
cosmopolitan masculinist 59
creole linguistics 27–28
Curzon, Lord 212

Dakhini Urdu 257
Dalit feminist movement 181
Dalit literary movement 187
Dalmia, Vasudha 260, 301
Damodar Valley Project 134
Dar Commission 115
Das Gupta, Indrani 198–212
Das, Krishnabhabini 186
Das, Sisir Kumar 183
Datta, Dwidas 284
Datta, Dwijas 287
Datta, Kedarnath 284
Datta, Satyendranath 288
Dawood 283
Debendranath Tagore 278
Debi, Kailashbashini 186
Debi, Nistarini 186
Debi, Rassundari 186
Debi, Sarala 186
Defoe, Daniel 207
Dehlavı 255
de Man, Paul 79
Denodaya Press 313–314, 316, 319
Derozio, Henry Louis 202
Derrida 150, 152
de Selva, A. M. 28
de Swaan, A. 18, 20–21
Devi, Gulab 103
Devi, Radharani 181
Devi, Svarnakumari 186
Devi, Yashoda 104–109, 111
Devji, Faisal 36, 39, 44–46, 53
Dev Sen, Nabaneeta 180–194, 181–183, 187–189, 191–194; literary productions 182–183; marriage 182; upbringing and family 181–182
Dhardwadker, Vinay 82
Dharmapala 286
diasporic community 317
didactic manuals 92, 97
Dil, A. S. 28
Dodson, Michael 273–274, 290
Doniger, Wendy 166
Dravidianism 324
Du Bois 161
Durkheim, Emile 274
dynamic nominalism 208

Eagleton, Terry 3
egalitarianism 304
Ekatma Vijnana 172
Elite Indians 150, 288
emotions and language: experiencing 237; expression 237; investigation 237; of the Islamic public 247
Engels, Friedrich 2
English: as an instrument of socio-economic mobility 29; dominance of 19; as a global lingua franca 19; and Indian languages 24; joint hegemonization of 25; as a medium of instruction in Rwanda 19; neutrality of 20–22; in post-liberalization India 20; in South Asia 23–24
English and Hindoostanee 262
English as a global language (EGL) 18, 20, 30
English as a lingua franca (ELF) 21, 24
English-vernacular binary 17–18, 22–25
Ezekiel, Nissim 183

false consciousness 2
Faraizi movement 279
Fārān 38
female sexuality 107, 109
Fergusson College 127
Flowers of Poetry 57
Fort William College 256, 259–260, 265–266, 269n13, 270n20
Foucault, Michel 68, 77, 80, 85
Frazer 290
Friedman, S. S. 209
Friedman, Susan 209

Gadgil, D. R. 118, 129, 131, 133
Gandhi, M. K. 121, 126, 174
Gautama, Siddharta 282, 285–286
gendering bilinguality: feminist historiographies 186; guarded tongue 188; historical predicament 183; iconoclasm 188; Indianness 185; life-writings of women reformers 186; lowly women 186–187; print capitalism 183; *savarṇa* women's autobiographies 187; schizophrenic language identity 185; vernacular press 184; women's writing 184
geocultural imagination 226–227
German philosophic tradition 144
Ghosh, Abhishek 290
Ghosh, Amitav 91
Ghosh, Anindita 184, 198
Ghosh, Bishnupriya 210
Gilchrist, John Borthwick 259–260, 262, 266
Gill, M. 27
Gill, Robin 79
Gokhale Institute 131
Gokhale, Shanta 180–194, 181–183, 187–188, 190, 192–194; literary productions 182–183; marriage 182; upbringing and family 181–182
Golden Age of Islam 38
Goldsack, Reverend 284
Goswami, Bijoy Krishna 284
Goswami, M. 201
Goyandka, Jayalal 175
graded inequalities 120
Grammar of the Hindi Language 264
Gramsci, Antonio 23, 305
Grierson, George Abraham 260, 295
Griffith, Ralph T. H. 170
guarded tongue 188
Gupta, Aghore Nath 274, 284–286, 285–286, 290–291
Gupta, Charu 9, 90–111
Gupta, Indrani Das 198–212

Habermas 142
Hacker, Paul 165
Hacking, Ian 208
hagiographies 180, 257
Hali, Altaf Husain 38, 45, 245
Hallisey, Charles 165
Halqa-i-adab-i-Islami 38
Hannan, Muhammed Abdul 283
Hany Babu, M. T. 24, 29
Harder, Hans 1–13, 71, 205
Hardinge, Lord 238
Harishchandra, Bharatendu 263
Hasan, M. 11
Hatcher, B. A. 210
Hatcher, Brian 274, 290
Hegel 152
hegemonic 'savarṇa' feminism 181
Heidegger 152
hermeneutic fashion 152
"high caste" male patriarchy 64
Hijazi, Nasim 38–39
Hindavi 257, 260, 262
Hindi: colonial encounter and vernacular education 217; imperialism 17, 22; in late colonial North India 218; novels *see* novel of the new mechanical age; periodicals 296; public discourse language 217; translating Western science 218–219; Urdu influences 217
Hindi-English dictionary 169
Hindi heartland 11, 256, 262
Hindi movement 219, 224, 298–299, 305, 307
Hindi Nationalism 256
Hindi print-public sphere 91, 110
Hindi public sphere 217, 221, 298, 300
Hindi–Urdu controversy 35, 40–41, 44, 49, 53–54, 255
Hindi–Urdu prose tradition 11, 256, 258
Hindī sāhitya kā itihās 265
Hindu ideas of God 172
Hinduism 36, 61, 99, 102, 165, 168, 174, 177n1, 213n10, 289, 292n5
Hindū jā*tiy*oṃ ke vibhāg 303
Hindu philosophers 167–168
Hindu philosophy 166, 173, 176
Hindustani 54n3, 127, 135n3, 218, 221, 256, 299

Hiwrale, Anup 71
Hopf, Arian 8, 34–55
Howell, Philip 78
Hunshiyar, Heshoram 198–200, 206–211
Hunter Education Commission 263
Huq, Fazlul 288
Hussein, Moinuddin 288
Hyderabad Rashtra Yadav Mahajan Sangam 302
hypercentral language 20

ideologies: contested terrains of consciousness 12–13; language, literature and the vernacular public sphere 10–12; of vernaculars and English 7–9
impatient idealist 245
India: Bengal Partition of 1905 119; bi-and multilingualism in 27; call centres in 20; Damodar Valley Project in 134; domains of contemporary Indian public life 117; English in 18; English-vernacular binary in 18, 22; hierarchical multilingualism in 25; history of linguistic reorganisation 116; IT and business processing outsourcing industries 20; language within public–political life 117; linguistic diversity 115–117; linguistic states in 24; MBA programmes and management studies in 19; Montagu–Chelmsford Reforms 120; multilingualism 116; non-aligned foreign policy 19; public spheres in 142; recovery of grassroots multilingualism in 27–28; relationship between 'regional' languages and English in 18–19; renaissance in 26
Indian Constitution 21, 24–25, 118, 122–123, 125, 157
Indian Institutes of Management 19
Indian Merchants Chamber 132
Indian National Congress 115; Nagpur session of 121
Indian religion and literature 152
Indo-Aryan language 256
Indo-Muslim culture 8, 35, 41, 50–51, 53–54; and Urdu 44–45; Urdu as symbol for 45–49
intellectual history for India 274, 281, 290
intercultural mimesis 165–167
"internal" colonialism 71
Iqbal, Muhammad 38, 48
Isfandiyar, Kaykhusraw 276
Islam 12, 35–40, 44–46, 48–49, 52–54, 92, 98–99, 102–103, 110, 167, 171, 176, 240, 246–247, 274, 278–284, 286–287, 289–291
Islami adab ki tehrik 37
Islam, Kazi Nazrul 274, 287–291
Ives, P. 23, 29

Jainism 61, 167, 171, 173
Jain Mahasabha 297
Jaisingh II 277
Jalibi, Jamil 49–53
James, C. L. R. 161
Ja̱nōpakāri 316, 324
Jawi Peranakan 314, 322, 324
Jayakar, M. R. 127, 129–130
Jenkins, J. 24
Jigyasu, Chandrika Prasad 96
Jinnah, Muhammad Ali 36, 46, 121, 125
Joshi, Svati 79, 85

Kachru, B. B. 24
Kader, Shah Abdul 283
Kale, Shobha 71
Kale, Sunila S. 71
Kalindi, Queen 285
Kallol 79
Kanya-kubja Brahmans 305
Karve, Iravati 301
Kaul, Suvir 78–79
Kaviraj, Sudipta 9, 82, 90, 141–163, 286
Kayastha Ethnology 304
Kayasthas 296, 298, 303–304, 308n25
Kellogg, Samuel H. 264
Kemper, Steven 286
Kerslake, Patricia 205
Keshab Chunder Sen, comparative religion: Bengali linguistic environment 281; Bharat Ashram 278; Faraizi movement 279; intellectual history and labour 281–282; literal and dynamic translation 284; Muslim development in Bengal 279; new Brahmo Samaj of India 278; non-Muslim readership 280; prolific translator 281; reformist activity 281; religion of Islam 278–279; religious communalism 282; rise of Islam 282–283; "vernacular" Bengali 280
Khan, Insha Allah 262
Khan, Muhammed Akram 280

Khan, Saiyid Ahmad 239, 243, 245
Khan, Sayyid Ahmad 45, 48, 283, 287
Khan, Syed Ahmed 283, 291
Khaṛī bolī 255, 257–260, 265–266, 267n3, 268n7, 269n13
Khusro, Amir 242
Kidwai, A. 27
Kippenberg, Hans 290
Kothari, Rajni 148
Kshatriyahood 300–301, 303–304
Kshatriya identity 296
Kumar Dutta, Akshay 203
Kumar, Uday 90
Kurmis 298, 303–304

Lal, Lalluji 256, 259, 262, 264
language: experience and analysis 149; family resemblance in 155–156; sociological settings of 149–155; time inside 162; trafficking 20; workers 20, 146
Laureate, Nobel 192
Laws of Manu 62–63
Lazarus, Neil 75, 81
Leavis, F. R. 80
Lenin 170
Lentriccia, Frank 86–87
Leyden, John 312
linguistic cosmopolitanism 185
linguistic diversity 9, 115–117, 119, 122–123, 134
linguistic heritage 115
linguistic landscape 2, 5
linguistic territorialisation 9, 118–119, 130, 135
literary foremothers 180, 188, 191
Liu, Gautam 11, 255–270
Loomba, Ania 78
lost/found in translation 9–10
Lucknow Pact of 1916 121, 124, 126

Macaulay's ideology of language 26
Macaulay, T. B. 26, 68, 77, 161
MacDonald Award 125–126
Madurai Tamil Sangam 314
Mahasthabir, Kripasankar 285
Mahdi-rebellion 322
Mahir-ul-Qadri 38–39
Mahopdeshak, Shiv Sharma 93
Maity, A. 199
Majeed, J. 7–8, 17–30, 275
Makhdum Sahib, K. 313, 316, 319
Malleus Maleficarum 176
manas 143, 153
mandamus 143
Mandir, Ram 189
Manjapra, Kris 79
Mannheim, Karl 3
Manto, Saadat Hasan 46, 80
Manu mindset 70
marginalized feminisms 181
Marx, Karl 2, 141, 170
Mascaro, Juan 174
"masculine" language 58
Masica, C. P. 28
Masjid, Babri 189
mass print cultures 91
Matbaᶜ Saᶜīdī 314
material culture of 'alien' science 224
Max Müller Bhavans 83
Mazoomdar, Protap 286
Menon, Nirmala 81
Menon, Ritu 84
Meston, James 247
metaphysical philosophy 35, 48, 53
Miller, Barbara Stoler 174–175
Mishra, Chaturbhuj 261
Mitra, Rajendralal 285
Mitra, S. 204
Modern Standard Hindi 255, 262, 267n3, 268n9
Mokashi-Punekar, Rohini 72
Monier-Williams, M. A. 168
monolingualism 1, 239
monolinguality 150
monotheism 275, 277, 281, 284
monotheistic religion 167, 175
Montagu–Chelmsford Reforms 120, 124–125
Montaut, A. 27–28
Moore-Gilbert, Bart J. 78
Mother English (poem) 57, 62–63
Mukharji, Projit 274
Mukherjee, Ashutosh 203
Mukherjee, Meenakshi 85
Müller, Max 285, 290
multilingual public sphere 322
Muṉājāttuttiraṭṭ*u* 313
Murthy, K. M. K. 170
Muslim World 279, 287, 321
Muslim Zion 36, 53

Nagari Pracharini Sabha 219, 298
Nanak, Guru 282
Nandy, Ashis 157
Narayan, R. K. 6

Naregal, V. 9, 115–136, 185
nāstika 165–170, 172–173
nationalism 3, 29, 50, 71, 122, 131, 135, 154–155, 157, 161, 163n16, 213n8, 218–219, 229, 231n14, 256, 286, 290–291, 311, 321, 324–325, 326n8
national language 1, 13, 21, 34, 36, 40, 50, 130, 231n15, 265, 324
Nehru, Jawaharlal 133
Nehru Report of 1928 123
Nehruvian era 80–81
neo-Hinduism 165, 177n1
new Brahmo Samaj of India 278, 284
Nicholson, Andrew J. 165–168, 173
Nikhilananda, Swami 174–175
North American postcolonialism: coloniser vis-à-vis the colonised divide 76; hegemony 78; Indian academia 75; *Kallol* 79; *Masks of Conquest* 77; *Orientalism* 77
novel of the new mechanical age: *Bāīs*^{l}*vīṃ sadī* 221–223; *Candrakāntā* 221; exemplary naturalism 220; Hindi novel reading 221; paraliterature 221; Premchand era 220; pre-Premchand 220; *Svarg*^{l}*purī* 221–223
Novetzke, Christian Lee 8, 57–71
Nyaya and Vedanta philosophies 173

Official Languages Commission 115
orientalism 76–77, 87n3, 249
Orsini, F. 237
orthodox Hindu Indian society 60
orthodox Hindus 167–168
Our Midwives *96*
Oxford Hindi-English dictionary 169

Paik, Shailaja 65, 71
Pakistan: geography 39–41; history with the Indus Valley Civilisation 41; independence 35; Indo-Muslim culture 35; Islamic identity of 35, 39; pre-Islamic history 41; regional languages of 49, 52; society and its identity 41; Urdu as national language 34, 36, 40
Pakistan Educational Conference 40
Pakistani identity 8, 34–55
Pakistan: *Literature and Society* 41
panchayats 296, 302
Pande, Aparna 82
pan-Islamic fervor 246
Pan-Islamic Organ 324
Paranjpye, M. R. 127
Park, Shivaji 190
Parry, Benita 78
Pathak, Shridhar 256
Pernau, M. 11, 237–250
Persian historiography 260
Persian printed newspapers 239
Perso-Arabic element 260–262
phenomenon of vernacularization 297
Phillipson, R. 18
Phule, Jotirao 8, 57–58, 60, 69–71, 72n3
Phule, Savitribai 8, 57–71, 186
Piṉāṅkuñāṉācāriyaṉ 316–317
Poddar, Hanuman Prasad 97
Pollock, Sheldon 273
Poona University 129–130
postcolonial India 151
postcolonial theory 8, 75–76, 79, 81–82, 86
Prabhavananda, Swami 174
Practical Sanskrit-English Dictionary 168
Prasad, Munshi Kali 304
Pratt, M. L. 209
pre-Independence movement 40
pre-modern India 185
premodern linguistic economy 142–143
Prem^{l}*sāgar* 11, 255–258, 265–270; language of 259–264
prophet Mani 176
prophet Muhammad 38, 41, 286
proselytization 68, 183
Proto-Australoid 42
public narratives 211
public sphere 57–58, 104, 184, 218, 223, 238, 279, 298, 325
Pulavar, Mohamed Abdulkadir 313
Puranic literature 264

quotidian revolution 59

Radhakrishnan 174
Raghuvanshi, U. B. S 96
Rahman, Tariq 45–46
Rai, Amrit 257
Rajan, Rajeswari Sunder 85
Rāj^{l}*pūt* 297, 300–302, 307n5
Rāj^{l}pū*t ke niyam* 299
Ramabai, Pandita 186
Ramakrishna 83, 281
Ramakrishna Mission Institute of Culture (RMIC) 83
Ramamsamy, E. V. 320
Ramanujan, A. K. 82

Ramayan 93, 170, 180, 262, 289
Ram, Chhotu 306
Ranciere, Jacques 93
Ran̄ī Ket^{l}kī *kī kahānī* 262–263
Rao, Desiraju Hanumanta 170
Rao, M. S. A. 305
rasa 143, 156, 200
Ray, Jagadananda 203
Ray, Praphulla Chandra 203
Ray, S. 198–200, 206–208, 210–212
Raza, Rahi Masoom 264
reading humour: bedroom 193; final auspicious journey 193; private spaces 189; productive labour 190; sense of place 190–192; sites of feminist enquiry 189; unfailing comical touch 188
Rebellion of 1857 127
Reddy, G. S. 306
Red Flag societies 313
Rege, S. 187
regional languages 2, 4–7, 17–22, 29, 40, 43, 49–50, 52–53, 83, 116–119, 127–130, 134–135, 160
Reider, John 205
religious conversion: conversions to Islam by widows 99, 102–104; Dalit women's conversions to Christianity 99–102; vernacular depictions 99; by women on the margins 98–99
reverse translation 9, 165–178
Riaz, Fahmida 41
righteousness 174–175
Rita Welinker 193
Roy, Arundhati 91
Roy, B. C. 149
Roy, Modhumita 78
Roy, Raja Rammohun 202, 275–278, 280–283, 288, 290
Roy, Rammohan 160
Rudolph, Lloyd I. 302
Rudolph, Susanne Hoeber 302
Rupchand Pakshi 201

sabhās 296–298, 300, 302, 306, 308n20
Sadana, Rashmi 90
Said, Edward 76, 78
Said, Muhammad 314
Samanta, S. 210–211
Samyukta Maharashtra movement 118
Sāṃkhya 166–167
Sankrityayan, Rahul 286
Sanskrit-English dictionary 167–169
Sanskrit intellectual history 273
Sanskritised Hindi 91, 256, 262, 265, 296, 299–300
Sanskritisms 262
Sanskritization 29, 286–287, 304–305, 308n23
Sanskrit neologisms 256
Santram BA 104–109, 111
Sarangapany, G. 320
Sarkar, Tanika 185–186
Sastri, Haraprasad 285
Schultz, Anna 82
Schweig, Graham M. 175
scientific modernity 200, 203–204, 210, 218, 225–226, 228
Seely, Clinton B. 82
Seidlhofer, B. 24
Self-Respect Movement 320
Sen, Amartya 191
Sen, Girish Chandra 12, 274, 279–281, 284–285
Sengupta, D. 201, 205, 207
Sen, K. C. 278, 282–286, 288, 290–291
sense of cultural anxiety 194
sense of place 188, 190–192
Sen, Suddhaseel 8, 75–88
servants and sexual anxieties: appropriate behaviour for girls and women 92–93; class and caste difference 94–95; didactic manuals 97; embodied allegories of inequality 93; legitimisation of servant–employer relationship 94; 'proper' behaviour for Hindu women 93; seclusion for the Hindu mistress 97; sexual liaisons and illicit romances 95; surrogate 96
Setalvad, Chimanlal 127–128
Seth, S. 207
sex and sexuality in colonial India: anxieties *see* servants and sexual anxieties; sexology *see* vernacular sexology from the margins; sites of desire *see* religious conversion; sites of enquiry by drawing 92; vernacular imaginative texts 90
Shabda Sagara Sanskrit-English Dictionary 169
Shagir, Shah Mohamed 283
Shahidullah, Muhammed 288
Shah, Sultan Ilyas 279
Shakespeare 207
Shankar, S. 90
Sharar, Abdul Halim 38
Shariatullah, Haji 279

Sharma, Krishna 173
Shikoh, Dara 288
Shiva Prasad, Babu 35
Shiv Sena 59
Shukla, Rohini 72
Shukoh, Dara 288
Sibnath Sastri 284
Singh, Bhagat 170–172
Singh, Chakkar 207
Singh, Ishita 10, 217–229
Singh, Jai 186
Singh, Lakkar 207
single-language public spheres 142
Sircar, Mahendralal 203
Smritichitre: *The Memoirs of a Spirited Wife* 180
Snell, R. 26
social cognition 152
social inequality 59
social theory 144–146, 150, 163n3
South Asia: language of Islam in 40; Muslims of 36, 48, 51
South Asian languages: and English 1–2; vernaculars 4
South Asian vernaculars 311
Speaking like a State 40
Srinivas, M. S. 304
Stewart, Tony K. 282
Straits Settlements: multilingual environment of 319; Tamil in 312; Tamil-language publics in 312–314, 321; Tamil Muslims in 323; Tamil press in 317; Tamil publishing in 314–317; vernacular press in 321–322
structuralism 144
Study English (poem) 65
Sugathpala, W. M. 28
Supreme Being 276–277
Supriya Chaudhuri 79, 82
Svati Joshi 78
Swami, Paramhangsa Soham 171–172

tabula rasa 200
Tagore, Debendranath 283
Tagore, Rabindranath 154–155, 192, 200, 285
Taḥrīk-i adab-i islāmī 37–39
tall-tale-therium 207, 211
Tamilians 132, 317–318, 324
Tamil-language periodicals 313–314
Tamil linguistic identity 312
Tamil newspapers 311, 314, 316–318, 321, 323–324, 326n4
Tamil print industry 311–312
Tamils Reform Association 320
Tamiḻ Muracu 316–317, 321
Tattvabhusan, Sitanath 286
technoscientific modernity 218, 225–226, 228
territorial reorganisation 119, 125
The Diary of Professor Heshoram Hunshiyar 198
The English (poem) 66–67
The Location of Culture 76
The Modern Vernacular Literature of Hindustan 295
theorizing science in colonial India: applied science 200–201; history 200; tabula rasa 200; tripartite diffusionist model 200
Tilak, B. G. 61, 121
Tilak, Lakshmibai 180, 188
Toolan, M. 29
translating Western science into the vernacular 218–219
Trivedi, Harish 86
Trivedi, Poonam 79
Trotsky 170
true religion 275–277
Truschke, Audrey 82
Tschacher, Torsten 12, 311–326
Tylor 290

University Reform Committee of 1924 130
Upadhyaya, Ayodhyasingh 102
Urdu in Indus Valley Civilisation 41–43
Urdu journalism 239
Urdū kā tahẕībī pas-manẓar 41
Urdu public sphere 249–250, 300

Vaiśeṣika philosophers 167
Valmiki Ramayana 170
Vanita, Ruth 9, 165–178
varṇa hegemony 300
Vedic language 42
Venkatachalapathy, A. R. 91
Venuti, Lawrence 210
Verma, Nirmal 80
vernacular: glocalization 6; history of 5; multilingualism 4; print sphere 91; regional languages 5
vernacular emotions: history 239; in a multilingual situation 238; *vs* cosmopolitan 237–238

vernacularization 58–59; corpus planning 7; 'cosmopolitan' Sanskrit 6; of democracy 59; of English 2; regional 'vernaculars' 7
vernacularizing sciencep: colonial Bengal 199–200; contact zone 209; delectable news 206; The Diary of Professor Heshoram Hunshiyar 206; hunting expedition 208; model of polycentricity 209–210; multimodality 209–210; multiple levels of lost epistemologies 210; tall-tale-therium 211; translation of colonial science 210; travelling tales 207–208; upside-down adventures 208–209
"vernacular" literary scholarship: anti-empirical fad 82; Indian academia 85; library services 84; postcolonialism 80–81; vernacular-language research in India 83
vernacular sexology from the margins: archive of sexual sciences in India 104; heterosexual ethics 105, 109; Indian erotica 106; language of pleasure 110; legitimate sex 109; monogamous renderings 107; perversions 107
Vibhishana 176
Vidyabhusana, Baladev 277
Vidyasagar, Iswar Chandra 274
Vienna-Oxford International Corpus of English (VOICE) 24
Vindhyavati 58
Viswanathan, G. 77–78, 82
Vivekananda 165
Vīr̄[l]caritāvalī 300, 308n16

Wadud, Kazi Abdul 288
Waliullah, Shah 281
Waquet, F. 21
Wazir Agha 53
Weber, Max 274
Wendy Doniger 173
White Flag societies 313
William, Fort 11
William, R. 7, 22
Wilson, H. H. 167–168
Woolard, Kathryn A. 3–4
world of *bhakti* 290

Yadav, Meenakshi 12, 295–308
Yadav Sangam 302
Yadvendu, Ramnarayan 96
Yates, W. 168
Young, Robert J. C. 81

Zahurbakhsh 103
Zaidi, Nishat 1–13, 71, 307
zero-man 67–70
Zia-ul-Haq 40, 46
Zulfiqar Ali Bhutto 40

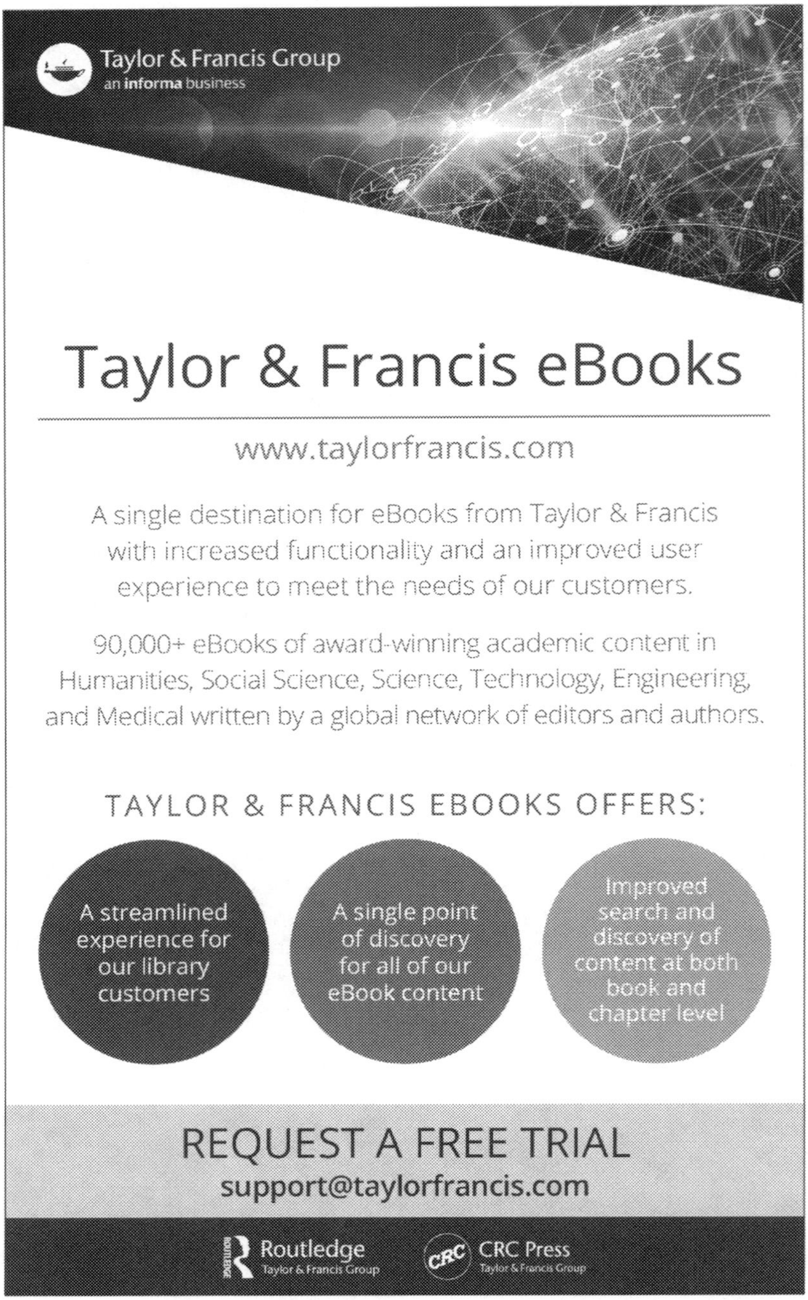

Printed in the United States
by Baker & Taylor Publisher Services